# UNTOLD GLORY

AFRICAN AMERICANS IN PURSUIT OF
FREEDOM, OPPORTUNITY, AND ACHIEVEMENT

## ALAN (B.) GOVENAR 1952

HARLEM MOON

BROADWAY BOOKS | NEW YORK

PUBLISHED BY HARLEM MOON

Interview of Josephine Harreld Love copyright © 1986
by Marlene Chavis.

Published in the United States by Harlem Moon, an imprint of the
Doubleday Broadway Publishing Group, a division of Random
House, Inc., New York.
www.harlemmoon.com

HARLEM MOON, BROADWAY BOOKS, and the HARLEM MOON logo,
depicting a moon and a woman, are trademarks of Random House,
Inc. The figure in the Harlem Moon logo is inspired by a graphic
design by Aaron Douglas (1899–1979).

Photo credits appear on pp. 399–400.

LIBRARY OF CONGRESS CATALOGING-IN-PUBLICATION DATA
Govenar, Alan B., 1952–
Untold glory : African Americans in pursuit of freedom,
opportunity, and achievement / by Alan Govenar.—1st ed.
p.   cm.
Includes bibliographical references.
1. African Americans—Interviews.    2. Successful people—United
States—Interviews.    3. Creative ability—United States—Case
studies.    4. Interviews—United States.    5. Oral history.    I. Title.
E185.96.G68 2006
920.009296'073—dc22
[B]
2006016986

ISBN: 978-0-7679-2117-6

PRINTED IN THE UNITED STATES OF AMERICA

10  9  8  7  6  5  4  3  2  1

FIRST EDITION

# ACKNOWLEDGMENTS

The journey that shaped this book began more than a decade ago when I was asked in 1994 by Lonn Taylor and Nianni Kilkenny to develop a public program at the National Museum of American History on African American cowboys. Subsequent presentations of that program at the Festival de Printemps in Lausanne, Switzerland, the National Black Arts Festival in Atlanta, and Colorado College in Colorado Springs refined my understanding of the questions often engendered by discussions of the migratory patterns of African Americans. Adrienne Seward and Sterling Stuckey suggested that I rethink existing literature on the American frontier, and Paul Stewart, Ottawa Harris, and Nudie Williams introduced me to the collections of the Black American West Museum and Heritage Center in Denver.

My involvement in the International Conference on African American Music and Europe at the Sorbonne in 1996, organized by Michel Fabre and Henry Louis Gates Jr., expanded the scope of my inquiry and provided me an opportunity to speak with Paul Oliver and Francis Hofstein about misconceptions of African American culture in southern and western regions of the United States.

In 1999, Saul Bellow, after an intense conversation about Ralph Ellison and race relations in America, urged me to contact his son, Adam, who was intrigued by my efforts and later introduced me to Janet Hill. Over the years, my dialogue with Janet, which began with her interest in publishing an updated edition of my book *African American Frontiers,* encouraged me to create a substantially new work through the arduous process of revision.

Clyde Milner II, who invited me to participate in a panel he assembled for the 2005 national meeting of the Organization of American Historians in San Jose, broadened my perspective on the idea of the frontier and compelled me to reexamine the fundamental premise from which my work advanced.

Kim Gandy, president of the National Organization for Women, recommended new interview subjects. John Slate assisted me in surveying historical archives across the country. Marlene Chavis graciously provided her interview with Josephine Harreld Love. Jay Brakefield transcribed many of my interviews, often checking facts and dates. Alan Hatchett helped in the preparation of the photographs for publication.

My wife, Kaleta Doolin, shared her insights as the final conceptualization of this book emerged. Tara Neal, Amanda Campbell-Wyatt, and my daughter, Breea Govenar, aided in the organization of references and primary source materials. My son, Alex Govenar, challenged me with his thoughts on the interplay of cultures in music and film, and inspired me to delve more deeply into the unexpected stories of people I heard for the first time.

# CONTENTS

*UNTOLD GLORY*

# INTRODUCTION

*Not in word alone shall freedom's boon be ours.*

—FROM "TO MISS MARY BRITTON" BY PAUL LAURENCE DUNBAR[1]

Paul Laurence Dunbar, ca. 1895.

PAUL LAURENCE DUNBAR'S POEM "To Miss Mary Britton" was first published in 1893 in his collection *Oak and Ivey,* the same year that Frederick Jackson Turner delivered his paper "The Significance of the Frontier in American History" to the American Historical Association in Chicago. Dunbar had traveled to Chicago that year, too, carrying copies of his *Oak and Ivey,* hoping to sell them for one dollar a copy at the World Columbian Exposition, the first World's Fair. Needless to say, Turner and Dunbar never met each other. In fact, they lived worlds apart.

While Turner proclaimed, "The frontier has gone and with its going has closed the first period in American history,"[2] Dunbar was envisioning a different America, where God might "speed the happy day/When waiting ones may see/The glory-bringing birth of our real liberty." The term *frontier*, Turner said, "is an elastic one, and for our purposes does not need sharp definition," but he did affirm the position of the United States census director in offering one concrete definition: The frontier was a place occupied by fewer than two people per square mile. The frontier, Turner observed, marked the divide between civilization and "savagery," and taming the frontier helped to shape such values of the American citizen as personal independence and participatory governance. Furthermore, the advance of American settlement westward onto "free land" explained not only the development of the United States but also American democracy and the nation's character. "The wilderness masters the colonist," wrote Turner, giving him "a buoyancy and exuberance which comes with freedom." Certainly, African Americans in 1893 did not enjoy such freedom. Though they had been emancipated from slavery, Reconstruction had ended and racism was rampant. Dunbar, in the published introduction to his poem "To Miss Mary Britton," extols the virtues of a schoolteacher who protested "in a ringing speech" against the passage of a "separate coach bill" in Kentucky. "Her action," Dunbar said, "was heroic, though it proved to be without avail."

Though little is known about the life of Mary Britton, a similar protest by Homer Adolph Plessy two years later, in 1895, triggered a landmark court case that became the basis for legalized segregation nationwide. After Plessy sat in the "white section" of an East Louisiana Railroad train car, a conductor confronted him and ordered him to leave. When he refused, he was arrested and jailed in New Orleans, charged with violating a recently enacted law mandating separate seating for "coloreds." Plessy was light-skinned and only one-eighth African American, but Louisiana applied the "one drop rule," meaning that anyone with "one drop" of nonwhite blood was by definition colored.

With support from the Citizens' Committee to Test the Constitutionality of the Separate Car Law, a group of Creoles and blacks in New Orleans, Plessy argued that the Separate Car Act violated the Thirteenth and Fourteenth Amendments to the Constitution. The presiding judge, John Howard Ferguson, ruled that the state could choose to regulate railroad companies that operated only within Louisiana, even though in

an earlier decision, he had declared the Separate Car Act "unconstitutional on trains that traveled through several states." Plessy appealed to
the Louisiana Supreme Court, which upheld Ferguson's decision, and
then to the United States Supreme Court, which ruled once again in favor of the state. Justice Henry Brown, speaking for a seven-person majority, wrote in his opinion:

> That [the Separate Car Act] does not conflict with the
> Thirteenth Amendment, which abolished slavery . . . is too
> clear for argument. . . . The object of the [Fourteenth
> Amendment] was undoubtedly to enforce the absolute equality
> of the two races before the law, but in the nature of things it
> could not have been intended to abolish distinctions based
> upon color, or to enforce social, as distinguished from political
> equality, or a commingling of the two races upon terms
> unsatisfactory to either.3

In response to Brown's opinion, the lone dissenter, Justice John
Harlan, stated:

> Our Constitution is color-blind, and neither knows nor
> tolerates classes among citizens. In respect of civil rights, all
> citizens are equal before the law. . . . The present decision, it
> may well be apprehended, will not only stimulate aggressions,
> more or less brutal and irritating, upon the admitted rights
> of colored citizens, but it will encourage the belief that it
> is possible, by means of state enactments, to defeat the
> beneficent purposes which the United States had in view when
> they adopted the recent amendments of the Constitution.4

Ultimately, the admonitions of Justice Harlan proved true. The
"separate but equal" principle upheld by the United States Supreme
Court in *Plessy v. Ferguson* effectively legalized racial segregation and discrimination. Local and state governments across America passed laws
that restricted African American access to public facilities, to housing,
and to virtually every conceivable place where blacks and whites might

interact—from restaurants and theaters to restrooms and schools. Surely, there were hundreds of square miles, if not more, that were thus not occupied by a single African American, let alone two per square mile.

By 1940, more than 25 percent of all African Americans lived in the North or West. During World War II, migration into the western United States expanded exponentially, propelled by the opportunities of higher-paying jobs in the shipyards, aircraft factories, and other wartime industries. In the 1940s, the population of the region grew 49 percent, from 1,343,930 to 1,996,036. This growth was most dramatic in urban centers. Between 1940 and 1944, the African American population in the San Francisco–Oakland area rose from 19,000 to 147,000; in Portland, from 1,300 to 22,000; in Los Angeles, from 75,000 to 218,000.[5]

After World War II, the labor organizer A. Philip Randolph established the League for Nonviolent Civil Disobedience Against Military Segregation. Randolph had been a staunch critic of government policy since World War I, when he cofounded, with Chandler Owen, a magazine called *The Messenger,* advocating more jobs in the war industries and the armed forces for blacks. In the 1940s, Randolph focused on the problems related to African American employment in the federal govern-

African Americans driving wagons in the first '89er parade, Guthrie, Oklahoma.

ment and in industries with federal contracts. He warned President Roosevelt that he would lead one hundred thousand blacks in a protest march on Washington, D.C., and Roosevelt yielded to the pressure, issuing Executive Order 8802 on June 25, 1941, barring discrimination in defense industries and federal bureaus and creating the Fair Employment Practices Committee. After Roosevelt's death in April 1945, Randolph worked to influence his successor, President Harry S. Truman, and urged him to issue Executive Order 9981 on July 26, 1948, banning segregation in the armed forces.

While integrating the armed forces was a major step forward, most of the United States was still segregated. Tuskegee airman Charles McGee recalls that after World War II, he continued his training to become an aircraft maintenance officer and that one of his first assignments was in Salina, Kansas, but he was unable to relocate his family. "It was too difficult," he says. "Couldn't rent or buy back in those days in Salina if you were black. And this kind of discrimination not only applied to housing in town but to restaurants, movie theaters, you name it."[6]

During the 1940s the NAACP intensified its efforts, working in coordination with its newly formed Legal Defense and Education Fund to spearhead the brilliant strategy devised by Charles Hamilton Houston and his colleagues at the Howard University School of Law to end the legal segregation sanctioned by *Plessy v. Ferguson*. Houston assembled a core team of lawyers that included Thurgood Marshall, James Nabrit, Spotswood Robinson III, A. Leon Higginbotham, Robert Carter, William Hastie, George E. C. Hayes, Jack Greenberg, and Oliver Hill. Together, they worked on many fronts, seeking out local attorneys and civil-rights activists who might be able to help them find the right test cases to take to the Supreme Court. Houston and his colleagues understood that to overturn *Plessy v. Ferguson*, they needed to bring together a number of court decisions that questioned the viability of separate-but-equal laws.

In 1951 and 1952, five district courts in five cases from four different states—Kansas, Delaware, South Carolina, and Virginia—as well as from the District of Columbia, ruled on the constitutionality of separate but equal. The state cases were based on the equal protection clause of the Fourteenth Amendment, and the District of Columbia case was built upon the due process clause of the Fifth Amendment (denial of liberty by such discrimination). In its ruling, the Supreme Court consolidated the four state cases. The District of Columbia case was considered at the same time but, because of the different issues it raised, was not consolidated with the others.

When the cases were first argued before the Supreme Court in 1952, no consensus was reached, and the court set the cases for reargument the following term. In September 1953, before the court convened, Chief Justice Vinson, who had opposed overturning *Plessy*, died of a heart attack, and when the court finally heard the reargument, his replacement, Earl Warren, was able to craft an opinion that was unanimous: "We conclude that in the field of education the doctrine of separate but equal has no place. Separate educational facilities are inherently unequal." A year later, the Supreme Court consolidated the four states with the District of Columbia when it ordered the desegregation of all schools with all deliberate speed.

In many ways, African Americans did not have true access to the frontier Turner described as shaping personal independence until the 1954 United States Supreme Court ruling in *Brown v. Board of Education* struck down the separate-but-equal doctrine set in motion by *Plessy v. Ferguson*. Personal independence was, by definition, impossible in a segregated society, where African Americans were denied access and opportunity.

The enforcement of *Brown v. Board of Education* proceeded slowly and was met with resistance on many fronts. On December 1, 1955, Rosa Parks, a seamstress in Montgomery, Alabama, was sitting in the "colored section" of a city bus when a white man asked her to give up her seat to him because the "white section" was full. Parks refused and was arrested and fined for violating a city ordinance. The next night, fifty leaders of the African American community, led by a relatively unknown minister named Martin Luther King Jr., gathered together to discuss a course of action that led to the Montgomery bus boycott. The entire African American community boycotted public buses for 381 days until the law legalizing segregation was overturned. Finally, in 1956, the United States Supreme Court ruled that segregated bus service was unconstitutional. Parks, in her autobiography, *My Story*, recalled that she was "tired of giving in" and that her involvement in the NAACP and the

Highlander Folk School had helped to imbue her with the strength to not give up.

Clearly, the action of Rosa Parks and the landmark Supreme Court rulings related to her case and to *Brown v. Board of Education* had profound effects on the civil-rights movement and the course of American life. However, resistance to the Supreme Court's rulings related to the dismantling of legalized segregation has persisted, and the debate about their meanings and ramifications is ongoing. Attorney Oliver Hill, who worked closely with Charles Hamilton Houston and Thurgood Marshall and is now ninety-eight years old, says, "We still have a long ways to go. *Brown* declared *Plessy v. Ferguson* unconstitutional and made it unlawful, so far as the law was concerned, but the de facto segregation is almost as bad now as it was then, fifty years ago. You must remember that without the rule of the law, we would still be second-, third-, or sometimes fourth-class citizens."[7]

Parks was not the first African American to protest segregated seating in public transportation. The little-known Mary Britton, referenced by Paul Laurence Dunbar, had articulated her objections, as did Adolph Plessy, Irene Morgan, and Jackie Robinson, among other well-known figures.[8] No doubt many other African Americans resisted as well, but their stories were never told. The difference with Parks's action was that after she was arrested she was handpicked for a test case by civil-rights lawyers because of her immaculate moral character and reputation, and her protest ultimately succeeded. If we perceive the frontier as an obstacle to freedom and achievement, Parks and those she represented finally breached it after many other tries by others had failed.

Of course, the *Brown* decision and the ruling two years later striking down segregation on public transportation did not solve all the problems of racism and segregation. As Hill remarked, much segregation remains. And it is now widely acknowledged that these breakthroughs created unforeseen problems by eroding a sense of physical community African Americans had when all were forced to live together. Many who could flee traditionally black neighborhoods did so, leaving behind those with fewer economic and social resources to cope with inner-city life in the era of downsizing and outsourcing. The struggle goes on.

In recent decades, historians have largely rejected Turner's thesis of the frontier. Many see the word *frontier* as outmoded and, in their search for a better term, have stressed cross-cultural interactions. The idea of Turner's frontier is implicitly ethnocentric, failing to take account of the significance of persons of African descent, American Indians, Mexicans, and migrant Asians, among others, who came to America in pursuit of freedom and opportunity. However, despite the objections of historians, the idea of the frontier has continued to expand long after Turner's death and has taken on a multitude of transmutations and metaphorical uses in the English language. A quick Internet search of the word turns up about 14,000,000 results.

"*Frontier*," historian David Wrobel maintains, "has become a metaphor for promise, progress, and ingenuity."9 Yet, as historian Patricia Limerick suggests, "the relationship between the frontier and the American mind is not a simple one. Clear and predictable on most occasions, the idea of the frontier is still capable of sudden twists in shifts of meaning, meanings considerably more interesting than the conventional and familiar definition of the frontier as a zone of open opportunity."10

The twists and shifts in meaning to which Limerick alludes are evident not only in the debate among historians concerning Turner's thesis but also in the proliferation of the term *frontier* in the contemporary world. Certainly, the usage of *frontier* has evolved considerably from its etymological roots in the old French *frontiere* (c. 1400) and the Latin *frons,* meaning literally "the front line of an army," to its more current definitions as "the borderland separating two countries," "the extreme limit of settled land beyond which lies wilderness," and "the extreme limit of understanding or achievement in a particular area."

Senator John F. Kennedy set forth the idea of a New Frontier in his speech at Memorial Coliseum in Los Angeles, July 15, 1960, accepting the Democratic Party nomination for the presidency of the United States. In the speech, he challenges the notion that there is "no longer an American frontier."

Today some would say that those struggles are all over—that all the horizons have been explored—that all the battles have been won—that there is no longer an American frontier.

But I trust that no one in this vast assemblage will agree with those sentiments. For the problems are not all solved and the battles are not all won—and we stand today on the edge of a New Frontier—the frontier of the 1960s—a frontier of unknown opportunities and perils—a frontier of unfulfilled hopes and threats.

This speech by Kennedy expressed what many in America were already thinking, especially African Americans, who were beginning to mount a systematic attack to dismantle Jim Crow discrimination. Buoyed by the passage of the Civil Rights Act of 1957, the NAACP, Southern Christian Leader Conference, CORE, and other African American community-based organizations aligned themselves with the agenda of the Democratic Party to help narrowly defeat Richard Nixon in the 1960 presidential election. While some African American leaders were skeptical of Lyndon Baines Johnson as Kennedy's running mate, they nonetheless believed that the Democratic Party presented the greatest hope for advances in civil rights.

After the assassination of President Kennedy on November 22, 1963, the Johnson administration was committed to the passage of civil-rights legislation. Johnson successfully won congressional support for many of Kennedy's New Frontier proposals, and in 1964, he secured passage of a sweeping Civil Rights Act and an Economic Opportunity Act. He moved beyond the New Frontier to declare "war on poverty" and outlined a vast program of economic and social-welfare legislation designed to create what he termed the Great Society in his first State of the Union message of May 1964.

The question remains whether or not the term *frontier* is still useful in understanding the process of history and, specifically, better comprehending the relations and interactions of cultural groups to each other and to the mainstream of American thought. Does broadening the definition of *frontier* dilute its meaning or enhance our ability to make sense of the world in which we live? For artist Laura Jean Lacy, who believes her family descends from indentured Africans brought to the Jamestown colony, the frontier has a very distinct significance for African Americans. "If, from a black perspective," Lacy maintains, "we think of

Unidentified couple, ca. 1890–1910.

Africans brought to America as the civilized (in a non-Western sense of the word *civilized*), the wilderness was occupied by white Americans, who were their captors. For blacks, white Americans, not necessarily American Indians, were the savages. . . . This, of course, may sound ludicrous, but for me, the word *frontier* has a life-affirming cache. Why do whites have a frontier, and blacks, what many call a boundary? The word *boundary* is more negative. In the frontier is hope . . . the boundary is an obstacle."[11]

While the symbolic meaning of the word *frontier* may be useful in understanding aspects of the history of Africans in America, specifically as it relates to issues of freedom and opportunity, it does not sufficiently express its consequences. For African Americans, there were many frontiers that not only involved geographic movement but also engendered new ways of thinking and acting. Certainly, *Brown v. Board of Education* helped to shape the personal independence described by Frederick Jackson Turner. Yet, perhaps most significant, equal access truly marked "the glory-bringing birth of our real liberty," envisioned by Paul Laurence Dunbar. In this context, the word *glory* not only encompasses the frontier but also fulfills its promise. Glory is achievement—the honor and admiration that is bestowed upon somebody who does something important. Glory may lead to fame, but in the everyday world, it may simply be defined in terms of the personal triumph over adversity or in that satisfaction that comes from strengthening the bonds of family and community. Among African Americans, especially during the years of segregation, there were countless events and ceremonies that were designed and organized to bolster self-esteem by conferring admiration or praise. The enduring significance of these celebrations of glory is often enshrined in photographs and in the stories that people tell.

Consider three of the photographs on the cover of this book: in one, a Pullman porter in uniform poses with his wife in a fancy dress on the front walkway to what is apparently their home with a well-groomed lawn in an unspecified location. On the back of the print, the couple is identified as Mr. and Mrs. Williams, and judging from its mounting and size, the photograph was probably made between 1910 and 1920.[12] In another photograph, Martha Fergurson (second from left) jokes around with her friends, Josey, Gloria, and Teenie—four freshmen at Talladega College in Alabama during the 1943–1944 academic year.[13] The third photograph documents a more politically charged event—an NAACP picket on a Dallas, Texas, street in 1965.[14] Two men in the second row carry a placard that reads "Freedom at Any Cost." This image was made by Marion Butts, a community photographer and managing editor of the African American–owned *Dallas Express* newspaper, who was proud to say that two of the men in the front row, C. Jack Clark and Travis Clark (left and middle) were "two of the first black millionaires in Dallas."[15] While these three photographs are significantly different from one another, they all stand as testaments to untold glory—one reminds us of the dignity of the Pullman porter in a relatively undocumented past, one celebrates a moment in the lives of four African American girls during their first year at college, and one marks a protest organized by community leaders committed to social change. Clearly, over the course of day-to-day life, glory inspires feelings of joy, wonder, thanksgiving, and pride.

*Untold Glory* explores the lives of twenty-seven people whose struggles, aspirations, and achievements speak to the power of determination in confronting and overcoming discrimination. The frontiers they discuss are personal in nature, but the glory they have achieved is profoundly revealing. While there are common concerns that many of the people interviewed share, the subjects discussed are complex. Individually and together, they bring forth insights on a broad range of issues, including the dilemmas of day-to-day life in a segregated world; civic action and social protest; the consequences of integration, social mobility, and stratification; interracial and cross-cultural relations; and the ways in which education was and remains fundamental to obtaining and sustaining freedom.

Personal life experiences chronicle the complexities within the course of daily life in America. The broad subject areas covered include art and culture, business and commerce, politics and government, religion, and social and demographic change. The emphasis is upon the people themselves and the ways in which they participate in the process of history through what they say and do. These stories of everyday life enlarge our comprehension of the multifaceted human dynamics through which different personal frontiers were conceived and explored, and the ways in which they provided the incentive for unprecedented accomplishments.

To study the perspectives of a cross section of African Americans, I engaged in extensive fieldwork, researching existing collections of oral histories and conducting interviews with as many individuals as possible. My principal focus was upon those regions of the country where the idea of the frontier seemed most relevant to geographic movement and the migratory patterns of African Americans. Initially, I explored the historical collections and archives in the states west of the Mississippi River, but as I began interviewing specific people, the scope of my work expanded. I began to understand that while the West did offer untold promise, the frontiers for African Americans were manifold and were based more upon the context in which opportunities and glory might be realized than upon geographic movement and relocation.

Bruce Lee, a biologist, for example, grew up in Buffalo, New York, in a region that he calls the Niagara Frontier, in a "community of coloreds," referring to his mixed African, Anglo-Saxon, and Indian background. For Lee and his family, this region of Upstate New York, prior to World War II, provided the greatest opportunity for economic and social advancement. The Bruce Lee interview resulted in an account that was a kind of oral autobiography or life history and served as a model for others.

For Jacob Lawrence and Gwendolyn Knight, the frontier was New York City, a mecca for black artists during and after the Harlem Renaissance.[16] For Herb Jeffries, it was creating the role of the black cowboy in the western movies of the 1930s; for John McLendon, coaching and struggling to integrate basketball; for Lawrence Douglas Wilder, becoming involved in local, state, and national politics and running for public office; for William Waddell, teaching at the Tuskegee Institute and achieving success as a veterinarian; for Marvin Williams, playing Negro League Baseball and trying out for the Boston Red Sox; for Reverend

NAACP picket. Front row (left to right): C. Jack Clark, Travis Clark, Roosevelt Johnson; second row: C. B. Bunkley, unknown, George Allen; third row (right): Tony Davis; fourth row (right): Pettis Norman; fifth row: Frank Clark.

Richard Stewart, attending Perkins School of Theology and serving as an Army chaplain; for Jeni LeGon, moving to Hollywood and breaking through as a film actress and dancer; for Geraldine Miller, founding the Household Technicians Union and working as an advocate for domestic workers; for Richard Harris, building a career as a journalist in Pennsylvania and Arizona and self-publishing six books; for Reverend Nicholas Hood, earning a divinity degree and representing his community in Detroit as a city council member; for James Emanuel, writing poetry and exploring life outside the United States as an expatriate; for Marion Kramer, fighting for the rights of welfare recipients; for Paul Hudson, building on the efforts of his father and grandfather as president of Broadway Federal Bank in Los Angeles; and for Mark Dean, developing three of the nine patents that led to the introduction of the personal computer.

In each interview, I asked people to talk about their birthplace, parents, education, and work, as well as obstacles imposed by segregation and racism, the extent to which the concept of the frontier was relevant to their experiences, and the ways in which they were able to actualize their goals and achieve a sense of personal glory in their lives. In editing these interviews, I deleted those elements of speech, including hesitations and interruptions, that might impede understanding. My intent was to make their speech fluent in written form.

*Untold Glory* strives to energize the dialogue about written history and the oral tradition by exploring the lives of people who defy generalization. These remarkable individuals personalize the process through which history is established by recounting the circumstances that shaped their lives. They speak to the ingenuity and tenacity that enabled them to pursue opportunities against all odds not only to achieve their personal goals but also to better the world for us all.

NOTES

1    Paul Laurence Dunbar, *The Collected Poetry of Paul Laurence Dunbar*
     (Charlottesville: University of Virginia Press, 1993).

2　Frederick Jackson Turner, *The Frontier in American History* (1920; reprint Tucson: University of Arizona Press, 1986), 2.

3　Justice Henry Billings Brown, "Majority Opinion in *Plessy v. Ferguson*," in *Desegregation and the Supreme Court,* ed. Benjamin Munn Ziegler (Boston: D. C. Heath and Company, 1958), 50–51.

4　Justice John Marshall Harlan, "Minority Opinion in *Plessy v. Ferguson*," in Ziegler, 61.

5　For more information, see Quintard Taylor, *In Search of the Racial Frontier: African Americans in the American West, 1528–1990* (New York: W. W. Norton Company, 1998).

6　Interview with Charles E. McGee by Alan Govenar, April 6, 2005.

7　Interview with Oliver W. Hill Sr. by Alan Govenar, August 31, 2005.

8　Ten years before Rosa Parks, the case of Irene Morgan was accepted and litigated by the NAACP, which was able to overturn state segregation laws as applied to actual travel in interstate commerce, such as bus travel. The Rosa Parks case applied to all segregationist transportation laws, not only those related to interstate travel. Jackie Robinson, when he was stationed at Fort Hood, Texas, objected to an Army officer who asked him to move to the back of a bus. Robinson faced court-martial, but was acquitted.

9　David M. Wrobel, *The End of American Exceptionalism: Frontier Anxiety from the Old West to the New Deal* (Lawrence: University of Kansas Press, 1993), 145.

10　Patricia Nelson Limerick, *Something in the Soil: Legacies and Reckonings in the New West* (New York: W. W. Norton, 2000), 75.

11　Interview with Laura Jean Lacy by Alan Govenar, February 7, 2005.

12　Unidentified couple, ca. 1910–1920. Courtesy of Texas African American Photography Archive, Dallas, Texas.

13　Martha Fergurson (second from left) with Josey, Gloria, and Teenie, Talladega College, Alabama, 1943–44. Reproduced with permission from the collections of the Iowa Women's Archives, University of Iowa Libraries.

14　NAACP picket. Front row (left to right): C. Jack Clark, Travis Clark, Roosevelt Johnson; second row: C. B. Bunkley, unknown, George Allen; third row (right): Tony Davis; fourth row (right): Pettis Norman; fifth row: Frank Clark. Photograph by Marion Butts, Dallas, Texas, 1965. Courtesy of Texas African American Photography Archive.

15　Interview with Marion Butts by Alan Govenar, September 16, 1994. For more information on Marion Butts, see Alan Govenar, *Portraits of Community: African American Photography in Texas* (Austin: University of Texas Press, 1996).

16  For more information on the Harlem Renaissance, see Arna Bontemps, *The Harlem Renaissance Remembered: Essays with a Memoir* (New York: Dodd, Mead, 1972), and Nathan I. Huggins, *Harlem Renaissance* (New York: Oxford University Press, 1971).

*Magistrate Sidney Barthwell Jr., Detroit, Michigan, 2005.*

# SIDNEY BARTHWELL JR.

COURT MAGISTRATE

*Born September 1, 1947*

*Sidney Barthwell Jr. is a magistrate in Detroit, and in this capacity he is a judicial officer in a lower court whose jurisdiction is limited to the trial of misdemeanors, moving vehicular violations, and preliminary hearings on more serious charges. After attending what was then called Cranbrook School for Boys, he enrolled at Wayne State University, where he graduated in 1986. He taught second grade for half a year and was admitted to Harvard Law School in 1987. He received a law degree from Harvard in 1990 and was hired by Dickinson Wright, a major law firm that at the time employed 230 attorneys. After two years, Barthwell left Dickinson Wright and decided to focus his career on issues critical to the African American communities of Detroit. As one of the six magistrates appointed in the city, Barthwell works at the Thirty-sixth District Court and feels that through his efforts he can have an "impact directly on people's lives every day."*

I GREW UP ON THE NEAR WEST SIDE of Detroit in an area known as the Boston Edison neighborhood. I think we moved into that house in 1949. My father was a pharmacist, and he lived in that house until the day he died, June 23, 2005. He owned a chain of drugstores. He also made his own ice cream. He had thirteen flavors. He used to make a half million gallons a year of ice cream. It was very popular at the time—Barthwell's Ice Cream. He was from Cordele, Georgia, originally. It's the county seat of Crisp County, Georgia, and it's about sixty-five miles south of Macon, Georgia, straight down I-75. His family migrated to Detroit around 1919. His father's name was Jack Barthwell. I think my father had seven brothers and sisters.

My grandfather's work was agricultural in the South. But when he came up here, he worked at Ford for a lot of years in the foundry at the River Rouge complex. And eventually, he died as a result of iron particles in his lungs.

My father died in his one hundredth year. I think he had eleven pharmacies at his height. He had three ice-cream stores. You know, back in those days, pharmacies all had soda fountains.

Well, I grew up in a black middle-class environment. Detroit was kind of unique, but it wasn't totally unique. There are certain components of what I'm about to identify in a lot of major urban areas, but Detroit and Washington, D.C., are places that come to mind. Maybe to a lesser degree Chicago. It's unique in that there was this commingling between economic classes in the black community. So what you had when I was coming up, you had guys who were of a middle-class background whose fathers were professionals or whatever, in the black community, hanging out with guys who were street guys. So there was a lot of that intermingling because if you wanted to go party, for example, as a teenager in Detroit, you had to be able to fight—or at least have some kind of strategy so you didn't get your ass kicked every time you went out to a party. My entrée was basketball. I was a good basketball player, so I knew all the basketball players around the city, because I used to play at all the playgrounds. That's where all the good games were, and you got to know all the guys playing ball, and they were also the hoodlums. So you go to the party at night, and a guy might say, you know, "Don't bother him. He's my boy."

These days, I might shoot a few baskets occasionally, but it's too physical for me. I just run. Right now, I run and play golf. I'm an average golfer. I was still playing a lot of ball when I was living in New York in the seventies. I played all over Harlem.

In Detroit, there wasn't much black-white commingling. I don't know what you know about metropolitan Detroit, but residentially, it's an extremely segregated scenario, and it still is. There's more diversity in the South than there is in the North, even though it was unintended. It was just an unintended result of the proximity of the races from another era.

During the time I grew up, the neighborhood was all white. When I started elementary school in the early 1950s, there were just two African Americans in my kindergarten class. This was a public school called Roosevelt Elementary School. By the time I came out of the sixth grade, I think there were maybe five or six white people in the class of thirty-five. So it was a neighborhood in transition.

It was Jewish and Anglo prior to the time we moved in; my next-door neighbor was Carl Levin, who's now a U.S. senator from the state of Michigan. His brother's named Sander Levin: He's a congress-person from a suburban district in Detroit. The house we moved into was once occupied by the brother of Cardinal Mooney, who was at one time leader of the Archdiocese of Detroit. So, it was an interesting neighborhood.

Detroit was a place where there was a commingling of socioeco-nomic classes in very close proximity. So the public school that I went to in elementary school drew from a cross section of socioeconomic fami-lies. The street I lived on, which was Boston Boulevard, was definitely upper class at the time. Really big houses, four, five, six thousand square feet. That sort of thing. Three-car garages. But the neighborhood did change. Today, Detroit is virtually all black. I think the city's probably 85 percent African American now.

In the fifties, the percentage was maybe 10 or 15 percent African American, 25 percent, possibly, something like that. So what changed is the fact that so many white people left Detroit. White flight. I think at its height, Detroit was approaching two million in population, which was in the early 1950s. And now it's about nine hundred and fifty thousand, maybe. So a little over a million people left the city in about a thirty-five-year period, but most dramatically between, I would say, the early 1960s and maybe 1990. The bulk of those people left at that time, and they were almost all white and almost all middle class or upper middle class. [But many of those who left in the late 1980s were probably more black than white.] So what you're left with is a city full of predominantly low-income people. And it's not a phenomenon that's unique to Detroit, though I think that the extremeness of the phenomenon is kind of unique to Detroit. It was so pervasive, and the riots in 1967 obviously ac-celerated the process.

In retrospect, my childhood probably was [difficult], but I think when you're a child, you don't know anything else. Obviously, when I was five, six, seven, eight years old, I wasn't aware of the demographics of white flight or transitional neighborhoods or things like that. I was aware of the fact that the color of my classmates was changing. And it was a period of time when there was great social upheaval in the country. The civil-rights movement was arguably entering its highest period of activity, or certainly a high period of activity shortly after or during the *Brown v. Board of Education* period, and all of the struggle against segregation—legal segregation, in the South, de jure segregation—was a topic of the highest national concern at that time. And it was something that African Americans were and continue to be extremely aware of as an oppressed people, if you will.

It was something that I was aware of at the time, but I wasn't fully aware of it. I wasn't well versed on the sociological impact of things. But I was aware of the fact that there was a civil-rights movement going on and that I was a black man in America. And I was aware of the fact that there was discrimination in America, in the metropolitan Detroit area. I went to elementary school in the Detroit public schools. It was a school called Roosevelt Elementary School, named after Theodore Roosevelt. And it was a big elementary school; there were about two thousand students. They used to have really big schools in the public school system in Detroit. I was on a campus with a middle school and a high school. The middle school was called Durfee Junior High School at the time. And the high school was Detroit Central High School.

After the sixth grade, I went to private school. I went to a school called Cranbrook School for Boys, which is in Bloomfield Hills, Michigan. It was a boarding school. It was named after a village in Kent, England, which is where one of the founders' antecedents came from. The founder of Cranbrook was a gentleman named John Booth. He was the publisher of the *Detroit News.* And he founded Cranbrook in the mid-1920s.

One of my classmates was Mitt Romney, current governor of Massachusetts. Other graduates of Cranbrook included Daniel Ellsberg of the Pentagon Papers fame, and there was someone named Peter Dawkins, who was a Heisman Trophy winner, as well as a military man back in the fifties who was a graduate of Cranbrook. But there were a lot of distinguished and not-so-distinguished graduates of Cranbrook. I was the only black person in my class, class of 1965.

Well, the cultural change between being in the inner city and being out at Cranbrook was extreme. Being in a virtually all-black environment in Detroit as opposed to being in a virtually all-white environment out in Bloomfield Hills, which is twenty miles north of Detroit, was very dramatic. And living there as a boarding student from the seventh grade on, from age twelve or thirteen . . . I was out there for six years.

The good thing was, I could go home on weekends. They had a policy: You couldn't go home every weekend, but you could go home roughly two out of four per month. So I had lots of access to going home. But at the same time, I was really separated from the city. Culturally, I was totally separated from the city. The cultural chasm between what was going on in the inner city in Detroit and what was going on in Bloomfield Hills was huge, immense.

An ongoing tension throughout the entire time I was at Cranbrook was the fact that after a couple of years, I really didn't want to be there. In my youthful, inimitable wisdom, I decided that I'd be better off at Cass Technical High School, which was the top public school in Detroit—which, incidentally, was the alma mater of my father. But that's not why I wanted to go there. I wanted to go there because it was coeducational. There were a bunch of fine young girls there. And I was a basketball player. I wanted to play in the Detroit Public School League.

[From Cranbrook] I went to Wayne State University in Detroit. I started in the sixties. I dropped out, moved to New York, did different things—was writing poetry and just kind of hanging out, for lack of a better term. Then when I came back to Detroit, I worked with my father for a number of years, and then I went back to college. I went back in 1984. I was a sophomore in '84. I was on academic probation. I had dropped out of school without doing it officially. As a result, I got a few E's. You know, it didn't help my GPA any. But in any event, when I went back, I did very well. I graduated in December of '86. Then I taught in the Detroit public schools, second grade, for a half a year. Then I went to Harvard Law School in September of 1987, and I got my law degree from Harvard in June of 1990.

When I was younger, I had an alcohol problem that I overcame by myself, basically. It's never by yourself, but when I say by myself, I mean without the benefit of Alcoholics Anonymous or any of those kinds of organizations. I quit drinking, and six months later I quit smoking, and I started running. I've run fourteen marathons since then.

I'm a child of the sixties, so to speak. So I was involved with everything there was to be involved with. See, my background is the black power movement, or militant black politics, particularly in the sixties and the seventies. Now, I'm a magistrate.

A magistrate is a judge. But we don't do trials. We do traffic court for the city of Detroit. We do small-claims court, claims of three thousand dollars or less. We do all of the felony arraignments for the city of Detroit. Civil infractions. It's a challenge. I've been a magistrate for about eight months. Prior to being appointed magistrate, I was a solo [law] practitioner for fourteen years.

When I came out of Harvard, I worked at a big law firm, called Dickinson Wright, for the first two years. At the time I worked there, there were 230 attorneys in this firm. It's a big majority-white law firm. That's a whole issue for another book; maybe I'll write that one. It's really amazing to me. You think of the law—at least I did, before I got into it—as being a very progressive area. You think that laws by their nature are inherently concerned with fair play and people being treated properly and things of that nature—antidiscriminatory practices. But in fact, what I found out—and I really didn't know about this until I got to Harvard, even though I was forty years old when I started Harvard and considered myself to be politically aware—I was not aware of the fact that the legal profession was so conservative and so backwards in terms of their own progression and in terms of promoting diversity. And they still aren't [promoting diversity]. It was shocking to me. I had no idea that the profession was lagging so far behind even American society. But it's a bifurcated profession. Eighty-five percent of all lawyers in this country are in firms of five lawyers or smaller, or they're solo practitioners. The other 15 percent are in big firms and/or corporate in-house lawyers or doing public-interest work of some sort. And those are the lawyers who run the profession. That 15 percent. They're also the lawyers who make the big money, and they're not who was involved in the civil-rights movement. The lawyers who were involved in the civil-rights movement were people like Thurgood Marshall and their cohorts.

[A lot of local people who fought these cases on a day-by-day basis were up against the corporate legal system. The corporate lawyers were the obstacles. That's whom they were fighting in the courts.] Exactly. And that's who continues to be the obstacle. I think there's 257 large firms in this country that are normally monitored for various demographic information, and in those firms, they're all majority-white firms, and they all have two hundred or more attorneys in them. And in those firms, the lawyers make the really good money, big money. They're the firms that Harvard and Yale and Stanford, etc., etc., feed. Those firms continue to have 4 percent of their numbers or less African American, and 2 percent African Americans or less are partners. That's today, and the numbers were identical at the time I started Harvard Law School, at the time I graduated, and the percentage of African Americans just hasn't changed. The structure of most major law firms in the United States is so resistant to change, it's unbelievable. When I was at Harvard—Harvard is a great place. Harvard believes in diversity; they've been diverse since the late 1960s in real numbers. Their numbers match societal numbers in terms of percentages and diversity. But when I was at Harvard, each class at Harvard Law School had 540 students, year in and year out. There were sixty-five African Americans in my class, and of the males, which was roughly half of that number, nobody got hired for a summer job from these majority-white firms—almost nobody—until almost the end of the first year. It was amazing to me. These were all folks, including myself, who sent out hundreds of letters seeking summer internships. And my white colleagues, counterparts, classmates, rapidly received multiple offers, seven, eight, nine apiece. It wasn't about grades, because at Harvard Law School, there were no grades [in the late 1980s] for first-year students until the end of the year. So everyone who sent out applications had the same qualifications. But those big firms were just not hiring black male students from Harvard Law School as summer associates, even at that late date.

To me, that is one reason alone enough for me to vote for a Democrat. Just because of the dramatic impact Republican administrations have had on the courts. We've got an interesting fight going on right now. The Republicans kept Clinton's nominees from being confirmed. And I know two of them personally, from Detroit, who were nominated to the Sixth Circuit by Clinton, and they sat there for three years, and their nominations were never brought to the floor of the Senate by the Republican-controlled judiciary committee. So they stonewalled Clinton's nominees. Absolutely stonewalled his nominees.

We're living the result of that legacy right now. The courts are unbelievably conservative. I could go on all day about that because they're not following the Constitution. They've enacted laws and policy that in my opinion have nothing to do with the tenor or the demeanor or the philosophies of the Founding Fathers, the people who wrote the Constitution. And it's really a shame.

I really enjoy going to Europe, and not just because of racial tolerance, but a kind of more progressive atmosphere generally. I was in France and England a couple of years ago. I was in Italy last summer, and I'm going to Spain this summer. And I'm not so naïve as to think that Europe doesn't have its problems or that it might not even be the genesis of the racial problems that exist in America. But they seem to have kept on evolving socially.

In France, [there's a tremendous interest in African American life and culture]. And England is interesting, too. England doesn't get enough credit, in my opinion, for the progressive nature of the culture—the modern England. I really enjoyed being over there. I enjoyed listening to the BBC. To get news from a perspective that's not tainted. Everything we get here is so tainted.

[In the United States, newspapers are not as interesting as they used to be.] Based on what we have to choose from, the *New York Times* is far and away better than anything else, simply because it makes an effort to cover news stories that the rest of the media in the United States doesn't even give the shortest of shrift to. But then you go to England, and the newsstands are full—the *Guardian* and what have you, I mean—in addition to the front-line papers. There's just so much there.

There's a black paper, the *Michigan Chronicle,* in Detroit that's been around for a long time. But all that paper today is about black social life, and you can virtually buy your way onto the front page. Well, philosophically, you have other forces involved. You have people that are willing to kind of sell their ideological purity down the river for a few bucks.

There are a lot of huge barriers facing the African American community with regard to . . . it's even difficult now to identify what the goal is. By that I mean, in the sixties, you had different ideological schools of thought in the African American community. You had a revolutionary school of thought. You had people that were interested in advances. The NAACP, the Urban League, folks like that, you had the black church, whatever it was they stood for, which to me is still a mystery. But clearly, it was for the most part in-system politics. At the time, everybody was kind of in favor of these kinds of amorphous terms *freedom* and *dignity,* and things of that nature. But when you got down to pragmatic definitions of what it was black folks really needed, then you had people who were espousing different things, and you had people who were kind of living a radical lifestyle but who really had no ultimate direction whatsoever. They were just into the lifestyle. The Black Panther Party had a Ten-Point Program, but if you asked them, "What are your specific goals for the future of black people?" then they would get lost in terms of what the ultimate ideological goal was.

Well, if you're asking today, what's the ultimate ideological goal of African Americans, I think you'd have a hard time getting an answer— well, not necessarily, because a lot of folks have just adopted the rote sort of American response to the question, "What are my goals?" You know, "My goal is to be wealthy, to obtain wealth," or something of that nature. I'm from the old school. I don't think that materialism is going to ultimately lead to happiness, either racially or in any other method. But I'm not so naïve as to not understand. I am a pragmatist. From a pragmatic perspective, I think what black people need is, we need better jobs, better education; it's the same thing you hear from everybody else. We need more money. We need more middle-class black people staying in the communities to uplift the level of services in the communities. And we need white people, too. I didn't use to believe that. I think we need more diversity. In a place like Detroit, Detroit needs white people back in the city. We need upper-middle-class white people living in the city. We need to raise the standard of living of everybody. I don't know how you get it. In terms of the black community, what we're left with now in places like Detroit is a huge central city of poor people who are disempowered, who virtually have no impact on public policy. Even though they elect officials, they're uneducated, for the most part. And the result is pretty disastrous. If you look at Detroit internal politics right now, from the mayor's office on down, you've got a bunch of people who are unqualified, in my opinion, running the city. And they're an embarrassment to me.

The current mayor of the city of Detroit is called the hip-hop mayor. He's thirty-two, thirty-three years old. He's a young guy. He kind of became mayor by default. Dennis Archer resigned, or chose not to run for reelection rather unexpectedly and late in his second term, which left nobody really to step up to run for mayor. The folks who normally would have been in that position thought Archer was going to run for a third term, so nobody really stepped up to the plate. The current mayor at that time was a state legislator. He had ascended to the state legislature by running for the seat that his mother had abandoned when she became a U.S. representative. And due to the overwhelming force that name recognition has in these kinds of elections, her son was able to step right into her old district and win. She had been the state representative from that district for sixteen years prior to his stepping in. So he just kind of ascended to her elected position, kind of as a rite of passage. And then from there, within four years, when there became this vacancy, this vacuum for candidates for the mayor's position, he was able to step right in and fill that void. He had an organized campaign. His father was a deputy executive of Wayne County, and that's another big political machine in metropolitan Detroit, the county government. Now, the county government, that's where Jennifer Granholm, the governor of Michigan, came out of that office, Wayne County executive's office. She also went to Harvard Law School, incidentally.

I think the underlying problems are the same as they've been for fifty or a hundred years. You still have this huge segment of the black population that is, as a result of cultural discrimination, undereducated or underemployed or unemployed and uneducated. We have a system, a national government that does not have as a public policy a priority to try to set straight the oppression and the degradation that was placed upon African Americans as a result of the cultural history of slavery and discrimination, which was the law of the land up until thirty years ago. It would take a massive . . . I feel it would have to be a high-priority kind of public-policy issue for African Americans to come out of this kind of perpetual bottom-of-the-barrel sort of situation that we're in now. As long as it's not a high priority, I'm not optimistic for the future of African Americans as a people in terms of uplifting ourselves. It's slowly happening. Affirmative action has been huge in helping black folks ascend to middle-class positions and professional positions in this country. It has been absolutely huge. And I think the assault on affirmative action is probably the most serious threat to black people becoming a mainstream part of the American system as anything there is out there. Everybody I know has benefited from affirmative action, every African American I know in my age group or younger. I'm fifty-seven. Every African American I know has benefited from policies that came out of the idea of affirmative action. It's an eminently fair way of dealing with societal oppressions that have existed for hundreds of years. And yet it's under attack. I laugh when I hear people talk about reverse discrimination. It's so absurd. The idea that you can enslave somebody and then try to say it's reverse discrimination when the folks are trying to get one or two spots out of a hundred in a professional program or something like that. If it weren't so tragic, it would be laughable. But that's been a very successful program. And those are the kind of programs that are needed to eventually erode or dissipate the vast inequities that we have societally as a result of the legacy of slavery and discrimination. But it's going to take a lot of time. You know, unless it's a massive kind of a program. There's nothing that can be done today or tomorrow, literally.

We live in a society that has this huge guilt complex about the whole African American situation, to the degree that they want it to go away. It's politically incorrect to say "racism." It's politically incorrect to play "the race card," which is, to me, a diabolical insinuation in and of itself. Because racial politics is not a race card. It's a real reflection of oppression and discrimination that's been wrought upon people for centuries.

One of the things about our society that's really insidious is the fact that there are African Americans who are getting jobs in a Republican administration, and some folks like to point at that as evidence that things are okay, that from a racial perspective, fair play is the law of the land and is part of public policy, without dealing with the ideology of the people that are in these positions. But the dilemma lies in the underlying mechanics that resulted in them getting these positions and how their ideology helps or hurts the bulk of African Americans in the country. I think that it is really important to understand that Clarence Thomas and Condoleezza Rice and even Colin Powell, who I respect as an individual, but these people hurt as much as they help, or they hurt more than they help. In the case of Clarence Thomas, his role has been extremely destructive to black progress.

My definition of that phenomenon [which has led to certain African Americans being appointed to high-level political positions] is that you simply have black people who have bought into the ideology of white racism. They have become conditioned and have bought into a system that has at its core a racially biased position. It's white racism that is covert rather than overt. It's unconscious rather than conscious. It's so deeply ingrained in our culture—and by our culture, I mean American culture—so deeply ingrained in American culture that the Americans that are affected by it don't even recognize that that's what they're being affected by.

I think that that phenomenon, the recognition of that phenomenon, would go a long way to accelerating the process of curing the ills that are afflicting the African American community in the United States of America. But that hasn't even begun to happen, because saying that there is still a racial problem is considered politically incorrect with the powers that be. George W. Bush would scoff at the idea. He'd just say, "Look at Condoleezza Rice. Look at Colin Powell. Look at all these other folks that I have in my cabinet." You know, as Reagan used to say, "There's not a racist bone in my body." Well, I mean, sure, if you don't recognize how racial politics in the United States molded how people think, but people don't look that deeply. The educational system, the courts. It's like the Supreme Court saying you can't use statistics to make a racial argument, because obviously, if you used statistics, you would come up with pervasive racism, pervasive discrimination. But the Supreme Court had the nerve to say "societal discrimination doesn't count." That's a quote, too. In terms of making rulings on some of the affirmative action cases—Bakke and some of those cases—[the court began dismantling affirmative action].

As a magistrate, as a judicial officer in the city of Detroit—and I'm one of six magistrates in the city of Detroit—I work at the Thirty-sixth District Court, which is the district court for the city of Detroit. We are very busy. The magistrates hear more cases than any other judicial officers because we hear all the traffic stuff in addition to the other things I mentioned, small claims and felony arraignments, and so that's a lot of cases. And what I'm able to do, though, that I'm really happy about is, I'm able to have a direct impact on people's lives every day. And they're primarily African Americans. And also, they're primarily Detroiters. And this is a system that has, in other times, been used to oppress black people. And now, as a judicial officer, as an African American male judicial officer . . . and I think it's important to understand that the treatment of black females and black males has differed dramatically and continues to differ dramatically in terms of opportunity. Black males are a unique problem, in terms of dropping out of school, in terms of being incarcerated, in terms of all these things. But one thing that I'm really happy about in terms of my own situation is that I am able to make an impact daily and to make a ruling based on my own background, as an African American in this city, based on the fact that I know the environment in which these people who come before me have come out of, and based on the fact that I can take into consideration subcultural kinds of powers that have influenced folks' lives [into making decisions that may not have been legal]. And maybe I can help some of these folks that come before me, help ease their burden a little bit. And I don't mean by being soft on crime or anything like that. But I do mean understanding that sometimes people wind up in situations for different reasons.

[Interview by Alan Govenar, May 23, 2005]

*Josephine G. Cooke, Los Angeles, ca. 2003.*

# JOSEPHINE G. COOKE

BUSINESSWOMAN

*Born May 5, 1931*

*Josephine G. Cooke was the third child born to Harry E. Cooke and Marion E. Cooke. When she was fourteen months old, her father passed away, and two years later, she was diagnosed with rheumatic fever. Because of her illness, she was unable to attend school for much of her childhood, but with her mother's encouragement, she completed her studies and graduated with her class in 1948. Cooke attended Virginia University in Richmond, Virginia, with a major in elementary education and, while she was a student, found out that she had the genetic disease sickle-cell anemia. Against the advice of her doctors, Cooke attended Cheyney State Teachers College in Pennsylvania and, after graduation, got a job teaching functionally illiterate adults in Philadelphia.*

*In 1967, Cooke moved to Los Angeles, California, where she obtained a position with a mortgage company as a clerk and over the years was promoted to the position of vice president. In 1983, Cooke started a new mortgage company, Cypress Financial, Inc., for three investors and worked with them as senior vice president of administration until 1991, when she founded the Quality Control Audit and Consulting Company for Mortgage Bankers. She closed that company in 1997 and became an independent consultant and auditor.*

*Through the years, Cooke has been active in service organizations, including Volunteers in Aid of Sickle Cell Anemia, Delta Sigma Theta Sorority, and Zonta International. She served as president of her local Zonta Club and went on to become international president of the organization. In 2005, Cooke was elected to the board of the Sickle Cell Foundation of California. She is a member of New Philadelphia African Methodist Episcopal Church in Rancho*

*Dominguez, California, where she not only worships but also is a member of the adult choir.*

MY FATHER PASSED AWAY when I was fourteen months old and left my mother with three small children, approximately two years apart in age, and I was the baby. And my mother had not worked prior to that. She was a housewife. My father, I understand, was a very ambitious person. He was a chauffeur. He was able to care for the family. He owned a car, a motorcycle, and a house, all of which my mother in short order lost because she had no business sense to keep it all together. And in those years— we're talking about 1932—women didn't know what to do. So my mother said she moved thirteen times in twelve months just because she couldn't pay the rent on the places [we lived]. But we finally did settle down in a house when I was three. We had a four-bedroom house on a very small street in Philadelphia. And those were happy times for me. I didn't know that my mother was having that hard of a time at the time. She was a very resourceful person.

She did finally get work. It started out as housework for an Irish family. And she wasn't the best person to do that. So they convinced her that she should be their cook. And this was good for us because when they shopped, they shopped for their house and our house. I remember we would be delighted when Mother came home, because she always had goodies for us from the family. And they encouraged her to go to beauty culture school while she was working for them, and they paid the tuition. And by the time I was five, my mother had graduated from beauty culture school and had acquired her teacher's license at the same time, and she was able to assist the teaching and get paid for it. And in I think it was 1935, we moved to Nicetown in Philadelphia, in a four-bedroom large corner house. It was a two-story house, but it started on the second level because on the first level were two businesses, two storefronts, and my mother took one of the storefronts and made it her beauty parlor, so she could work and be home with us.

Through all of this, my grandmother Daisy Washington, who was living in New York when my father passed, finally saw that my mother was having such a hard time. She moved in with us, and so we always had someone home to care for us. We didn't know we were poverty-stricken and oddballs. We were kind of happy kids. We ate three squares a day. My clothes were my sister's hand-me-downs because she grew a lot faster than I did. And the only new things I really got were shoes. That was the order of things, but once my mother opened the beauty parlor, it got a little better.

My mother worked all the time. She'd get up in the morning, six o'clock, and she did hair until eight, nine o'clock. But we were structured in our house. We ate breakfast together; we ate dinner together. We were very regimented in our home. And when I was about three or four, my sister and I were diagnosed with rheumatic fever, but we took two different roads with the illness. She defied it. She went out and did everything they told her not to do. She skated, and she did all of those things. I didn't. I read books, played with my doll babies. I was kind of a loner and thought it was okay. I never felt sorry for myself for that. I just made do with what I had and stayed around my grandmother a lot.

My mother remarried when I was nine, and he had two children living with him and one not living with him. My mother's name was Marion Cooke until she became Marion Holloman. My stepfather's name was William Holloman. And after they married, we moved, and he bought us a home in west Philadelphia in a very nice neighborhood, moved my mother's beauty shop, and she continued her business. We had a good life with two parents, a grandmother, and five children in the house.

I went to school every day and wasn't allowed to lean on my illness. I had to go to church every Sunday. My mother made us do what was expected of us. And when we were sick, she would go to the school or have one of the children go to the school, get our work, bring it home, and say, "When you feel better today, you can start working on your work." So I've always been driven.

They didn't have a lot of money, but my stepfather was an entrepreneur. He worked at the Philadelphia Navy Yard, but at the same time he opened a tailor shop. Then he bought an apartment building in north Philadelphia and opened a billiard parlor in that building. And we had to work—when you turned thirteen, you had to work somewhere in our house. It didn't matter how sick you were, you had to have a job. And we could pick where we wanted to work. Of course, with my mother having the beauty parlor, I always did things with her. I'd help with manicures or help her when she was busy with shampooing. And then, because she had her teacher's license, she was able to teach my sister and me cosmetology, and by the time I was eighteen, I had my license for cosmetology. And my sister did the same thing. We were able to work in the shop and make a living, and on Friday night we had to pay—we had to make a payment for our rent. We were told we had to pay if we were making money. I don't know how much, a dollar, or whatever it was, we had to give it to my mother.

Finally, when I was seventeen, they opened the restaurant called the Haverford Grill at Fifty-second and Haverford in Philadelphia. And they made us a deal about higher education. Of course, they insisted that we all graduate from high school; that wasn't an option. But we had a choice to go to college or university, and this was the deal, that we work all summer and we pay the first semester's tuition—not the books or any of the other stuff, but the tuition, and they would pay the rest for the balance of the year, whatever it took. So they figured we had to be committed, and they weren't going to waste their money. My brother was the first to go. He went away to Virginia Union University. We had an uncle who was dean of political science at Virginia Union. And my grandfather, my mother's father, lived in Richmond. His name was Joseph Teal. I don't know too much about his background, other than he was a Native American mix and he had remarried somewhere in the scheme of things because my grandmother also had remarried and divorced, and that's when she came to us.

My grandmother Daisy Washington was born in South Carolina. Her mother was a slave and her father, my great-grandfather, was the [white] master [slave owner]. I know my great-grandmother's name was Cherry Rogers. My great-grandfather had died sometime before my grandmother was born, so I don't know very much about him. My grandmother was a very interesting lady because she was one of those African Americans who looked more white than black.

I don't know where my father's family originated, but they settled in Maryland, Eastern Shore. My father ended up in Philadelphia, but I can't tell you how. As far as my mother is concerned, she was sent to Philadelphia to my grandmother (to her mother), but my great-grandmother raised her for most of her early years, and she was sent to her mother, as I understand it, when she was about thirteen. And my grandmother was already in Philadelphia.

Interestingly enough, it is my understanding—I never heard it—but my mother and my grandmother used to talk about how after my father passed and she was trying to make her way, people used to think she was a fast woman because she had these three children who looked different. So they claimed we all had different fathers—my brother, Harry Cooke, and my sister, Daisy Cooke. My brother was very dark, and when you look at the family, he looks like my grandmother, except his skin color is very dark. He had the deep-set eyes and the long face. My sister, when she was born, she was born very fair, but not white, and has almond eyes. And she's the one who, as we grew up and got to know our people, she looked like the Teals, my mother's father's people, the Indians. She had all of the Indian in her. I, of course, turned out looking like my father, just a little lighter color in skin, with big eyes.

As a child, we were not allowed to talk color. That was a no-no. My mother made us feel equal all of the time. We weren't taught about discrimination. But we knew there were places we didn't go. We never had to sit in the back of the bus. We didn't do that in Philadelphia. But we weren't about to go to Stouffer's for lunch. We could go to Horn & Hardart's for lunch. It was a kind of a cafeteria. And you could get sandwiches, but they were in machines. You put your money in. An automat!

Schools were integrated. We didn't have that kind of discrimination in Philadelphia, as I remember it, at that time. But there was discrimination. When we lived in Nicetown, it was largely a Jewish population, along with affluent African Americans, along with, you know, Caucasians. And when we first moved to Nicetown in Philadelphia, they used to throw rocks in our window and burned a cross on our lawn. But my mother and my grandmother never told us why. They just told us there were good people and bad people. We know the Jews didn't put a cross on our lawn. Eventually, the neighborhood settled down and accepted us. We didn't know who was throwing the rocks, because we didn't know the difference. How I remember that is because when we'd sit down to listen to the *Lone Ranger* on the radio at night and things like that, we had to sit on the floor with our backs against the wall away from the window so that if the rocks came in, they wouldn't hit us. Oh, [I was] about five. But we were never told anything other than they were bad people. We weren't told how come and what for.

My real first taste of discrimination came when I went away to Virginia Union University, a black Baptist college in Richmond, Virginia. Well, my very first weekend there, my roommate and I wanted to go shop for some little things to dress up our room. And we left and went to Sears. And I walked through the millinery shop. Now, keep in mind that Virginia Union is a religious school. At that time, when you went to church or vespers, you had to wear a hat, women had to wear hats. So I was kind of a hat-crazy person. So I went through the millinery section and saw this hat and I put it on, tried it on, and didn't want it, and I put it down. And this lady came up to me, and she said, "That'll be two ninety-eight." And I said, "I don't want the hat." And she said, "You tried it on. You're going to buy it." And I said, "No, I tried it on, and I don't want it." Oh, and she called the manager, and they called the police. My poor girlfriend, she hadn't done anything. And she was trying to tell me, "Pay them! Pay them! Pay them!" And I said, "No." I'm kind of stubborn. And the sheriff said, "Gal, where you from?" And I said, "Philadelphia." And he asked my roommate where she was from. She said, "New York." He said, these were his words: "They send you little Yankee niggers down here and don't tell you how to act." I knew the word *nigger*. But I'd never been called a Yankee nigger, and I knew it was not a nice word. And he said, "You put that hat on, you greased up that band, and you're going to buy that hat." So, of course, I'm crying by now and boohooing, and my girlfriend made me pay for the hat, and we got out of there without going to jail. Of course, I called my mother up. "I want to come home. I don't want to stay here anymore." And she said, "Oh, no. You will stay there, and you will learn how to cope with it." She wouldn't let me come home. Of course, with my [grandfather's] people in Richmond, I got to meet and know them. And they kind of told me what the real world was about. They guided me, and I had to cope. So I abided by the rules. I sat in the back of the bus, and I went to the balcony for the movies. That was a very unhappy situation, but as I do with most things, I coped until I got home [to Philadelphia]. Then I explained to my mother that I didn't want to stay there, and she said, "You're going back." And back I went because I did what my mother told me to. She was trying to make me understand what the real world was about.

So I just stayed, like everybody else, stayed to myself until one night—this was really the eye-opener about discrimination in America.

We had African students at the university. And one of the young men wanted to take me to the movies one night. And I said sure. And his name was Titus Mosolun Apoeso. Well, we got on the bus, and he sat on the very first seat that was empty. And I said, "No, no, no, no, no. We don't do this." Keep in mind he was very dark in color. And he said, "Sit down." And I did. And of course, the next stop, a white lady got on the bus, looked at us, and went to the driver to tell him to make us move. And the driver pulled over. Well, by now—and we're talking about 1950, okay?—there were people in our university, young people, who were on the move. They were getting on the bus, intentionally sitting in the front, getting dragged off, going to jail. That had started going on. And I didn't want to be a part of that because I didn't have the background to do that, you understand? I hadn't had enough experience to understand all of that. So I wasn't even a part of that at the time. And here I am, sitting in this first seat, and they're going to think I'm an activist, and they're going to drag me off. I was scared to death. And the driver came back and he looked at Titus and he said, "You have to sit in the back of the bus. The white line's back there." And Titus went in his pocket and came out with his passport or visa and said, "I am a British subject. I sit where I please." "True," the man said, "I apologize," and he walked back to the lady, "You will have to sit somewhere else." I'm sitting there sweating ink because if they had said anything to me, I don't know what I would have said. "No speak-a the English." I didn't know what I was going to say. But we rode down Slaughter Street to the theater. And we got to the theater and he purchased two tickets, orchestra tickets, and that's where I drew the line. No balcony tickets. "No, I sit in the orchestra, first floor for me." And I said, "Okay, you sit by yourself, because they're not going to ask you for a passport in there." And I caught the bus back behind the line and went back to school by myself.

I wasn't out there for the movement. I wanted to go to the show. And to go to jail for that just didn't make any sense to me at that time. Anyway, as it turned out, I didn't go out with him anymore, and I kind of stayed "in my place."

I used to go back and forth home [to Philadelphia] by train, and one of my stops had to be in Washington, D.C., our dear capital. Well, I caught the train, and of course, the trains were also segregated. We couldn't go in the diner to eat. They had, like, a little kiosk or something for the Negroes. But we couldn't go into the diner for food. So I waited until we got to Washington. I had to change trains to go from Washington to Philadelphia, and I went into the restaurant, to the counter, and sat there to eat. Well, the waitress kept going back and forth, bypassing me, going to different people, and not waiting on me. And there was a gentleman who sat next to me, a white gentleman, and she came and asked him, "Can I help you?" And he said, "This lady doesn't seem to have been waited on yet." And he sounded like a Northerner. I don't even recall his name now, but it was an interesting situation. And she said, "I asked if I could help you." And he said, "Yes, after you help her." So she came over to me and said, "What you want?" So I ordered some eggs, and then she went to him, and he gave her his order, and when she brought the food back, she gave him his food first, and she took my food and she slammed it down on the counter and the food went off the plate a little bit. This must have been about 1951. And this gentleman looked at me, and he said, "Do what I do, please." I didn't know what he meant. And he said, "Please, do what I do." And I looked at him, and he took his plate and he turned it upside down and threw it back on the counter. And he said, "Do it," so I did it. And he looked at the waitress, and he said, "You eat it, and I'm not paying for it, and come on, gal, let's go." And he took me to a restaurant across the street, outside of the train station, for breakfast.

He was white. I don't remember his name, but I'll never forget that incident that I was in—and his beef—that we were in the capital of the United States, you know, Washington, D.C., and this should be going on. It was just ridiculous.

I majored in elementary education at Virginia Union. And it was around this time I was diagnosed with sickle cell. I was nineteen. I was at the university, and I was bleeding when I passed my water. I was taking my final exams. I think it was January, and I went to the infirmary. I told them I didn't know what was going on because I was passing clots in my urine. And they sent me to a doctor, and this doctor examined me and he says, "Well, I think your kidney is bleeding through your bladder. When do you go home?" And I told him I was going home the next day, and he said, "Well, I want you to take two Alka-Seltzers four times a day until you get home. Take your two finals and go home and see a urologist." And so I did that. And when I got home, of course the first thing I had to tell my mother was, "I've got to go to the hospital." I had no pain, but my doctor sent me to the University of Pennsylvania to a urologist, who was a Cuban doctor, Dr. Figueroa. And he did tests on my kidneys, and he said, "Well, your kidney is hemorrhaging. However, the kidney is not itself damaged. I want to test you for sickle cell." In his broken English, he said "sickle cell." I had never heard of sickle cell. He didn't use the word *anemia*. He just said "sickle cell." And I thought he said "syphilis." Here I am, away from home, and this man is suspecting me. I'm having syphilis. My mother will kill me. And that's all I could think. I got all upset. And he said, "No, no, no. We'll test you." So they took blood. And I still don't know what sickle cell is. And they came back the next day, told me—they had six doctors at the teaching hospital, in the ward—and told me yes, it was positive. I had sickle-cell anemia. That's when they tagged on the "anemia." And they said they were going to give me blood transfusions and they needed to test my family because it was genetic. Then they proceeded to tell me that my life expectancy was about twenty-nine to thirty years—that I shouldn't go back to school, not to get married. "Don't have children. Don't go in any altitude more than two to three thousand feet. And we'll give you pain medication for the pain and treat you for the illness, but there is no cure." Okay. I wallowed in that for about fifteen minutes.

They tested my family and my mother—at that time, the tests were not as sophisticated as they are—they didn't know what they know now. In those days, they thought you either had the trait or you didn't. We now know that there's a combination of factors—my mother had to have some of the combination, but my father was probably the one who had it because he died of a stroke at about age thirty-two.

Sickle-cell anemia is a blood disorder; it's a genetic blood disorder. We who have the sickle-cell gene, some of our red cells that we produce look like a sickle that you cut grass with. It has a hard covering, so it isn't as pliable as the others. And the more of these that we produce, the greater the chance we're going to have painful episodes. And that causes a crisis that is generally very painful. And if you get a lot of these sickle cells, these crescent-shaped cells, they do what they call logjamming, and they cause hemorrhages in your body because they can't make it through the vessels and you get pain in your joints, in your bones. If you get a hemorrhage in your brain, you get a stroke. You get a hemorrhage in your eyes, you go blind or you have what I had. I've had five surgeries, putting my retina back from hemorrhages in my eyes over the years. And of course when these vessels break, when they heal and close up, they create scar tissue. And the bones don't get as much blood, as much nutrients as they should, which is why I lost both of my hips, because I had a lot of pain in my legs, arms, and hips, and the bones deteriorated. It causes bone-degenerative bone diseases. I've had heart attacks; I've had blood clots in my lungs. You name it, I've had it—everything but a stroke.

Anyway, I went back to Virginia Union University, but I was convinced that I should be near home because I had these doctors. Actually, when they found out I had this incurable disease and my sister had it— my brother has the trait; he's a carrier—my Blue Cross dropped us like a hot potato. My stepfather had us all covered under Blue Cross. And we had an incurable disease, and they would not cover us anymore. So there were a group of doctors at the University of Pennsylvania, hematologists, who wanted to do some research on this. And that gave me at least, if not free, affordable health care. I was one of the first twenty-five patients. So I moved home and went to Cheyney State Teachers College. It was a black teachers college. And I never did quite finish. I met someone by the name of Joseph Robinson and I got married. And I got pregnant. I had a very difficult but successful pregnancy, and I have a beautiful daughter who has the trait.

My husband wanted to move to New Jersey, and I went to New Jersey. By then, I had joined the NAACP, this is 1955—and we were marching [protesting]. It was the same year that the young man Emmett Till was murdered. And things were going on [in the civil-rights movement].

In Jersey, they had private swimming pools. They called them private clubs because it was restrictive. And the NAACP went after them, and I worked with them. Here I am very pregnant. And what they [the NAACP] would do is send two or three of us, the blacks, to go in. But they would keep us out because they would say it was full. "You aren't a member." And we'd say, "Well, we want to apply for membership." "Well, we don't have any more memberships open." And then they would send two or three white members right behind us, and they'd get in, and they'd get memberships. And I was doing that while I was pregnant, trying to break them, and through court, we did get those swimming pools opened up in New Jersey. That was in New Brunswick.

My husband was a postal worker. The marriage didn't last long, but by being married to him, I ended up with good government medical coverage. But I was twenty-nine years old. He tried to cope with me, but it was very difficult. He knew I was ill, but he didn't fully understand. One minute, I'm fine, I'm healthy. I'd go to bed, I was okay, get up in the morning and I'd need help to walk to the bathroom because my legs hurt so badly. I think sometimes he thought I was a hypochondriac or something, and lazy at that.

My marriage lasted until 1959. That's when I took the real nosedive. My daughter was four and a half. . . . My daughter's name is Tracy—back then, her name was Michelle Marion Robinson. She legally changed her first name to Tracy when she was thirteen. She wanted to change it. She was born in 1955.

Anyway, this must have been 1960. And my kidney was acting up again, and they decided to do exploratory surgery to probably remove the kidney. What they said to me was, they left the kidney, but they removed my spleen because the spleen had enlarged. The spleen is a holder for your cells, for your red cells; it's like a storehouse. And sometimes your spleen gets enlarged. This is a normal difficulty with people with sickle cell. Well, I found out in 1982, '81, I still had my spleen. How do you like them apples? But that's another story. Well, I was very sick [in 1960]. I went down to eighty-two pounds. I wasn't going to make it, and I think he [my husband] might have prayed for that to happen to free him because he wanted my daughter. I had to fight to keep custody of my daughter during that very bad illness. But he and I are friends today. We're fine. He's been a great dad, but I got the divorce [and I moved back to Philadelphia]. I went to the board of education because I couldn't teach. I didn't have my credentials for teaching. But I had to work and raise my kid. So I was given credentials to teach the functioning illiterate adults. I couldn't handle the children. I wasn't physically able. I didn't weigh a hundred pounds and was hurting most of the time. But I taught for about five years, six years, till I came to California.

I came out to California on a [travel] tour. Everything I do is hooked to this illness. It's really hysterical. We had a travel group, a few women who every summer would go somewhere up and down the East Coast. East Coast people generally don't go west. But we decided we wanted to go to California and Las Vegas this particular trip. I couldn't fly. So we took a train from Philadelphia to Los Angeles by way of Chicago and came to California. About my third day here, my kidneys started hemorrhaging again. The hotel had to call a doctor. And this is all part of this story, so you have to hear it. And the doctor who came—and this was at night—he came and talked to me, Dr. Jack Lewis. And after talking to me, he said to my mother [who was also on the trip], "I'm going to have to put her in the hospital. She's going to have to leave the tour." He got an ambulance, took my mother to his home with him and his wife so she wouldn't have to be in a hotel by herself. This was a Jewish doctor from Beverly Hills. Very nice guy. While I'm there in the hospital, of course, he started me on a sodium-bicarbonate regimen intravenously. I didn't understand it. But he did it and it helped. And while I'm in the hospital, my roommate called a friend of hers because I hadn't seen anything in Los Angeles. She called this friend and said, "You've got to come and meet this great gal"—here I am, in the hospital, right, with an IV hanging out of my arm. And she explained why I was there. And he came to the hospital, met me, and later took my mother downtown to buy me some clothes because my mother was sure I was going home in a pine box and had sent all of my clothes back to Philadelphia with the tour. And after I got out of the hospital, he took us around Los Angeles and showed us a few things. And when we got ready to leave [for Philadelphia], he gave me an engagement ring, out of the blue. I thought the man was out of his mind. My mother laughed all the way home, all the way to Philadelphia. We said, "What is the matter with this character?" He was a widower, had two children. And sure enough, he courted me for a year or so, came back and forth to Philadelphia. And I decided, why not? So my daughter and I came to California in 1967 and I got married. His name was Chester Gudger.

Well, the marriage went well; parenthood did not. By 1971, we were divorced. His children had some problems, psychological problems, and he didn't want to do anything about it. And when I had a heart attack in 1970, I knew that I had to get out of this relationship or I was going to die. I had my Dr. Lewis for my doctor, which I think is really the reason I stayed in Los Angeles.

So I got a job in a travel agency, and I taught myself to type thirty-five words a minute. And they sent me to work for a mortgage company because they needed a person of color [to meet their quota]. It's my understanding they had been put on notice by HUD that they had to integrate the company, but they kept telling me they were concerned how I would be treated when I got there. And I asked [my supervisor] did they grow oak trees in the company, and he said, "Well, no." And I said, "Well, they can't lynch me. I'll do fine." And he said, "Well, with your sense of humor, I guess you will." I stayed there fourteen and a half years and left as a vice president. Got my mortgage-banking certificate on them. They sent me to school.

Then, my boss at the time, with two other mortgage bankers, decided to start their own company, and they asked me if I would put it together for them. I quit my job and put it together for them, and then they quit their jobs and came in after me. We're still all friends. We opened that company in 1983, and I left in 1990, a growing company, to start my own mortgage quality-control company. And in 1997, when my mother got ill, I decided to close my company, and that's when I started doing my consulting work, and I've been doing that ever since.

Well, when I was learning to become a mortgage banker, I got involved in Zonta International, a business and professional women's service organization. As I said, they sent me to mortgage-banking school, and while I went to Stanford, my roommate was a lovely gal who worked for the Veterans Administration. She was also a student that they sent, and she was a Mormon from Salt Lake City. And she and I got to be great friends. She was in Zonta. So she recommended my name to the Zonta Club of Los Angeles [because there wasn't a Zonta Club at Stanford]. And of course, you have to know, they didn't have one of me, either. I was the first. But it didn't bother me. I'm a screwball in that regard, because part of my success in doing what I do is I don't have any anger. We weren't raised to be angry about who we are.

For me, the appeal of Zonta was its Amelia Earhart Fellowship (to provide scholarships to young women pursuing careers in aviation and aeronautics), but I knew nothing about the Zonta organization in general. And when I learned about what they were doing for women in areas of education, I thought, "Oh, great! This is a good thing to do."

Well, I went to Zonta meetings for about three months and they invited me to become a member. And of course, I accepted. I was probably the youngest or next to the youngest one in the club at the time; I was in my forties. But we got along. And the next year, I was elected the president of the club. And they supported me wholeheartedly. I went out and said, "We live in an integrated city. We need to look like the city." And we went out and got Asians and Hispanics and some blacks to join our club.

I was taught if you're going to do anything, you do it well. So the very next year—I joined in February—they nominated and then elected me to be a director of our club. And I'm one of those people, you give me a job, I say, "Okay, I'll try. I'll do my best." Then the secretary died at midterm, and they asked me if I'd take that job over, so I was secretary, which qualified me when we had elections at the end of my first year. They wanted to know if I would run for president of the club because they were older ladies. Most of them had been president one or two times. And I said, "Okay." And so I went on to become president. And in the next two years, I was nominated to area director. Then I was nominated to lieutenant governor, and the only racism I really encountered in Zonta came when I was lieutenant governor of this district. The gal who was running for governor was campaigning against me because [she said] it wasn't time to have a black governor in District 9—[one person was saying this] openly. And I was furious. In fact, I almost left Zonta because of it. But the then-governor, I went to her, and I said, "I'm going to pull out of the race. I can't handle this. I've never been a racist. I don't know how to fight racism. I'm not going to do anything to anybody." And she and her husband talked to me and said, "Josie, if you pull out, you're selfish. You're doing it for yourself. Zonta needs your leadership. And if you pull out, you will not be doing our organization any good. We need you." I thought about that, and I thought, well, if one person thinks that, I don't know what else I could do. So in my speech, I just told them that if I were elected, everybody would have a permanent suntan and permanently curly hair. I was elected hands down. Everybody laughed. They thought that was funny after they realized what I was saying to them. But this woman, I had to spend two years as her lieutenant governor. I got to tell you, it was awful. But I survived it, and she survived it.

Well, from district governor, I was asked if I would run for international director. And I said, "Okay." I joined [Zonta] in '76, and I was president from 1996 to '98. I went from director to vice president to president-elect. I didn't have a break in my leadership.

As president of Zonta International, I looked at the multitude of issues that Zonta focuses upon to advance the status of women worldwide—education, health issues, cultural issues, social issues. And I decided that the focus of my biennium was going to be issues related to violence. Violence against women is prevalent anywhere you go. But there are different kinds of violence, whether it's domestic violence or genital mutilation, whether it's burning the girl child if she's firstborn or trafficking women and children, all of those things. In my travels around the world during my years of leadership, I recognized these problems. Whether it's prostitution, or forced prostitution, there is an issue about violence against women. And it's everywhere. What we need to do is to say, "Okay, here's a program that focuses on violence against women. We're going to eradicate it. But we're going to allow our clubs, our district, our regions to focus on the issues that face them." And that's why we now have ZIS-VAW, which is my baby—Zonta International Strategies to Eradicate Violence Against Women, and the tag that's not in the [acronym] is "and children."

My district has been very active in women's issues, but we've acted very quietly. In my own club, for years, we have sponsored the House of Ruth [which is a domestic violence shelter for women and children] financially and with our hands-on service. We would go down and read stories to the children while the parents went out to look for a job. We would have a party for the children. We were actively involved with issues [that really mattered to women and children]. We also supported the Spastic Children's Foundation, which is now a part of the Cerebral Palsy Institute. These are the kinds of things. We've focused a lot on education for the woman returning to work and scholarships for women who are returning to get an education in order to get on their feet. Each club should look at their community and focus on the needs of that community.

I was so very pleased at the end of my term [as Zonta International president] the board recommended that ZISVAW should be an ongoing international project, and it is. It isn't going as strongly as I would like, but I'm happy with what's going on. There are real issues that are being addressed.

The frontier to me is something new. Uncharted waters are a frontier. It's a new venture. Something that isn't fully developed is a frontier. It's a beginning. ZISVAW. I would like to see the day come when ZISVAW is no longer needed. That's the goal. Zonta is not a frontier for me. It's a vessel through which frontiers can be explored.

The saddest thing about the African American movement, in my estimation, I kind of tighten up a little when I hear people talk about "the slaves were freed." You cannot free a people who are not educated and have no resources. The slaves were let go. We are still in a constant cycle of being freed.

As we become educated, as we have resources, become property owners, and achieve economic success and it is a continuum—we have not arrived. But it's not just African Americans who haven't arrived, okay? Anybody out there who is not educated to some degree, who has no resources, they are enslaved in poverty.

In addition to ZISVAW, when I was Zonta International president, I worked with UNICEF—talk about a frontier—to advance the education for the black girl child in South Africa after apartheid. And it was a failure. I say failure, but maybe that's not really the word—my goals had not been met. Neither had UNICEF's to the point that they returned our funding. I had the opportunity because of that project to visit South Africa in 1996 and found a country with wonderful resources—wealthy— and yet stricken with poverty, crime, segregation, and discrimination. Unbelievable.

In the United States, we had black and white schools. We had segregated schools, okay? White children went to one school; black children to another. They called it separate but equal when it wasn't. But it was separate, and we talked about equality. That's a whole other story for me; something's wrong with that. But then I went to South Africa and found out that they have three separate educational systems—black, colored, and white. For the blacks, the staff does not have to be credentialed, and the school edifices were located in the middle of fields and were old, broken-down farm buildings with leaky roofs, no electricity, and no running water. I went there and talked to the children. I had one little girl talk to me privately, and she said she was being raped on her way to school mornings or afternoons because she had to come through the fields because her parents could not afford to pay for the bus ride to school. I also learned as I went from the elementary school to the middle school, I started seeing fewer girls in school. Middle schools were a little better equipped in terms of the building. They didn't have too many holes in the ceiling. I'm still talking about the black schools. And by the time I got to the high schools to visit, I saw very few girls, and I had to ask, "Where are all of the girls?" Well, when girls get pregnant, they cannot go back to school. How do they get pregnant? Well, the teachers, officials, invited them to their houses to clean up for them. They use them, abuse them, just like this little girl was getting raped in the field. She gets pregnant; education is not a part of her goal. Can you believe that? I went to a library at the senior high school, and there were no books on the shelves. And we here in Los Angeles have a whole building locked up, full of books that could be used.

Zonta tried to help with this. I visited the white schools, I visited the colored schools, and couldn't do anything. UNICEF is the one who put the skids on it [Zonta's efforts] because it's all too political. And the crime element. They've got a long way to go.

You can't free a people who have no education and who have no resources. I don't care whether it's here in America or in South Africa or Timbuktu. And it seems we're moving backwards in our movement with education. How can we ensure an acceptable level of education for the majority of the people? It has to start with family leadership. I listen to some of the young people talking. I'm going to talk about the young. And it's not just now. That's the sad part about it. It's not just the African American.

Keep in mind, the African American is a product of the slaves who were brought here, who were deprived of their language, their culture. They were robbed. They were absolutely robbed. Raped—and I'm not talking about just sexually. They were robbed of who they were. The institution of slavery totally decimated the family.

Other immigrants come here, and they have something that they know, that they remember, that they hold onto. We don't have that. The Hispanics come here; they are Hispanics. They have their own culture. We don't have a culture. By the time you get to my generation, I don't have a culture. Why? Because I'm so mixed up. I'm Irish, I'm Indian, I'm African. Who am I? I lived through the whole thing of what to call me.

When I was a kid, if you called me black, I'd be angry. You called me Negro, that's what I am. You called me nigger, you were mad at me. Then all of a sudden, we go through this metamorphosis of, "I'm black, I'm African American, I'm all of these things." I don't even know who I am.

As the president and an officer of Zonta International, I would never allow anybody out there when I was going to speak to introduce me—and some wanted to say, "Josie Cooke, the first African American president." How dare you! I'm an American in an international organization. I wouldn't let them introduce me that way. If you weren't blind, you knew. Okay? And if you were blind, you shouldn't care, if my message was okay. And it doesn't say an awful lot for an organization that started in 1919, that in 1996, they got the first African American president, and they're proud of it.

Around 1994, I was asked to be the keynote speaker at the Zonta Club of Santa Clarita Valley, which has a Status of Women program every April. It was the same year that here in California on the ballot was the abolishment of affirmative action. And I was Zonta's guest speaker, right? And they are a very politically active club—some of their members are politicians. But I talked about affirmative action, the pros and the cons. And yes, I am a product of affirmative action. I don't want you to forget that, because I think that's important, that my getting into mortgage banking was affirmative action. I was given an opportunity because they had a need to showcase me. However, I took that opportunity and I built on it. You open the door, I'll get it for myself. And I went into that company. They opened the door and let me in there and didn't even have a j-o-b for me. Okay? My boss and I created and developed a department called inventory control. I took advantage of all of the things that would help me grow as a person after getting the opportunity, as a worker, as an employee, as a career path.

I guess I've had the pleasure of having more positive results than negative results in my effort. And there's an old religious song that we sing, "I've had some good days, I've had some bad days"—"Hills to Climb." "I've had some lonely days, I've had some sleepless nights, but when I look around and I think it over, all of my good days outweigh my bad days." If it doesn't go right, I turn around and make another path. I don't blame anybody. I guess that's really part of where I'm coming from. I don't blame anybody for my illness because I think all of this—I was telling them last night at choir rehearsal. We do a prayer and praise [report]. If you need a prayer, you ask for a prayer for something. If you have something to be happy about, you stand up and tell them. And to-day marks my second anniversary of when I went on life support. Two years ago today. I can shout about that because I didn't die. I'm back out here kicking and screaming. I know I have to do something with the rest of my life. And I don't know what that is; I don't know what that purpose is. But I look at all opportunities as a purpose, as a purpose for me, to do something good for somebody else. That's what I do with my life.

[Interview by Alan Govenar, September 3, 2004.]

*Quoqueze Desiree Craig modeling Calvin Klein, Dallas, Texas, 1977.*

# QUOQUEZE DESIREE CRAIG

FASHION MODEL

*Born December 21, 1941*

*Quoqueze Desiree Craig was born in Dallas, the daughter of Quo-*
*queze and Douglas Moore. She attended segregated schools in Dal-*
*las, including K. B. Polk Elementary and Booker T. Washington*
*High School, where she graduated in 1960. Growing up, Craig*
*learned about women's fashions from her mother, who made her*
*clothes, and had a sophisticated "sense of style." While Craig was*
*working as a technician at Texas Instruments, her sister-in-law*
*encouraged her to try out as a model for Neiman Marcus, which was*
*then looking to hire an African American. Craig became the first*
*black fashion model to work at Neiman Marcus in Dallas and in*
*other store locations around the country. She discusses her modeling*
*career in the context of her family life and professional aspirations.*

MY FULL NAME IS Quoqueze Desiree Moore Craig. My mother and I have
the same first name, and my father and brother have the same first
name—Douglas. My mother's friends called her Kokeeze, and then later
my friends and I only knew her as Coke. I tried to call her Mother or
Mom, but it just never worked. Everyone knew her as Coke.

I'm not really sure about the origins of the name Quoqueze. I just
know that it's Indian. At one time, when I worked at TI [Texas Instru-
ments], I was told that it had something to do with Sunflower or Sun
something. I'm not really sure. I was born in Dallas.

My father came from Uniontown, Alabama, and then he moved to
Detroit and then to Dallas, and met my mom. That's history. Douglas
Moore. No middle name. He was one of the first black icemen in Dallas.
He went from house to house with an ice pack and the picks and all of
that, worked for the Southern Ice Company. He got into the business

through my mother's father, who was the first black iceman in town, and he went around town with one of those horse-drawn ice buggies.

My father came to Dallas because he thought it was a progressive city and had more to offer him than Detroit did. I would think it was in the thirties. I'm sure it was. He settled here, got a foothold here, and loved everything here. And when he wasn't working as an iceman, he played the alto saxophone. In fact, my brother and my son played the alto saxophone, and they both ventured into the baritone sax as well. But my mother sang at Boll Street [CME Church], gave recitals. So I'm from a musical background. My mother was a singing artist. In fact, she was compared to Marian Anderson. She sang contralto. And I can still hear her voice ringing in my ear when I go to church now on Sunday.

By the time I was born, my father wasn't playing in bands. And he just worked as an iceman. He passed in 1975; he was going to the store. My little daughter Deb—Deborah—wanted to use the facilities before their little trip. She came out and there he was on the ground. He'd had a massive heart attack, and of course, my mother was so thankful that they weren't on the road at that time, because it could have happened while he was driving the truck.

We were all born in my grandmother's little house at 2608 Munger Avenue. And if you could see her then, you would compare her to Granny on the *Beverly Hillbillies,* because, I swear, she looked just like Granny. Her name was Eddice Josephine Thomas. Sparks was her maiden name.

I never met my grandparents on my father's side. They moved to Detroit from Alabama. Several of his brothers are still living there. I don't know why they went to Detroit, but I do know that my father had five brothers and one sister.

My father was so fabulous. We truly were a sweet family because we didn't do the kidding around and everything. Ours was just true and honest love. My mother and father met, and they planned their children. They wanted a son first and then, because they desired a daughter, that's where my middle name, Desiree, came from. But actually I was named after a woman in the Long family, who owned the Practical Drawing Company. They supplied all of the school supplies to the school system then. And her name was Desiree Long. My mom worked in their home. And Mr. Long was known as the king, and she was the queen.

We had such a wonderful childhood. I used to have little colored chickens. They were dyed pink to match my shoes for Easter. Oh, it was fabulous, it really was. My father was always at home. In fact, I wasn't accustomed to men being out at night. He was always there. Got up at five in the morning. He was home by 2 P.M. and he brought whatever we needed. We were always just a little close-knit family, just the four of us.

My mom worked in the Longs' household. But other than that, she was a stay-at-home mom. I have memories of coming home in the winter to hand-made "corny" dogs. It was fabulous. She always was able to attend the PTA meetings. A lot of parents, because of work, weren't there. But she was always there for us, and so was my father.

We had a little community there, which was called North Park Addition. But as you know, boundaries change. North Park is now Northwest Highway. But this was actually there at Mockingbird Lane. That's when Mockingbird Lane was a little black dirt road. Well, I've only lived in two places in my life. I was born on Munger, as were my mother and my brother. Then, we moved from there, which was my maternal grandmother's home, to North Park. And from North Park, I went to Oak Cliff. So I've been in the same house all these many years. But growing up in Dallas was different. We went downtown very seldom because of the fact that then you couldn't use the public facilities, and it just felt degrading to my mother.

I have a very personal sense of segregation and racism. Even today, that's the one thing; it's always as though you have to apologize for the color of your skin when you get into any kind of event or any kind of interaction with people. It's terrible. But yes, I did feel it. And I must tell you, I know it shouldn't, but it disturbs me.

I love seeing history. Just the other day, when I saw [footage] of Martin Luther King Jr. on TV, I found myself crying because honest and truly, things have changed, but not that much. It was something that he said that I found myself saying to this day, and that was about feeling like you're nobody. The nobody-ness. I have found that out daily, on a constant basis. If I have been talking, having a conversation with someone in my office, and all of a sudden, someone else walks up, the conversation that I was having with this other person just sort of disappears and goes into the air. No one says, "Excuse me." They just start the conversation as though I'm not there, and I'm the only black person in the office. And I feel like a nobody. And I think, "Now, this is something from fifty years ago, that's what Martin Luther King was talking about." And to this day, there's still that little underlying feeling.

I enjoy a lot of music, but I also find it interesting, too, how much blacks are copied. You find that we are criticized for being a certain way, and then you turn around and the very people that criticize us are doing the same things. I never will forget how funny I thought it was to see Bush on TV high-fiving somebody. But my family doesn't high-five. But it's one of those things that you think, "Okay, they talk about us being so down to earth and natural, but there is something about our naturalness, the way we dance, the way we sing, and whatever that must be appreciated by somebody because we're copied an awful lot."

Once you are exposed, then it's a matter of it just coming naturally to you. You see it in sports as well—Tiger Woods in golf . . . in basketball, football. Used to be, if you look at old TV stations and everything, they said that there were predominantly white teams. And now a lot of them are black. And then, didn't they say that we couldn't be quarterbacks? Excuse me, look now! Who's going to the Super Bowl? [Donovan McNabb, Philadelphia Eagles.]

But like anything else, it takes people with the right attitude in their heart to pass it on to others. When they see that something is wrong and they know that it's wrong, you have to speak out. You hear it on TV, but rarely do you really see a person speak out and say, "You know that's not right." It happens to me all the time in the office. I can't tell you how many times. I even had one guy do this "Yowzah" thing. "I'se a need some business cards." And I called him on it, because my mom always said, you have to do it then. Of course, he apologized. He sat me down and said he had moved to California to get away from racism. But yet and still, somewhere in his body, in his mind-set, it's there, because he said it. It happens all the time in my office, and here it is, what, 2005?

As a child, I went to K. B. Polk Elementary School. I was their first queen. Then, you won with contributions, and I won with twelve dollars and fifty cents to become the first queen of K. B. Polk. It was a black school in North Park district. It was quite an honor, of course. but basically you just raised the money to become the queen.

You should have seen the dress that I wore for my elementary school graduation. My mother has always been so stylish. She found this picture, an illustration, of course, probably from Neiman's, and it was a square-necked gown, sleeveless, white organza—it was in three differ-ent layers, close to the body, and then at the bottom it flared out, and it was just a little above my ankles. So it was different, for me to graduate from elementary school in this dress—no one else had, of course, a dress like that. She had had it made.

I had an interest in fashion from early on because of my mother. She always wore colored stockings. People would stare at her maybe, but she had a sense of style about her. She did, in the fall mostly, the red hose and the blue hose and fishnets. That was one of her trademarks. So she's always been very stylish, and so was her sister, Clementine Northcutt. She was a minister's wife, and she had furs—she was just very glamorous with her hair pulled up on top of her head.

So in the ninth grade, I went to Booker T. Washington. It's now called the Arts Magnet. I found out later, though, that a lot of the history, when it became the Arts Magnet, was just thrown in the trash. I don't know why history would become so obsolete, perhaps the name changed a little bit on the school, but history is history. And that was where J. L. Patton Jr. was the principal.

We had several memorable teachers—one of the most influential was Miss Holloway, Hazel Holloway. She was in charge of the pep squad. Now, we had the pep squad, and there was a drill team, majorettes and cheerleaders. And it was all considered the pep squad. And Miss Hol-loway would perch on the second floor of the school building to look down on us so that she knew what we were doing wrong. She'd watch the girls and make the lines straight. But she was the one, also, who taught us in physical education just the way to hold yourself and to respect yourself. Miss Holloway, you always had to have your starched white gym suit, white socks, tennis shoes. Kids don't exercise like that anymore. And I think that's why they're talking about the world having an obesity problem. But Miss Holloway would have us in line, with her little pad and pencil, and she walked down the line and took note of everything, whether our hair was combed. The gym suit had to be immaculate. White socks and tennis shoes. And then we exercised and showered after-wards. It was really fun.

The training I got as a majorette was important. And it was fun. You know, being on the field, high-stepping in front of everyone and hear-ing the crowd yell. Yeah, it was nice. I think I still remember the routine,

Quoqueze Desiree Craig, Dallas, Texas, 1977.

too. Give me a baton; I can do it now for you. It's the truth. But that was another thing, too, I always kind of felt a little different. I've always felt that I was never really understood. I would meet kids, and when they finally got to know me, it was like, "Oh, I didn't know you were like that. I thought you were stuck up and everything." And I said, "No, I don't understand how I've gotten that role in life, or how people see me that way," but I generally just tend to stick to myself, do the things that I need to do, and leave everybody else alone.

For the majorettes there was a store that always made the uniforms for our school. But my mother insisted that mine had to be done by the same lady that did my dress when I graduated from high school. She took the time to find fabric similar to what the other girls had, and there was a certain braiding on the skirt that had to be done, the tassels and all of that. I mean, there were at least fifty-two tassels on the bottom of the skirt, the little red skirt with the white little tassels and everything. And then the jacket was white. Our colors were crimson and gray, but because that's such a dark kind of color, we just did red and white. It was easier to find. And then, there were the high hats and the plumes and the boots and the tassels. Oh, man, those games at Cobb Stadium [where the black football games were played] were really out of sight. And then we'd walk from there to [Old] North Dallas and have our little barbecue or whatever and then catch the bus and go home. And that was basically the only outing that I did as a teenager.

Maybe we had parties at the YMCA, evening dance things at the Y or whatever. It was, of course, segregated. But then in the summertime, there was a six-week course where you would learn hobbies and other crafts, and that was very enjoyable. And you got a chance to mingle. There were only three [African American] schools then—Booker T. Washington, Lincoln, and Madison, which came later. But you got a chance to meet some of the other kids that were in town, rather than just people in your little area. Still, traveling [around the city] wasn't done that much. I used to think driving to Oak Cliff was long—it was like driving out of town. But now the streets, the roads are so different. There's no problem. You can just drive anywhere now and get around town in thirty minutes anywhere.

I graduated from Booker T. Washington in 1960. But I had already gotten married while I was still in high school. I must have been seventeen, eighteen. It was unusual. So after I graduated, I was busy raising my family—my son, my husband—taking care of them. And then, shortly after that, I was hired at TI, Texas Instruments. Man, that was something: my first job. And I think that helped to mold me in life as well, because we had to bond little, tiny strands of gold thread that were one-eighth the size of human hair. With a microscope and sharp tweezers, we had to bond [these threads together]. It was interesting. These were some of the units that were used in the first space programs, so we were responsible for being perfect. My mother not only taught me to be like God—"You have to be like God; that's what we're supposed to be, that's what he intended"—but there at TI, we had the little ladies in the white jackets, the quality control, and they came by every thirty minutes and got your rack of bonded units and tested them and came back to tell you how many were wrong and all of this. So you always tried to be perfect. And that's why I think I am as I am.

I really had thought of going to college, but I was not impressed by the idea of getting more education, because I felt like I could only be a teacher or work in a beauty salon. You couldn't be a stewardess. You couldn't be anything. There weren't very many opportunities. So you either went to school, or you became a mom, or you just got a job. So that was basically all.

I really hadn't even thought about modeling. I was content working at TI, and there was a beauty hair competition. Tony Davis and a little group there on Forest Avenue (now Martin Luther King Jr. Boulevard). There was a little beauticians' building, and they had a little competition there for hairstyling. In fact, I did my own hair. But of course, the person that had asked me to be in the competition took credit for it. And that was sort of my first opportunity to be in front of a crowd. So some time not long after that, my sister-in-law was working at a little club, and someone told her that Neiman Marcus was thinking of having their first black model, and she said, "Oh, no. I'm too short and my nose is too big and too wide, and I'm a little bit wide back here, but I think I know someone. I'll tell her; she's my sister-in-law." She was the sister of my former husband, Charles Eddie "Bubba" Craig—Chuck is what I called him—and she told me about it. There I was at TI, working the second shift. I called the store to make an appointment.

Daria Retian, she's from Egypt, and she had a fashion flair about her no one in Dallas had. When I called to make an appointment with her, I didn't know that I was talking to the desk on the second floor in the couture shop, which had nothing to do with the modeling business. The third try (what do they say about the third try?) I tried again and met with Daria Retian and Diane Yost from the modeling department. And I put on the smock that the models wore then and the shoes, which were a size 9—and I wore a 10, and so my feet were cramped. It was terrible. But Daria took me up to the Zodiac Room, and they had a ramp there that went from one column to another. And she taught me my turns, and I practiced at home with my little daughter running behind me trying to do my turns, and that was it. Actually, Daria and Diane asked me to let them know when I lost weight and call them. That was in June, and I think, in July of 1968 I called them back, and they booked me for their first show, in September. It was an annual show called "Under One Roof," and it was presented at the Sheraton Hotel in Dallas, downtown.

Bill Blass was the guest designer. And we came from underneath the stage, upstairs to appear on a huge podium. I remember my leg just shaking because it was just unreal. We'd rehearsed it, but to do it in front of a large crowd and to hear the music and the lights and then it's "Action! Okay, first changes." And then there you are. It was really something. But I got through it. It all worked out well. And from there, I met Kim Dawson [to represent me], and then of course, Daria and Kim Dawson talked and they thought, "Mmm." They wanted to get a black model into the store. And that was something different for Neiman's. It was 1968 and they had never had a black model on staff. They had black salesladies on the floor, but no one on the staff of models.

I did know of Naomi Sims. She was out of New York and working out of Oklahoma, maybe, or somewhere in another state. I would see little blips of her on TV or something, and of course, I paid attention. But then I also loved fashion magazines, and that I think I got from my mother, her taste. And just by looking at the magazines, I became fashion conscious. Actually, before the "Under One Roof" show, I had only stepped inside of Neiman's once. Years before, I'd gone in, stepped up to the counter, and asked if someone could help me. And I quickly left. Later, when I went to the fittings as a model, I was still wearing a garter belt and hose, but then everyone else had pantyhose on. I was trying to pull my dress down so the other girls wouldn't see the tops of my stockings. That was really something. And Louise Kahn also helped me with my makeup, and of course, I needed some help. That's something you develop.

Neiman's had ten staff models. There were four on the second floor, which was the couture floor. One was a fur model, and one did the Trophy Room. And then there were two other main models. But the Trophy Room then moved to the third floor, and there was a sportswear model on third floor, one on fourth floor, the Galleria Department, then your junior floor was the fifth floor, and then four up in Zodiac. So every day there was a luncheon fashion show from noon till two o'clock. So the girls only popped in a little bit before noon, and they did the four changes, and then they were out of there by two o'clock. And it was very, very nice.

Peggy, my sister-in-law, helped convince me to try modeling. My mother was saying, "Oh, no, maybe you'd better stay at TI." But Peggy talked me into it, and everything worked out. I left TI and started modeling for Neiman's exclusively. I had to buy my own shoes, though. See, there's always a little catch. No one else on staff had to pay for their shoes, but I had to buy my own. Well, I will admit, my foot was a little bit larger than theirs, but they provided shoes for them, and not that they didn't have the size in the store. But I did. So therefore, I was on the third-floor sports shop from nine-thirty to five. We worked a full shift. But then, two months later, someone asked me, why don't I try to become a Zodiac model, because someone was leaving. And there they only worked from twelve noon to two o'clock, so that would give me more opportunity to be with my kids and also get more bookings, working through the agency. Then I could do designer shows and fabric shows, market shows, but not anything for any other store in town. And that continued from 1968 to 1978. It was very interesting. They always used agency models.

Daria came in one day while one of the girls was knitting. And, of course, they jumped because they should have been up modeling, and there she was knitting. So they decided, instead of having full-time models on staff, paying for their insurance, and having to cope with whether or not they were late or sick, they decided to use freelance models through the Kim Dawson Agency. And then I became in charge of the models. Not only did I pull the clothes, I was also asked to stay and model. Before, the young lady that pulled the clothes, she modeled, but after that, they just had the young lady just pulling the clothes and not modeling. Not only did I pull the clothes for the various floor models, I pulled the accessories as well—the scarves, the jewelry, the hats, the purses, and all of that—to make outfits that people would want to buy. It really was fun. I really enjoyed that. It made me think so much of what I loved as a child. And that was playing with paper dolls. It was just like dressing my little paper dolls. Occasionally, though, I did have friction with some of the girls because you could tell that they didn't like the authority that I had. But I have some friends that are still modeling, and they thank me for all of the input that I gave them and the fashion savvy and the flair, and I taught them how to accessorize things. And that all came to me from just looking in the magazines.

Rarely did I see a black person at Neiman's. My first little romp through the Zodiac Room, I had one lady call me over to the table. She

QUOQUEZE DESIREE CRAIG | 45

said, "Turn around." And I turned around because we were supposed to show them the outfit, tell them where they can find it and the accessories, and how much it was and all of this. And she said, "Ah! You have nice broad shoulders and everything. You're nice and thin. But they should never put gray on you." And she just flipped off and went into another world. Well, they would tell us to go to the tables that seemed interested, and because I was the first black model, everyone was interested in looking at me. Then I'd walk up to the table, and they would stick their heads in the menu, and there I stood, feeling like a fool, really. But I did my little thing.

Actually, there were several black designers in town, as well as photographers. Martin Ames was well noted for his designs in Dallas. And he, of course, did fashion shows, and I would do those for him. I think this was the latter part of the seventies, into the eighties. He came along after Willie Smith in New York. Willie was prominent in the seventies.

There were really not that many black fashion models in Dallas, and in the U.S. at that time. Really and truly. And because I was the first black model in town, I did commercials. I did videotapes. I did photography. Not only was I considered for fashion or runway, I also did advertisements in photographs in business attire and things like that. I got a chance to do all of that because there was no one else. And during one of the interviews, they asked me if I knew of someone else, and I thought of Evelyn Phillips, a young woman I knew locally. And I called them when I got home and said, "I think she would possibly be a candidate for a model." And Evelyn Phillips became a model.

We sometimes did shows out of Dallas. Being with Neiman's, I did all of their openings, the openings in Bal Harbor, the openings in California, the various store openings—we traveled to those locations and did shows for them.

Emilio Pucci asked me to travel with him to Europe, but I didn't. I was a mother, and parenting was first for me. Modeling was a job and not a career. So I didn't take him up on it. I wonder what would have happened, though, had I gone to Europe. Everyone says Paris is my city. But I've not gone there yet.

In fashion, at that time, Dallas was third, after Europe and New York. Yves Saint Laurent, Chanel, Carl Lagerfeld—all of those fashions were the beginning of the trend for the season, and then they would trickle down. It was Europe, New York, Dallas, and then maybe Atlanta or whatever. But recently, the Apparel Mart [in Dallas] has closed. And I guess they do the shows out of the Design Center. But Dallas is no longer the fashion hot spot that it used to be. I've heard that people love going to Las Vegas. So now Las Vegas is a fashion city. Can you imagine that?

There have been some ladies that were given the opportunity to gracefully decide when they were going to stop modeling. For me, it was a total surprise. I noticed my name on one of the runways—they have a list of models, and you have a lineup of how they're to appear on the stage. And I noticed that near the finale, my name was listed, not up with the other girls, but it was near the bottom with the society ladies. And I questioned that. I said, "You know, is there something here I need to know?" And it was like, "Oh, well, uh, yes, we're, uh, highlighting you as this being your last show." "Oh, really?" So, see, it was quite a surprise to me, so I ran home, got my little bio so that they would have something to say about me when I was on the runway as they were going to talk about the others, and of course, can I tell you, the commentator, a woman named Carlotta, never said any of the things that were printed for her to say. She just mentioned me being the first black model at Neiman's. Kim Dawson was in charge. It's her agency, and the shows came out of the agency.

It wasn't a matter of being racist, because Carlotta's black. But there were people in the agency that moved up, and there were people in the agency that moved out. And I was one that moved out. In fact, I said to Kim, "You know, Kim, by the way, if there's a way that you can use me, you know, after this or whatever," and she said, "Use you? Oh, darling, I don't want to use you." And I thought, "I think you know what I mean, and I didn't mean it like that." So I just sort of blew it off. And can I tell you—I'm sorry, I have a little love-hate relationship with the agency. And not only did they do that, but my last photos, which someone re- minded me that I paid for and had done by a photographer, were just thrown away instead of, when they came back from the printer, being given to me. They knew my address, my telephone number. All they had to do was say, "The pictures are in." But instead, they just discarded them. It hurts. It hurts, basically, because it means that you mean nothing— there goes that nobody-ness. I didn't mean anything to them.

So I started working as an office temp and got a chance to see what the business side of the world was like and got a chance to work at insurance companies, computer companies, and found out how the staff was treated. I learned to use computers, so it was really a move up for me, as far as being in the business sense of it, and found myself in securities and found that I could also check the companies out, just as they were checking me out. And then I went to Cavanaugh Securities and stayed there for several years. They were bought with the mergers and acquisitions starting to take place in the nineties, and then I moved to Barrow, Hanley, Mewhinney, and Strauss, where I'm presently employed. I provide administrative support to portfolio managers and other investment staff. It is a progressive firm. And it's a wonderful firm to work for.

Do I feel like I was going where no one had gone before? In Dallas, yes. Mainly because I was asked to do articles and *PM Magazine.* Leeza Gibbons hosted *PM Magazine,* and they highlighted me in one of the segments, showing what I did on a daily basis and following me around and everything. That was exciting. There were other things, too, articles written on me about how I handled motherhood, being a mother and modeling as well, because as I still say, it wasn't a matter of being a single person and being able to just travel all over the world like that. I had to think of my children first because I divorced shortly after becoming a model.

I'm detail-oriented. I love the various details of things. My son makes me laugh when he's cleaning up his room. Just like on TV, he'll take off a piece of clothing and put it down, and the next day he'll put something else down. I tell him, "It wouldn't be a chore if you hung up your clothes every day. It becomes a chore when you have to stand there, and you have four or five days of things to hang up."

I've always taught my kids, whether it's cutting the yard or whatever, you want to be able to stand back and look at it and say, "I did that," and be proud that you did that, and do it in a way so that it's presentable to people.

[Interview by Alan Govenar, January 25, 2005]

*Mark Dean in his office, IBM Almaden Research Center, San Jose, California, 2005.*

# MARK DEAN

ENGINEER

*Born March 2, 1957*

*Mark Dean grew up in Jefferson City, Tennessee. His mother, Barbara Peck Dean, was an educator, and his father, James Edward Dean, was supervisor of three large Tennessee Valley Authority dams. As a child, Dean showed an aptitude for math, engineering, and the emerging field of computers, building Heathkit electronics and an early Altair computer. After graduating from high school, he received a minority engineering scholarship to attend the University of Tennessee in nearby Knoxville. Dean earned highest honors with his bachelor of science degree in electronic engineering. At the urging of one of his professors, IBM recruited Dean to join a small research team in Boca Raton, Florida, that was developing the personal computer. In Boca Raton, Dean flourished and invented technologies that were in three of IBM's first nine basic patents for the personal computer (PC). One invention—the industry standard architecture (ISA) bus, which permitted add-on devices like the keyboard, disk drives, and printers to be connected to the motherboard—would in 1997 earn Dean and colleague Dennis Moeller the U.S. Department of Commerce's Ronald H. Brown American Innovator Award and election to the National Inventors Hall of Fame. Dean's responsibilities grew with the popularity and impact of IBM's PC. He developed the Color Graphic Adapter (CGA) method for displaying color on PC monitors and led the design of several PS/2 subsystems. After earning his Ph.D. at Stanford, he managed increasingly complex areas in the development of the PowerPC processor, video servers, and the RS/6000 workstation in Austin, Texas, and in 1995, he was named an IBM fellow.*

*In 1997, Dean became director of the Austin Research Lab. Achievements there during his tenure included testing the first giga-*

*hertz CMOS microprocessor, designing a high-speed DRAM (with latency less than 5 nanoseconds), and developing the cellular server architecture, which is optimized for managing, storing, searching, distributing, and mining complex data, such as video, audio, and high-resolution images. Dean moved to the Thomas J. Watson Research Center in Yorktown Heights, New York, in 2000 as vice president for systems, where his team began incorporating the cellular architecture into the Blue Gene supercomputer design. He was also responsible for the research division's initiative for low-power processors. In 2002, he moved to Tucson as vice president for storage technology in the IBM Systems and Technology Group Tucson, where he led the global development of storage-systems architecture, design, technology, and strategies. His technical achievements and leadership have led to many distinguished awards, such as being named Black Engineer of the Year (2000), election to the National Academy of Engineering (2001), and an honorary doctor of science degree from Howard University (2002). Currently, Dean is lab director of IBM's Almaden Research Lab in San Jose, California.*

I WAS BORN IN JEFFERSON CITY, TENNESSEE, and my father worked at the Tennessee Valley Authority (TVA) at the time, and my mother was a teacher. We moved around a little bit, but when I was about five years old we ended up settling in Jefferson City, which was where my grandparents and my great-grandmother lived. So we had family. My grandfather was principal of the black school, the Nelson Mary School, which was a grammar school and high school all together. I went to that school, where my grandfather was principal, because it was still segregated when I was old enough to enroll. My first two years, I was in a classroom that covered the first through fourth grades, so there weren't a whole lot of students, and teachers had to teach four grades. So that was good for me, because I was doing fourth-grade math in the first grade, and that turned out to be one of the big catalysts in my getting into engineering. That worked out in my favor, even though it was still part of a segregated environment. Third grade was my first year I went to an integrated school; they integrated that year. And, you know, like all stories, it was tough. It was tough in a lot of ways. I was ahead in math, way ahead of everybody else, so they had a tough time keeping my attention.

They were starting to abolish segregation, and it was always a challenge. Kids can be tough, tougher than most, because they don't have the . . . I don't know, training or the skills to keep their mouth shut when they should, maybe. That's okay; it's just the way kids are. I went to grammar school and high school in Jefferson City, played sports—basketball, football, and track—made good grades. I was at the top of the class. As I think back, I didn't have any people that I stayed in contact with over the years, though I developed some friendships, I think. I would call those people friends now.

My grandfather's name was Eugene Peck. And my grandmother's name was Ophelia Peck. My grandfather was principal of a country school. Almost all of Tennessee is rural. When does it stop being rural? It was part of a town, but it was pretty sparse. My father's parents lived in Alabama, Monroe County, near Mobile, near Monroeville. Prichard was where most of them lived.

My mother went to what is now Tennessee State. My father did not have a college degree. He went into the service. After he was discharged, the Tennessee Valley Authority trained him for his particular job. And he went up through the ranks and he was actually a supervisor for some of the dams in the Tennessee Valley Authority. My grandfather was educated, and to be honest with you, I don't remember off the top of my head what school he went to. So I had some intelligent grandparents and parents, let's put it that way.

One of the reasons I became an engineer was through my parents' guidance and my father's interest in building things. He was always building things. He built a tractor from scratch, and I got to help a little bit with that. He just had ability to build just about anything that needed to be built or fixed. So I learned a lot from helping him with those kinds of things.

My parents taught me to ignore any racism or discrimination—that many individuals don't know any better, they're not born racist; it's something you learn. It's something that also can be unlearned, once they've experienced the truth. So I kind of held that, and I ignored most bigotry and racism, and I think that helped me get through most of it.

One thing that happened to me, just a comment that was made by one of my friends that reinforces this thinking, was when he came up to me and said, "You're not really black, are you?"

He said, "You're not black. You make good grades, and you interact with us," and he says, "You're not black."

And I said, "No, I really am black." The stereotypes that he had come to learn weren't true, and he was associating certain stereotypes with black, and since I didn't fit the mold, he didn't want to call me black. So I thought that was telling, in the fact that he only knew what he had learned, and he had just created this label, and the label wasn't valid. So it just takes, sometimes, time for people to learn it differently.

I think any visual or spoken word that provides a little bit more realistic view of the way things are is helpful. And it just unfortunately takes decades of time to change that opinion. And blacks and whites aren't the only example. It's an interesting challenge, because [for example] we're trying to hire as many women and minorities into engineering and computer science as we can find, and the pool is not high enough. We need more people, more of that gender or race, to get into these disciplines. And you've just got to interest them into it. They can do it; that's not the problem. It's a matter of getting them interested and guiding them into it, such that we have people we can choose from. But it's hard, something you have to stay on all the time.

I had an extra challenge because I couldn't read very well. Numbers were easy for me, but reading was harder, so I had that extra challenge. I remember in the third grade, I was pretty confident that I was as smart as anybody else in that room, so I didn't have a lack of confidence or self-esteem during that time, because I thought people really kind of needed me. I helped people with math and the science classes that we had, so I developed friends, at least people that needed my help, anyway, fairly quickly. And I had my share of people that challenged me on both sides. It's interesting how if you do well and become successful, you develop jealousies within your own race, where people want to hold you back. That's another challenge that kids have, and maybe grown-ups as well, in that if you do well, the people in your race that aren't doing well, they don't want you to do well. They want to hold you back. They call you names, give you a hard time, because you're focused on doing well, and they've been less fortunate, let's say. So if you want to do well and you're young, and that was my case, you would have prejudices from both whites and blacks for different reasons. It really makes it hard for kids, especially, to want to do well. You have to have a tremendous amount of support from your parents, and encouragement, because there are so many factors that want to pull you back and keep you from doing well.

All through grammar school, I went to Jefferson Elementary after I left Nelson Mary, and then in high school I went to Jefferson High School. So I was there for my entire schooling. [After I graduated from high school] I went to the University of Tennessee for my undergraduate work, and I went to school at night and got my master's while I was working at Florida Atlantic University. I was working for IBM in Boca Raton, Florida, at the time, and I went to school while I was working. I must have been twenty-two [when I got my first job with IBM]. I was fresh out of undergraduate school. Now, I had worked for Alcoa Aluminum while I was getting my undergraduate degree, as a co-op. I'd work a quarter and go to school a quarter; it was the co-op program at

Mark Dean views the world from a favorite spot on his 1947 Chevrolet in the parking lot behind the gym at Jefferson High School.

University of Tennessee. So I worked for Alcoa Aluminum, I think it was for six quarters. We were on the quarter system at the time. And that paid my way through school, that and a scholarship, which was part of the program that I'd gotten from the Minority Engineering Program at the University of Tennessee. That really was another key factor that led to my being an engineer. Getting that scholarship at University of Tennessee made a tremendous difference. It was through a fairly new program that Fred Brown started and made happen. It was called the Minority Engineering Program at University of Tennessee.

I can't say enough positive things about Fred Brown. He was one of the early African American leaders, black leaders, in the community, and he was associated with the University of Tennessee, and he started this Minority Engineering Program that would bring in blacks, essentially, at the time. [That] was really what it was focused on, [helping to get blacks] into the University of Tennessee as freshmen and then to provide mentoring, guidance, and funding to put them all the way through an undergraduate degree. That program required you to co-op, so you had to work in the co-op program as well as being in an engineering field, and of course then they would give you a small stipend each quarter as part of the program. You had to keep your grades—I think you had to have a 3.0 grade point average. And that was a struggle for many of the students. I had good grades. I graduated at the top of the class, so that was less of a problem for me. I had to study a lot. I wasn't really that much smarter than anybody else, but I guess I enjoyed it a lot.

I decided [that science and engineering was my field] when I was in the eighth grade. I even knew at that time I wanted to work for IBM, because I wanted to work on computers, and fortunately during that time I started building Heathkits and little digital devices and even a small working computer in high school. So I knew I wanted to be an engineer. I knew I wanted to be an electrical engineer and work on computers. And I wanted to work for IBM. And this was back in the eighth, ninth grade. [I was introduced to computers] through magazines—*Popular Electronics, Popular Mechanics.* My father, although computers were crude at the time, had access to some [computer] systems at TVA. So when he would take me on tours, I would see all the controls for the dam, and I was pretty interested early on. [That] was in the early seventies. They [computers] were pretty new, but I knew that was going to be something that I would be interested in. It felt like I could do pretty well. I didn't care [that I was entering a field where there wasn't much precedent for African Americans]. I was having fun. That's all I knew. And that was simple for me. It was just a matter of what I enjoyed. Maybe that's what got me through most of it, because I ignored most discrimination, because there was always a way around it, and I always had something somebody else needed because either the things I could build or the things I could design or invent had value. And I think that helped me get into opportunities.

In college, there was [still a sense of discrimination], just an undercurrent. I think not getting into certain activities or being chosen for certain things, you feel it. Again, as long as I got to study and work on and learn electronics, most of that other stuff really didn't bother me. If I wasn't chosen for something, that's fine. And I think that kept me focused, more than anything else. There's something about being—what would you say, "Bliss"? Or you know, absent of what you're missing, knowledge of what you're missing, maybe? Because it allows you to focus on the things you really want to get done. I was aware enough. One of the things I got from my grandfather was a sense of history because he was a history major. He taught history. When they integrated schools and he stopped being a principal at the black school, he was a history teacher at the integrated high school. He always gave me all the knowledge that you could get from a black-history standpoint, which you don't get in schools. I was quite aware of the trials that he and his generation and my parents' generation had gone through, so that was always there. And I benefited from not having to have those same struggles. So I thought I had it easy compared to what they had. I didn't have much to complain about. They really had to struggle. I never remember having to go to a "black" bathroom or drink from a "black" water fountain or go into a different door in a restaurant. I never remember that. But I know they did. They had to deal with that. Tennessee was a little more neutral than some of the other states, I think. In certain areas, you see more discrimination, and it's more a part of the culture than at least the part of Tennessee in which I grew up.

All I knew at the time was that if you wanted to do computers, IBM was the big dog on the corner, right? Nobody else was even close. When you talk about computers, IBM was synonymous with computers. And so my rudimentary brain said, "Okay, that means I should work for IBM. If I want to do computers and design them and work on the state of the art, nobody's doing that but IBM, so I should work for them."

I started [working for IBM] in Boca Raton, Florida, in 1979. It was by chance, actually. I had done some work for a professor—I think his name was Professor Wong. His son and I did projects together. His son was also going to school at that same time as me. And I was really good at building these projects. I would always get them done early, and that set a positive impression in this professor's mind. So when the recruiter came from IBM looking for top talent, he talked to my professor, who had been his adviser at the University of Tennessee. And fortunately, Professor Wong told him about me, so I got interviewed, because it was hard to get interviews with IBM. They invited me to come to Florida for an interview. My grade point average was high enough to graduate at the top of the class. I would have been an easy pick whether I was black or white. It was fortunate for IBM that I was black, right, because they were going to get a top candidate, plus they'd start to help their numbers, so we both kind of came out winners there.

I was a junior engineer at the time. I was fortunate to work on the original PC, the first one. I was part of the team. I did the graphic adapter and monochrome adapter for the first PC. And I did most of the monitor interface cards for the original one. On the PCAC, which created the ISA bus, I was responsible for that entire design.

The ISA bus, that's what the present name is. We called it the PC bus at the time. It's the way adapters are interfaced to the computer. It's kind of the backbone of the system. And so all communications between components of the system go through this interface we call the bus. The industry coined the term ISA for "industry standard architecture." Before the industry called it this, we called it the PC bus. And I would say of my claim to fame, that and the patents that we held in support of that interface were the keys for my success. Those are my primary contributions.

The first PC was introduced in 1981. It's funny. You could call it cutting-edge. Actually, it was built with mostly off-the-shelf components. So that's why it was so successful. When we built the PC, we thought we might build 200,000 of them, and that would be the end, and we'd go off and build something else. Little did we know it would catch on and be so successful. Well, the primary reason it was so successful was because of two things. The first are the components we used; anybody could buy them. They weren't custom; they weren't special. And the second, we gave away the logics and the input-output system, the software. The code to run the system and the design for the system, we gave away. We put it in our technical reference manual. Just like you get diagrams in the back of old televisions, you know. They always would put the diagrams for the television in the back of the television. When we did it, we put the complete logic design, complete schematics, and the typed-out software in text form in our tech reference. So anybody that wanted to build an exact copy could build one, exactly, 100 percent compatible. And that's why it was successful. It wasn't the best system at the time. Apple actually had, I think, a better design from a software-hardware standpoint. But we let more people play. From this information we provided, people could build adapters, they could build exact copies—they could participate in the industry. And that gave customers options, and it caught on. And that was the best decision we ever made, and I think it happened by accident. We may have made some poor decisions that followed some of that, but that particular decision, to give away logics and the code, was the best decision we ever made.

After working for IBM ten years, I was able to go back to college. IBM actually paid my way to go back to school, to get my Ph.D., and I went to Stanford University from 1989 to 1992 and got my Ph.D.

I have almost forty patents now. I've got some still pending, but it's approximately forty. There are three major ones that led to my induction into the Inventors Hall of Fame. These were the three patents that were part of the original PC design and mostly had to do with the ISA bus and the graphics interface for displaying characters and graphics on the screen. [At that time], there were nine key patents, and I was on three of them.

IBM owns all the work that was done, since they were paying my salary. But I've gotten a couple of awards from IBM for the prevalence of the use of these patents. We do track how often both IBM and non-IBM vendors use IBM patents, and there's a significant amount of, I would say, revenue and profit associated with the use of the patents that I own. So they were fairly valuable patents.

At the time, we were just having fun. I did these designs, and they worked, and that was great, and then we were off designing the next thing. We never designed anything thinking there would be any fame associated with what we were doing. For me, in particular, I enjoyed building them and watching them work, watching people use systems that I was responsible for, and I just enjoyed making things and watching them function. I never did anything for the fame, because that wasn't tangible. I always did stuff because it was just fun to do, and I think that's important, because without the fame, I'd still be as satisfied with what we did.

I've been based in San Jose, California, at the Almaden Research Center, since September 2004. [Before coming to California] I worked in our storage systems group in Tucson, Arizona. After working in Florida, I got my Ph.D. at Stanford and went back to work with IBM in Austin, Texas. I worked for a few years in the research group in New York. And then I went to Tucson, Arizona. And now I'm in California. So I haven't moved around a whole lot. I was actually in Boca Raton, Florida, for ten years, and I was in Austin, Texas, for a little bit more than ten years. So most of my career has been in, essentially, two locations.

I think now what keeps me going is the opportunity to work in an environment where anything's possible. If you walk the halls of this research center or any of the other IBM research centers, you have the opportunity to work with the tops in their field, and those fields range from anthropology—we have some anthropologists at my lab here—to biology, chemistry, computer science, electrical engineering, mechanical engineering, material science, physics. We have the tops in their fields, and they get to work on stuff that is leading-edge. And I get to be a part of that. There's very few locations, very few organizations that can give you that breadth and depth. And the possibility of discovering some new stuff is always kind of there and keeps me going. So it's fun. For the people around here, there's nothing you can talk about where they will say, "Oh, that can't be done." It's an environment where anything's possible. And that's pretty neat.

[Interview by Alan Govenar, March 7, 2005]

*Mary Lovenia DeConge-Watson, Baton Rouge,*
*Louisiana, 2003.*

# MARY LOVENIA DeCONGE-WATSON

MATHEMATICIAN

*Born October 4, 1933*

*Mary Lovenia DeConge entered the Sisters of the Holy Family in
1949 when she was sixteen years old. She earned a B.A. in mathematics and science from Seton Hill College (Pennsylvania), an
M.A. in mathematics from Louisiana State University, and a Ph.D.
in mathematics (with a minor in French) from St. Louis University.
DeConge was a nun until 1976. She married Roy Cedric Watson in
1983 and has remained active in her Catholic church.*

*During the 1950s and early 1960s, she taught in high schools in
Louisiana. She was a teacher at DeLisle Junior College from 1962 to
1964, when she decided to pursue a doctorate. After completing her
Ph.D. in 1968, she accepted a position of assistant professor of
mathematics at Loyola University in New Orleans. In 1971, she was
appointed to the mathematics faculty at Southern University in Baton Rouge, where she served as professor, chair of the mathematics
department, and vice chancellor. She retired in 2004. DeConge is
the author of research notes appearing in the* Proceedings of the
National Academy of Science (USA), *the* Notices of the American Mathematics Society, *and the* Journal of Mathematical An-
alytical Applications, *and is coauthor (with Denise Bourgeois) of a
college-level geometry book,* Parallels of Euclidian and
Hyperbolic Geometry.

MY FATHER WAS A BARBER and a part-time farmer in the early years.
And my mother didn't work at all. I am one of nine children, the seventh
child of Alphonse DeConge and Adina Rodney DeConge. I was born in
Wickliff, Louisiana, about three miles outside of New Roads, Louisiana,
about thirty-five miles northwest of Baton Rouge. I knew only one of my

grandparents, my mother's father, and his name was Joseph Rodney. All the others were dead by the time I was born.

My father's father was white, and we lived across the street from his [my father's] sister. Our relationship with his family was sometimes cordial, but New Roads was a very bigoted town. We were brought up in a small cocoon with my family and cousins and all. Between my mother's brothers and sisters and my father's family, we were about sixty first cousins. And so we had a little community of our own. We were allowed to work and play. I went to a Catholic school and with those kids in my family; we didn't have to have that much contact with other races.

My father's father died before I was born, but he raised my father from about the time he was thirteen, because his mother died when he was about thirteen. It didn't make any difference in those days. Everybody knew my father's father was white, but nobody talked about it. I guess it gave my father a little more privilege than most people; everybody respected him. So he didn't sometimes go through some of the things a lot of black men went through when he was growing up. His father came from Canada, and he must have been married in Canada, or I don't know what happened to his wife, but he came with one daughter from Canada, but I don't think he ever remarried. He was French Canadian. I don't think he lived together with my grandmother. My father's mother was from Independence, Louisiana, which is a good distance away from New Roads, about a hundred miles.

I don't think any part of my mother's family was ever in slavery. I think they were free people of color, because my great-great-grandmother was the daughter of a white gentleman from the Poydras family who had two daughters. And one of those daughters was my mother's great-grandmother. My mother and father both spoke French, and I understood it, but I really didn't speak French per se as a child. I studied French in school all the way through my doctorate degree and became fluent, but I've lost a lot of it.

Everybody in our neighborhood spoke French. I grew up listening to music people call zydeco today, but we didn't call it zydeco then. It was just the fiddle music, banjo, that kind of thing. There were dances, mostly dances at people's houses. We never went to any big hall that had a dance when I was growing up. They weren't expensive instruments, but they weren't handmade. It was mostly family [that played music]—uncles, cousins, whatever. There were family get-togethers.

I started school at St. Augusta Catholic School, and I went to that school until I was in the fifth grade, and then we moved, and I went to Corpus Christi Catholic School in New Orleans, Louisiana. Well, my family moved to Baton Rouge. My sister was living in New Orleans, and I went to live with her for one year. And that's when I went to Corpus Christi. I stayed there one year, and I came back to Baton Rouge, where my family was. I went to St. Francis Xavier Catholic School.

After the eighth grade, I entered the congregation of the Sisters of the Holy Family. I'd always wanted to do it, since before I ever knew any nuns. I had never seen any nuns until I was in the sixth grade, because I was taught at Catholic schools, and there were only lay teachers at the first school I went to. The first nun that I saw was in the sixth grade; her name was Sister John Mary of the Blessed Sacrament sisters in New Orleans. She was white, and she was a very good teacher, I can say that. She was an excellent teacher—it was a self-contained classroom. The thing I remember about her most was she had influence upon my reading. And we did a lot of diagramming of sentences. She was a pro at that. Oh, I kept in contact with her for at least twenty years after that.

So I entered the convent and continued my schooling. I went to St. Mary's Academy in New Orleans, and I got my high school diploma from there. All of the nuns in the Sisters of the Holy Family were black. At the time I was there, there were about four hundred, four hundred and fifty nuns. They have about one hundred and some right now, a hundred and twenty-five maybe, and they're all elderly now, except for very, very few.

[In the convent] I would say we were on a very strict schedule and had a lot of manual duties. We had classes every day. Some of the classes had to do with the study of theology and the Catholic life as a nun. We also took secular classes. We studied a lot. We got up in the morning about five o'clock, and after we got up, we had some duties to do before we went to Mass, set up the dining room for breakfast, and that kind of thing. Then we went to Mass and prayers, and after that, we went to breakfast and cleaned up after breakfast. Each person had her own particular duties. When I was in novitiate, which is where you study, we were about fifty people in there.

Sister Sylvester, Mary DeConge, New Orleans, Louisiana, 1958.

We went to bed about nine o'clock in the evening, but we had what they call recreational periods. Some of us read, some just sat and talked, some played cards. We did different things, played the piano, and sang, whatever we wanted to do. We had time after lunch and about an hour of recreation in the evening. It was not very difficult. We had prayer in the morning, and then when we were first in novitiate, we had prayers before lunch and then, in the evening, around five-thirty. The prayer in the morning was the longest because we had Mass. And then we had vocal prayers, which was the singing of prayers, and then we had meditation for half an hour. It was very structured. I made lifelong friends there. Sometimes it was lonely. You missed your family a lot, because during the novitiate period, I had very, very little contact with my family. But I felt I had a spiritual calling. I stayed a nun for twenty-six years.

After high school I went to Seton Hill College in Pennsylvania, where I studied for a degree in mathematics. I had a double major, mathematics and French, and I was there four years. I was with the Sisters of Charity at Seton Hill—a small school, about five hundred girls. I taught mathematics and French for two years at a Catholic school in

Opelousas after I had my college degree in 1959, and then I went to Louisiana State University for a master's degree. I was on an academic year grant, and I was there about eleven months. I got my master's degree in mathematics in 1962, and then I went back to Opelousas and taught for another year. In 1964, I went for my doctorate at St. Louis University in mathematics and got about thirty-five hours in French while I was there, too.

I was always good in mathematics from the time I was very, very young, and at the time I was sent to study for a doctorate, the Sisters of the Holy Family had a junior college, DeLisle Junior College. DeLisle was the founder of the Sisters of the Holy Family. I wanted to keep my heritage in French, because it was a very good break for me from mathematics to French. It was much easier and I enjoyed it. I mostly studied French literature—I had literature from the tenth century all the way through the twentieth century.

I went to France in 1975, which I enjoyed, because I was able to communicate. I've used my French several times. I went to French-speaking Africa. I used it there and also in Canada. When I went in 1975, it was just on a trip that somebody had given a group of us. I was still religious then, and we went to several countries—to Portugal, to Spain, and through France and Italy. I loved it. I got to see some very interesting things. It was a bus tour. But in Paris, a group of us just broke away and started just taking the Métro to go different places. It's easy to travel on the Métro in Paris. So we went to Versailles, we went to several churches—Sacré Coeur—and then we went to Ile-de-France and traveled around Paris. I went to Lourdes. Their French was nearer to what we speak here than it was in Paris. It was more of a patois in that area.

I wrote my mathematics thesis in geometry, but we had five areas that we had to study. I studied algebra, typology, real and complex analysis, and geometry. After I finished my doctorate, I taught at Loyola University in New Orleans for three years, and I came to Southern University in 1971. So I taught from 1968 to 1971 at Loyola, and part-time at DeLisle before it closed. Then I took a job in Baton Rouge at Southern University, and I have been here since. I retired four times. I retired the first time in 1998, and then I was home about six months. They called me back to serve as an associate vice chancellor of academic affairs. And then I left again, and then they called me back the second time to serve as associate vice chancellor in 1999 and then again in 2001. The next time I went back as vice chancellor, in 2003–2004. And since then, I've finally stopped working at the university.

In mathematics, I'd say my biggest contribution was my teaching. I did a little writing. I wrote, with a friend of mine, Denise Bourgeois. We wrote a college-level geometry book called *Parallels of Euclidian and Hyperbolic Geometry,* which we both used. My friend was teaching at Ohio State University in Columbus, and I was teaching at Southern. We used it as a textbook for about ten years.

I first met Denise when I was studying for my master's at LSU. She was there, and then I went to St. Louis University first, and then she came after I was already there. So we were together at St. Louis University. And then when I taught at Loyola University, she was teaching at Dominican College in New Orleans. She's in New Orleans now.

I stayed in the convent for twenty-six years. I left in 1976 because of my health. Well, at the time that I left, I was sick and didn't know what it was. Later, I found out it was lupus. I was just extremely fatigued all the time, and I thought I needed a break, and then when I left, I took a year's leave to rest, but I didn't. I worked at Rockwell International in Anaheim. I did research. We were working on a submarine for the navy. I was there one year, and then I came back to Baton Rouge again to teach at Southern, and I've been in Baton Rouge since.

I had entered the religious life when I was very young, and after delving into it for many years, I couldn't reconcile some of the things I saw happening, what I thought it should be. When I do things, I don't expect any reward. I don't have an ulterior motive. I didn't have the idea of getting married when I left the religious life. But about six years later, I was living alone and felt that it was a good idea to have some companionship. I met a man who had been in my class as an adult, who had been away from education for many years, but decided to come back and get a degree. He was in my class around 1978 or 1979, and I didn't have any interest in him, but we met again in 1982 and I realized that he was someone special. I got married in 1983. My husband's name is Roy Cedric Watson. He worked as an operator for an oil company and is now retired.

I'm the kind of person who's not satisfied if I have a problem and I can't find a solution. That applies not only to math but also to life in general. I'm always looking for a solution. I'm the same way in my spiritual life. I'm not satisfied with just knowing the surface of things. I am always delving for something deeper. I want to know the deeper meaning. I question a whole lot of things that happen, whether it's religious or not. I always want to try to analyze that kind of question and find an answer, a solution, if that's possible.

At Southern, I was nominated as master teacher several times. I think I touched a lot of kids. A lot of them have gone on to study for doctorates. I was chair for ten years, and during those ten years, I think I was able to turn the math department around. I brought in a lot of researchers. And while I was chair, the math department was written up by MAA [Mathematical Association of America] as one of the model schools for revision in the teaching of mathematics. In 1968, I was the fifteenth black woman in the United States to receive a doctorate in mathematics.

I think women bring a little bit of heart to mathematics. Sometimes men are more interested in the subject matter than they are in people. I think women mathematicians are interested in the subject of math, but they are also interested in people. As teachers, they are more empathetic with students, and able—I know I've had students who came into my class very deficient, and I was able to work with them on an individual level and try to bring them up, if they had the intelligence to do it and the will to do it. I would work with them until I got them to a point until they felt confident in themselves. And some men do that—I know a lot that do it—but on the whole, I know that men are sometimes overconfident.

I didn't sense the discrimination [from men] when I went to St. Louis University, because it was a different atmosphere, but at LSU, it was downright racist [toward] women and blacks. My friend Denise was hit as a woman, and I was hit as a woman and a black. The chair of the department at that time, he would come to class and say all kinds of things. The professors tried to intimidate me by asking what I was doing there in the class. When he asked me that, I asked him, "What are you doing here?" He wasn't teaching, for sure. But little things, they just felt you should not be there because it wasn't a subject for women—the things that they would say, the way you were graded, being ignored. I know one woman who went to LSU, she finally got her doctorate, but it took her seven years, and she was white.

I think men may have more three-dimensional insight. It seems that they were always able to solve three-dimensional problems, but it was always harder for me. I don't know if that's the way they grew up playing with different types of things. Women are more detail-oriented than able to see the big perspective. Most of the women I met had to really understand something in detail before they could put their teeth in it. I don't think it's genetic. I think it's the way they were brought up to think.

I went to an all-girls high school and college at Seton Hill, and they had brilliant women there. One of my best black friends from eighth grade has a Ph.D. in mathematics. She's also retired. Her name is Dolores Spikes. She was the first woman president of Southern University. I have a lot of women friends in engineering. One in particular, I taught when she was in college. She has a Ph.D. in civil engineering, and she's really doing well. Right now, she's at Prairie View. She just went there as the dean of civil engineering. Her name is Judy Perkins. I taught her from when she was a freshman until her senior year at Southern. She got her doctorate at Georgia Tech. She has had a very interesting life also, because she has a high ranking in the army.

I have another student, Robert Johnson Jr., who has a Ph.D. in mathematics. He's at the University of Maryland at College Park, and he's making a big difference. His father has a doctorate in mathematics, too. The interesting thing about Robert is that I helped him get a scholarship at St. Louis University, so he went back there to study, and he was the first black to get a Ph.D. after I did and that was thirty years later. I received mine in 1968, and he graduated in 1998.

I'm into a little bit of everything. These days, I'm working mostly with my church, Immaculate Conception Catholic Church. I'm on several committees there, chair of a couple. I'm a lay minister for the church, and I'm director of adult formation, small-group meetings studying the church and doctrines in the church. I teach a Bible class every Tuesday, and I serve as eucharistic minister. I taught the confirmation class there for twenty-eight years.

I've been a member of the Alpha Kappa Alpha sorority for twenty-one years. I joined in 1983. In fact, I had never heard of it until I came to Baton Rouge, and I was recruited to join. I like it because you get to know a lot of women on your level and work with them on all kinds of projects. I've gotten to know a whole lot of people through the sorority. I was president of the sorority for four years. I just stepped down in 2004, and I've been the treasurer [since then]. Alpha Kappa Alpha was founded in 1908, and it's had a very important history. We give out scholarships. We have health seminars. We have leadership classes year-round; we have around thirty boys and girls in the group and give them leadership training for a year. We do art camps with the kids and a lot of service work—tutoring. We adopted a school and we go there once a week and work with the kids in Louisiana who are having difficulty passing their classes. We work with them tutoring once a week.

The state of Louisiana has a program called the Louisiana Assistance Initiative Program, where you train [retired] teachers to go back into the schools and teach. I've worked with that for about ten to fifteen years, bringing in thirty teachers and working with them intensively in the summer and meeting them once a week on Saturdays for a year, training them to go back into the classroom. It was a mixed group, I'd say about fifty-fifty, black and white teachers.

This year, for the first time since 1989, my sorority had a social dance and dinner, and we invited friends who had been supporting us through the years. That was very nice. The tradition of the social tea was common in sororities at one time, but they've moved away from that kind of thing. They're more service-oriented now. We meet as a big group once a month, and then we meet in small groups. We always have something going on.

I don't recall the Catholic Church being involved in civil-rights activities. I was in a unique situation being a member of an order. The order didn't get very involved, except the day-to-day workings with people. I was a member of the Friendship House in New Orleans in the 1960s, between 1963 and 1964, when I was there, and then when I came from 1968 to 1971, I was involved in that organization. It was interracial, and we'd meet with police and leaders in the city, and we'd talk about problems that were going on and try to influence them to change. I guess in an indirect way, the Church had a lot of influence, working with kids, and then we did a lot of social work, visiting families—that was more of the order—helping people individually. The order never got involved, but individually we did marches. I know I did the marching thing in St. Louis, and I still have those calluses under my feet. When Martin Luther King was shot, we marched from one end of the city to the other in protest. That was mixed—black and white. I was in St. Louis finishing up my doctorate when Martin Luther King was shot. We just marched all the way from the Mississippi River to Park Forest Park, and that's about eight or nine miles. We walked through the city and had speeches and that kind of thing. But it wasn't a world-shaking thing. When you look back on that period, you had a lot of great people who made a difference.

When I think of all the things I've done, my faith has brought me through a whole lot. You need to touch individual lives. It's a good thing to stand in front of a group and talk, but unless you have that one-to-one contact with people, you can't make a difference in their lives. I think you need both, but I think the one where you touch people individually and bring them from one level to another is more important. When you make a difference in that person, then they go out and make a difference in other people, and you get it spreading that way.

[Interview by Alan Govenar, September 19, 2005]

*James A. Emanuel at his desk in his Montparnasse apartment, Paris, France, 2005.*

# JAMES A. EMANUEL

POET

*Born June 15, 1921*

*James A. Emanuel was born in Alliance, Nebraska. He earned a B.A. from Howard University, an M.A. from Northwestern University, and a Ph.D. from Columbia University. Among his books of poetry are* Jazz from the Haiku King *(1999),* De la rage au Coeur *(Thaon, 1992, translated by Jean Migrenne and Amiot Lenganey),* Whole Grain: Collected Poems, 1958–1989 *(1990),* The Quagmire Effect *(1988),* Deadly James and Other Poems *(1987),* The Broken Bowl: New and Uncollected Poems *(1983),* Black Man Abroad: The Toulouse Poems *(1978), and* At Bay *(1969). He is also the author of* Langston Hughes *(1967) and the editor, with Theodore L. Gross, of* Dark Symphony: Negro Literature in America *(1968). Emanuel's essays and other writings have been included in many anthologies and periodicals. Among his honors are a John Hay Whitney Award, a Saxton Memorial Fellowship, and a Special Distinction Award from the Black American Literature Forum. James Emanuel has been a professor of English at the University of Grenoble and the University of Toulouse, among other universities. He lives in Paris.*

I HAVE TWO BIRTHDAYS. All my young life, I was told that I was born on the fourteenth of June. When I got a passport, for which I needed my birth certificate, I found out that the fourteenth had been scratched out and the fifteenth was put in. So I celebrated two birthdays that year, and have ever since then. I don't get two sets of presents, but I get a little joke out of it.

Now, Alliance, Nebraska, where I grew up, is in the northwest corner of Nebraska. Nebraska itself is just south of South Dakota, and it is immediately east of Colorado. Every winter it got to at least thirty-six degrees below zero. It was prairie land. If you walked outside of the town—there were about five thousand people there—all you could see would be brown prairie. Everywhere you turned, you saw brown prairie. There weren't any trees. So it wasn't in that sense a very exciting place.

As far as race—Americans always seem interested in race—in my town, I suppose there were eight or nine African Americans. I was raised around relatively few African Americans. The first school I went to was Grandview. My kindergarten or first-grade teacher was named Agnew. And I went to Alliance High School. It had excellent teachers. In my graduating class, there were 153 students, and three of us were black. There were so few blacks, people I guess didn't think about it much. I left home, Nebraska, when I was seventeen years old, and went to a CCC camp, established by Franklin Roosevelt. And boys that went there— these camps were of course segregated because life was segregated in the United States then—and each young man that went there got, I think, twenty-one dollars a month. Eight dollars were for him, and the rest of it went to his family. I spent a year and a half in this camp in Wellington, Kansas.

From there, I went to Des Moines, Iowa. I was still in the West and Middle West. I worked as an elevator boy in Des Moines making five dollars and eighty-six cents a week. And that included working on Sundays. So I left Des Moines, and I had a very small amount of money. I got on the bus saying goodbye to my friend, and I had about five dollars and eighty-four cents. I asked the bus driver, "How far will this take me?" And he says, "That will take you to Davenport, Iowa," and I went to Davenport, Iowa. When I got off the bus, I had nothing, nothing. I saw a bridge that crossed the Mississippi River, and I immediately thought of crossing the bridge, going across to the town on the other side, which was Rock Island, Illinois, and hunting for a job. But I didn't get far on the bridge before the man asked me for the toll. To the cross the bridge, you needed to have five cents. I didn't have five cents. So he says, "Sorry. There's a free bridge," and he pointed far to the east.

I'm seeing myself walking down the street in Davenport, and a lady from a barbershop—she was the owner—she stopped me. Now, this was like a black woman called Mary in Ralph Ellison's novel *Invisible Man*. And she was the same character, I think, as Mary was. Anyhow, she asked me what I was doing, and she got out of me that I had no money and that I was looking for a job. And she offered me a place to sleep for the night underneath a stairway. I said, "I'm going to cross that bridge and see if I can find a job." So I crossed the bridge into Rock Island, Illinois. It was a long bridge. I didn't find a job, so I was coming back to Mary's barbershop, getting ready to get on the bridge from Rock Island to Davenport. And I looked down at the beginning of the bridge. I saw a junkyard, and I went to the office of the junkyard and said, "I need a job." I went inside, and the man said, "What can you do?" And I told him a lie, I said, "I can do anything." So he put me to work, said, "Come back the next morning."

That's how I got a job in a junkyard when I couldn't get any other kind of work to do. I stayed at that place called Brady's Iron and Metal Company until I took a series of tests for the civil-service jobs. It's interesting as I look back on all of those tests. I got scores in the nineties, but they never called. One day, however, I got a letter, inviting me to come to Washington, D.C.—by the way, there were two young black boys who took the test with me. I crossed the bridge with them now and then, and they didn't look any brighter than I was. I had been the class valedictorian. I thought maybe I was just as smart as any other ordinary person.

So I went to Washington [in 1940] and I became the private secretary of General Benjamin O. Davis, who was the first black general in the army of the United States. [Davis was promoted to the rank of brigadier general (temporary) on October 25, 1940. He was retired on July 31, 1941, and recalled to active duty with the rank of brigadier general the following day.] I worked for him, and my life changed immensely, of course, because I started to go to classical music concerts. I went to an opera. I did things I had never done before in my life. I stayed in Washington with General Davis until World War II broke out. I went for my physical exam. I failed it deliberately, because reading the war department manuals, I found out how to stay out of the army, if you wanted to stay out. So I thought I'd have a little bit more fun in Washington. Later on, I wrote the draft board saying I'm ready to go into the army, and of course, I passed the physical and went into the army.

I trained in a training camp in Massachusetts. I'm interjecting things that ordinarily, perhaps, I wouldn't even remember. The things that have to do with the difficulties caused by racism do stay in one's memory. I say that about this camp in Massachusetts—Fort Devins—all of us in the camp took an exam for officer candidate school. I took the exam. The captain who was in charge of my training, his name was Richard A. Cain from New York. He told me one morning, "I'm proud of you. They tell me that you got the highest score of the whole regiment." He says, "You'll make a fine officer." The army, the government, however, did not send me to officer's training school, even though I did have the highest score. They sent me overseas to Manila to work in an ammunition company for the army until I was sent to New Guinea. There was an officer in New Guinea who had known me at the Office of the Inspector General in Washington. So he pulled me down to be his secretary, and I spent the end of the war in New Guinea.

I came back to the United States in 1946, found out that I was the only man in the entire unit—many, many men there—who didn't have enough days of service to get out. I lacked seventeen days [because of my date of enlistment]. So they kept me. I was the only one they kept. Everybody else went home. When it was time for me to get an assignment, a captain told me, "Well, we'll send you to a camp in Alabama." I looked at him and I said, "By God, I won't go." He looked at me and said, "Well, Sergeant, the best that I can do is send you to Fort Benning, Georgia. And I can give you a fifteen-day furlough on the way there."

So I went across the United States twice trying to have some fun. Then I went down to Fort Benning, Georgia. I won't say much about my experiences there, except all the time I was in Fort Benning, I stayed in the camp, because I knew that if I went in town, I might not come back alive because I was the kind of fellow who did not take abuse. A man in charge of the court-martial section at Fort Benning took me to town because I was the only man in the whole organization that wrote shorthand. And he needed to take a deposition from a black soldier who had been shot. So I went in with them and the soldier was lying in bed and the adjutant general started to question him. The soldier was in such bad shape that he had to put his lips right up to my ear, and I wrote down what he said. He said a lot, but I'll tell you what he said mainly. He said, "I came into town here on assignment and I really didn't know where to go. So I was walking down the street in my uniform. A policeman came up to me and stopped me. And he told me to take my hands out of my pockets." Then he said in words so faint I could hardly hear him, "I guess I didn't take my hands out of my pockets fast enough, because he started shooting. He shot me eighteen times."

Well, I thought later, maybe the boy didn't have the right count of the number of times he was shot, but he died. And I didn't go out of the camp to town at all [after that]. When I was discharged, I went directly to Washington, D.C.—anyway, in Washington, D.C., I went to a little café near Union Station. I had on my military outfit with my battle stars and ribbons and my staff sergeant insignia. And I asked for a Coca-Cola, and the girl came over to me with a sweet look on her face and said, "We don't serve Negroes here."

I waited two hours for the manager to come, and I blasted him. I told him what I thought of him, that he was worse than Hitler. And I strode away, but I never, to this day, I never, never, never forgot that.

I decided to go to Howard University. I was going to study and try to make something of myself, taking advantage of the G.I. Bill. So I spent four years, of course, at Howard University, graduated summa cum laude. I had all A's. As a matter of fact, although it doesn't really mean much, my grades were all A's from the eighth through the master's degree. That's just an indication of how hard I worked.

But after I got my degree in 1950 and left Howard University and went to Chicago, I couldn't get a job doing anything, even as a laborer. I tried everything in the newspapers and nobody would hire me. I tried to get a job as a coal hiker, a man who just shovels coal. They wouldn't hire. I was walking away from the reception desk, and the young man at the desk kind of looked around and beckoned to me with his fingers, and he whispered to me. He says, "I couldn't hire you because you're a Negro." So it didn't do me any good to be summa cum laude.

Somehow I ended up in the office of a Jewish man who later became a high official in state politics. He said to me, "I don't understand why your people don't help you." Of course, the words "your people" kind of hung in my mind, because I wasn't sure who my people were. And he sent me to the *Chicago Defender*. He says, "Go there and ask them for a job, and if they don't give you a job, you come back to me. And I promise you, I will get you a job." And I never forgot him either. His name was Abrams.

Anyhow, the *Chicago Defender* gave me a job as all-errands boy. I'd get cigars for the public-relations man. And they would let me tamper with the speeches that the president of the Johnson Publishing Company was going to make, because I knew how to point to the places where he should pause on a roll of tape, so that he would sound okay when he was talking.

I got married in Chicago, got a master's degree at Northwestern University in Evanston in 1953. And I headed east again because my goal was New York. I wanted to go to the toughest place, and I wanted to go to the top. So I went to New York to study for my Ph.D. at Columbia University. I had the John Hay Whitney Fellowship grant.

When I got to Columbia University, I was called into the office of the head of the English department, by Marjorie Nicholson. I think she was the only woman who was the chairman of a department at that time. It was 1953. And she said to me—we talked, and she asked me what language I had to offer. I said, "Spanish." And she said, "That won't do."

I said, "But the bulletin said that Spanish was all right."

She said, "No, that won't do." And she talked a while; she said, "I hardly ever ask a candidate for Ph.D. to get up on one language, but I'm going to ask you to get two languages."

Well, I felt like a soldier again, and so I got up and I walked out like a soldier. I said to myself, "I'll teach her."

Even though I was teaching at the Harlem YWCA Business School, and sometimes I would work at the owl's shift at the post office, I learned three languages in one year—French and German and Latin. I taught myself two of them. So I worked like a slave. At the end of this academic year, she called me into her office, and I took my little boy with me. I took him everywhere because my wife was working. I know she was testing his intelligence by something, feeling his head, looking for the Walt Whitman chart of bumps, I guess, and she said, "Mr. Emanuel, you have done very well." And I said to myself, "I know damn well I have done well," but I didn't say that, of course. I got a Ph.D. at Columbia University in 1962. All of my degrees—major subjects—were in English and comparative literature.

I had an area of interest that ultimately cost me another year or two. I had chosen the Romantic period in English literature, but I said to myself, I should know something about Negro literature, as it was called then. So I started delving into African American literature at Columbia. I took anything that might have something to do with it. And this cost me another two years, but I finished in 1962. And I tried to get a job at Columbia in the evening school. Vernon Loggins, who was famous as the author of the book *The Negro Author,* headed the school. He was the first great scholar on black literature. And I said to him I'd like a job teaching in the evening school. His answer was, "Why don't you try Howard University?" And I said to myself, "He didn't learn much in studying Negro literature. He didn't learn much about black people."

So I talked to some people in the city. I said, "I'd like to work for City University." Everybody said to me, "You're wasting your time. There is nobody [black] in the English department. You're wasting your time."

Therefore, I wrote a letter directly to the chairman of the English department at City University asking him for a job. He hired me. He was kind of an unusual man. He'd been an air pilot. He had been a boxer, but they told me in later years, he had one uncanny talent. He could put his fingers on good men. He hired good men, all of whom became much more than the average in later years.

I started writing on black literature. I was, I think, probably the first writer in 1961 and 1963 to publish essays urging the United States to pay attention to black literature. That's my claim. I don't know of any earlier works doing that. So I started on black literature, continued on until the time of retirement, went to Europe, taught at the universities of Grenoble, Toulouse—Warsaw, in Poland—until I was able to take what they called early retirement, which I jumped at, because I wanted to write poetry. That was my big aim. And as of now, I'm still writing it. I've published almost four hundred poems in fourteen volumes of poetry, plus critical books, critical essays, but my love and challenge has been poetry.

Frederick Douglass once said to somebody, "No man can insult the soul of Frederick Douglass." That was the way I felt. I was not going to be stopped from pursuing my deepest aspirations.

I moved to Paris the last time in 1984—June, during the celebration of the Normandy invasion. I came to Paris because I didn't know anybody here. I didn't go back to Toulouse, where I had taught at the university for four years, because I had too many friends. What I wanted to be was a writer, and I had learned that when you make friends, you lose much of your time. So I didn't really try to make friends.

I started writing poetry, I guess, when I was a child. When I went into the army, I wrote a poem that was put on the bulletin board of the ship, stuff like that. But I started seriously writing a poem when I got a prize for a sonnet in 1958, "Sonnet for a Writer." *Flame* magazine gave me a special prize for that poem, and from then on, I knew that's what I wanted to do. I had done much of it before, but I knew when that poem came out that I wanted to be a poet.

Paris gave me the opportunity to be alone and not be bothered by a certain atmosphere. There's an atmosphere that I had lived through in the United States that I never wanted to experience again, never. It's a wretched, cruel thing.

Countee Cullen wrote a famous sonnet "To France." It's about the fact he found a lack of racism here [in Paris] and that he would prefer to die in Paris [rather than live in the U.S.]. He said, "among a fair and kindly foreign folk." And I knew exactly what he meant.

Paris, I think, means something special to all people who spend a lot of time there. I don't how they express it, but I think they feel the same thing that I feel. I think there have always been black writers in Paris, but I never tried to seek them out.

I was always a solitary person when I was young. When I worked, for example, I'd work in a grain field in Nebraska, where you just turned around in a circle and all you could see were those fields that you had to work with nobody to help you, because I worked for an old farmer who never spoke to me except to give me a command. So I became a solitary person. By the age of seventeen, I was a solitary person, and I think I did not change. It's been a long journey.

There were seven of us children, three boys and four girls. My mother's name was Cora Ann Mance; my father's name was Alfred Andrew Emanuel. He was a westerner. My mother would say things about him, but one thing she would praise him for. She would say, "I've seen him ride wild horses that no other man could ride. I've seen those horses jump eight feet into the air." My mother was slow to praise. She liked famous men. She had high standards. She liked people who were something.

My family was among the early Nebraskan pioneers who followed

Pap Singleton in the 1890s. He's well known. My mother said, "I knew Pap." She didn't think much of him. He led the groups from Georgia and other parts to the West. They were homesteaders. They went there in the days when if you stayed on your land and improved it for five years, it became yours. This was true in several states in the West—Arizona, Nebraska, and others—the Homestead Law. My parents went there when they were relatively young.

There is an article written by somebody called Beryl, and it's called "The Lost Pioneers." It came out in the *Negro Digest,* I think the year was 1964, 1965, and my family is mentioned there. And my grandfather Mance is mentioned as the pastor of these pioneers.

As far as I know, my mother was prominent among black people in the town. I don't know how she did it, but she knew all of the important white people [too]. I never figured out how she did that, but she did. Whenever any important black people would come through the town, they would come to see her. The West provided more opportunity than was found in the South.

My mother lived in Georgia, I know. Some of my ancestors came from Luxembourg. My translator, Jean Migrenne, he told me he looked in the phone book in Luxembourg and he found a number of Emanuels. My family must have been mixed, because I remember when I was a child in school, I had an assignment to find out about our racial ancestry. I asked my mother and she told me, "African, Indian, and German." Whether she mentioned French, I don't know, but she mentioned German and Indian and something else I don't remember. Of course, most black people were mixed after a couple of generations—mixed and mixed up for some.

Well, my mother was a Christian Science practitioner. I think really she became a Christian Scientist because a number of the powerful people in the town went to the Christian Science Church. And I think she wanted them to know her. She had practical reasons for doing a lot of things. I don't like organized religion. I had an experience in Washington. There was me and a brilliant young man who later became the chief of cardiology in Harlem Hospital. We were on the street one day and the air-raid alarm—you had to practice where to go and you were supposed to go into the first public building. Now, for us, the first public building was a church. We went up there and I knocked on the door of the church and the minister came out. He had on his ministerial garb. He was white, and when he saw we were black, he slammed the door in our faces. I never forgot that. I believe in the religious thrust of the human spirit. It's one of the best, but you know when people get together, they act worse than when they are alone.

I don't think about my age, because in Christian Science, they say that age is a human error, a human falsity. They don't believe in it. I come up the stairs two and three at a time if I don't have groceries.

My father's dreams might not have been fully realized, because by heart, he was a rancher. I remember once I was on the threshing crew—different families got together in those days and went to a particular farmer's property and they threshed his grain. I was fifteen, sixteen years old. I always worked with men, by the way, never with boys. I always did a man's work. My father saw me, and at one point, a little boy, seven or eight years old, he was there. And the grown-ups were talking about a certain big rancher, and the boy said, "He said that ranch wouldn't amount to much if wasn't for Emanuel." I know he was imitating what his parents had said, that it was my father that held that ranch together and kept it going, but he didn't have enough money to buy his own. I think he would have wanted to be a rancher and raise cattle and horses.

There's a real frontier, and there's one in the head. The real one, of course, moved west gradually from the Mississippi and went on finally to California, that Thoreau didn't want to be a part of. But that is an entirely different thing. I often think about the frontier in my head. That's the frontier to do something that's never been done before. And to do something good that no one has done before, which I've tried to do in poetry and am still trying to do. Just do it better than other people do it. And let it be a good thing that advances people rather than kills them and tortures them. If you try to follow this way of thinking, at least you won't be—what's the word Faulkner liked to use?—retrograding. You'll be going forward, at least, instead of backward. Try to do something good not only for yourself but for other people, and do it well.

[Interview by Alan Govenar, June 8, 2005]

*Richard E. Harris and his wife, Laura Dungee Harris, Phoenix, Arizona, 1964.*

# RICHARD E. HARRIS

JOURNALIST

Born September 12, 1912

Richard E. Harris has been a writer and social activist for most of his life. Growing up in Chester, Pennsylvania, Harris realized that he wanted to be a writer while still in high school, but was not allowed to write for his school newspaper. While the school was integrated to the extent that both blacks and whites attended class together, black students were not afforded the same rights and privileges as their white counterparts. After graduation, Harris became the first African American to write for the Chester Times, covering local sports and community events, but was not hired for a full-time job at the paper until he was twenty-seven years old. In 1945, he started his own newspaper, the Delaware County Crusader, and in his first edition, in a front-page editorial, he called for equal rights for African American servicemen returning home from World War II. Over the years, Harris worked for a number of African American newspapers, including the Philadelphia Afro-American and Pittsburgh Courier. At age fifty-two he became the first black reporter at the Arizona Republic. After moving to Phoenix, Harris not only worked as a journalist but was actively involved in the civil-rights movement, challenging segregated schools and housing, and fighting bigotry and injustice. In 1965, he married Laura Jane Dungee, whose family settled in Phoenix in the early 1920s. Over the years, Richard and Laura Harris have worked actively to advance civil rights and opportunities for African Americans in their community. He is the author of six books: The American Odyssey of a Black Journalist (2003), Estevan: Black Comrade of Conquistadores (1999), Politics and Prejudice: A History of Chester, Pennsylvania Negroes (1991), The First Hundred Years: A History of Arizona Blacks (1983), Black Heritage in Arizona (1977), and Delinquency in Our Democracy (1954).

I WAS BORN IN EASTERN MARYLAND, and we came to Chester, Pennsylvania, when I was eleven years old. And I was there until I moved to Phoenix in 1960.

We lived in Easton, [Maryland]. My father worked at a furniture factory. And I had an uncle who had a grocery store right across the street from us. We moved from Maryland so my father could look for a better job. There were six children in my family. And when we got to Pennsylvania, there was a lot of segregation. It was kind of ironic. You would think there would have been more segregation in Maryland, but there wasn't that much. Well, you know, it was "sit upstairs," and when I finally came to Phoenix, Arizona [as an adult], it was the same thing, and it was much worse [than Maryland and Pennsylvania]. [In Phoenix,] I became one of the community leaders who helped to break down segregation in the schools and everything like that. I have quite a few citations for my work.

I got started as a writer when I went to high school. In Pennsylvania, we couldn't go to high school until the tenth grade. Back then everything was all segregated. And so when I finally went to the tenth grade, only reason I went there, I had to go to school, and I wanted to play football and track. In the tenth grade, we were able to take a foreign language, and that was for the first time. And my teacher told me—and I was flunking English, and my teacher told me, "Don't take any foreign language." And I said, "Oh, to hell with you," you know, and so I took Latin. And me and another student, a Jewish boy—his father was a doctor—we talked a little. He and I were the top students in our Latin class for the next two years. So that's when I got really interested in writing.

I wanted to compete against the whites and compete against them in class also, which I did. I was the only black in the Latin class, and the Jewish boy was nice in class. But we just went to the class at the same time. We didn't sit together or anything. I don't know whether we even much spoke. There wasn't any real integration in classes. If he had been friendly with me, he would probably have been ostracized. So that didn't happen. The black and white students didn't mix. They might have been in the same room in class, but that was about it. I went to that "integrated" school for tenth, eleventh, and twelfth grades.

After I graduated high school, I was the first black to write for the local paper, the *Chester Times.* I went in there and told them I wanted a job. And I wrote a column five or six days a week about news in the black community, at first, and then later on, I wrote sports—football and track—for the same paper.

From the *Chester Times,* I went to work for the *Philadelphia Afro-American* newspaper. That was the name of it. It was owned by blacks. It's still running now. It was one of the first completely black newspapers. They gave me a job as city editor. I was in charge of five or six people. I worked there about three years, and went back to Chester. I had also been with the *Philadelphia Independent,* another Philadelphia paper. You see, the *Chester Times* had gone on a strike for a couple of years, and then when they went off strike, I went back to them. And I wasn't there very long before I went to another black newspaper called the *Pittsburgh Courier.* The *Pittsburgh Courier* was distributed all over the country. So was the *Afro-American.* The *Afro-American* is still in operation. In fact, one of the daughters of one of the publishers got out of journalism and became the first black presiding elder at an African church. They're still in Baltimore. They had a chain [of newspapers]. They had about six different papers, in Philadelphia, New York. They were the Murphys.

I cover this in my last book. It is called *The American Odyssey of a Black Journalist* (2003). I wrote that, rather modestly, I can claim myself as being one of the few surviving members of that generation of black newsmen proudly following in the traits forged by those gurus of the Harlem Renaissance.

Beginning in the post-Depression days, I have labored with at least ten newspapers, starting with the *Chester Times, Philadelphia Afro-American, Philadelphia Independent,* and *Pittsburgh Courier,* and later on with the *Cleveland Call Post, Akron Record, Los Angeles Sentinel, Arizona Sun, Delaware County Crusader,* and *Arizona Republic.* It's what I call an odyssey. I've published six books. My first book was *Delinquency in Our Democracy.* I did that in 1954.

Unlike many of the past and more recent fellow journalists ordinarily operating from specific stomping grounds, my quests carried me to numerous large and small cities. And during those periods, duties ranged from that of ordinary reporter to roving correspondent, columnist, associate editor, labor writer, city editor, sportswriter, and religion editor. In addition to my home bases in Pennsylvania, Ohio, California, and Arizona, my investigative assignments concerning Negroes often resulted in my spending considerable time in Boston, Memphis, Harlem, Gary, San Antonio, and Maryland's Eastern Shore. Other cities visited were Houston, Baltimore, Oklahoma City, Los Angeles, Omaha, Oakland, and Kansas City.

I'm self-taught as a writer. But I had a role model in Chester, and he went to Syracuse University. I used to ask him how'd he got into it. First thing he told me, "Three words: Write, write, write." And then he gave me a list of things. But here's the curious thing about it: He left the *Chester Times,* and he was doing something; I don't know what he was doing. But he supposedly had a degree in journalism. But they gave him a job, janitor or something. He took it. But anyhow, he left there and went to the first independent newspaper. And when I got there, he was supposed to be an editor, or something like that, but anyhow, he gave me hell. He'd just take my copy and throw it in the basket. I mean, that was tough, boy. His name was Ted Graham. I thought he was a mentor, but I'm not so sure now.

That was his method of teaching, but it did teach me that I had determination. He worked there three, four months, five months. And then they got rid of him. That's when I went back to the *Chester Times.* He didn't do anything for me. In fact, some of the other people on the staff used to tell him, "Why are you treating Harris like this?" He had a problem. And he was black. I could never quite understand why he acted the way he did.

The fraternity of African American editors and journalists has long commanded an influential and unique position in this nation. And along with the churches and some fraternal lodges, their print media represents a dominant vanguard in the continual campaign for justice and racial equality. *Freedom's Journal,* widely recognized as the forerunner of race-owned papers, was founded in 1827 by Samuel Cornish, a Presbyterian minister, and John B. Russwurm, who later became governor of [a province of] Liberia, the American-sponsored African colony. While scores of other similar efforts followed the short-lived *Journal* and Frederick Douglass's *North Star,* most nevertheless espoused the latter's policy of "keeping the Negro public informed on vital issues, creating an open forum for voicing Negro sentiment, exposing racial injustice, urging Negroes to become conscious of their past achievements, and striving for opportunities for betterment."

My journalistic sojourn fortunately carried me through some of the most significant, controversial, yet exciting years of our modern history, which was coincidental to the prime time of the Negro press's progress and prestige. The great majority of those papers were members of the National Newspaper Publishers Association, whose credo was, "We believe that America can best lead the world away from racial and national antagonism when it accords every person, regardless of race, creed, or color, full rights. Hating no person, fearing no person, the black press strives to help every person in the firm belief that all are hurt as long as anyone is held back."

The Second World War period witnessed increased militancy by Negro papers, vigorously taking the nation to task for its hollow treatment of race on both the home front and in the armed forces. Just prior to U.S. entrance into the conflict, its industries were earning millions from Allied war contracts, yet ignoring the jobless plight among black Americans. The onetime journalist A. Philip Randolph, head of the Brotherhood of Sleeping Car Porters, under the threat of leading a million-person protest on Washington, forced President Franklin D. Roosevelt to issue Executive Order 8802, the Fair Employment Practice Act, outlawing discrimination in federal contracts.

During the war, the Negro press had permission to send their own correspondents to the war zones. But much to the chagrin of some federal authorities, these reporters were often dispatching news of discriminatory incidents against colored servicemen. The *Pittsburgh Courier*, while exposing these negative revelations, also advocated its "Double V" theme, calling for "Victory at home as well as Victory overseas." Negro servicemen stationed at camps in both the North and South were victims of flagrant injustices, and sometimes even death. In fact, so disturbing were the frank criticisms of the "war efforts" by the Negro press that the U.S. Department of Justice once threatened twenty of the editors with acts of sedition. Almost simultaneously, many of the papers began experiencing difficulty securing adequate newsprint. An apparent compromise between paper owners and federal authorities eventually settled the controversy.

Postwar years were equally crucial for many blacks insofar as discrimination in jobs and public accommodations were concerned, and while their papers continued campaigning vigorously for racial equality, some unwittingly found themselves victims of their own missions. White editors were apparently beginning to recognize the double potential of the Negro press. First, its vastly increasing readership could possibly pose threats to the establishment press, as minimal as it may have been. Second, it seemed a very practical business decision to hire a competent Afro-American reporter, rather than send a white reporter to cover stories in restless Negro neighborhoods. As an incentive for a Negro reporter going to a daily, a salary double or triple that earned at a Negro paper, awaited him or her. Furthermore, such a move spelled a good public-relations gesture for the white editor and welcome prestige for the daily's first black reporter.

From personal experiences, I might speculate on the role of the colored reporter with a white-owned operation. On two separate occasions, widespread, to be sure, I served such companies. During the dying Depression days, I stepped into my first paying job as a correspondent for a Pennsylvania company. And at the height of the civil-rights revolution, I campaigned to become the first of my race to become a reporter with the *Arizona Republic*. True, the events represented a span of twenty-five years and twenty-five hundred miles apart, yet the results were basically similar. With the Philadelphia paper, I was to write a six-day-a-week column on civic, church, and social-club items from "my community." With the Arizona paper, my assignments were to cover the city antipoverty programs, which ordinarily dealt with Negroes and other minorities. While with either paper, I proved to be as capable as most white peers and soon found news stories outside the stereotype bounds suggested for me.

When I first came to Phoenix, the owner of the *Arizona Republic* wrote the *Pittsburgh Courier* people asking about me, and he heard good things. So they hired me right away. But I only worked there for three and a half years. Then I went to the Urban League because I could be involved more in my community. I worked with the Urban League in Phoenix for about twelve years. My first task was to initiate activities aimed at helping to satisfy students' questions concerning their own heritage. I developed a youth program. I set up speeches, and we had a newspaper. The white students in the schools didn't allow our young people [African Americans] to work on their paper. So we set up our own paper called *Youth United*. And we had a few Chicanos in that group that got along with us [African Americans]; they volunteered to work with us. There were eight or ten schools; all of them had their own papers. But when blacks got there, they couldn't get on the paper or participate in other activities. We had to do our own thing. Besides writing news, short stories, and poetry, they [the students] interviewed community professionals and later composed black historical skits in which they acted. Such experiences were unavailable in the public high schools where these students were enrolled. Thus, through such outside extracurricular activities, they were presumably beneficiaries of vocational counseling, work experience, and increased racial pride.

The NAACP wasn't too strong in Phoenix, compared to some [chapters] in other cities. See, when I first came out to Phoenix, I got on the picket line with the NAACP. In fact, I was on the picket line in front of the state capitol the day before I was hired [by the *Arizona Republic*]. I tell people I just wanted to get on the picket line so they could see where I was coming from. I showed up, reporting for duty. No problem. I never had any problem after that.

We were picketing the statehouse about the segregation policy. Blacks couldn't do anything here. They didn't have any jobs in any of the [big downtown] stores or anything like that. In fact, there wasn't even any civil-rights legislation. We had to get something from the city to act on the problem of segregation before we stopped the picketing. And it went on for seven or eight months, maybe a year, after I was the first [African American] hired. None of the blacks were being hired. There was complete segregation in schools and in the workplace, you name it. The only professional blacks, the majority, were teachers. One of my close friends who I mentioned in my book, Dr. Eugene Grigsby, was a black artist. And he was one of the first ones hired by ASU [Arizona State University]. He had his Ph.D.—he has three degrees. He was one of the top artists in the country.

As far as I was concerned, I was just interested in helping those kids who were in a segregated high school. I was pulling them in my way [to protest and to work on their own newspaper, *Youth United*]. I even got

Richard E. Harris (fifth from left) surrounded by students from his writing workshop, Phoenix, Arizona, 1972.

those kids to picket the segregated schools to get them integrated. They were supposed to be integrated, but there was a lot of segregation going on as far as the subjects that were being taught and the way social activities excluded blacks.

Some of the students, after they got through our program, still keep in touch with me—and some of the programs are still going. One of the young men in my group has become a writer. He started on radio here in Phoenix, and he's still active. In fact, most of those kids—I call them kids [though they're grown-ups now]—are still writing. After college, some embarked on careers in public relations, radio, television, drama, and print journalism. One now is down in Louisiana, in Baton Rouge, and has developed a similar cultural program that focuses on writing and is directing a similar program that I had. And he still gets in touch with me every once in a while.

[In recent years] I helped develop a new building here in Phoenix. I was more or less a pioneer here. When I came here, they didn't have [an African American] museum, so we took one of the schools, one of the black schools, and set up a committee. My wife was a member of that group, and so we bought the school and set up a museum, and it's the first one [African American museum] there. And they are exhibiting a lot of things that I had collected—antiques, photographs, articles, and books.

My wife [Laura Jane Dungee Harris] was one of the women who graduated from there in 1941. It was called Phoenix Union Colored High School, and they later changed the named to Carver Union High School. And when I married her [in 1965], I was already getting into that [civil-rights] field. My wife's family came to Phoenix in 1923 from Oklahoma City, and at that time, there were very few blacks. There was a black lawyer living in Arizona, and he was hired by the whites to go to Arkansas and Oklahoma to find blacks that wanted to come into this area, free of charge. They wanted the blacks to do domestic and field-work. They let them off in Eloy, Arizona, but her parents didn't want to work in the fields anymore. So they came to Phoenix, where her dad worked in a hotel, and her mother did domestic work in private homes. My wife went to segregated schools and worked various jobs. She eventually became a nurse's assistant at the state hospital for fourteen years. It was called Arizona State Hospital, at Twenty-fourth and Van Buren. She helped care for people who were mentally infirm and with geriatric patients.

I've kind of slowed down. I write letters to people. I don't know what keeps me going. Have a good meal and everything and exercise. In fact, when you called, I had just come in from helping the guy to get my septic tank. I was out there doing a little digging, stuff like this. I have some exercise I do quite a bit. But I'm slowing down anyhow.

I went to the doctor the other day, for the first time. Something was in my eye; that's all it was. And they said, "How old are you, Mr. Harris? You look like you're only about sixty years old." I don't know, I'm just an ordinary guy, that's all.

[Interview by Alan Govenar, January 14, 2005]

*Chester Higgins Jr., New York City, 2004.*

# CHESTER HIGGINS JR.

PHOTOGRAPHER

*Born November 1946*

*Chester Higgins Jr. has worked as a photographer for the* New York
Times *since 1975. His interest in photography began when he was
a student at the Tuskegee Institute and met the photographer P. H.
Polk, who let him borrow his camera. At the end of his junior year of
college, Higgins went to New York looking for a critical response to
his photographs and to explore the possibilities of finding freelance
work. In New York, the Farm Security Administration photographer
Arthur Rothstein, who was then an editor at* Look *magazine, took
an interest in Higgins and became his mentor. After graduation
from Tuskegee, Higgins moved to New York and secured a contract
for his first book,* Black Woman *(1970). In the years since, Higgins
has published* Drums of Life *(1974),* Some Time Ago *(1980),*
Feeling the Spirit *(1994),* Elder Grace *(2000), and* Echo of the
Spirit *(2004). Higgins's photographs have appeared in* ARTnews,
Newsweek, Fortune, Essence, *and numerous other magazines.
His work has been exhibited in museums and galleries in the United
States and abroad, including the International Center of Photogra-
phy, the Schomberg Center, and the Smithsonian Institution.*

I WAS RAISED IN A LITTLE COUNTRY TOWN of six hundred people in the
southwest corner of Alabama, where Alabama, Georgia, and Florida come
together. My father was a small-businessman. He and his father owned
a dry-cleaning business; he was the only black dry cleaner in town.

My mother was an educator, a schoolteacher, and probably, unlike
most other kids, education was very important when I was a child. I grew
up in a house filled with books. I remember learning my ABCs on my
mother's typewriter and having encyclopedias and dictionaries to take

up the time when my mother wouldn't let me go out of the house or play with the other kids. She always seemed to have hundreds of chores for me to do. But in that kind of exacting educational environment, I grew up and essentially looked forward to the day I'd graduate out from under my mother to go to college.

I went to Tuskegee University because my mother always wanted me to go to Tuskegee. She went to Alabama State. Her home is in another part of the state, in one of the two coastal counties of Alabama, Baldwin County. I grew up in an environment where, because of my mother and her friends—a mix, women and men—everybody was ambitious about learning. Learning was very important. In my book *Echoes of the Spirit*, I talk about how my mother and her friends made sure that our own curriculum in school was augmented with the knowledge of the contributions of blacks in history. They would pull these essays and curriculum together and make sure that we had that understanding about ourselves. I also learned the Negro national anthem ["Lift Every Voice and Sing"], which I realized when I came north that few Northerners, when they rise to sing it, know it. But it's something we had to learn at an early age.

So, because I grew up in such a small town, mostly agricultural, all of my friends who came from less means than my parents had to spend their summers working in the fields—cotton fields, cornfields, watermelon fields, peanut fields—and I went and worked with them because otherwise, I had nobody to play with during the summer months. And that was great because work was a noble endeavor for everyone in my community. It wasn't until high school that I began to work for plying trades, first with a plumbing company in the summer, and then with an electrical company, and then with a television repair group before leaving for college.

As a child, at the age of nine, I had a vision one night, and my grandfather, who was also a minister, interpreted it as a call to the ministry. So as a young man, I became very active in the church as a young minister, ministering and preaching at my church and visiting other churches, so that my Sundays became very full. And the Bible became an additional book that I began to study and spend time with in addition to my academic books.

Not until I reached college did I become interested in photography.

I had seen a book called *Ain't Everybody Got a Right to the Tree of Life* by this Vista worker. It was on the Gullah Islands off of South Carolina. My interest in college was the civil-rights movement period, and this was the first positive picture book I'd seen on black people. You could always see pictures in the press of black people, but the pictures that you saw would always be pathological images—women who were accused of being prostitutes or men who were accused of some criminal behavior.

At the time, I was majoring in business and sociology, and I came up with an idea, as the business manager for the student newspaper, to get local businesses to place larger ads in the newspaper. Other than just using a business card, we could illustrate the ad with a photograph. So I hired a local photographer, a campus photographer who was an older man, and asked him if he would go and make pictures of these establishments or their principals, and we convinced these businesses that we should run his pictures in addition to just the type. Well, he was late getting these pictures to us, and we were on deadline at the printer. So I went to his house that day, and I said, "Mr. Polk, I need these pictures now." Luckily, he had already shot them. He just hadn't processed the film.

The photographer was P. H. Polk. And I said, "Well, I'm not leaving here until I get these prints." So he went to process them, and it was magic. I had never been in a darkroom before, never seen negatives processed. And being there when he was printing them and seeing the prints come up in the solution of the fixer was magic. But my more immediate concern was fulfilling my obligation to the paper. And while I was there waiting, I noticed that behind one of the curtains he had some pictures of people who looked like they were farmers or sharecroppers, people from my part of Alabama. But what was interesting about them was they had such great dignity, decency about them, and that's the thing that's always missing with the images of people of color when outsiders make our pictures. We're often seen as objects, but our humanity oftentimes gets sacrificed on the altars of our condition. And it ends up that three things are always missing—decency, dignity, and virtuous character. It was like an outsider just could not comprehend that people of color or black people could have the attributes that they would normally give to themselves. So when I saw these pictures, I said, "Mr. Polk, I want to go do this first, discharge my responsibility, but I want to come back to you and talk to you about these pictures."

So I came back the next day, and I said to him, "Look, these pictures remind me of people from my community. And as a student on a student budget, I don't have the money to hire you to go down and make these pictures. I'd really love to have pictures of these relatives because I've never seen any pictures of them. And I know them very well." My mother and my father; I'd seen those pictures. But my great-uncles and my great-aunts, I had never seen photographs of them. There may have been a war photograph, but nothing that captured them in their old age. I said, "Would you teach me photography?" And he looked at me. He thought about it, and I said, "You know, would you let me use your camera to learn photography?"

So he says, "Let me see if I understand this. You want me to loan you my only camera that I make a living with to learn how to make pictures?"

I thought he was questioning my sincerity, and I said, "Well, yes, sir, Mr. Polk, that's right."

He looks at me a little longer. Finally, he says, "You know what, I'm going to be as big a fool as you. If you're fool enough to ask me, I'll be fool enough to help you."

I didn't realize what he meant for a decade. But after about the second time, I realized that he really didn't want me using his camera—he was reluctant, and that was okay. He had a Pentax, a 35mm SLR, and then he also worked with a twin-lens Rolleiflex, for himself. But the Pentax was a lot simpler for me to use and compose. But it didn't have a light meter in it, and I messed up a lot of film because I couldn't get the light right. But I didn't ask him for his camera the second time, but instead I would keep coming to him and talking to him, asking him questions about the thousands of pictures that littered his studio and office, while saving my own money.

That summer, I was in Manhattan, Kansas, for a national meeting of the National Students Association because I was involved in student government. And I walked past this camera shop, and there was a camera, a Praktica with a screw-mount lens for about sixty or seventy dollars. And I bought it. It was my first camera. And that's the camera I came back to Tuskegee with and started making pictures that summer.

I made pictures with that, and I studied. I used my business background, my sense of business from growing up in a business, that's the
dry cleaners, and doing all kinds of business enterprises as a young high
school student, to my college business training. And what I did is, I said,
"Well, I've got to make money with this thing." So I figured out that I
could do portraits of faculty members, and I could charge faculty members so much, five or ten dollars, for their portrait. But in order to do
this, I would have to process the film, and I did that a couple of times and
was miserable. I couldn't do it. So I asked Mr. Polk if I could hire him to
process the film and make the prints for me. And still, I was able to
charge a reasonable fee that left me a profit. And from that, I was able to
save enough money to graduate to a better camera, to a Nikkormat.

And from there, with that Nikkormat, I guess after a year, almost a
year working, perfecting my skill as a photographer, I went back home.
And then I began to make these pictures of my elders, my great-uncles
and great-aunts. I remember one of my great-uncles, Uncle John, who
worked his whole life on the railroad, said to me when I went to make his
picture on his porch, "Well, Chester, that's a pretty camera." He says,
"How much did that camera cost?" And I probably said, "Uncle John,
two hundred and fifty dollars." And Uncle John says to me, he chuckled,
he said, "Well, if it costs that much, it should make pictures by itself."
That was a love moment.

Well, my goal initially was from the heart, from love, to document
people that I love, that I cherish. And so, I had a mission. It wasn't just
to pick up the camera because I wanted to snap a picture here and snap
a picture there. I had a purpose for picking up the camera. And Mr. Polk
helped me understand how to approach people, how to approach
strangers, because he had such a personable way about him. He was one
of those people who sort of convince you that with people, you have to let
them know that you accept them and love them right away, uncondition-
ally. That was a way to disarm them. And he also had other ways of dis-
arming them by telling jokes or using some pat phrases he would say to
people. Like he would say to a woman who was very uptight, he would
say, "Oh, you must be a twin." It would distract her, make her think
about something else, and she would say, "No," and that would happen
several times, "No," and finally she'd get so frustrated and upset with

Chester Higgins Jr.'s great-aunt, midwife Aunt Shugg Lampley, making her evening prayer
before bed in New Brockton, Alabama, 1968.

him. "Mr. Polk, I keep telling you I'm not a twin. Why you keep saying
that?" And Mr. Polk would say, "Well, I just don't believe that one
woman could be so beautiful." And then he would get this beautiful
smile. He would set up these moments. If one thing didn't work, he
would find another way to get over these barriers. So I learned so much
by coming over to visit him from time to time and just be able to ask him
questions and also watch when he worked when people came in, when
he shot, or to ride out with him in the countryside and just watch him
stop. He'd see something, a picture he liked. It gave me a sense of how to
work with people. But my purpose was still to photograph—because I appreciated the love and dignity that he put in his own pictures. That made
me realize that this was the man to learn from. And when I went back
home, because of that love, that's what I did.

Now, that love as a mission, as a purpose, changed during the civil-
rights movement. It became politicized—I can say I've always photographed with my heart. But the civil-rights movement caused me to
photograph with my head. It caused me to be politicized. And that happened because we at Tuskegee, the students, would go over from time to
time to Montgomery, the state capital, and we would protest against the

then-governor, racist governor, George Wallace. And when we'd come back, the media that evening, and on television and in the newspaper the next day, the pictures were very disturbing that were produced about our protest. Instead of seeing us as American citizens exercising our right to petition the government, the photographers invariably showed us as potential thugs or arsonists or rapists. And it made me realize—this was the first time I had become disturbed by it because I was a part of it myself, and I knew that the reality was quite different from how it was projected. At the same time, I realized, though, this was nothing new, and this was how we've always seen ourselves projected in the press and that I think black people have sort of become numb to that particular kind of depiction because it's always a racist depiction. But it made me realize that there was another part of the story here that had not been seen and that I could show it. But what really made me put that together was having dinner one night with one of my professors, a visiting professor from the University of Michigan who taught me industrial relations. And I came over to his house that evening with he and his wife, and I was very upset and obsessed with what happened.

And he says to me, "Well, Chester, have you ever heard the story about the father who would read the bedtime story to his son each night about the man fighting the lion?" and part of me, as I'm sitting there, wanted to say, "You know, you old stupid white man, what are you talking about?" But as a child growing up in my little country town, I remember spending hours sitting down listening to old people, and old people would talk a lot in parables, that things weren't quite as obvious as what was said. So, keeping my mouth shut, I listened to his story.

I said, "Well, how does the story go?"

So he says, "Well, there's this father who will read a bedtime story to his son, and the son's favorite bedtime book was the fight that the man and the lion had."

And I said, "Well, okay."

He said, "Well, it goes like this: The man goes into the jungle, he comes upon the lion, they have a big fight, the man takes out his knife, and he kills the lion. So this particular night, the son says to the father, as he reads the book, he says, 'Dad, I don't understand. Why doesn't the lion win? Look. The man went into the lion's house. The lion's got a right to protect his house. The lion is bigger than the man. The lion has four big claws and a big mouth with all those teeth. I don't understand, why doesn't the lion win?' he says to his father. And the father says to the son, 'Son, the lion will win when the lion writes his own book.' "

For me, that clinched it. I understood immediately what I needed to do. It was not to just say, "These photographers are racist and the media is racist," but to take my frustration and show another point of view that other people can't see and try to get these pictures published in their media and other media. But realizing that these people can't see this and calling them racists won't make it different, but trying to preserve those images myself, hopefully to be used now, to use my salesmanship skills to get those pictures published in major media, and then also for historical purposes because I can see, from Mr. Polk's pictures, that something off the wall thirty years ago, looking back at you, also has a great deal of importance.

That professor from the University of Michigan was Michael Ryder. He was also a mediator with the American Association of Mediators. He helped me see the purpose and the path of how I could use the camera from a political point of view. So, in my work, I've attached both of those—I'm sort of like, you know, in the old days, they had those wagons with two mules. Well, my camera's sort of attached to two mules. One is attached to the head, and one is attached to the heart. The one out of the heart is out of love, and the one out of the head is an awareness of what time it is in history and what time it is in the human drama that's going on before.

While I was at Tuskegee, I was able to get published in a couple of national media, like Johnson Publishing Company had *Jet* magazine; I had a couple of pictures in *Jet*. And they also had a magazine, an intellectual magazine, called *Black World,* in which my first essay was published. And then in '69, I went to New York with a portfolio of images that I had been photographing of women. I spent the summer trying to peddle this around to a publisher. And at the same time, I took a smaller portfolio. What I first did was, I went to a newsstand, and I picked up all of the magazines that use pictures. And I looked to see who the picture editor was, and I called them up, and I said, "Look, I'm a student from Alabama. I want to be a photographer. We don't have a photography school in Alabama where I go to school. But I know you see all the best photographers. Would you please take a look at my work? I'm not asking for a job. But would you please take a look at my work and tell me what it is that I have yet to learn?" And I went around to all these picture editors, and they were very nice. They took a look at my work because I'm sure they thought that maybe, hey, here's a freelancer that maybe we can use in the South if something happens. Who knows what their motivations were? But this is what I said to them. And I got some good advice from *Newsweek*, from *Life*, from *Time*. And then I was at *Look* magazine one day, and I was showing my work to the picture editor there, a young man by the name of Sam Young.

And when Sam and I were finishing, a baldheaded man sticks his head in the door and he tells Sam something. I didn't know he was Sam's boss. He saw me, saw the pictures. He says, "Sam, what's this?" So Sam told him. And so he says, "Sam, when you're finished, send him into my office."

Sam says, "Okay." I didn't know what this was. But I want criticism; I want some input. So I'll talk to anybody. So I go into this man's office, and he takes a look at my photographs, and I tell him the same thing I told Sam: "I'm from Tuskegee, I'm a student, we don't have a photography school, I want to learn photography, I want to get better. I know in my environment I'm very limited, so, here, you guys see the best photographers. Look at my work and tell me what I need to learn." So the guy starts looking at my pictures, and immediately, after he goes through all of them, he takes a picture, and he takes out four pieces of white paper. And he lays the paper on top of the picture, leaving an aperture, an opening. And he says to me, he says, "Look." He says, "There's your picture." And I looked, and it was incredible. He had taken all this other stuff out from the picture and just zeroed in on where the strongest elements of that picture were. And he did another one. And he did another one. And he did another one. And he says, "Well, this is what's called cropping a photograph." And he says, "You crop a photograph to take out everything that's insignificant that competes with what is the central view."

I was astounded. So we went through all my pictures. I say, "This cropping is a whole different thing." And he says, "In the process of cropping, as you cropped, what made that work is that you had to understand composition, design, and balance."

So, one thing after another, he kept using these words, and this vocabulary of seeing began to grow. And at the end of this hour session or so—I don't know how long it was; he was very generous with his time—I say, "Look, Mr. Rothstein (his name was Arthur Rothstein), would you do me a favor?" I said, "My head is bursting with all this stuff you've been telling me. Can I go out—I want to go out, and I want to shoot something the rest of the day and tomorrow, to see if I understand this new information you've taught me and see if it's clicking."

So he says, "That's a great idea." He says, "Look, let me give you some film." Because I had been using film, you know, you buy a hundred-foot roll. And I rolled my own film. It was cheap; I'm a student. I don't have money. He gave me fresh packages of black-and-white film. He says, "Okay, go out and shoot this." He gave me about three or four rolls. "Bring it back, and I'll process it, and we'll sit down, and we'll go over it in a contact sheet."

Sure enough, I went out, I shot stuff. I came back, and we went through the contact sheet, and he was pointing to me where I succeeded, where I almost succeeded, where I failed, and why. And then I said, "Well, you know, could you give me a practice assignment, so I can be more refined with this project?" So he gave me a practice assignment of working at trying to follow bicycle messengers. And we went through that. And every day, there was something. And finally, I found myself, what started out as maybe seeing him a couple days a week, after a couple weeks, became almost daily.

Finally, he said, "Look, I can't tell other photographers here to pay attention to you. But I can let you come in and let you see if you can develop your own relationships with the individual photographers, because they will always be traveling." And he says, "See if they will let you—when they come back in and go through their works, their take, in the light box or the contact sheet—if they would mind letting you look over their shoulder."

So gradually—I think, in the beginning, most of the photographers at first didn't know what to make of this. They knew Arthur liked this kid, and the kid had a lot of energy and had a lot of questions. They didn't know if Arthur was grooming me to be the next staff photographer or what. I didn't even realize those issues until much later. But what it became for me that summer was essentially an intense university without walls.

Arthur and I would talk day after day. We would talk nothing but visual linguistics. He gave me a list of things to study, about movement of the face, the meaning of angles and what they can do; or space, negative and positive space, all these things. There was no way that I would ever learn this sort of stuff at Tuskegee. So that whole summer I spent with Arthur. And Arthur sent me to a museum one day. I'd never been to a museum. And he says, "I want you to go, and I want you to look at these particular paintings." And they were realistic paintings of masters. And he says, "It doesn't matter to me if you like the painting or not. What matters to me is that you have a reason for not liking it or a reason for liking it. And I want you to look at composition, design, balance, lighting, and content. And those are the things that we're going to talk about."

So I went, and I came back, and we sat, and we talked about the paintings I saw at the Met. Then he sent me up to the Frick collection, and we talk about those things. He sends me down to maybe the city museums, and we talk about those. And then he sent me over to the Modern to look at stuff, but at the Modern, he sent me not to look at realistic paintings, but he sent me to look at the photography collection. And the woman who was head of the photography collection was a woman named Grace Mayer, bless her heart. And he told Grace, he was on the phone, he said, "Grace, I'm sending this photographer over there, and I want you to show him the work of the FSA (Farm Security Administration) photographers—Dorothea Lange, Walker Evans, and all those other people." So I'm there [at the Museum of Modern Art]. I'm spending a day going through these pictures, just really blown over by great photography, because most of it also is in my element, in the rural South. And that's where I'm from. And then I come across a picture that had Arthur Rothstein's name on it. I say, "My God, this is Mr. Rothstein." See, I had no idea who this man was, other than he was some sympathetic person who saw my work, but I could tell he was a good teacher. And because he was a good teacher, I worked very hard to learn from him because I only had a limited time to learn. I had from June to September to cram as much as I could, and I was just blessed to have a guy who was a good teacher, willing to spend time with me. So I say to Grace Mayer, "Well, this is Mr. Rothstein." Then she tells me who this guy is. I go back to his office. I said, "Mr. Rothstein, they have some of your pictures over there." I was able then to ask him questions about FSA—because Grace had begun to tell me what FSA was—and how he got started. And that same summer, he began to take me to some of his gallery openings. He would have some openings. I didn't know that this man would never stay in the city at night, past five o'clock. He'd get on the train and go home. But he had a couple openings, and he invited me to come to them. And then he introduced me to photography people. He introduced me to *Life* photographers. He introduced me to Cornell Capa, who was a brother of Robert Capa. He introduced me to Gordon Parks. He called him up and said, "Look, I want to send this photographer to talk to you." And that began a lifelong relationship with Gordon Parks, good advice from Gordon. When I met Cornell Capa, he was in the midst of starting a program at New York University, and he invited me to come, and I didn't have to pay. I just had to show up. And Cornell would take me out with him in the group afterwards for dinner. He would be taking his guests out for dinner and his wife, Edie, and a couple of other people, and I was the youngest one in the group invited to come along and listen and talk. So this went on, you know, for years, and then Cornell eventually started the International Center of Photography. Cornell single-handedly made photography an art, a respected art form in America, because before, it was really a stepchild. And he used to put on these exhibitions wherever he could. I remember he put on a Cartier-Bresson exhibition at the Metropolitan. Wherever he could get a space. The Jewish Museum would sometimes let him produce exhibitions. So then that lifetime relationship began with Gordon, Cornell, and Arthur Rothstein. And at the end of that summer, that September before I returned to school, luckily, I finally found a contract for my book, *Black Woman*, to publish those pictures that I had brought up to New York with me. An editor at *Ebony*, Peter Bailey, who had seen my photographs, brought my work to the attention of Orde Coombs, a new editor at *McCall's*. I went to see him; he loved what I had done and felt that if I could add more images and structure the text, there was a book here. I had to go do some more work, fill in some more gaps, but I had a contract. I went back to school now with my mind fully developed about the linguistics of photography, being trained by the best people in photography, and having a book contract going into my final year of college.

I graduated from Tuskegee in 1970, and I moved to New York. I was offered a job in business at 3M in Madison, Wisconsin, and I went up there. I walked through the building. I was doing an orientation, walking through, and after an hour or so in this, I thought, My heart is not here. I'm looking at these people sitting at their desks, and looking at this office, and all of a sudden, things just looked very fossilized. It looked like a tomb rather than a life. And I turned to the people, and I said, "You know, I don't think this is for me. Thank you very much." And I changed my ticket, and I flew to New York, and I called Mr. Rothstein up, and I say, "You know, I'm here. I want to work." And he didn't have anything for me at that point. But that was okay. I started freelancing, because from my summer with him, I understood now that with my drive and my sense of business, I could find work here and there. I knew how to do the portfolio, I knew how to present my work, and I understood the needs of editors and understood the meaning of deadlines. And I began to find freelance work. I found an apartment. I lived with a friend for maybe the first two weeks.

And eventually, Rothstein called me up one day and he says, "Come in. I need to talk to you." And I went in, and he says, "I have an assignment for you. It means you've got to travel for about a week all across the country, and this is what you're going to be doing. And let's talk about it." What was very important with Rothstein, I had learned the summer before, was an issue called previsualization, that you don't just go out on the story because you're just running after it. You have to think about what are the many different picture possibilities that are going to present themselves in that particular story that you're doing. And you try to work up a sheet of at least thirty or forty picture possibilities that you know are there and that you're going to look for in the course of looking for everything else. So that those thirty or forty things, you know if you can bag those, you've got it, and they may happen at different points within the shoot. And they can pivot off—while you're looking for them, they can pivot off into something else. So we spent the afternoon previsualizing the images from this story, what it would be like. And I think the next day or two, I met the editor, the writer who I'd be working with the next day. And the next day, I had a ticket with the writer, and we were gone for a whole week, crossing the country, following up this personality, doing the story that wound up to be my first five-page spread in *Look* magazine. And then I did two other stories, but those stories didn't run because then in October, end of October 1971, *Look* went out of business. I didn't know at the time, but there was a suit hanging over *Look*'s head by the mayor of San Francisco, because *Look* had run a story by two freelance writers who had accused him of Mafia connections. And the mayor of San Francisco sued and prevailed in this suit to such an extent that the magazine went under. So, that was my *Look* magazine experience. But at that point, at least I had more in my portfolio to help me get more freelance work. Because of Cornell Capa, I had made other contacts with *Time* magazine, *Newsweek*. I was able to stay afloat. And then, because of my educational background, I understood the process of writing proposals and getting grants, and I was getting grants from Ford Foundation, Rockefeller Foundation, because I had other projects that I wanted to work on. All of my work was about bringing a new vision to people of color, to my people. So all my projects were, I guess, a visual census, in a way, investigating different aspects of black life and culture. And with that, I was able to get grants. And Cornell and Arthur Rothstein and Gordon Parks, among others, were always people I could rely upon to write letters of recommendation for these particular grants.

I started working for the *New York Times* in 1975. During my period of freelancing, from the time that *Look* went out of business, I had a grant from Ford to go to Africa. But I needed money to continue my work. And I had a project that Margaret Mead was one of my sponsors, and Dr. Elliot Skinner, who was head of the anthropology department at Columbia and was looking at the transition of African culture from traditional culture to modernity. And on one of these trips, I ran into a *Times* reporter I knew, Tom Johnson, who was now the West African bureau chief. And he was pointing out to me the story of the drought up in the Sahel [that band of African countries just below the Sahara Desert and above tropical ones: Mauritania, Senegal, Mali, Niger, and Chad]. He was in Dakar at the time. I had run into him. And I came back to New York after that trip, and I went around looking for funding to help finance a trip for me to go to the Sahel because people were dying of drought, and it was a huge area of land and the desert was moving south. And it was too much for any one government. The problem was just too big. I figured that it really needed America's help, America's attention for airlifting food. But that was only going to help if I could get the media involved. So I went to different church groups and other groups, and I was able to pull together enough money. I flew back to this area. I hooked up with the NGOs (nongovernmental organizations) which were involved, and I flew into Niamey, Niger, and I took a French government airlift into Agadez and then hooked up with the NGOs and went off to this refugee camp. It was so far in the desert that if anything had killed me, it would take a year for New York to find out about it. But here I was determined to make pictures to show the gravity of the situation and try to bring about change. And in return for the help of one religious group, they were able to make use of my pictures to make posters to use for fund-raising. But what really helped is that I went to the *New York Times*, to the op-ed people, and I showed them these pictures. And to my good luck, there was a writer who was, I guess, a former Peace Corps writer, who worked for a think tank, who was also aware of this problem and trying to get the government to be concerned about it. They had the piece, but they had no illustrations. So, because of my illustrations, we were able to do two of his pieces in the *New York Times* op-ed page. And those two pieces caused our government, our U.S. aid people, to spend millions of dollars to airlift food into this country in the Sahel, in Niger, to help prevent further dying. And because of that piece, the *Times* asked me if I would like to be a photographer for them because I had shown great initiative. They knew of my experience, they knew of Cornell—and I mean it was a tight circle of people. They all knew each other. So that's when I was offered a job, in March of '75.

I've been a staff photographer for the *New York Times* now for thirty years. And since then, I've done six books because I really have all these projects in mind. And for me, my dream is to pull together a visual encyclopedia on the life and times of people of color, of African descent, obviously, as I see it and experience it. My community has just gotten larger. I'm still that little community photographer, except that my community is just much larger, that's all.

One or two voices are not enough. It's easy for people to marginalize and ignore. And obviously, a hundred doesn't mean that you're going to break down the wall, but as the mass grows, as the mountain grows, at some point, you can't ignore the mountain in the middle of the room. So I'm glad to know of all these people out there.

Don't get me wrong. I have my limitations, too. The Dallas museum hasn't called me up to say, "Let's have an exhibition of your work." The Metropolitan Museum of Art, or MOMA, hasn't called me up to say, "Let's have an exhibition of your work." As you can see from my Web site, I have a lot of exhibitions. Some of them have been in white museums. Most of them are in black museums. But you know, the opportunities—we have to just keep working for them. That's all I'm saying. The lack of opportunities just means that there's a challenge here. And how we overcome that challenge is what we have to keep working at every day. But none of us are where we want to be. I'm not where I want to be. I may be further along than some other people think that they are, but I still have my frustrations, too. I want to be a mainstream photographer.

It's the ghettoization and marginalization that bothers me. It's the difference between being a writer and a woman's writer. It's that marginalization. It's that "other" that people want to put you in, because I find it always interesting that a white photographer can do a book about black people, and Barnes & Noble will put it in the photography section, somebody you never heard of. But me, when I do a book about black people, it's not in the photography section, it's in the African American section. So, that sort of frustration, that sort of otherness, is still a problem.

What keeps me going is discovery, because I discover every day. I also have a huge library of a few thousand volumes that are broken up into three major areas. One is on the Diaspora, American and African Diaspora. Another one is on Ethiopia, ancient Ethiopia (or Axum), and another one's on ancient Egypt (or Kemet). So I'm a consummate reader of nonfiction, history, and anthropology and archaeology. And that is how I also prepare myself. Each year, I take a month and I travel somewhere, over five weeks, to two places that fit within my research. I'm always researching. I always take busman holidays. So I use my books to study up on what are the picture possibilities and what is the history and what are the social dynamics in this place I'm going to go. In September,

CHESTER HIGGINS JR. | 111

I go to Morocco to photograph the royal visit of the king of the Ashantis with the Moroccan king. And then, in January or February, I'll be in Ethiopia and Sudan working on my evolution-of-religion project. So, what keeps me going is discovery. Photography is my way to search for the many different pieces of myself. I realize that there are many quilts; there are many pieces to the quilt that make up who I am, the person who I am, the representative, the member of a people, who I am as an African American, as a Western-born African, as one of the original people. I'm so many of all these different things. So I find it immensely gratifying to go and actually make visual evidence of the many manifestations of who I am and who we are as people of African descent. In addition to seeing other people, as well.

I hope that some little kid who is trying to find his way or her way stumbles upon a book of mine and finds there's something else that's real that they can attach their imagination to. And that it helps lift them out of being unaware and broadens their world and broadens their sense of self and value out of what neighborhood or what town they're in and explodes in their mind a possibility of a larger world, of a larger meaning that they can find, that opens up a cerebral or cognitive space of water that they can swim out into, to the horizon.

[Interview by Alan Govenar, June 2, 2005]

*Oliver W. Hill Sr., Richmond, Virginia, ca. 2004.*

# OLIVER W. HILL SR.

CIVIL-RIGHTS ATTORNEY

*Born May 1, 1907*

*Oliver White Hill worked as a civil-rights attorney for more than six decades. He was born in Richmond, Virginia, and lived there until the age of six, when his family moved to Roanoke. He graduated from Dunbar High School in Washington, D.C., and then enrolled at Howard University. While Hill was a student, his uncle, a lawyer, died. His aunt gave him all of his uncle's old legal books, which he read, prompting him to decide to become a lawyer himself. In 1933, he graduated from Howard Law School and was second in his class only to Thurgood Marshall. In 1938, he established his first law firm, Hill, Martin, and Robinson, and joined the NAACP's legal team, led by Charles Hamilton Houston, to fight the "separate but equal" principle, upheld by the Supreme Court in 1896 in* Plessy v. Ferguson. *In 1940, working with Marshall, William H. Hastie, and Leon A. Ranson, he won his first civil-rights case,* Alston v. School Board of Norfolk, Virginia, *and the city of Norfolk was ordered to pay black teachers the same as white teachers. In 1942, Hill co-founded the Old Dominion Bar Association, the first organization of its kind for African Americans in Virginia. In 1948, he was elected to the Richmond City Council. In 1951, after hearing that students in Farmville, Virginia, had walked out of their dilapidated school, he became involved in their case to challenge the separate-but-unequal educational facilities. The subsequent lawsuit,* Davis v. County School Board of Prince Edward County, *later became one of the five cases decided under the landmark* Brown v. Board of Education.

*During the 1950s, Hill and his family were subjected to constant threats, and a cross was burned on the front lawn of his home. Not deterred, Hill persisted in his efforts to fight against racism and discrimination, and worked on numerous cases related to the de-segregation of public transportation and public facilities, free bus transportation for black public school children, and the rights of black citizens to serve on juries and participate in primary elections. Hill has received numerous awards over the decades, including the Presidential Medal of Freedom, awarded on August 11, 1999. Students at the University of Virginia honored Hill when they founded the Oliver W. Hill Black Pre-Law Association. Hill retired from Hill, Tucker, and Marsh at age ninety-one but has remained active in community affairs.*

I WAS BORN HERE IN RICHMOND. My maternal grandmother died, and my mother and her new husband came to Richmond for the funeral. My father had deserted us before I was one year old. I didn't realize how poor we were until many years later. I never was hungry in my life, and I always had a place to sleep. We moved to Roanoke, and I lived in Roanoke until 1923.

When we went to Roanoke, my mother and stepfather lived in a house with another family, the Pentecost family. It was a black family. My stepfather and my mother had met up in Hot Springs, Virginia, at the Hotel Homestead. He was on bell, and she was a porter for the Southern Springs guests. When we came to Roanoke in 1913, he had opened up a pool hall. But in two years, Virginia went dry. He was going to teach me how to play billiards and pocket pool. But Virginia going dry kept me from doing that.

I went to school the next year, when I was seven. I don't know why my mother held me up. But anyway, when World War I started, my step-father went to Washington and got a job in the naval yard. I didn't like it then because the Pentecosts were upper middle class economically and very well respected. And Christmastime, they had a great big Christmas tree, and it was loaded with gifts.

I went to live with my mother and stepfather in Washington. My mother's name was Olivia Hill, and my stepfather's name was Joseph C. Hill. My [biological] father was William Henry White. My grandfather, his father, Rev. William Henry White, he was the founder of Mount Carmel Baptist Church.

I really don't know [if my grandfather had been enslaved], but I imagine he was. My grandfather's brother was born in the mid-1800s, so it's possible that he could have been born in [slavery]. He also could have been born after the Civil War.

I went to Dunbar High School. We had everything the white boys had. As a matter of fact, I finished at midterm. I only lived three or four blocks from the campus, but I needed to wait until September to go to college. My total ambition was to be a physical education major. I never was close to any teacher except the first teacher I had. When I was in college, I finally got conscious of the fact that the Supreme Court had made us second-class citizens, and Congress had done everything it could to give all the civil rights to a white person. So at that time—that was in 1928—we couldn't get a law passed by Congress to make it a crime to lynch a Negro, much less give him any further civil rights. I decided that the only thing was for somebody to carry another case to the Supreme Court that convinced them they were wrong in 1896 when they came up with *Plessy v. Ferguson*. I didn't look around for somebody else. I began to inquire as to what I had to do to go to law school. A whole lot of things happened at that time. Mordecai W. Johnson, the first Negro president of Howard University, had decided that Howard University [should have] a law school.

Charles Hamilton Houston (1895–1950) was a professor at Howard who became the vice dean of the school. He was a brilliant scholar. He was a graduate with honors of Harvard Law School and [the first African American to become] a member of the [editorial board of] *Harvard Law Review*. He was a wonderful man.

Charlie decided to make the school—from the time it was founded in Reconstruction, it had been a night school, evening school, and without a settled plan. And all the professors, teachers, were adjuncts. And they moved around from house to house and all that sort of stuff. But Charlie decided he was going to make a first-class day school with a proper library and a full-time state faculty, and that's what he did. All the adjuncts were white and had jobs in government. But anyway, about the same time, a white boy named Garland, his father died, and he inherited his estate. He didn't need it; he didn't work for it. So he turned it over to the NAACP to fight segregation.

Garland's story is in a book called *Simple Justice: The History of Brown v. Board of Education and Black America's Struggle for Equality* by Richard Kluger. In 1929, Garland's estate got wiped out. The NAACP didn't get a chance to get the full benefit of his contribution. Anyway, one of Houston's classmates at Harvard did a study on how to attack segregation. He recommended filing suits all over the South to open up the public schools. To attack segregation head-on—this was 1930 now—would be banging your head up against a stone wall. And of course, subsequent events proved he was right. He thought what we ought to do was attack segregation at its weakest point. Everything was separate, but nothing was equal. So the weakest point was the inequality. We had a battle plan, and we held to that until we got *Brown v. Board of Education.*

When I went to law school in 1930, another brilliant youngster who had graduated from Lincoln with honors was in the class. His name was Thurgood Marshall. He was my classmate. It so happened that the total enrollment of that freshman class was an even number, twenty-eight or thirty. And before we graduated, the *Washington Post* carried an article, "A Class That Never Had an Officer." We used to go to school at eight o'clock and get out at eleven-thirty. Back in those days, there were a lot of prophets, like Father Divine, from Tennessee. Father Divine operated a restaurant down on Ninth Street [in Washington, D.C.], and you'd go in and raise your hand and say, "Peace is truly wonderful." They'd give you a fine lunch for twenty-five cents. Thurgood and I used to go in there, to Father Divine, and have lunch together, and we'd come back. Thurgood and I would study. Well, the members of the faculty and the dean saw us every day in there studying, and we got to be good friends.

You see, Thurgood had come to Howard because they wouldn't let him go into the University of Maryland Law School. He was living in Baltimore at the time. His mother was a schoolteacher in Baltimore. He had a brother who was at Lincoln University [in Pennsylvania], and his father was in charge of the service at a very prominent club that was situated outside of Baltimore.

Thurgood and I graduated from Howard in 1933. Several of the Howard students took the D.C. bar [exam], and Thurgood took the Maryland bar. But when I had missed the Virginia bar, there wasn't another bar till December. The man who later became one of my partners, S. W. Tucker, had a very precocious boy, and he was a freshman at Howard. We

Oliver W. Hill, Richmond, Virginia, ca. 1950s.

happened to meet one day, and he asked me what I was doing, and I told him I was studying for the bar. I asked him what was he doing. He said he was studying, too. He was very precocious. His father operated a real-estate business. Insurance companies had offices with a lawyer named Watkins, and Mr. Watkins took an interest in him. From the time he was twelve till he finished law school, he was a paralegal. And so, that's the reason—see, his father had taken the bar several times, but he never had passed it. I passed the bar, and I was still in Washington, but I had given my address as Roanoke, where I had gone to high school, the Pentecosts' address. And I was waiting to hear from them, and I hadn't heard anything in January; this must have been around February or late January. I went to a dance, and we were feeling pretty good, with bootleg liquor, and he said, "Congratulations." And I said, "Congratulations on what?" He said, "Hell, you don't pass the bar every day, do you?" And boy, next morning, I was down at the library, and I looked in the Roanoke paper, and there it was in great big letters: Oliver White Hill.

I started practicing law in 1934, in Roanoke, Virginia. Thurgood was in Baltimore. And Tucker had gone to the WPA, one of the relief programs at that time. Everything was separate, but nothing was equal—they were denying Negroes to serve on juries, denying Negroes having bus transportation to schools, which were totally inadequate, couldn't live where we wanted. So I went down to King George's County and asked them, "Why you going to call secondary schools for whites [preparation for] high schools, and secondary schools for Negroes, training schools?"

They said, "Because for Negroes, we train them for work that they can get a job doing." You see, most of the time, Negroes, they were limited to labor. I went to law school so I could go out and fight segregation, and that's what I did.

[In 1951 and 1952, years of coordinated work around the country came together among a dedicated group of lawyers, led by Charles Hamilton Houston and Thurgood Marshall and including James Nabrit, Spottswood Robinson III, A. Leon Higginbotham, Robert Carter, William Hastie, George E. C. Hayes, Jack Greenberg, and Oliver Hill. Five district courts in five cases from four different states—Kansas (*Brown v. Board of Education*), Delaware (*Gebhart v. Belton*), South Carolina (*Briggs v. Elliott*), Virginia (*Davis v. County School Board*)—and the District of Columbia (*Bolling v. Sharp*), all ruled on the separate-but-equal principle. All of these state cases were ultimately consolidated with *Brown v. Board of Education*, and in 1954, the Supreme Court ordered desegregation of all schools "with all deliberate speed."]

The Supreme Court ruled on all of them. Four cases involved the Fourteenth Amendment [based on the equal protection clause]. And one case, in the District of Columbia, involved the Fifth Amendment [based upon the due process clause]. Of course, the District of Columbia was our state.

Well, I think if you want to stay alive, you've got to keep active, keep doing things. That's all I know. And besides, we still suffer from [discrimination]—*Brown* declared *Plessy v. Ferguson* unconstitutional and made it unlawful, so far as the law was concerned, but the de facto segregation is almost as bad now as it was then, fifty years ago. Not quite as bad, but a whole lot of things have changed. You must remember that without the rule of the law, we would still be second-, third-, or sometimes fourth-class citizens. That's what we were when *Plessy* was in force.

What would make the world a better place is if we got enough common sense to recognize the fact that we don't need these damn countries; all we need is to recognize the fact that we are human and earthlings, human earthlings. And recognize that we all have the same requirements, so far as our life is concerned, and that a person ought to be able to get himself the best education he can get and training he can get, and work for the benefit of the common good.

We need to get the majority of people to know something about history—American history and foreign history. We talk about juries. Well, the majority of people don't realize that African tribes settled their civil suits [by jury] when various Anglo-Saxons were settling their complaints by combat, riding forth, knocking each other off horses with a spear.

After World War II, I was going to a town called Lynchburg, [Virginia], one Sunday morning, and I had already decided that I wasn't going to ride segregated anymore. And I was getting on a car, in the back, and there was a long, tall white girl with stringy hair. And back in those days, practically all, especially white women, had a nasal sound to their voice. And she was saying, "I'm free, white, and twenty-one! Pure-blooded Anglo-Saxon." That's the last I heard, because by that time I had got on the train. So I thought about it: How the hell can anything hyphenated be pure-blooded? I doubt that you could find a person without African genes or genes from some European section of the world. It was a long time before we realized that there are certain blood types spread all over the world. And how many people's lives were saved by being able to use blood plasma, rather than that nonsense about white blood and black blood.

I still think that eventually we will get sense enough to recognize the fact that we're going to be much better off thinking of people as human earthlings rather than as Englishmen, Chinese, and all that stuff. We need to recognize the fact that you don't do yourself any good by hating.

[Interview by Alan Govenar, August 31, 2005]

*Nicholas Hood Sr., Detroit, Michigan, ca. 2004.*

# NICHOLAS HOOD SR.

MINISTER AND CITY COUNCILMAN

*Born June 21, 1923*

*Nicholas Hood grew up in Terre Haute, Indiana. After graduating from high school, he attended Purdue University, where he received a B.S. in chemistry. While he was an undergraduate student, he decided to pursue the ministry and enrolled in Yale Divinity School. He was awarded a master of divinity degree in 1949, and he then moved to New Orleans, where he served as pastor of the Central Congregational Church. In 1958, he accepted a position as senior minister of the Plymouth Congregational United Church of Christ in Detroit, Michigan. Over the years, Dr. Hood led his church, which was located in the middle of an urban-renewal area, in rebuilding forty acres of former slums in the heart of Detroit with town houses, apartments, a senior citizens' high-rise building, and facilities for developmentally disabled persons. In addition to leading a fifteen-hundred-member congregation, Dr. Hood was the second African American to be elected to the Detroit City Council, on which he served for twenty-eight years.*

*Dr. Hood was a founding member of the Southern Christian Leadership Conference (SCLC) with Dr. Martin Luther King Jr. He was a member of the advisory board of the Federal National Mortgage Association in Washington, D.C.; president of the Ministers Life and Casualty board of directors, Minneapolis, Minnesota; member of the board of directors of Hutzel Hospital, Detroit; president of the Hannan Foundation, Detroit; and founder of the Cyprian Center and the Cyprian Foundation, whose chief mission is to assist developmentally disabled persons.*

MY PATERNAL GRANDFATHER WAS A FORMER SLAVE who became quite proficient in brick making. He was the general manager of the brickyard in Martinsville, Indiana. My father was Orestes Hood, and my mother was Daisy Eslick Hood. My mother was from Springfield, Ohio, and my father was from Martinsville, Indiana. My mother was a teacher and social worker. She was a graduate of Fisk University in Nashville, Tennessee. And she probably taught everything in those days. My father was an electrician. He did three years at Purdue in electrical engineering and had to drop out because he ran out of money. So he began teaching in East St. Louis, Illinois, and that's where he met my mother. She was a teacher there. And then they left there, went to Gary, Indiana, where he became an electrician in the steel mills. And then, the Exide Battery Company contacted him to go to Terre Haute, Indiana, to be their representative because he was one of the few people around who knew anything about the electric storage battery. And the electric car was a big thing in those days, and so he went to work in Terre Haute and then opened up his own radio shop in downtown Terre Haute and had it until the crash wiped him out in '29.

It was horrible [growing up in Terre Haute]. Racially, it was very tough because everything was separate. Even though I lived in what we would now call a racially integrated neighborhood, I could not go in the drugstore to eat my ice cream with my little white friend. And a lot of things I couldn't do that he could do, which was a rather difficult kind of experience.

I went to grade school—Booker T. Washington—in Terre Haute, and I went to Wiley High School in Terre Haute. It was not a very good school, but I went to grade school, and I finished high school. The grade school was all black, and I began going to integrated schools in junior high. Well, they were integrated, but that's all there was. It wasn't a matter of integration; there wasn't anything else. But they made a real distinction. You knew that you were not—well, you weren't that well accepted in that school. It was very difficult, when you stop to think about it.

I graduated high school in 1940. My goal was to go to college. Well, what happened was that I had a birth deformity, so I had to go in the hospital for a year following high school to get this spinal deformity corrected. And during that time, I decided I wanted to be a physician so that I could pay back society.

I went to Purdue University at West Lafayette, Indiana, and got a bachelor of science in zoology and chemistry. I was a premed major, but at the same time, I was working in the student religious center there, and I became interested in working with young people and trying to build bridges across racial lines. And I said, "Well, look, that's what I want to do. I don't want to be a physician. I want to do this." And it just turned out that some of my advisers, a couple of my advisers, were white, and they said, "Well, you ought to go in the ministry." And I hadn't even thought about it. And one of them was from Yale, and he said, "Well, why don't you go to Yale?" Hey, I didn't know Yale from anyplace else. So I applied and was accepted for the following year. I'd also been accepted at Meharry Medical School for that fall, but that fall, I took a year and went to a little liberal-arts college over in Illinois, just to get some liberal arts, because I'd gone through Purdue during the war years, and everything was science. They were turning out scientists, and that was the big concern. So, to get a more balanced background, I went to North Central College in Naperville, Illinois, for one year, and then I went on to Yale in the fall of 1945.

[When I was at Purdue] blacks could not live in West Lafayette, where the university was located. But there were a couple of white ministers who had opened up their homes to black students. They were eventually run out of town because of that, but they set up an international house, a house where blacks and whites and foreign students could live with a housemother, and that's where I lived during my years at Purdue. But what happened was, I was so impressed with what these two ministers had done, the sacrifice that they had made leading to them being forced out of town, that I began to look at the ministry in a different light. They didn't try to influence me or anything else. But I just observed what was happening in their lives, and to me, that was quite an experience.

You didn't have [overt racial] violence [in West Lafayette] in those days. Everything was too subtle for that. We were catching it otherwise. For example, we couldn't get our hair cut in West Lafayette. Leon Higginbotham, the former federal judge, or deceased federal judge, and I went to the president to ask why we couldn't get our hair cut in the student-union building barbershop. And he said, "Well, I'll put some hair clippers for you in the storeroom, and you guys can go there and get them and use them." I mean, that kind of thing. So you felt the racial feeling there in the town, although while I was there, I sang in the white Methodist church choir. And I guess what really caught me were the extracurricular activities. I began working in the student Methodist group. They had a student group there on campus, and they had a building, and once inside the walls of that facility, I was completely free, and I wasn't burdened down by racial concerns. And I think all of that was having an effect on me.

Leon Higginbotham came a year after I'd been there, but the racial feelings were so strong, he couldn't take it. So he left and went to Antioch. But the irony of it all is, I'm the first one to receive an honorary degree from Purdue, an honorary doctorate. I'm the first black to receive an honorary doctorate from Purdue. It was in the seventies.

Well, Yale [Divinity School] was obviously an entirely different kind of experience than Purdue. We lived in the quadrangle there, and it was a very good, wholesome kind of experience, although I spent much of my time down in the black community, working in a black church, working in the housing project. So I worked while I was there, and it was a very good experience.

After I was ordained, I was trained in student work. That was my training at Yale, as my emphasis. But when I came out, there weren't any jobs for blacks in colleges, and the minister with whom I was working had been invited to come to New Orleans to look at a church there, and he wasn't interested, so he recommended me. I'd never been down South, so I went just for the trip. But when I got there, it was such a tremendous experience that I said, "Oh, hey, this is where I want to be." So I accepted their offer to become their pastor, and I was there for nine years.

I was ordained in 1949. And I was in New Orleans from '49 to '58. The church I went to was Central Congregational Church. Not a big church, but a very nice church, and the Congregational Church has more of the intelligentsia—you know, the doctors, the lawyers, the teachers— as the base. And it just fit me perfectly, and so that's where I landed.

That [church] was at the corner of Bienville and Tonti. And at that time, the street on the side of the church had no sewers. It was dirt and no sewers. But one of the things I did while I was there, I got those streets paved, got the sewers put in, and I led the community group that did that. It was quite an experience. Also, while I was there, I became quite involved with the Baptists in the freedom movement. Our particular kind of church wasn't really in the forefront, but when I went to New Orleans, the parsonage was not ready, and I had to move in. My wife and I had to move in with a family of the church. And it just happened to be the family of Andrew Young Jr. He was away in college, and I met him. I was young and anxious to work, so I was leaving the house about six o'clock in the morning to go down to work at the church, and he was coming in from a party. And that's how we met. And then, later on, I was invited to come over into Texas to work with a youth group in a summer camp, and I asked him to drive me over there, and he did. He had friends in Dallas; he figured he could go to Dallas and party while I was at the camp. Well, he didn't realize we were five hundred miles from Dallas, and he was stuck out there in the camp with nothing but the kids and the Bible. And we were there a week, and out of the experience, his life was completely changed, and he committed his life to God, and the rest is history. And his whole life just exploded after that, in terms of creativity and service. And, you know, he went on to do great things.

It was a Disciples of Christ camp somewhere in Oklahoma, just beyond the Texas border. It was a youth camp, the same thing that I had enjoyed doing so much back at Yale, just working with young people. See, while I was at Yale, in the summers, I just went from one camp to the next, doing music leadership and worship leadership. Weekends and summers, that's what I did, and so, it's what I really enjoyed doing, just working with teenagers and helping them to see religion in another light.

When Martin Luther King Jr. began his movement in Montgomery, he got Baptist clergymen all across the South to form improvement associations patterned after the Montgomery Improvement Association. So, in New Orleans, we formed the New Orleans Improvement Association. And because of my relationship with Andrew Young, who was then Martin Luther King's chief of staff, I became a part of that with these clergymen that I would have had no association with otherwise. And I was perhaps better trained than most of them, so I became the secretary of the group, and I was the person who kind of kept it together and kept it in order and all that kind of thing. So our big project there was to get the buses and streetcars desegregated. And you would have thought that we were trying to steal something. All we wanted was the opportunity to ride on the public transportation in some kind of respectful manner. Oh, it became quite heated there at times.

We had marches and protests. I was the negotiator. I would be the guy on the inside, trying to convince the white businessmen that it was to their best advantage to support the movement to remove the segregation signs on the buses and the streetcars. I left, though, when they began direct action against stores. I had come north by that time. I came north to Detroit in 1958.

In Detroit, I became pastor of Plymouth Congregational Church. It is a church that was formed in 1919 by a group of blacks who had come to Detroit from Montgomery, Alabama, to take jobs at the Ford Motor Company for five dollars a day. The church had been located in a couple of houses, and then in 1927, they bought this old synagogue, where you were beginning to get movement [out of the neighborhood] at that point. And it stayed in that synagogue until 1975. But when I got there, it was 1958, and the community had changed considerably, and there was a lot of prostitution and crime and all of that all around the church. Yet I saw potential in the church. It had a strong group of men who were willing to take leadership positions. And after I'd been in Detroit about two years, I picked up the morning paper, and there was a big headline that four hundred and fifty acres would be cleared for urban renewal. And as I looked at the maps, I said, "Hey, that's where my church is located." So I began approaching city officials about, "Can't we change this?" They said, "No, you cannot. Your church will be torn down. You have to get out." So I organized all of the storefront churches and the large churches, black churches, in the area. I got them organized, and we began protesting this action of the city. Well, that particular city administration wouldn't hear us at all. So we joined with other labor and liberal and civil-rights groups and defeated that particular city administration, and overnight, the whole policy about blacks relocated into the urban-renewal area changed. And that showed me the power of politics. And out of that experience of trying to save my church, I became involved in politics. And after being in Detroit for just six years, I was elected to the city council, the second black elected in modern history to the city council. So I carried my activism to Detroit, but it took a different form. It was political activism in Detroit. Of course, that's civil rights, too, but it was purely a civil-rights kind of activism when I was in New Orleans.

Ultimately, the Plymouth Congregational Church purchased five acres of urban-renewal land to build a new church and a facility for the handicapped, and since then, we have purchased forty-two acres in the same area and have completely renewed it with housing, town houses, and apartments and facilities for the handicapped.

That area is called Detroit Medical Center, and one of the housing developments of twenty acres is called the Nicolas Hood Sr. Medical Center Courts. And the other sixteen acres is called the Medical Center Village. And I built all of that.

Oh, it was a complete slum area. But at the same time, the urban-renewal program was to benefit the hospitals in the area. And at that time, the hospitals would not admit blacks to their staff. But the physicians found out that you could not discriminate if you used urban-renewal land. So I joined with the physicians in fighting the hospitals' expansion until they put black physicians on all of their staffs. There was a different kind of civil-rights activity in the North than there was in the South. It was very subtle, very silent, but very, very significant.

Well, the Jews, of course, represented the liberal community. And I was able to be elected to the city council because I put together a coalition of Jews, labor, liberals, blacks, whites, and Christians. I built a coalition. But the Jews were central because they really had the money, and they were a power. It's interesting, now—what, thirty, thirty-five years later—the Jews have largely moved out of the city. In residential succession, blacks would move into their areas, and they moved out, and they've moved on beyond the city limits. So Jews are in the minority now in the city.

Jews and blacks were aligned together. I mean, they had their own kind of oppression, but they had the money. For example, they weren't welcome in the leading hotels, so they bought the leading hotels. And then, blacks could go into the leading hotels. There was always a very good relationship between the Jewish community and the black community, with the exception of some of the more radical elements of the black community, the Black Panthers, the Freedom Now Party, and some of those kinds of things.

The Jewish community was basically in the northwest, and when urban renewal began taking the homes of blacks, they had money with which to buy, and so they went to the northwest. And the Jewish community was the place where most of the blacks chose to live. We had some blocking of schools by parents who didn't want the blacks to come in, but that was short-lived because there was such a wave and there was so much money available. Well, there was highway construction that was going through the black community; there was urban renewal that was going through the black community. You had all that money that was being given to black families that they could go out and buy something with, and the blockbusters came in with all of their sales pitch, and they helped to use the scare tactic to clear out many neighborhoods, also. So residential succession is the same here as it's been in most places.

I was on the city council twenty-eight years. And I was pastor of the church, and I just had a bunch of good folk who allowed me to do that, and it worked very well. And I did all of that development during the same period. I built a whole series of facilities for mentally retarded adults. I was young, I had plenty of energy in those days, and I just had good folk at the church. I took a cut in salary so that we could bring in additional leadership, and it worked out quite well. Matter of fact, I had a white associate for, oh, ten years, which is unheard of, an associate pastor. I was fortunate.

During the Detroit riot [in 1967], being the only black councilman, I was sort of a focal point, so I met regularly with the governor and the chief of police and the mayor as they tried to work out strategies. There wasn't much strategizing, other than to try to keep the troops that they brought in from just going berserk. But I was sort of the focal point during that period.

I think the riot was a culmination of a whole lot of things. It didn't just happen. But there'd been a lot of police brutality. There had been a campaign of stop and frisk, where they could stop a black person anywhere and frisk them and rough them up. And all this boiled over. The precipitating cause was they raided a blind pig [a place where liquor is sold or served illegally; also called a blind tiger], and the folk just fought back. It was on the weekend, and the police were down at their lowest number there on the weekend, and the folk that they broke in on just got tired of being harassed. And they fought back, put up a resistance, and then the thing just exploded.

Well, I don't know that you'd say Detroit's become a better place, but it became a more civil place in terms of police respect for citizens, especially black citizens. And it opened up the door for an explosion of political activity in the black community. It led to Reverend Albert Cleage's forming the Shrine of the Black Madonna, and that became a center of political activity in the black community. And they began actually influencing elections by getting people out to vote and registering people. And it led to more blacks being elected, both in the state legislature, the board of education, city council, so, really, it began a whole series of changes.

Reverend Cleage's church is still functioning. He went on to form a black—well, a denomination; I don't know what you would call it. He has since died, but the church has gone on. It's not as powerful as it once was, but they have left their influence. I mean, they've been able to put people in at every level of government. It's not as powerful as it once was, but they have opened the political doors to many for whom it had been closed.

[When I was on the city council], there was work being done at the city level and at the state level. We got a lot of black representation in the state legislature out of that whole experience. And also, with this movement out [of the city of Detroit] that we were talking about earlier, that left some void, so you got a change in the state legislature, at the senate level and at the house level, which meant that many, many changes were made in legislation, not only in the city level but at the state level, also.

We made a lot of changes. History will judge whether or not it was progressive. There were a lot of progressive things done during that period, though. There was just so much that changed. We could never get more than 3 percent of blacks in the police department. We changed the exam, changed leadership. But still, it was always 3 percent. Well, the first black mayor [Coleman A. Young] was elected [in 1974]. And he came in and said, "We shall have 50 percent." Well, overnight, that 3 percent changed. You got significant changes like that, so while the police department at the administrative level was all white, it slowly became integrated, and now, of course, it's black, after three black mayors. So change in the legislature was very important. A very subtle change that isn't talked about much is, the local symphony was changed because they were on hard times; they needed money from the state. But the black legislators said, "Until you start putting some blacks in the symphony orchestra, you will not get any money." And that has made a complete change in the symphony, in the cultural life of the community. So there have been many changes, not so dramatic, but significant.

The educational system has gone through a complete change. We began getting blacks on the board of education, and then it got out of hand some kind of way, so the state took over the board. They became in charge, and we're just getting out of that now, and whether we won or lost, it's hard to say, but the schools are in bad shape. I don't know if it's a backlash or what it is, but our schools are not better off than they were, that's for sure. The system is just getting back to community control, local control, so we don't know what's going to happen. I mean, it's in flux at the moment.

Of course, affirmative action has been in process. This whole police department thing was a part of it. The fire department had to go through that. One of the most significant things I did was to create a procedure whereby [that could be addressed]—the fire department was very underrepresented with blacks. In order to get it up to affirmative-action standards, I was able to get through a measure that would allow the fire department to receive city employees into their training program, make a lateral transfer from one department to the fire department, and go into the academy. That was very significant in changing the racial balance in the fire department. There were so many things like that, I've never documented them, but very, very significant. And there were so many of those things—everything was segregated at that time, and so the whole process of desegregation was just step by step, and it wasn't as dramatic as school desegregation. But we had to go through every department. For example, one illustration was the auditor general, the person who monitors the finances of the city. That job is independent of whoever's in the mayor's job. Well, I kept saying to the auditor general when he'd bring his reports up to the city council, I said, "Can't you get any black auditors?" He says, "I can't find any qualified." So the person doing my taxes was a CPA, a black female CPA. And I put her name into the hopper. And she was elected. [The auditor general] wasn't even a CPA. He was just a white career individual, and he couldn't find any qualified blacks. So I got rid of him by simply bringing in a qualified black person and getting the votes. There were a lot of things going on like that.

I served on city council for twenty-eight years. That's kind of unusual. But I worked hard, and I guess that was the reward. I stepped down from city council in 1992. I had resigned from the church in 1985, and my son, who has the same name, had worked with me for seven years, and he became the minister.

I'm retired now. My son—Rev. Nicholas Hood III, who followed me as senior minister of Plymouth United Church of Christ—is the one who's involved now. He ran for mayor against the present mayor and lost. He's the one who is the person out front. I just stay in the background. I've served my time, and it's time for somebody else. My other son, Stephen Hood, is an official with the county of Wayne, and my stepson, Victor Irving Chenault, is an electrical engineer. I've got a good wife, and I spend a lot of time doing Web pages. And that's about it for me. I remarried in 1993 [to Doris Chenault Hood, a retired public school administrator]. My first wife [Dr. Elizabeth Hood] died. My advice for young people is: Just work hard, study hard, and prepare yourself. You've got to be prepared.

[Interview by Alan Govenar, June 3, 2005]

*Paul C. Hudson, Los Angeles, California, ca. 2004.*

# PAUL C. HUDSON

BANK PRESIDENT

*Born May 8, 1948*

*Paul C. Hudson is the president and chief executive officer of Broadway Federal Bank in Los Angeles. Broadway Federal Bank was founded in 1946 by his grandfather, Dr. H. Claude Hudson, and a group of civic-minded African American men and women seeking to provide financial services to their community and others not served by the existing institutions. Building on an initial investment of $150,000, H. A. Howard, a real-estate broker and investor, managed the operations of the bank until 1949, when the leadership transitioned to H. Claude Hudson, who chaired the board of directors and supervised bank operations for the next twenty-three years. In 1972, Dr. Hudson's son, Elbert T. Hudson, became the bank's president. He, in turn, passed the leadership on to his son, Paul, in 1992. Paul, like his father and grandfather, is a lawyer and community activist.*

*The headquarters of Broadway Federal Bank was located at the corner of Forty-fifth and Broadway in Los Angeles in a building renovated by Paul's maternal grandfather, the noted architect Paul R. Williams (also a founding director), and the bank now has four branches. Over the years, Broadway has nurtured the mission of its founders and has provided training for minorities entering the financial industry. "We firmly believe that there is a need in the marketplace," Paul says, "for community institutions that reflect the local history, culture, and aspirations—institutions that are managed by their neighbors or classmates or a friend's grandson or granddaughter."*

I GREW UP IN THE WEST-CENTRAL MIDCITY AREA of Los Angeles, west of downtown, roughly in between Beverly Hills and downtown Los An-

geles, in a predominantly African American middle-class neighborhood. Growing up, I'd say my childhood was fun. Safe. Happy. Kind of
carefree, kind of an ideal youth.

My mom's family had been in California for three generations. My
dad's family came here around 1920 from Louisiana, basically for a better life, to escape Jim Crow and the discrimination that was going on in
the South at the time. My dad is a lawyer, my dad's dad was a dentist, and
my mom's dad was an architect.

My mother's maiden name was Williams. Her father was Paul R.
Williams, the architect, who is the subject of two books by my sister,
Karen Hudson, *The Will and the Way: Paul R. Williams, Architect* [1994]
and *Paul R. Williams, Architect: A Legacy of Style* [1993]. My dad's family
was prominent, too. My paternal grandfather was a well-known civil-
rights activist, dentist, and head of the NAACP here in Los Angeles. My
father went to UCLA and Loyola Law School here in Los Angeles.

I went to public schools all the way through, and they were all integrated, although they were predominantly white and Asian—Twenty-
fourth Street Elementary School, John Burroughs Junior High School,
and Los Angeles High School. I didn't feel any real discrimination. I was
student body president of my junior high school and was active in my
high school. I was involved in a lot of different clubs and sports. I had no
frame of reference [for comparing Los Angeles to other cities]. But
looking back, Los Angeles clearly was more progressive than most of the
South.

My paternal grandfather integrated the beaches out here in Los Angeles, so I was maybe one generation removed from segregation. Still, I
had a fairly sheltered and protected upbringing, so I really didn't feel it.
My architect-grandfather was well known and often took us to some of
the finest restaurants in the city. The African American community was
still pretty much segregated. School was integrated, but a lot of my social
life was among African Americans, predominantly, mostly middle-class
African Americans.

My father's father was H. Claude Hudson; he was a dentist/banker/
lawyer. He was president of the NAACP in Los Angeles, and he was one
of the founders of the Broadway Federal Bank. It was founded in 1946.
About eight financial leaders in the community pooled their resources

to start the bank and get a bank charter. And my grandfather was one of the people that put money in initially, and he was on the original board of directors. He had gotten his dental degree [from Howard University], but then he went to Loyola Law School. In fact, he was the first African American graduate of the Loyola Law School. He got his law degree so he would be better able to serve the NAACP. There was a lot of litigation going on in those days, a lot of lawsuits. That's why he got his law degree. And then he went to a school to get a banking degree also. So he ended up with three hats. He served as kind of the port of entry for a lot of the immigrants, African Americans moving here from Louisiana, especially northern Louisiana. He had a network of people that knew him from Shreveport, and many of them would come here and ask for Dr. Hudson. My great-grandparents came out to California afterwards. He brought them out after he got out here. Back in Louisiana, I'm sure they worked the land; they weren't professionals.

Broadway Federal Bank, ever since its inception in 1949, has had the same mission, to serve African Americans, but [over the years] the mission has expanded to include other underserved communities—Latinos and African Americans in the Los Angeles area, particularly. So the original mission has survived, primarily because the leadership of the bank has been maintained consistently since its inception. Dad, who took over in '72, followed my grandfather, and I took over in '92.

I went to UC Berkeley, and I received my law degree from there also. I started in '66, got my undergraduate degree in 1970, and my law degree in '73. I went straight through. But it didn't occur to me [to pursue a career in banking] until 1980, almost seven years after I graduated from law school.

I was politically active and became socially aware, socially conscious, during my days at Berkeley. I was there during the rise of the Black Panthers. I was there during the demands for a Third World College. I was there for People's Park. I was really involved in the movement for a Third World College, where minority students were pressuring for a more diverse curriculum, including African American, Latino, Asian, and Native American studies courses accepted as legitimate core courses at the university. We went on strike for most of my junior year in '68. And I was arrested and tried and ultimately found not guilty. Then we went on strike my first year in law school because the college seemed to be admitting a lot of minority students and then flunking them out the first year. We were making the argument that the law school wasn't spending enough energy in trying to retain minority students once they admitted them. We definitely had issues with the way the administration was running the affirmative-action program in 1971.

I benefited from affirmative action, and I think it's still needed; affirmative action is important and makes an important contribution to our society. Any efforts to say it's no longer needed or to say that it's reverse discrimination ignore the legacy of this country. We still need to create a level playing field.

After I graduated from law school, I worked for a law firm in Washington, D.C., for two years, doing mostly corporate transactional work. And then I spent a couple years practicing here in California. My dad's old law firm was still in existence, so I worked at his firm—it was a two-person firm—I worked there for a couple of years. And I worked on different business-venture-type ideas in between.

I knew I wanted to do business, but I didn't know what business, and one day I woke up and asked myself why I was trying to reinvent the wheel and why I was trying to beat my head starting something from scratch when my family had invested probably at that time close to thirty-plus years in a business. And it was an important business in the community that I could help grow. It fit my desire to be in business, and it seemed it was a socially responsible business to be in. I could help build the legacy that my grandfather started. I owned and ran a painting business at the time, and it just was back-bending hard work. So a lot of things came together at the same time, and I started at the bank with the idea that I would quickly move up in management. But my dad started me as a teller, and I had to work my way up the management ladder. I learned the business. I took it very seriously, and I didn't assume that anything was going to be given to me. So I worked hard.

I think this bank has played a role in helping to level the financial playing field, providing credit and financial products and services to underserved communities that, without such, would have a harder time creating jobs, wealth, and other financial benefits. It's tough. I realize people have options, and a lot of people operate based on convenience, and it's getting harder to compete on convenience if you don't have branches, if you don't have ATM networks, if you don't have all of the products and services. It definitely is more challenging. Each year becomes more challenging.

We have four branches—south and west. We've always pretty much served the southwest part of Los Angeles. We started off as a mutual bank, and during my administration, we converted to a publicly traded company. And so we have shareholders, and it's always been my goal to create wealth for the shareholders. The idea was that the communities and the people that had been doing business with Broadway would own Broadway and buy shares in Broadway, and so the goal was to create wealth for our shareholders. And that's still the goal. We pay a dividend, and our stock has increased in value. We're trying to get to $500 million in assets and a 15 percent return on equity for our shareholders.

We're still promoted primarily by the African American community, and I think the challenge for us is to continue to make efforts to get our name and our mission in front of African Americans. If anything, we're guilty of not doing a better job of marketing and getting our message out and looking for ways to make ourselves easily accessible to African Americans. But in spite of all that, we're still predominantly supported by African Americans.

If Broadway can continue to be successful, then we can demonstrate that there are still opportunities and there is still a willingness and an interest in supporting African American businesses by African Americans. I just think it becomes harder because there's not the same concentration, geographic concentration, of African Americans. In California, at least, there's a much broader dispersion of African Americans throughout Southern California. And there is a lot more competition for the business. At one time, communities were redlined, and banks didn't want the business. Now they're seeing the profits that can be made. It's still possible. It's going to require different models and different business strategies to maintain the links between community businesses and the communities they serve.

There are some big demographic shifts going on in Los Angeles that are changing not only the residential composition but also the business composition. There's a major shift toward Hispanic families and Hispanic businesses in areas that were traditionally African American. So I would say the [1992] riots had an impact—changing demographics has an impact. Crime, educational opportunities have an impact. Where you can afford a house has an impact. There are all sorts of variables that go into the changing buying habits and geographic centers—all those factors have contributed to the fact that African American businesses in Los Angeles are not as concentrated, not as strong, not as many. But then you have little pockets of communities in San Bernardino County, Orange County, and Ventura County. We're also evaluating moving into those communities with the out-migration of African Americans. We definitely have to come up with a plan to provide more branches in more diverse communities.

There are probably fifty or less African American banks in the country today, and many are members of an organization called the National Bankers Association. Everybody's kind of dealing with the challenges of local competition and meeting shareholder demands and growing their businesses at the same time they're trying to work together with other African American banks across the country. I think the interaction is less on a day-to-day business basis and more on a macro basis—what are we doing to address the macro challenges that African American banks face? We talk on the phone. Probably twice a year we have meetings. When you have a particular issue, you may call up a fellow banker in some other bank across the country.

What keeps me going? I'm internally driven, so I don't need external drivers. I am a competitive kind of guy who doesn't like to lose or fail. Personally, I have been and still am focused on self-discovery, a self-realization journey of trying to get to know myself better and understand what I'm passionate about and what additional things I can do to improve the quality of life for myself and others. I've always liked helping people. And I think the bank is one way to do that, but I'm still looking for other outlets to give back. I haven't completely figured it out yet. But it's never too late to try to self-improve.

[Interview by Alan Govenar, May 23, 2005]

*Herb Jeffries, Dallas, Texas, ca. 1973.*

# HERB JEFFRIES

ACTOR AND ENTERTAINER

*Born September 24, 1911*

*Herb Jeffries, the son of a dressmaker and an entertainer, began his career as a jazz vocalist in Chicago in 1933. Jeffries became interested in acting a year later while he was touring with the Earl Hines band in the South. He was repulsed by the segregated theaters where blacks had to wait in long lines to see white western movies. After numerous investors rejected his idea to introduce the black cowboy in westerns as a positive role model for young African Americans, Jeffries approached Jed Buell, who had produced* The Terror of Tiny Town, *a western starring midgets. Buell liked Jeffries's idea immediately, and together they made four westerns:* Harlem on the Prairie *(1937),* Two-Gun Man from Harlem *(1938),* The Bronze Buckaroo *(1939), and* Harlem Rides the Range *(1939). In the 1940s Jeffries joined the Duke Ellington Orchestra and recorded the hit song "Flamingo" for RCA Victor. In the 1950s, Jeffries moved his family to Europe and opened a jazz club in Paris. Over the years Jeffries's career has been characterized by perseverance and determination. During the 1990s, Jeffries recorded a CD entitled* The Bronze Buckaroo, *reviving the music of his westerns of the 1930s. He currently lives in California.*

I'M A MONGREL. I come from a very mixed racial family in Detroit, Michigan. My mother was 100 percent Irish, born in Port Huron, Michigan. My grandfather and grandmother were both Irish, from County Cork, Ireland. And my father was a mixture of Italian, French, Chippewa Indian, and Ethiopian. That's what I am. I'm a mongrel that came from many different nationalities, and so I celebrate all of them. I celebrate St. Patrick's Day, and I celebrate the American Indian holidays. I celebrate the Italian holidays as well as the Afro-American holidays, though I prefer being called an American. This is my nation; this is where I was born. However, the identity I chose for myself is Afro-American because I descend from the Ethiopians, the Moors, and black Irish.

At any rate, I lived in a neighborhood in Detroit that was very mixed. We had a high concentration of Jewish neighbors, we had some Italian neighbors, and then we had Polish neighbors. My father's name was Howard. My mother's name was Mildred, and my mother was a costume designer. She was a dressmaker who designed a lot of costumes for many [touring] shows that came through Detroit. And my father was a singer, an entertainer who sang around in our region of Michigan, [in cities] such as Saginaw, Bay City, and Flint.

My neighborhood did not know discrimination. We shared our cultures, and we were very close. The immigrants coming in were very happy to be accepted, and we were learning things from them that they brought from the old country. We were a little bit below the middle class at that time. We weren't in a ghetto, but were damn close. We all had to work in our family; there were five of us, two sisters and two brothers beside myself and my mother. My father died when I was around seven, so I didn't get a chance to know him very well. All I know is what I've heard about him and what people told me about him.

My father sang all kinds of music—classical music and music of the times. He was not a jazz singer. Jazz was very popular in Chicago; it was coming up from New Orleans, but we didn't have any great exposure to that kind of music around my neighborhood. My father sang classical-type songs, things like "The Road to Mandalay" and "Never Had a Sweetheart Till I Met You," those great old songs that were being played and published during that particular time, from World War I on up into the twenties.

I started my career about sixteen, seventeen years old, singing in some of the carnivals that came through and wherever else I could [get a job]. I was around music all my life. We had a home with a piano in it, and many different entertainers would come to visit. And they would play piano and sing songs. We had piano rolls that we would pump on, and there were all kinds of wonderful popular tunes that you could get on a piano roll. When I started singing, there were songs like "Stormy

Weather" and "Sweetheart of Sigma Chi" and other wonderful pop songs like that that were around. And then at the age of about nineteen, I started singing in cabarets.

My mother did things for the Shubert Theater. I couldn't remember the names of those shows if my life depended upon it. I was too young at that time, and I was more concerned about what was happening with my career and with the singers that I could hear on records. I collected records and played them on the phonograph.

My younger brother next to me also got into singing, and he was a very good singer. His name was Howard Jeffries. And he did sing around later in life when he became an adult in some of the nightclubs around, and he tried very hard to follow in my footsteps. He never got a recording contract, even though he had a very fine voice.

Well, in 1933, I went to Chicago to spread my wings. I had been as successful as I could be in my hometown, and I wanted to get into broadcasting. And I knew that there were some opportunities during the World's Fair to get exposed to some of the big bandleaders. And when I got to Chicago, I got a job singing with a bandleader there called Erskine Tate, who had the orchestra pit band at the Regal Theater. Well, one night, Earl Hines came in and caught me singing and offered me a job at the Grand Terrace, where there were live broadcasts over the national networks of his performances. And when I joined his band, I recorded two songs with them. "Blues for You, Johnny" was one of them, with Baby Dodds on drums, and I believe there was Earl Hines on piano, and Sidney Bechet, one of the great-grandfathers of the soprano saxophone.

Jelly Roll Morton was in and out of Chicago a lot, because at that time, music was coming from everyplace. It was coming out of Kansas City, St. Louis. It was coming heavily out of New Orleans. That was right at the very beginnings of the swing era. There were a lot of different kinds of music—a lot of blues, Dixieland, and then of course, the new music, which was jazz. And jazz was becoming more sophisticated all along because there were great arrangers such as Earl Hines and Fletcher Henderson, who was doing a lot of charts. It was really an exciting period; new innovators were coming in and out all the time.

There were many little after-hour places in Chicago. It was right after Prohibition, so there was a lot of celebration. Plenty of people were drinking and having the freedom to go to clubs and drink because it was legal. Back then, jukeboxes were starting to become a very big thing, and most of the jukeboxes had bands like Lucky Millinder and Cab Calloway, Duke Ellington, Count Basie, Jimmie Lunceford—bands of that class that were swinging. And we danced to that kind of music, and I was highly influenced by it.

Around that time, I was starting to get some sense of the discrimination that black people had to face. I sensed it around the perimeter of where I lived. There was a migration coming up from the South to go to work for the automotive companies, and many of these people were blacks and some were whites coming up from the same place. And they hated each other down South, and so when they got to Detroit, those kinds of hateful feelings were beginning to drift in and leak into the outer perimeters of our community.

The fact is that when I finally did go down South, I found out that most animals were treated better than black people—a black dog could sit on the porch of a white place in Mississippi, but black people could not. They'd be out there in their little community cities, their little city halls, and they'd be sitting around the cracker barrels and the spittoons, and the dogs would be sitting beside them, black dogs and brown dogs, and they were well treated and well fed and well kept. But a black person had to walk off the sidewalk so that a white person could pass by. Black people were looked upon as some kind of a domestic animal, like a cow or some horse that was doing a service for them. And certainly [blacks] weren't paid any amount of money whatsoever, because if you look at their communities and see the way they lived, you would see that they didn't live too much better than animals. Some of their homes had dirt floors, didn't even have flooring on it. I saw those places. I saw people living in hovels that were unbelievable. And they had no political representation, plus they couldn't vote. And they had no hygienic education whatsoever. So, of course, a disease doesn't give a damn who catches it. It doesn't care whether it's white, black, green, yellow, pink, or blue. And so here were people living in these conditions, and some of them were disease-ridden, and that disease could be transmitted on to anybody. Syphilis was in a great flurry down in the South at that time, and blacks had major problems, because they had no doctors or very few doctors that could care for them. So that only made matters worse.

It put fuel on the fire because signs went up, "Don't drink out of this fountain," "Don't use this toilet," don't do this, and don't do that. It was unreal. And when I saw it, coming from where I came from, it infuriated me. And it made me want to represent black people even more. I said, "Hey, this shouldn't be." And it should have never been in this country. The Constitution of the United States of America says, "All people are created equal." You know what I mean? The animals were treated better than the blacks were treated in the South, and I'm sorry if it this offends anybody, but I'm being honest, and the truth will set you free. I don't mean to bear down with a militant attitude against any other race. I'm not saying that the people who did this were terrible and bad people. I think they were ignorant.

Well, I got the idea to make black movies when I was traveling through the South in 1934. Even in the capital of the United States blacks could not sit on the first floor with whites. They had to sit up in the balconies. And these balconies were very tenderly called "Nigger Heaven." That's the way it was. And when I saw that, I was repulsed by it, because I'm a kid who put my hand over my heart in school and said, "I pledge allegiance to the flag and to the republic for which it stands. One nation indivisible with liberty and justice for all." And then when I saw this going on down there, I said, "What have I been doing here? This is not true. Maybe in my little section of the town, I saw it, but down here, I didn't see it." So all of a sudden, I just said, "Wow! You know, here are these discriminated theaters."

And the further I traveled south, I began to see that blacks could not go to any theater, that they had to have their own little tin-roofed theaters, and they had thousands and thousands of them. What were they playing? White cowboy pictures. White cowboy pictures. I said, "Well, wait a minute. This is not what I read in my hometown. This is not what I studied in school." I studied that after the Civil War, there were thousands and thousands of blacks who escaped and were taken in by the Indians all over the place. The blacks went with the Chippewa, the Sioux, the Mohawks, the Cherokees. They all took the blacks in because they were in sympathy with them, and they felt that if they were ever captured, they would be made slaves, the same as the blacks were. And they were right; when they were captured, they made slaves out of them. So, of course, many were very compassionate to the blacks. They could relate to the slave because when slaves went into the Indian camps, they were at home. Why? Because it reminded them of Africa. In Africa, what did they use? Bows and arrows and spears. And what was their dress? Feathers. And what was their war dress? Their identification, whether they were hunters or warriors—they wore paint on their faces. And the hunting tribesmen were like the American Indians; they worshiped the elements, and they had witch doctors and medicine men just the same as the American Indian tribes did. So the black slaves were right at home with the Indians; they could assimilate very easily.

Many blacks after the Civil War were fabulous horsemen. They could ride bareback, and they made great cowboys. One out of three cowboys who helped to pioneer our country were black, one out of three. And the blacks were great drovers, because the cattlemen preferred using them in many instances because they could wheel and deal with the Indians, and they could speak their tongue. And so they could get their cattle through with the black drovers a heck of a lot easier than they could with the white ones. So, you see, when I saw thousands of black theaters all throughout the South playing white cowboy pictures, I said, "Wait a minute. Here's a chance to take something bad and make something good out of it. Let me see if I can find someone that'll finance an all-black cowboy picture." And it took me two years to find the backing to make the first black western.

That was in 1934. I was traveling through the South with Earl Hines. We were playing at tobacco warehouses, and immediately after our engagement and the dance was over, the concert was over, there would be two cars of sheriffs heralding us out of their community, making damn sure that we were in the next community and out of theirs, a bus of black musicians. I can't tell you how many times I saw signs that said, "Nigger, don't let the sun set on you in this community." Big billboards. So, you see, that was enough to give me the driving force to say, "Wait a minute. You know, let me make a picture where a black man is a hero." We didn't have that. Even with Bill Robinson and men who were making big money—and mind you when I say that, I have great love and respect for Bill. I knew him very well. But even then, he played subservient parts for Shirley Temple. So we [blacks] didn't have national distribution of motion pictures that showed a black man as a hero, that little children could identify with.

Who'd I go to? I went to everybody. I went back to Chicago to the "policy" [numbers] barons. And I talked to the policy barons back there, who paid as much for one racehorse as what it would cost me to make a picture: $80,000. They'd buy a racehorse for that. And I spoke to several of those guys back there that I knew. I had met them when I was working at the Terrace with Earl Hines. They came in there, too, to show off their wealth and their popularity and power. And I met them and they weren't interested. They said, "Don't know nothing about motion pictures, and that's not our business. We're not interested." I went to see two playboys (two brothers) in Chicago that were Oklahoma multimillionaires. I spoke to them. And they pretty much passed their money around in luxury, playing with big cars and things. And I tried to raise money in the black community.

No one wanted to give me a chance. So finally I read an article in a magazine about a man who had produced a picture called *The Terror of Tiny Town*. It was made with [a complete cast of] midgets, little people. And I figured if this guy would do a picture made with little people, an entire western, that he might be interested in doing a black motion picture. So I went to Hollywood and walked into his office. His name was Jed Buell. In fifteen minutes, we agreed that it was a good idea. He called to Dallas, Texas, and spoke to the man who owned Sachs Amusement in Dallas, [a man] by the name of Albert Sachs. And Sachs said, "I'll take as many as you got. How many you got?" So we were in business, and we started on the first picture, which was called *Harlem on the Prairie*.

Well, Jed Buell asked me, "Who's going to write the script?"

And I looked down on the floor and saw a bunch of scripts piled up there, and I said, "What is that?"

And he says, "Those are some scripts we did about six or seven years ago."

I just yanked one out and I said, "What's the difference? Why don't we use this one?" I said, "By the time we put black characters in there and have someone write some black humor in it, nobody's going to recognize it anyway."

And he said, "Gee, that's a good idea." I mean, this guy was right on the ball. Any suggestion, he was ready for any new ideas, and so he said, "That's a good idea. Who's gonna write the black humor?"

I said, "Well, I know some guys down on Central Avenue who are comedians," and I said, "I think that they could take this script and write in the black humor for the sidekick and the comedians in there, and we'll just use the same story line." It was originally called *Sunset on the Prairie*. And we changed it to *Harlem on the Prairie*. Using the word *Harlem* would definitely let everyone know it was a black film.

I loved it in California. California was mild on its discrimination. There were places in Hollywood at the time where they may have frowned upon blacks fraternizing, but they did play in the clubs there. The head of the chamber of commerce, he frowned upon it, but it didn't do much good because the black bands were very popular bands out here. They were more or less black and tan. There was some discrimination, but not like I had seen it in other places. And the climate was so wonderful; I loved it out here. I saw some good possibilities. At first, I lived in the black neighborhoods, and then after I got moving fairly well in the picture business, then I moved into the west side of the city, which did not have too many blacks, but blacks were starting to move out in the areas around Western Avenue.

Central Avenue was wonderful. It was like a small Harlem. They had some wonderful clubs. They had the Club Alabam, which was a big club that had chorus girls and a big band and was sort of our Cotton Club out here. Then there were little mushrooms coming up, night spots and after-hours spots, and many of the movie stars, the big movie stars, came down to see the entertainment—black entertainment, the black shows and the clubs. It was quite black and tan. Many of the big stars came down; Clark Gable and Carole Lombard came down. Oh, I saw people like Buck Jones; he would come down to watch the shows. And there were a lot of Texans in that area around Central Avenue. As a matter of fact, when we made the western pictures, we had a good choice of some of the black Texas cowboys that were around.

I made the first record of "Angel Eyes." Yeah, it came to me, and at that time, Buddy Baker—he was out of Kansas, I believe—he came out to spread his wings. He was a brilliant arranger, and we put a big orchestra together—big, lush band with strings—and we recorded "Angel Eyes." It was brought to me first. But we were with a small company that was just beginning to be called Exclusive. It was owned by Leon Rene, who wrote "Sleepy Time Down South," "Someone's Rocking My Dreamboat," and

"Swallows Come Back from Capistrano." Leon formed this small label in 1945, the first, in my mind, independent black-owned major-category label—certainly the first in California. And if anybody's name should have been on the sidewalk as a pioneer of the independent record company, it should be Leon Rene. I don't think it's on there, though. But at any rate, I made the first record of "Angel Eyes," and because we were a small company, we were covered by several major companies. Sinatra, of course, covered it, and he was with a big major label that could really do a great job of publicity on it. I don't think Sinatra needed too much help because he was the rage at that time.

I guess my shepherds into the film business were Tom Mix and Buck Jones and Ken Maynard and people like that that I went to see in the movie theaters in Detroit as a youngster. I would go into the movies on Saturdays about eleven o'clock in the morning, and then my sister would have to come and get me out at eight o'clock in the evening because I'd watch the same picture over and over four or five times. So she'd come and get me at seven, eight o'clock to come home and have dinner. And these were my heroes—Tom Mix and Buck Jones—and of course I wanted to be like them. I always had that desire inside of me, as most youngsters do, to ride off into the sunset with the fair maiden. And it was my tenacity, I guess—and then I should say my anger—that made that dream happen.

I think that once you're a performer on the stage, you're taking acting lessons, because you have a live audience in front of you, and that's why we call our performance an "act." You say, "What is your act?" My act was singing. And so when I was on stage, I was always performing for a live audience. In nightclubs, I had a different type of an emotion to deal with. I had to deal with people who came not only to hear the music and to see the show but also to drink and to maybe make contact with someone of the opposite sex. Then there was the audience who came to just sit in the theater and listen, and they didn't drink, and they didn't do anything but maybe have popcorn and soda pop. And then, of course, there were the concert audiences, the larger audiences. I think what makes a good actor is the trial and error of life, falling down and getting up and falling down and getting up in many of your efforts in your career. And especially if you have the lows and the highs, you learn how to perform any of those emotions. You know how it is to be hungry. You know how it is to be drunk. You know how it is to be high. You know how it is to be rich. You know how it is to cry sadness. So you experience all those emotions as you try to become successful in whatever your career may be. And I think that's what makes the better actor, rather than the canned ones, the ones that come out of a can.

I never knew [the producer] Jed Buell until I walked into his office for the first time; in fifteen minutes, he bought my story. And later on I did finally meet that other wonderful man, Albert Sachs, out of Dallas—Sachs Amusement—who when Mr. Buell spoke to him on the telephone, he said, "Yeah, great, I'll take all [the movies] you got." So that was encouraging, and he was always a great supporter, and this, of course, was a man who had national distribution.

I don't mean to take anything away from Oscar Micheaux and Spencer Williams, who were great pioneers of the black motion-picture business. I have a great deal of respect for them and I love them very much. I never met Mr. Micheaux, but Spencer, of course, I worked with. They were brilliant men. But unfortunately, in their earlier days, they didn't get on the track [into the mainstream] because they were making small-budget pictures with low finances, probably black financing or whatever money that Micheaux could get out of his own pocket. His distribution in those days, as I recall it, was in churches and small theaters that he could set up any kind of contact with. And at the same time Sachs Amusement had national distribution to all these theaters and was putting his white cowboy pictures and white pictures in these black theaters all over the United States.

Well, I was fortunate enough to strike it rich the first time my ax went into the mine, through Jed Buell. Of course, that was a great atmosphere to be around, because it was totally professional. Mr. Buell had made numerous white cowboy pictures and was good and accurate at it. And our movie locations were good locations. The first one was at Murray's Dude Ranch in Victorville [California].

The other ones we made in different locations. Some at Murray's and then in Saugus out there in the rock country. Murray was an Afro-American who owned that particular ranch in Victorville, California. So Mr. Buell was a learning tree for me. We had Sam Newfield as our director; he was a wonderful director, had done many, many, many white

Westerns. And I sat at his shoulders, and then learned how to go in and use a Moviola and learn to cut and to be a film editor. And of course, film editing is really the true way to learn directing. So thorough Sam Newfield, I was able to have that environment around me, of learning, and he was a wonderful man and a good friend, and I took good direction from him because he was a very understanding person. And so any success that came from my performances certainly came through Sam Newfield, the director.

Another actor I worked with was Clarence Brooks; he was wonderful. He was from New York and from the Lafayette Players. He had had a lot of experience working in New York onstage. He was a fine stage actor. And as a matter of fact, he was very light-skinned, and a lot of people thought he was Caucasian. In many instances, I'd have people say, "Well, who was the Caucasian that was working in the picture?"

Then again, we get into another element of the criticisms against Oscar Micheaux, which I'd like to defend. Micheaux was criticized for the fact that he used a lot of light-skinned actors all the time in his films. Well, I'm going to tell you how that was. Because, see, during those times, the light-skinned people had greater opportunities for education, and also you know, some of them could pass [as white] and go to school to be educated. And also, their job opportunities were a little bit better. It's like putting cream in coffee, you know, to lighten it up a little bit. And so the prejudiced man would be more [accepting of] the lightskinned Negro than he was the black, the darker skin. And of course, these [lighter-skinned] people had a better opportunity for education; therefore, a lot of them would go to the drama classes and learn drama. And so it was that more of these [lighter-skinned] people had a better understanding of drama. And when you would cast for a movie, you wanted to cast somebody who was more articulate and who could play the part. And so it seemed that you found that there were a lot more light-skinned Negroes who were interested in drama than darkerskinned Negroes. You see, so it wasn't that Micheaux preferred the lightskinned Negro—it was that they were more available to do the parts he wanted them to play. And it wasn't really that he used them to excess. When he found an actor, he picked them for their ability as an actor and not because of their skin color. It just happened to turn out that way.

Look, take me, for instance. You know, I'm a mongrel. I have many,

many races. I have preferred to represent myself as a black man because of my ethnic DNA, I guess. I chose to be black. But many times, I've been places where people have no idea that I have any black blood whatsoever.

When I went to make this cowboy picture, Mr. Buell did not want me to play the lead part. Absolutely not. He said, "No way." We screen-tested around twenty different people, dark-skinned actors. But either they couldn't ride a horse or they couldn't sing. Or if they could sing, they couldn't act. If they could act, they couldn't ride a horse, or were scared to death of horses. So we just couldn't find the actor that would have been able to play that part and not hold down production with somebody teaching him how to do it. You see what I'm saying? So, of course, this was our problem. He didn't want me to play it.

I finally went to him and said, "What are we going to do about the picture? I can sing, I can ride, I can act, I can do all this."

He said, "They'll never buy you."

I said, "What do you mean, they'll never buy me? I've been down South with Earl Hines, singing in places. They bought me down there." I finally said to him, "May I ask you a question? Have you ever lived in a black neighborhood?"

He said no.

I said, "Well, you're an Irishman. You know that I could take you right now down to Central Avenue and tell them you're my brother, and you would be accepted. Nobody would question you. I'd say you're black; they'd say, 'OK, cool.'"

I said, "First of all, what you don't understand is that black people (or Afro-Americans, or Negroes, which they were called at that time) come in a bouquet of colors." I said, "Obviously, you have never lived amongst them, so you wouldn't know this."

And he said, "I don't know."

I said, "Well, let me say this to you. Did you ever see a picture called *The Good Earth* [1937]?"

He said, "Yeah."

I said, "Well, there's a man by the name of Paul Muni from the Jewish theater who played a Chinaman. And also, an Austrian lady played his maid." So, I said, "If they can play Chinese, if I'm an actor, why can't I play any part I want to play?"

And on the basis of that, he called on the phone and said, "Give this guy a screen test and get him out of my hair."

So I took the screen test. I didn't know a cowboy song to my name. And I sang "Way Down upon the Sewanee River" for my screen test. And they accepted it. And we used it in the picture, opened the picture up with me riding a horse and playing the guitar, singing "Way Down upon the Sewanee River."

I learned to ride at my uncle's place in Toledo, Ohio. I spent my summer vacations there when I was a young boy. And my grandfather had a farm; he was a dairyman, up in Port Huron, Michigan. I brought many cows in when I was eight, nine, ten years old on my summer vacations. I had early experience in riding and knew animals very well. And then later on, I became very serious about it, when I went to live up on a ranch up there in California. I learned what cowboys really were about as far as branding and as far as going out on the trails. This was during the time after my first picture, right after I made my first picture in 1937. I have a ranch right now up in Oregon.

I worked with cowboys and I worked with some very good actors. One of these was Maceo Bruce Sheffield. He was a black policeman. Well, Sheffield was very important in the first picture because he really was the guy who helped to cast that picture. He helped to cast it. Because he was a policeman and was very well known, he knew all the actors [such as Leon Buck, Nathan Curry, Connie Harris, Ira Hardin, F. E. Miller, Mantan Moreland, and Spencer Williams] and all the people and everybody around in town, and he was a fairly good actor himself. Later on, he was a café and club owner. Yeah, he got into that later on. But his main character when I first met him, he was a cop. He was a detective. And he, I think, was responsible for the first all-black rodeo in California. He was a man who was very much interested in western things, and he was interested in the handling of firearms, being a policeman.

Of course, youngsters who desire to become a cowboy or western man, you know, always have this consciousness about guns. And it was to show that there were other things entertaining about the cowboy besides him just being out on the range, branding and bringing in the cattle and saving the girl from somebody who wants to buy her ranch or steal it from her. There were cowboys who could ride broncs and who were great bull riders and bull handlers and clowns, and so, of course, it was likely that Maceo would probably be the first guy that would bring a rodeo to California—a black rodeo to California.

Oh, I enjoyed working with him. I had a very good relationship with him, a very good communication with Maceo. We liked each other very much. I found him easy to work with when we would do our choreographing for our fight scenes. And we didn't have any doubles in those days; we couldn't afford them. And as a matter of fact, there were no stunt associations around at that particular time, like there are now. So we did all our own stunts, and we choreographed all our fights through our director, Sam Newfield. And many times, I took one on the chin, you know, that didn't come off the way we choreographed it. And vice versa. He took a couple of blows from me, too. That happens in the best of routine layouts in fighting. And in any kind of stunt.

Another actor I worked with was John Lawrence Criner. He was an older guy who starred in his first movie as early as 1926 [in *The Flying Ace*]. He had been a Lafayette Player. My uncle Romaine Johns was also a member of the Lafayette Players [started in 1915 by Anita Bush, a young Harlem performer who was a pioneer in the development of African American theater]. That's how I know about the original Lafayette Players out of New York. Well, I have a flashback into my long-range memory. We're talking over sixty years ago. And I think there are some people of my vintage who are not able to remember six years back.

In 1937, I made *Harlem on the Prairie* for Jed Buell. Well, as best as I can remember, we made these pictures in about five or six days, you know. Seven days at the most. A week would be over budget, really. They were quickies. We worked maybe fourteen or fifteen hours a day. In order for us to push a picture through in a five-day quickie formula, we were working from the time the fog lifted and we got the first ray of light coming over the hills until the last light, and then we went into arc lamps to do interiors. And sometimes we would work from six or seven o'clock in the morning till eleven, twelve o'clock at night. And so we were really pushed and occupied in our stunt routines, our dialogue memory, and things like that. Now, I can't tell you too much about the location, other than the fact that in Victorville, California, there's a lot of rocks. There was a ranch house there. When we shot, a lot of times, day for night, with our filters on, and then when we did interiors, there was an old house there that didn't have a roof on it, and we'd arc it up with the generators at that time, and we would shoot interiors right in this old house. We did our bunkhouses and our things there, with arc lights at nighttime.

Oh, we had several real black cowboys, yeah, that came out of Texas. Then we had another black cowboy that came up from just beyond Santa Barbara and the ranches that there were up there. And they groomed all the rest of our guys in the posses, you know, teaching them how to ride. Sometimes they would go out with these guys so that they'd get the look of being real cowboys. These guys were Central Avenue people [from the Central Avenue area of Los Angeles]. Some of them had never been on a horse.

There probably were some of them [real cowboys who sang] when we were out there at the ranch. There were several of them that would sing some songs. I don't recall any of them ever having any great voices. But I don't think you're going to hear too many great voices on cowboy records even today. You're not going to have any cowboys that can compare to Johnny Mathis or Frank Sinatra. Cowboy songs don't necessitate your having a good voice.

I've heard a lot of songs about the "range" in my travels. I'm sitting here with a pair of cowboy boots on right now. My closets are full of cowboy boots. I've always been a cowboy. I will die being a cowboy. I love the cowboy world, and it came into my life in my early stage, and it's still a part of my dream. I have a picture on one wall in my house that has two guns in harness and a hat over the top. I was inducted into the hall of fame of the International Western Music Association. I have that plaque. I just received a commemorative version of the original gun that I used in *The Bronze Buckaroo,* and I'm looking at it here on the wall. The duplicates of those original guns are being made by a company called America Remembers. They're called The Bronze Buckaroo, and they are engraved in gold. So my room is pretty well filled here with western stuff. It's an atmosphere I live in because I'm a cowboy at heart.

Do you know why cowboys sing? Everybody wants to say that singing cowboys were invented by Hollywood. That's the biggest lie that was ever told. Do you know why cowboys sang on the range? It quieted the cattle down. And do you know who brought that into the cowboy world? The black cowboy brought it in because he would get out there on the range with his guitar and sing the blues, and they found out that it would settle the cattle down. That's why you hear a lot of great white blues singers who have learned from the black blues singers. And that's why the blues influence is still in the cowboy business, whether they're black, white, Indians, or whatever. But that's how it started, and they'd notice that one of those cowboys was out there singing the blues and playing his guitar, and the cattle settled down. In my research that's what I found out.

The three pictures I made prior to *The Bronze Buckaroo* (1939) all had "*Harlem*" in the title—*Harlem on the Prairie* (1937), *Two Gun Man from Harlem* (1938), *Harlem Rides the Range* (1939). I grew sick of the name Harlem, but they did that because they wanted to identify it as a black picture. But I decided, "I don't want to use '*Harlem*' anymore."

They said, "Well, what do you want to call the next movie?"

I said, "Call it *The Bronze Buckaroo.*" So that's how the name came to be—but I wrote a lot of the music for the pictures, a lot of the music. And what we didn't have, I wrote. For the first picture there was a guy named Lou Porter, who did a lot of writing. And there was some other guy they brought into it. But the latter pictures, I did a good deal of the writing of music in the pictures, because we couldn't afford great musical scores in those pictures. Our budgets were too low.

Dick Cohn was another director I worked with. Well, yeah, let me tell you that story. See, Jed Buell made the first picture, but he was so busy with the success of the first picture, which not only played in black movie houses but also was playing in white movie houses, through Sachs Amusement, because of its entertainment value and because of its uniqueness, and he was so busy that he forgot to sign me for some other pictures. Well, all of a sudden, these things started to break loose and become successful. Richard Cohn got in touch with me and said, "Listen, I'd like to sign you for three more pictures." And he got to me with a better deal than I got from Buell. He didn't have to twist my wrist.

And then, of course, I had an opportunity to own my own horse to make a deal where I said, "Hey, if you want me in this picture, I don't want a rental horse. I want a horse that can fall in love with me and I can fall in love with it, and this could be my buddy horse, like the rest of the cowboys." So part of my deal was that he bought this horse for me, which was Stardust, which I used in all of my pictures thereafter.

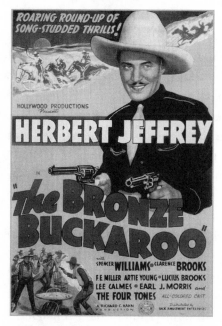

*The Bronze Buckaroo* movie poster, 1939.

Dick Cohn was with Hollywood Productions. He was a terrific guy, just a wonderful man, very compassionate and understanding. He felt that he was doing what needed to be done, that these pictures needed to be out there so that other little children—not just Afro-American children, but there were Indian children, there were Puerto Rican children, and there were Mexican children out there who were also getting bad treatment and had no heroes to identify with. And so we were trying to create an image that these youngsters could identify with. And in the pictures, we had moral standards. In none of my pictures did I drink. I faked drinking in one of them. I pretended to be drunk in order to get upstairs and get to the guy who I wanted to get to and get some information. I never shot a man unless it was in self-defense. I didn't smoke any cigarettes in the pictures. We had moral standards that I must say we did not create. These were the same things that were being used in the Roy Rogers and the Gene Autry pictures. We sort of tried to copy the moral principles that were in those movies.

I made a total of four of the black cowboy films. And then what happened after that was a very interesting thing. I went back to my hometown to make an appearance at a theater where my picture was playing. In Detroit. And while I was there [around 1940], the great Duke Ellington was playing at one of our well-known ballrooms, there on Woodward Avenue. And of course, I had met him before on several occasions. I had gone backstage to congratulate him some years prior to this appearance. We shared a professional respect for each other. Well, he was playing at the ballroom, and so I thought well, I'll just keep these cowboys clothes on. I'll just go to that ballroom that night. I'll stand in the front of the bandstand and maybe Duke Ellington will see me and remember me that way, and I might attract some attention to my personal appearance at the theater I was playing at. I was really on a sort of an advertising campaign. And when I went there, I had all my western regalia on, the big hat and all that, which of course created a focus of attention because nobody else was wearing those kinds of clothes. And then, too, people recognized me, as well, from my pictures, and it was a black affair. And when I walked down in the front of the bandstand, Duke looked down and he saw me. He not only recognized me, but he stopped the band and he said, "Ladies and gentlemen, I have standing in front of me the Bronze Buckaroo, Mr. Herb Jeffries, whose picture I just played with for the last week at the Apollo Theater."

He had been playing along with *The Bronze Buckaroo* in New York at the Apollo Theater, doing the stage show in between pictures. You know, a picture and then a stage show and then another picture and another stage show. He was well aware of me, and he introduced me and asked me if I would come up and sing a song with the band. So I went up and I sang something—I don't recall what it was. It probably was something like "Stardust" or something like that. Anyway, he had an arrangement in my key, and then after that he said, "Don't go away."

He says, "During intermission, I'd like to talk to you." So I went back in his dressing room during intermission, and he asked me, he said, "I'm doing this series of stage shows, and I'd like you to come and perform on our stage show and join my group."

So I went with him and he introduced me as the Bronze Buckaroo, and I didn't wear western clothes—I wore a tuxedo. And I started singing with his band. And then he asked me later on if I would record with his band and make some records with them. And we selected some songs to record, one of which was "Flamingo." Needless to say, "Flamingo" was a multimillion-record seller. And so I had another career going for me. I was a movie star who became a band singer. I went the other way because I realized that I was performing with one of my heroes and a man who I believed would go down in music as a Mozart, Beethoven of our times, Mr. Duke Ellington. No question about it. No question in my mind's eye.

Once upon a time, in England, I was asked on BBC if Duke Ellington had influenced me. I said, "Absolutely not. I was cloned by him." He was one of the most wonderful human beings I have ever met in my whole life. He was not only a great inspiration as far as education and articulation was concerned, but he was one of the ten best well-dressed men in the world. And besides that, here was a man, if you spent one hour with him, you forgot epidermis, you forgot about skin color. You became brain-conscious. He did not have a color. And one day that is what is going to break down the [color] barrier. We have another man who just proved that by the name of Colin Powell, who proved that education is the answer for discrimination. This is the man who not only was the head of the Joint Chiefs of Staff, but turned down the possibility of being president of the United States.

I grew up with so many people who helped to break down so many of the barriers that black people faced. In Detroit, there was the Olympian Jesse Owens. I knew him very, very well. He was a great, great guy. Well, I can only tell you that this was a man, Jesse Owens, who was a great uplift to me, because when I saw that he could become a champion, it only made me know that I was on the right track. A champion like that becomes a hero.

Jackie Robinson was the same way. He was a baseball champion who went through his trials and tribulations. That is a part of success, trial and error. But he became a hero, not only in the eyesight of his own ethnic group, but he was a hero to all people. And so was my friend Joe Louis. I saw him fight many times. And I went to the Brewster Center [in Detroit], where he would train. That's where I used to go, too, to take my athletic training. He was another great inspiration for me, to see the Brown Bomber become a man who was not well educated but still was a scientist of great intelligence as far as the science of the art of self-defense was concerned and who became one of the great heroes not just to his own ethnic group but to the world.

I heard a man say something, just the last week when I was at a stroke center where I usually go every week as a volunteer. We do a rap session with the stroke people here. I usually do it with a good friend of mine. He's an actor by the name of Richard Harrison. And Harrison and I were there doing our rap session with these people. Anyway, he said something that kind of bemused me. He's a Caucasian. And he says to all these people, who are disabled through paralysis. It's a rehabilitation center as well. But anyway, he said something that kind of really amused me, and I've mused over it ever since. He said, "You know, Herb, I'm beginning to think that black people are special people. My God, there are no athletes like them in the world. They're champions in everything they do. Look at these guys in basketball; my God, man. They produce nothing but champions."

I said, "Well, it's not that they're a superpeople, not at all. But what creates the super feeling, the super emotion, which is in me, is tenacity. And that tenacity is not to take no for an answer. I'm gonna be in your hair. I'm gonna bug the hell out of you until you say, 'Do something with this guy. Get him out of my hair.' " This is the way to forge forward. And it is this that creates champions; it's that you have to do it. You must do it.

I think the civil-rights movement started with the freedom riding. Freedom riding down through the South. And there were many people who also assisted in this. Now, we're going to talk about a man who happens to be one of my champions. I don't know if you like him or not, but he's a champion of mine. We're talking about Adam Clayton Powell, who tricked the president into the integration of the federal government. And he's been sort of forgotten about. I knew Adam Clayton Powell very well. I wanted to do his life story. I wanted to do the A.C.P. story. And so when I was at Universal doing a picture with a man by the name of Jim Drury—I was doing The Virginian and so Jim said to me, "You know what," he said, "I think I can get Universal interested in doing Adam Clayton Powell's life, and you should do it."

And I said, "I'd be interested in doing it. He's a very dear friend of mine."

He said, "You think you can get the rights?"

And I said, "I'm sure I can if I can get hold of him. He's in Bimini [in the Bahamas]." So through one of his aides who was teaching up at a university, who wrote a story called *The Kingfish,* I was able to get ahold of him and I said, "Get ahold of Adam for me."

He said, "I'll get ahold of Adam. But you're going to have to be at a telephone booth someplace at a certain time where he can call you back, because that's the only way you can communicate with him in Bimini."

So I was at the Mayfair Hotel in Washington, D.C., and I gave them the telephone number at the bar downstairs, and at seven o'clock, that specific time that night, the phone rang. I went into the booth; it was Adam, calling me from Bimini. And he said, "What can I do for you, Herb?" See, I had known him from Paris, because he had come over to Paris many times to visit with his son and with his wife, Hazel Scott [the jazz pianist], and I was living in Paris at the time. I had a big jazz club there, a successful jazz club, called the Flamingo. That was from 1950 till 1958 I owned that. It was just a half block off the Champs-Élysées, a block from Pierre Charon, about three blocks from the Georges V Hotel.

I had a very successful jazz club, and Adam Clayton Powell came to see me and talk to me about some things. And we became very close, and when I'd come to the city, New York, I'd always get together with him.

Well, Adam tricked Eisenhower into making a statement [after World War II], and then he released it to the newspapers the next day. He told Eisenhower that he was a man who had dealt with races success-fully in the services and that the federal government should be inte-grated, and it was time for us to stand behind the Constitution. And he said, "I think you could make yourself a very big man." And so Eisen-hower agreed to it, and he released to the paper the next day that Ei-senhower was going to uphold the bill of integration in the federal government.

It was actually Truman who initiated the administrative action to in-tegrate the armed forces. But Eisenhower was the guy who completed the picture. Adam Clayton Powell Jr. passed about fifty-two bills. He was an incredible congressman and an incredible man. But unfortunately for him, he never was really able to represent the race because he was too fair. And the militants came into the picture at that particular time and overshadowed what he was doing. But nevertheless, what's the dif-ference? The difference is, he got the work done.

Look at me. I was eighty-one years old before I signed a contract with Warner Brothers. And they came looking for me because of the black cowboy pictures.

I went to Europe in 1950. I went over to France. I tried to get agents to book me there. They wouldn't book me because they didn't want to split commissions. I was with William Morris at the time, had big success here. And my records were playing all over the world. And I was known, but they wouldn't book me there. They didn't want to split the commissions. So I woke up one morning and said to my wife and child, "We're selling everything. We're going to sell the house, we're going to sell our cars, we're going to sell all the clothes and everything, and we're going to go and get educated in Europe. I want to go." And we sold everything, and we got on a ship. We had booked it three months ahead of time, so that I'd have to leave. And we went to Paris. And we got a flat in Paris, and we lived around there for a while, and then finally I decided to go take a look at the south of France. I took a look at the south and then came back. We came back to Los Angeles, but I had no intention of staying because I'd sold my house. And so we rented a place for a short period of time, and I had analyzed the whole situation there and decided I'm going to go back [to Paris], and I want to open up a club. So I did. I went back in '51, found a spot, opened it up, and it was an immediate success. Parisians love jazz. And everybody came.

I knew Richard Wright when I was living in the south of France. I didn't live very far from him. I had a villa there. And Richard lived very close. He was brilliant. Then he opened up a club. He went into a business in Paris and became an investor in a club called the Ringside, which Eartha Kitt worked. The stage was built like a ring; like a fighters' ring. And it was quite successful.

Richard was a very intelligent man. Here again is the way, the only way we're going to get rid of this thing [racism and discrimination], and believe me when I tell you I believe that it's promoted. I believe the whole damn thing is promoted by the hierarchy. Because it's an old formula called divide and conquer. As long as they can keep us divided, racially, class, sex, age, think about it. There's not a living ass on the face of this world, regardless of his epidermis, that is not going to suffer discrimination. Because I don't care if you're white, I don't care if you're Oriental, I don't care if you're an Indian, or if you're Mexican, or French, or German, or Spanish, or whatever you are, you're going to get old, if you live long enough. And if you get old, you're going to be discriminated against. Age discrimination is the largest form of discrimination on the face of this earth. Even among your own family. Your own family's going to say, "Hey, let's put this guy in a home, man. He's starting to bug me."

So, you see, now we have what we call sex discrimination. And then we have racial discrimination. And we have class discrimination. My God, man, I mean, I'll tell you. And the hierarchy loves it because they can manipulate you and push you around and move you where they want.

Richard Wright was angry. Angry. You get angry about the situation that you know is hypocrisy. It's hypocrisy, and it's the greatest trauma for you to look me in my face and tell me you care for me and you care about me and what I'm doing, and then behind my back say that I'm not good enough to belong to your golf club, or I'm not good enough to belong to your social structure. C'mon. So when you go to Europe, you don't have that problem.

It's always been that way in France, and even from the days that I can recall and the days I've read about. That's the way Josephine [Baker] felt. Oh, I loved Josephine. I loved her to pieces. I mean, how can you not love intelligence? She was a beautiful woman. And she spoke French fluently. Here's a woman who became a part of the French underground, who was loved by the French, and who is still adored by the French. When you met her, you met class, you met elegance, you met nobility. When you looked at her profile, she looked like some kind of a queen from a lost African tribe.

For me, California was a frontier, and then Europe. In Europe there was a great sense of possibility. California was a frontier because the motion-picture business was a bit in its infancy; it was beginning, and the movie czars were building it. Still, as I looked about and observed then, being interested in history all of my life, I was curious about other countries. I wanted to go to travel. I went to Paris [in 1951], and then Paris satisfied a certain part of my life. And then, you know, I needed Italy, and I went to Italy for three years. And then I went to England for a while.

I studied in Rome [in the 1960s], studied music there. And while I was living in Rome I traveled around Italy, but I headquartered out of

Rome. It was my home. Then I went to London. I spent about a year in London. And then London is where I met a man who interested me in India, a man who was an Indian. And he was a guru, a teacher of the yoga philosophies. And then I became highly interested in the yoga teachings. I am ever grateful to it because I learned that I could not stop the aging process, but that I could slow it down, and that's what I've been able to do. And I still practice yoga. Every moment of my life. I'm practicing it right now.

I came back to the United States in 1958, 1959. Then I went back to Europe again. I would sometimes go and stay maybe six or eight months and then come back because I would miss the culture. And here in this country, we're suffering from cultural anemia. I've lived all over the world. I spent time in India. I came back, and then I wanted to see what the East was like. And I went to Malaysia, Singapore, Hong Kong, Philippines, all down through the archipelagos, into Australia, New Zealand. You know, when a man is eighty-six years old, he can go a lot of places during that time.

The wiser a man becomes, the more he knows how little he knows. And so, I'm hungry for knowledge. What I'm searching for is results. I want to help make new frontiers or be part of the new roads to be paved. I've only touched the tip of the iceberg. What keeps me going is that I'm curious. I want to know more. I've got places to go and things to do.

[Interview by Alan Govenar and John Slate, January 7, 1998]

*Gwendolyn Knight, Dallas, Texas, 1998.*

# GWENDOLYN KNIGHT

ARTIST

*May 26, 1913–February 18, 2005*

*Gwendolyn Knight came to St. Louis, Missouri, from Barbados when she was seven years old. In 1926, she moved with her family to Harlem, where she took art classes in public school. She attended the Division of Fine Arts at Howard University from 1931 to 1933, when she could no longer afford the tuition. She returned to New York and studied with sculptor Augusta Savage. While studying with Savage, she met painter Jacob Lawrence, whom she married in 1941. She continued painting but received little recognition. In 1960, she enrolled at the New School for Social Research in New York and studied art there until 1966. She then went to the Skowhegan School of Painting and Sculpture in Skowhegan, Maine, from 1968 to 1970. For most of her career, Knight was a figurative painter of portraits and still lifes, utilizing oil, charcoal, and ink in her work.*

WE LIVED IN THE CARIBBEAN until I was seven. My father, Malcolm, died when I was two. He was a pharmacist. I was an only child. My mother's name was Miriam. She died in 1984. She had a good life.

My early childhood was very pleasant. I remember going to a little school and passing the walls overgrown with flowers on the way. Just everyday life; things come back to me once in a while. I don't really think about them that much.

The Caribbean was a British colony. And it wasn't like the South or anything like that. It was quite different from the United States, I think. The people, the white and the black people, lived peacefully, I think. I wasn't there till I was an adult and grown up, but as a child, I don't remember any discrimination.

A family adopted me, and we moved to the United States. We went to St. Louis. It was amazing to me. There was cold weather, and snow, and different kinds of holidays. And so it was quite different and very wonderful, as far as I thought. But in St. Louis there was discrimination. I went to a segregated school. And there was lots of discrimination, because that was almost like a Southern town. I think you could ride buses and things, and sit anywhere, but it was a segregated town. It didn't really bother me at the time.

My foster sister was the one who adopted me. She was practically as old as my mother, I guess. My mother stayed in the islands. She had been crippled in one of the tornadoes, so I don't even know if they would have allowed her in at that time. But I kept in touch with her all the time. And so there was no missing Mother.

We went to St. Louis because my foster sister was working as a dresser for an opera star—Dorothy Francis. It was white opera. In St. Louis and Forest Park every summer, they had opera. So she came with Dorothy Francis to St. Louis, and she met and married someone there.

To me, it [St. Louis] was fine. I had lots of little friends, and we lived in a nice neighborhood. And I had good teachers. Our school was wonderful. I have no idea how I got interested in art. From the time I can remember, I've been interested in doing that. I always liked drawing and doing portraits. I loved to do portraits, even as a little girl. But everybody thought they were ugly.

My mother would say to me, "Oh, I'm not that ugly."

But anyhow, I really enjoyed it. Then I used to see some very glossy calendars that had maids with water jugs and all that, standing by the fountain, something Italian, and I thought they were gorgeous.

I read a lot. And I was very nosy and bossy, but my friend Sarah Turner—she was younger than I, so I was sort of the bossy person with her—and it wasn't that there was any antipathy or anything like that, I just assumed that since I was older, I would know better than she would know how to act. So when they had a show there, I asked everybody if Sarah Turner was still there, and then we found Sarah Turner, so she told me that after I moved to New York, I wrote her letters telling her how to behave.

I think that my foster sister had been in the United States for some years before. Then her family came. We arrived in 1920, and we went to live in New York in 1926, I guess. I finished junior high school in St. Louis.

When I got to New York, it was exciting. I had been living in a segregated city and going to a segregated school, and all my friends were black. In New York, I was amazed at all the different kinds of people, like Italians and Jews . . . so I was fascinated by that and loved the Italian names and thought it was wonderful.

We lived in Harlem. My sister had been here before, so when we first arrived, we lived with a family in a private house on 126th Street until my sister found an apartment. And then she found an apartment on 114th Street. And from there, we moved to 1851 Seventh Avenue.

I went to high school in New York. I went to Wadley. Wadley High School was the girls' high school and had a good reputation. It was mixed and was on 115th Street. Well, when I first came, Wadley had two annexes, and one was on Seventy-something Street and Amsterdam Avenue, and the other was on 103rd. I went to the one at Seventy-seventh Street and Amsterdam, and I met an art teacher there. She was a typical art teacher. She had short hair and wore long beads, and she was very interested in what I was doing. So I continued with my art there. I spent my freshman year at the annex. And then I went to the main building, which was on 115th between Seventh and Lenox.

While I was at the annex, I had the really good support of this art teacher. I can't remember her name. But anyhow, she made a great impression on me. She was white. She was very involved and very helpful to me, so I felt that I could do something. But at the main high school, it was a little bit different. I didn't know it at the time, but I think I ran into some people who did not favor blacks. So it was a little bit different.

After I was an artist and got to know the artists in Harlem, I had a sense of the Harlem Renaissance. Of course, I used to read a lot, so I had read some books by black writers, Langston Hughes and Claude McKay, so I knew the writers just by reading about them. I spent a lot of time in the library, too.

After high school I went to Howard University. This was 1931. I was a student in the art department. I had Lois Mailou Jones, and Mr. Porter was head of the art department. I only stayed at Howard two years, because that was just at the beginning of the Depression, and the money was not available after two years.

So I went back to Harlem. That's when we were living on 124th Street. My sister became a housekeeper for a very well known psychiatrist.

Well, after I came back from Howard University and was not going back to school again, I met a lady, Mrs. Welch, a black woman, and she got on my case and asked me what I was doing and all that kind of thing; why wasn't I doing something? So she took me up to Augusta Savage's studio, and I began to go there and study and meet the artists.

Mrs. Welch was a fine dressmaker. She thought that I was interested in art, and Augusta Savage's studio was well known in the art world at the time. And so it was the place that I could go and do the things I liked to do.

Augusta Savage had had some recognition, so I would have thought at the time. She must have been in her thirties, but now that I look at it, she must have been older than that. But you know, as a child, you either think somebody is ancient—or as a young woman, anyhow—or if you like them, you think they're close to you.

It's really incredible when I think about it because it was only for one year, and I'm always surprised when I think of it, because she had an influence on my life as an artist. I mean, I don't think that, had I not known her, I would have persisted in doing what I'm doing.

Augusta didn't give lessons. She got models for us, and we drew and she did her sculpture, and I guess she must have done some teaching because she was there, you know. She would come and say, "This is good," or that, but she was a sculptor, and I was a painter or graphic artist.

I was working from the model at the studio and at Augusta's place and doing charcoal drawings. And then I did little opaque watercolor works and things like that. But I did not really work very hard, I tell you.

Then the WPA, the art program, came on. And I got a job as an assistant to one of the master artists who was involved in the murals-in-Harlem project. Her name was Selma Day, but the head of that project was Charles Alston. He was kind of a mentor to Jake [Jacob Lawrence].

I met Jake at 306. That was the place where Jake worked and also the place where all the murals artists signed in for work. It was on 141st Street between Eighth and St. Nicholas. That was, I think, in 1933 or 1934.

I knew Jake all the time. I'm not sure when we started actually dating. We were married in 1941.

I thought Jake's work was wonderful, and he had the stick-to-it-ness. He just worked more than anybody. I thought he was a very good artist, and he was a nice young man, too.

I am absolutely sure that in other places, you wouldn't have had that kind of community [that we had in New York] because there was everything going on there, and especially at that time, the WPA time. Orson Welles's *Emperor Jones* played there, and all the arts were being followed in Harlem. I don't think any other place would have given me this opportunity. And on top of that, I began to know other artists, because in 1941 or 1943, Jake became a member of the Downtown Gallery.

The place I remember most is East 51st Street. And Edith Halpert had taken Jake as one of the stable in her gallery. So I got to know all those gallery artists, and there was Ben Shawn, all the well-known artists. There was a kind of mixing that went on in New York that couldn't happen someplace else.

Before the sixties, before the [civil-rights] movement, everybody was in Harlem. All the [black] intellectuals, all the professional people—the doctors, the lawyers—everybody lived in Harlem, and I guess we all cared about each other. So it was a rich community. It changed at the end of segregation. There was a wider opportunity for people to live places other than Harlem. And I guess people who could afford it moved out. And that was too bad, I think. And that left people who were not as able to defend themselves to try to better themselves. And children didn't get the same sense of knowledge and truth in their community.

When I got there [Harlem] in 1926, I was too young to be really involved in the arts scene. I didn't know anything about it, for one thing. So I think the twenties was the time of the Renaissance. I knew these other people because Augusta was one of the Renaissance people. I don't know whether she entertained people like Langston Hughes, but she did know a lot of people—Aaron Douglas, Claude McKay. She knew them, and the community was a small community, so you knew everybody. You knew all the artists. We could meet the writers and the painters. There were all these great jazz people—Duke Ellington, Billie Holiday. All the big bands. We used to go to the Savoy, and all the big bands came there. And we went to Small's Paradise. If you wanted to dance, you went to the Savoy. That was it. And Small's was fine. And there were several neighborhood places where you could go. I've forgotten the names of them.

I think Harlem was a mecca. That was the place to go if you were an artist. There weren't many opportunities for black artists elsewhere. I didn't expect that we'd be here [Seattle] this long. I had never really thought about the state of Washington. If I thought of the West Coast at all, I thought San Francisco or Los Angeles, where the movie industry was. And I just didn't think about it.

We had a friend who was a dancer, Perry. And he had gone into the service and had been stationed at Fort Lewis out here. And we met Perry one day on the street and he said, "I'm thinking about moving to Seattle." So we said, "Oh, isn't that nice." And then I said to Jake, "Why does he want to move to Seattle?" We were surprised, you know. But it's a very nice place, and it's been very good for us. Well, now it has a very vital arts scene. But it wasn't always like this.

I can't put my finger on the group of artists who are as cohesive and close as the ones I knew in New York. Well, it's a different time. I guess people are different.

I met one young woman on one of our trips, and she wanted to recreate that. She was so taken with the Renaissance and Harlem as the place where the arts flourished, and there was so much going on, and where it was so joyful at times. And she wanted to know how she could start back to that time.

Jake and I are quite different artists. I think I'm more spontaneous, in a way. He's interested in history and very controlled—he knows more or less what the painting is going to be like when it's finished. You know, he plans it, and it's done, and it comes out exactly as he was thinking about it. There may be some small changes, or maybe not. But I never know. So I find that doing a monoprint suits me fine.

I don't work very much because I get involved—we're busy all the time. But I do work. I just had a show of monoprints in the spring, and Jake has a big exhibition here at the Henry Gallery. And they have two portraits that I did: one a self-portrait and one of Jake.

I think it's the art [that keeps me going], it's the music, it's the paintings, it's the dance, it's all the arts. It's wonderful. We get the Sunday *New York Times,* we get the *New York Times* every day, and it's just wonderful to read about what's happening in the arts. And every time we go to New York, I visit a museum. So I think the arts are really what keeps me involved.

[Interview by Alan Govenar, September 3, 1998]

*Marian Kramer, Highland Park, Michigan, ca. 2003.*

# MARIAN KRAMER

*Born June 16, 1944*

*Marian Kramer has worked at the forefront of the civil-rights move-
ment since the 1960s. She is cochair of the National Welfare Rights
Union (NWRU), an organization dedicated to unity among low-
income public-assistance recipients and the unemployed. For
decades she has fought government programs such as "workfare,"
defended poor women against unjust prosecution for welfare fraud,
and led electoral campaigns to elect the victims of poverty to political office. She has helped organize summit meetings of grass-roots
leaders of poor people's movements, housing takeovers by people
without homes, and efforts to unionize in the South. She is the recipient of numerous awards for community service and is nationally known as a mentor to college students fighting poverty. Today,
she maintains her commitment to end poverty in America by empowering the poor, and especially women, as leaders.*

*Kramer was a contributor to* For Crying Out Loud: Women's
Poverty in the United States *(edited by Diane Dujon and Ann
Withorn, 1996), a book that focuses on issues related to poverty
by bringing together the perspectives of welfare mothers, social activists, and scholars. She has served as a delegate to the NGO (nongovernmental organization) Forum on Women in Beijing and has
worked extensively with the Lawyers' Committee for Civil Rights Under Law, the National Council of Negro Women, the African American Women's Caucus, the Women of Color Caucus, and the National
Organization for Women. Kramer was a board member of the National Anti-Hunger Coalition; a staff member of the Congress on
Racial Equality (CORE) in the 1960s in Louisiana and in Detroit; a
founding member of the Black Panther Party in Detroit, Michigan,
and the League of Revolutionary Black Workers; an organizer of
Welfare Workers for Justice based in New York in 1975; a staff mem-*

*ber of the Wayne County Welfare Rights Organization; a paralegal*
*for Wayne County Neighborhood Legal Services; president of the*
*Michigan Welfare Rights Organization, 1982–1989; a member of*
*United Auto Workers (UAW), District Council 65; and a board mem-*
*ber of the League of Revolutionaries for a New America.*

I WAS BORN IN BATON ROUGE, LOUISIANA, but we left there when I was about six years old. We lived in west Baton Rouge, which is Port Allen, Louisiana. And my grandfather, who worked in a bar across the street from our house, was assaulted by his young boss, who was white, three different times. The young man was young enough to be his grandson. And when he did it the third time, Dad retaliated and cut him. And for a black man during that period to do something like that in the South was time for white folks to come and hang him. But I remember my family coming together, my father's side as well as my mother's side, and collaborating with each other to see how they could get my grandfather out of there, because they knew what the repercussions could be.

I might have been about four or five years old at that time, listening to them trying to plan to get my grandfather out of there. In fact, they did, that night, and he left for Dallas, Texas, and moved in with his sister, Lily Bynum. And over the next year and a half, they planned out how to move the whole family to Dallas. And during that period of time, my father and mother separated.

My grandfather snuck back to Louisiana one night with some family members and an old truck—we had one of those big, old cars. And all the children and my grandparents were in the car, and the extended family was in the truck, and we got on the highway late at night and relocated to Dallas.

My mother, who is still alive, is still a fighter; her name is Viola Ross. At that time, she was Viola Bernard. My grandparents were Isadore and Alberta Hill. At times, my mother would have two jobs. They varied. One time, she was working at Neiman Marcus when black folks couldn't even come in the front door to buy. Or she was working as a nurse's aide. At the same time, she might be doing somebody's housekeeping, cleaning up someone's house. And every year, she'd get a second job at the state fair.

In Dallas, we lived in Oak Cliff, down in "the Bottom," we used to call it, over by Golden Gate Baptist Church. And we moved around a little bit. But Dallas was segregated, just like in Louisiana. Very segregated. You know, again, the thing that protected us was the fact that we had a close-knit family.

When I was about nine years old, in 1952, I participated in a march for the YWCA. That was the year that the churches—everybody in the black community—was boycotting the Texas State Fair. That was when the state fair was only open to blacks one day a week. My mother specifically told me, "Do not go beyond those gates of the state fair. Meet us right there at that gate. Don't move. Stay right with your group. And we'll make it up there to get you." And I went on the march, and we all wore these little white boots that were all shined up. And when I got to the gates of the state fair, I waited. It was hard for my parents to get up there. And some of my friends decided to go in, and I went on in with them and walked around in the state fair with them.

Well, my grandmother, Alberta Hill, was a very determined woman, and she came looking for me. But it wasn't easy for her. I think her right leg was locked—her knee was locked. When she was pregnant with my mother, she went to a baptism down at the river in Louisiana and caught a cold in that knee. She went to a doctor, and the doctor put a cast on that leg, and he left it on there too long, and so her bones locked together. So she had a stiff leg. We would say, "Mom, why didn't y'all sue at that time? Sue the doctors?" She'd say, "You know, at that time, black folks didn't sue no doctors or struggle against any white folks. This is what ended up happening to me." But even with that leg, my grandmother could get around, and she walked that whole state fair looking for me because she said what she remembered were those little white boots that all of us had on and trying to find us. And she found me. And I learned a lesson from that, what a boycott was all about, that we stick together, and I don't care how bad you want something, you do not break that boycott.

We finally won our demands with the state of Texas about the state fair. That boycott was very successful because we were then able to go to the state fair whenever we wanted. But after that, I didn't care about the fair anymore, because I had learned my lesson, and I didn't have any desire after that to go to the state fair. The lessons that I learned from my mother and my grandparents have stuck with me for years.

At the same time, my church was also playing a big role with us. My minister was giving us reports about the civil-rights movement that was developing. I remember in my younger years, even prior to high school, going to church and learning about how they were trying to move to outlaw the electric chair because the majority of the people that were being electrocuted here were black folks, for crimes they had not committed. I was beginning to hate this society that I lived in because why would the Constitution say that we were created equal and at the same time, black folks could not enjoy life like everybody else?

The NAACP was constantly organizing. We all were members of the youth contingent of the NAACP. But I would never go to any of the meetings because the youth were not the ones making the decisions. But I was very supportive, and my mother made sure that we were supportive and active in different things. Our church was our foundation for that. Dallas was so segregated. We only knew our communities.

In Dallas, city officials claimed that a black person—they used the word *colored*—was not equal to a white person, and discrimination was being practiced and carried out every day. When we left home and got on the buses, we saw it; in Kresge's we had to go to the little counter that said Colored Only. We had to go the "colored" bathroom. When we went to Louisiana to visit my family, we couldn't stop in any service stations or anything like that; we had to go to "colored" bathrooms, *if* they had one, or we had to stop and use the bathroom behind some trees. Right now, my children will tell you that when we travel, I always have toilet paper and paper towels—we didn't have paper towels at that time, or Wet Ones, or something like that in the car. We had to have toilet paper because we knew we were going to have to stop behind a tree to use the bathroom because there were no facilities for black folks at that time.

My mother kept us involved, not only in the church, but understanding what my grandmother and my grandfather used to say, "Look, you don't have to take what we've had to live up under. We've tried to fight back." And my grandfather was a prime example of that, fighting back. But my mother made sure we understood that we didn't have to take this mess out here. We could get involved. And once I went to Southern University in Baton Rouge, Louisiana, I was involved.

They desegregated the buses my senior year in high school around 1960–61, and in Dallas, we were able to ride the buses and sit anywhere we wanted. Anywhere we wanted! And we made sure—we had a pact with black students from all over—when we got on the bus, we'd sit in the front, and if there were several of us, all of us would sit in a different row. And if white folks didn't want to sit with us, then they had to stand. That was *their* choice to make. We made sure that we took the seat that we wanted, and we were waiting for that bus driver to tell us what they generally would tell us, and that is, "Move to the back." And we would never move. So we began to take a stand in high school, just on that bus alone. That laid the groundwork, but when I got to Southern University, I was told by my parents and everybody, "We're sending you to Southern to get an education. Now, don't get involved that way. Get your education first. That is the key to your freedom." Well, that became a contradiction with me because we had always been involved in the fight for our rights. And now my parents were telling me don't get involved because the president of Southern had expelled a lot of my cousins when they participated in the demonstrations.

By the time I got to Southern the next year, the students were not organizing. But CORE, the Congress of Racial Equality, at that time had come into the state and was doing some organizing for people to get involved in voter registration. I was interested, and I began to go to some of the meetings because those meetings were held at my aunt's café, which was located a few steps on the other side of the [Baton Rouge] city line in Port Allen. So we could stay open all night and everything. And my mother got involved, I got involved, and our whole thing was to try to integrate the schools there in Port Allen. Then my family started splitting somewhat around that, too, because there were different positions around how we should be moving as far as integration. And I saw the strength of my aunts on my father's side, the strength of my mother and all of them. These women were very influential. They really were my heroes because they stood strong, saying, "If y'all got to demonstrate against a store down the street that has shot a little black boy in Baton Rouge somewhere and had a store over there in Port Allen, we're going to be out here with you."

I'll never forget that my aunt who owned the café would be in her old pink Buick every day as we demonstrated in Port Allen. I'd go to school;

I'd come home and get in the picket line, until we closed down that store. That was a major victory for Port Allen, to close that store down. My uncle who worked at the port told me, "Stay involved." And he was one of the people that were instrumental in helping Port Allen to become a part of the boycott of the stores. He and my aunt Gert; her name was Gertrude Hardy. I called my uncle "Kink" Hardy so many times that I forgot his given name.

I was at Southern for a year and a half. And then I went back to Dallas. I went to Arlington State [in Arlington, Texas, just west of Dallas]. Arlington State had opened up, had desegregated. Some friends of mine I had graduated high school with, they had come back home, too, after a year and a half, and we all went to Arlington State for a semester. This was the first time I ever went to an integrated school. And I'm sitting up in this class, and it's obvious that my history teacher didn't like the idea of black people being in there. You could tell by the racial slurs he would make. And you could tell that a lot of the students didn't want us on the campus. One day, I was in my physical education class, and we had to team up for tennis, and I ended up with a young lady I had gone to elementary school and high school with. And we could tell that the white girls didn't want to play us. Their whole thing was to aim for our heads. We had never played tennis before, right? So we got pretty good at it, and we were able to retaliate also and hit those balls back in the same way. But it was obvious that we were not welcome on that campus.

From Arlington State, I went back to Southern. I got a call from my grandfather, who had gone down there for a week and had seen my uncle. My uncle, whom I was really close with, had gotten really sick, and my uncle was asking for me to come back. And so when I went back, it was at the same time that the March on Washington was being organized. I was on the train on the way back, and at that time, in Plaquemine, Louisiana, the Klan was attacking the rallies that were taking place around voter registration. They had taken their horses up in the churches in Plaquemine, stomped some people, and I got heavily involved there. I didn't make it to the March on Washington because my uncle was ill and too much was happening in Plaquemine, Louisiana.

Plaquemine was where the organizing drive started for the civil-rights movement in Louisiana. Voter registration was the first priority.

And because of that a young lady got stomped in her stomach by a Klan horseman, because they came up into the church where the rallies were being held.

Ronald Moore was head of the state project. And James Farmer was the director of CORE at that time. They had to be snuck out of Plaquemine in a casket, one in a casket and one in a compartment under the casket, in order to save their lives. The Klan would have tried to kill them. They did not want black people to be registered voters. Plaquemine was like the headquarters of what was happening at that particular time in building the civil-rights movement.

After my uncle died, I joined the task force for CORE. That was in 1964. We went through a week of training to be a civil-rights worker, because you had to learn civil disobedience, you had to learn the laws. You had to learn how to conduct campaigns and to achieve the goals we were trying to accomplish. We were not only trying to get everybody to become registered voters, but we were challenging the forms and policies that were used in Louisiana, in Mississippi, and different other areas in the Southern states to keep people from becoming registered voters. At one time it was the poll-tax situation that they would use. This particular time, it was the forms that they would use to block a lot of people from becoming registered voters, besides the intimidation and harassment. These forms that they used to be a registered voter were like filling out a form to try to get into your doctoral degree. So we had to learn how to fill those forms out as well as teach the people in the community how to fill them out. And at the same time, we were trying to get the federal court to change the situation in these states. So that was the campaign that year. But that year was a tough one, too, because I got assigned with a whole lot of other folks to Monroe, Louisiana, which is up in northern Louisiana.

Interesting enough, some of the people that helped us and helped to protect us and helped us to secure an office in Monroe, Louisiana, were the Black Muslims. People had said how much the Muslims hated white folks, but they were the ones that helped protect all of us—the black and the white civil-rights activists. The community in Monroe, Louisiana, was something for me because this was the first time I was in a city without my family being around. If I went from Dallas to Louisiana or vice versa, my family was all around, and the protection was there. When we demonstrated in Port Allen, my family was there to make sure to protect us when a lady tried to hit us with her car in a picket line. My aunt, who was sitting by the side in her car, rode the lady down and told her she better not ever try that again because "you harm the hair on any one of those children up there and particularly"—and she looked at me— she said, "particularly that one right there, that's mine, and you better not mess with her."

Well, the only people I knew in Monroe, Louisiana, were the people I had just met that summer. And this was the first time that I had worked closely, in particular, with white people, with Anglo Americans. This was the first time as far as planning out strategies and tactics and stuff like that, and being a part of some type of organization on my own. It was a new experience. We all lived in freedom houses. These were houses that people in the community had rented out to CORE. We lived with a lady who was a senior citizen. She lived alone. She was black. And she had three rooms, which she rented out to us. The agreement was that she would provide us with coffee, and we had food and other stuff we needed that we bought and put in her refrigerator. She was like our house-mother. Her house was in an alley in Monroe, Louisiana.

Every day we were testing for segregation—at lunch counters [and other accommodations]. We had groups of people going into places to see whether or not they'd be waited on and served. We found out that the community was more involved than what we thought. Sometimes in the evening I would go and sit on the porch with some of the folks in the community, and I found out that every night, the people in that sur-rounding area where we were staying were sitting up all night, watching over us to stop any possibility of Klansmen or people coming down that alley and trying to deal with us, because they had tried it one time, and the community got organized. The word was out that no white person could come down that alley other than the people in the civil-rights movement. Because in our household, our housemother not only had myself and another woman from the civil-rights movement, but she also had two males, one of them being Anglo American, and another Anglo American male that would be there at times.

We never stayed in any freedom house that a white person owned because you would get them killed. We had two freedom houses in Monroe, Louisiana, one that I stayed in and another one in another neighborhood where a lot of the other males stayed. There were four at our household sometimes, and then with the [civil-rights] recruiter, there were five. And then, over at the other place, there had to be about four or five. Every morning, diligently, we'd be having breakfast at 7:30 A.M. at a restaurant that we had contracted with, and then we'd be at the office by eight-thirty. And we would work at that office until five o'clock every day, and I was assigned to the office. And in the evening, we would have our lunch, and we'd have dinner, and then we generally had some kind of community function that we had to attend. That was a daily routine all during the summertime during the civil-rights movement. We either were going door to door or we were testing. That went on for months. And when we would have to go to our state meeting, we would have to go down to Baton Rouge at that time because the operation had moved from Plaquemine. We would have to get on the road with our people in Jonesboro, Louisiana, to try to hook up, where we could travel together. Now that became real dangerous because they knew all our cars, and they would be watching for us on Highway 55 to try to attack us, and we always made sure the most experienced drivers would be in the driver's seat. We always had an agreement: Do not stop, and try to stick together. Generally, we would get chased all the time on Highway 55, chased into Mississippi—Vicksburg, Mississippi—because that was a short way to go to Baton Rouge. You go from northern Baton Rouge on Highway 55, go into Vicksburg, Mississippi, and drop back down into Louisiana. But we would always get chased.

In one area off of Highway 55, we knew that we had a place that we could go and relax during that trip and kind of get them off our tail, and that was at the home of this black priest. Don't ask me his name because I cannot remember it. And if I could, he was a hero, because this man always would be available as soon as we called to not only hide us but to be able to give us some refreshments and allow us to stay there for a couple of hours to get the people off our tail.

Monroe, Louisiana, was something else because at that time, we found out in the biggest park they had signs up: Colored Only. They had split the park up. The best part of the park, where all the equipment, the swimming pool, and all that stuff was, it was white only. And then, one night, in 1964, after the civil-rights bill had been passed and signed, a couple of the young black males were going across the park to buy cigarettes. I think it might have been a nickel at the time, get one or two cigarettes for a nickel. And on their way back, a gang of whites whipped them. They came to our office the next day, and to see that was shocking to me, to see all these gashes in their bodies, for just being black. They came straight to our office the next day and joined the movement. That same week, or sometime during that period of time, a woman that was on the bus stop trying to go to work also got whipped by a gang of young whites. The whites had intensified the attacks because we had intensified our testing, our demonstrations. This woman had gashes all in her legs.

I was in Monroe, Louisiana, from June of that year until approximately October. I went back to Southern for one semester, and that was the beginning of 1964. And I joined the movement that summer, to become a direct task worker. I left in December of that year to come to Detroit with a man I'd met named Dave Kramer, because he had asked me to marry him.

Dave Kramer had taken a leave of absence from his job here in Detroit. He was working for Ford Motor Company at the headquarters. He was designing cars. And he took a leave of absence to come to the civil-rights movement. And once he got down there and began to be confronted with what was going on, he got beat up. See, Kramer was Anglo American. He decided to resign from Ford Motor Company and stay down there in the civil-rights movement and rededicate his life to that. We couldn't get married in Louisiana because of the miscegenation law at that time. We came to Detroit because he had worked with people up here. There was a community group that was trying to bring Saul Alinsky in from the Industrial Areas Foundation to train them to organize their communities. They had invited us up here for the holidays, and these were his friends. So we got married up here in Detroit. We were up here for two weeks. I met a whole bunch of other folks. And they approached him at that time about coming back and being an organizer.

Well, on our way up from Louisiana, we saw a lot of crosses that were burnt throughout the South the night before the election of Lyndon

Baines Johnson. They burnt those crosses all over the place. We were able to capture one, and we brought one up here on our trip so people could see what one of those crosses looked like. We brought up a White Citizens' Council sign to let them see how this stuff looked, because people were not aware up here that these things existed all over the South. We were trying to educate folks that the White Citizens' Council generally was composed of businesspeople who were doing the funding of a lot of the Klan's operations. We had to cover all that stuff up; we were in danger, because we had to make sure that we did not get stopped on the highway. Dave, on our way up here, had to hide in the backseat of the car because there were four of us that came—three blacks and one white. We went through Louisiana, Mississippi, and Tennessee at nighttime. We had to make sure that Dave could not be seen. But on the way back down, it was only Dave and me. By the time he and I got to the Mississippi border, I had to lay down in the back of the car on the floor with a blanket over me, where I could not be seen because if we had gotten stopped, it would have been our death. So I had to travel that way.

Once I left Louisiana, I had to promise Ronnie Moore and the staff that one of us would be back for the summertime's project and to help train new task-force workers. That person had to be me because Dave was going to take a job as an organizer for the West Central Organization [WCO] in Detroit. I began to work with him as a volunteer in building a community organization up here. The biggest fight was the question of urban renewal. I had never experienced urban renewal before. And I began to learn about the court systems. And then I got hired by one of the organizations, which was part of the WCO, the Hotel, Motel, and Restaurant Workers Union. It was my first experience with unions. I was hired as one of the clerical workers there.

The overall goal of the president of Hotel, Motel, and Restaurant Workers was to make me one of the representatives for the union. I wanted to learn contracts. I wanted to learn all there was about the union. I didn't know what being one of the representatives was all about. But I worked there, and I began to experience the discrimination against the workforce within the union. The membership was okay, but the administration had problems. But I learned about the contracts, and [the union president] put me over the organizing—picket lines and stuff like that—that was taking place against Travelodge. He put me over a lot of that. But at the same time, I was participating with WCO and doing the Alinsky-type organizing that was taking place in the community against urban renewal. It was a busy time as far as organizing in the community.

Then in 1965, we were told at WCO that there was going to be a poor people's conference in Syracuse, New York. WCO organized a bus that December to take a busload of community folks to this poor people's conference in Syracuse, New York. This was quite an experience for us. We went on that bus trip, and when I got there, I saw some of the people that were in the civil-rights movement with me. And they requested that my husband and I and a few other people sit down with Frances Piven and Richard Cloud [her husband], who were thinking about the concept, along with George Wiley (who had been in CORE with me), to talk about the need to build a welfare-rights organization. But I could not commit, nor could my husband at that time, to organize directly for welfare rights. I told him [George] we would help to organize some people to come to the meeting in Washington that he was talking about. A march was taking place from Cleveland to Columbus, Ohio, and they wanted people to be mobilized here or in Washington. So I started helping to do some cases here against the welfare department. I had never taken on the welfare department before. We began to have a committee that was dealing with nothing but social-services programs. So much was going on at that time. And after a couple of years, my husband decided he was going back to school to get a master's degree in social work. And I took the job at WCO and became an organizer. That's when I learned how to organize block clubs and organize against urban renewal. And then I had to face up to myself [and my own personal problems] a year later, and my husband and I separated.

Some ministers and all the rest of us were trying to save this particular community. I began to learn about condemnation court—how the city could condemn properties through the court system. Each step of the way, I was learning. But in 1966, we were facing federal penitentiary because in this area, Research Park (that Wayne State University was trying to get and use as a research area), the workers who lived in these homes took a stand and said, "We're not giving up our houses." And we decided as an organization, because we had been working over there with them, that we would support them. And the police arrested us. I got arrested with a gang of ministers from different denominations. And they put a felony on us, felonious assault and battery. Eventually, through our organizing, the charges were dropped, but the judge really didn't want to drop them. He wanted to send us to the penitentiary for seven years.

During the rebellion [the Detroit race riot of 1967], I was out there trying to help save our community, making sure the young people didn't get hurt. Later, we built the League of Revolutionary Black Workers, which was in a lot of the major factories around here, as well as in about fourteen high schools. The Black Student United Front and some of the elementary schools and some of the hospitals and clinics and some of the social workers and churches were all a part of the League of Revolutionary Black Workers. Our main goal was to get some justice for blacks within the factories and within the schools.

At the time of the rebellion, there was a lot of police brutality. A lot of injustice was going on at the time. Well, there was an after-hours joint down on 12th Street, which is now named Rosa Parks Avenue. And there was a lot of harassment by the police. And finally, the people just got fed up with them, and after they had brought everybody out on 12th Street that night, and people said they just got fed up and started rebelling.

Rosa Parks worked over in Conyers's office, Congressman John Conyers's office. I was in the South during the bus boycott. She had her own little organization. And when I came up here to get married, people asked me if I would escort Rosa Parks around Detroit—Fannie Lou Hamer wanted us both to go around together. Fannie Lou Hamer was very instrumental in the civil-rights movement. Detroit was and still is a hotbed of activity.

Well, around 1970, I was approached by some folks about going to New York and helping Welfare Rights to reconstitute itself. Welfare Rights had grown to over 100,000 members. I had maintained my membership in Welfare Rights, although I was not doing direct organizing. I had helped in WCO and made sure WCO had Welfare Rights as a part of it and helped organize the Welfare Rights in Jeffries Public Housing. George Wiley had called me and said, "Marian, why don't you come on staff of Welfare Rights?"

I said, "George, you know how we organize, to make sure that the people who are in control are the membership. I don't think the leadership in this area is going to appreciate that. And they're not going to hire me. So it's best that I stay where I am." And so I was not hired, but I still supported and worked directly with Welfare Rights.

In 1975, I started working full-time with Welfare Rights. Before then, I was active in our Welfare Rights group and maintaining another job. But when I had my baby in 1970 and I was separated from my husband, I got on aid, and I had to personally confront the welfare system. I had to go in there and fight it to try to get some help.

I went to the Welfare Rights second convention. It was held here in Detroit. And my cousin Charlie Granger, who had been a football player at one time, and his wife, Barbara, called me and said they were coming up to the convention, because Charlie was working with Welfare Rights also. And that's when I first met Annie Smart from Louisiana. They talked me into going to the convention—"Come on, Marian"—I wasn't going to go. I said, "Since it's at Wayne State, I'll go over there to this convention." So I went, and I got hooked again. I was so proud of these women, these women that were not only able to articulate their problem. These women were strong; these women were ready to fight for their children to have a better life—and not only for their children but for poor children throughout the country—to fight the battle against poverty.

So when I was asked in 1975 if I would go to New York and help bring recognition to Welfare Rights on a national level, I said, "Yes, I will come. And I will get on aid and try to organize if I don't get a job." And I went to New York, and I started organizing. I took the challenge, and I went there and began to do that work without any salary or anything. I got on welfare because Welfare Rights did not have any paid staff at the time. The second year, I was able to get a grant to go to school, which paid for a lot, coupled with my welfare check, because at that time, the grant was waived as far as trying to obtain an education. So I had a busy life in New York. We started Welfare Workers for Justice because of the economic crisis in the factories—a lot of people were laid off. We began to see a trend that technology was creeping in. And the reserve army of unemployed was beginning to join the permanent army of unemployed.

And so what we did in New York was, we didn't go to using the name New York Welfare Rights Organization. We selected the name Welfare Workers for Justice because our attitude was that we were all workers. Some of us were temporarily unemployed, in low-paying jobs or no jobs at all.

The first thing I did with Welfare Workers for Justice was to take on what I was a victim of myself. I made sure I went through the process. And that was standing out in the cold at four-thirty in the morning, trying to be one of the first people to get an application into the Department of Human Resources there in New York. People would be freezing to death. I mean, they would take the garbage cans and light them up where people could be warm. The fire department would come out, put the fires out, and people would light them back up because they needed heat out there. This was to be able to be in line to get some services from the welfare department. People were experiencing a lot of unemployment at the time, so those lines were long. It took us several days to try to get some help from the welfare department or to begin to process our case. But if you were eligible, you had to go through a process of a face-to-face redetermination every six months, which was very degrading. It was like being on probation. It was like starting all over again. So that began my challenge—how to eliminate this face-to-face redetermination. Even the vets had to go through it. And we were successful in getting redetermination eliminated in New York. Then we took on the whole question around being SSI [Supplemental Security Income] recipients, which included a lot of senior citizens. They were eating dog food because they could not afford any food. There was a thing in New York which said the state could opt out, and it's still there—either give food stamps or give ten dollars in their check. They opted to give the ten dollars to cover food for folks each month in their check. So dog food was more cost-efficient to the seniors than the actual food itself.

Another struggle that we took on when I was there involved a young kid who was hit by a car. He was an Italian American. And his mother didn't know what to do because of the fact that her husband was usually the person that took care of everything in their particular culture. And her husband was in Attica—you know, the prison. It hit the news, how the child might not live. Well, I got on the phone that night and found out where I could get more information concerning this family. And I

Marian Kramer speaking at the Up and Out of Poverty rally, State Capitol lawn,
Lansing, Michigan, 1991.

was able to get them to let the father out for three days to check on the family, and I was able to talk to the father, and I told him to meet me at Welfare Rights at the Department of Human Resources the next day, and we'd try to help him get some help for his family. And we did.

When I first moved to New York, I lived in Park Slope. My whole time in New York, I lived in Brooklyn—Park Slope, Crown Heights. I was in New York for two and a half years. And then I went back to Detroit, and I've been here ever since. I figured if we're going to make this organization successful, we need to be around organized labor. And what better place than Detroit. And I moved back here, and at the same time, I began to date General Baker Jr., who is now my husband (and whom I had met some years earlier when I started organizing in Detroit).

Welfare Rights was built on the heels of the civil-rights movement, and Welfare Rights was being built at the time the Dodge Revolutionary Union Movement (DRUM) was built on the heels of the rebellion. It was the spark that started a lot of union movements within the various factories here in Detroit. We were in fourteen different high schools with the Black Student United Front. We spoke to the problems that black students were facing in these schools in Detroit, as well as those that many were facing in the auto plants.

In the 1990s, Faith Evans, who had been in Welfare Rights and had been working with the National Organization for Women [NOW], and I sat down and talked about whether Welfare Rights and NOW could work together. Patricia Ireland was the president at the time. And I said, "Why should we? We have been treated so bad in the past by not only different women's organizations—be they black, white, green or yellow— why should we stick our necks out again?" I said, "Look, our meeting would not just consist of the women, but it would be some men who are in leadership also." So NOW helped, through Faith Evans, to raise funds and brought in twenty-five of us to meet with them. And that was a hell of a meeting that took place between us and NOW. And those women were in tears when they heard how we had been treated in the past. And we agreed to work together. We ended up being a part of all their marches after that, because they knew we had a stand also for choice. I told them, "Your overall struggle is for choice. The women we represent, they don't even have an opportunity to make a choice because they don't have the economic base. And yes, we're going to fight that the federal government should be responsible for women to be able to have that right to choice, whether or not they want to have a baby, or whether or not they want to have an abortion. That is our position. But you have to also fight with us." And we became instrumental in a lot of NOW's conventions.

I'm codirector, executive director, of Detroit NFI, Detroit Neighborhood and Family Initiative, and I'm working to build a back-to-basics community partnership. And a component of that is welfare-rights organization. I'm the chairperson, copresident, of the National Welfare Rights Union.

If this country claims that it cares about the well-being of children, it's a lie. It's a lie, and we're here to say that that is a lie. So I'm going to stay in this fight. I just tell people, "Bury me with my boots on." One of our women, Guida West, wrote the book *The National Welfare Rights Movement*. And she not only wrote it, Guida was a part of it and still is. She lives in New York. Guida is almost in her eighties. We have another woman there in Texas that's been very instrumental in welfare rights and one of our heroes, Irena Edwards, who lives in Houston. Irena is in her eighties and in declining health, but Irena kept Houston on the map. Originally from Opelousas, Louisiana, but she's a Texan now. So these women still exist around the country. There are not too many of us that started out at the beginning of the movement. But I've been fortunate.

What keeps me going? I've been fortunate to have known and learned a lot from these women and from the men that have been a part of fighting against injustice and fighting for a better world that we know can happen. We have enough here in this country to make sure—we can build houses on the assembly line in less than forty-five minutes, but yet the homeless population is constantly growing. Education is not the priority it needs to be. Quality education for everybody? We don't have it. So Welfare Rights has always stood on the premise—not always, but we framed the program back in the eighties—that said we wanted universal health care. We have changed that now. We want health care to be nationalized. We're calling for the nationalization of water now because right now in Highland Park, Michigan, where I live, they're trying to privatize our water. Our city is being run by nonelected officials. We've been taken over by the state. And if you want to learn something, see how they're moving on Detroit and all the other cities in the state of Michigan; this is what they're trying to do everywhere. We pay the highest water bill in the nation, probably in the world, in this little city. Forty thousand people in the city of Detroit, in one year's time, had their water shut off. We know that we don't have to live this way. And that's what keeps me going. I don't want my children—I don't want anyone's children—to have to live like that.

[Interview by Alan Govenar, March 18 and March 20, 2005]

*Jacob Lawrence, Dallas, Texas, 1998.*

# JACOB LAWRENCE

ARTIST

*September 7, 1917–June 9, 2000*

*Jacob Lawrence grew up in Harlem during the Great Depression. He was raised by his mother, who had separated from his father soon after the births of his sister, Geraldine, and brother, William. Because his mother was a domestic who was often on welfare, Lawrence was forced to work in a printer's shop and in a laundry to help support his family. At night, he attended classes in painting between 1932 and 1937. He received training in the Harlem Art Workshops, supported first by the College Art Association and later by the Federal Art Project of the WPA. Lawrence attended the American Artists' School in New York City from 1937 to 1939. He had his first one-person exhibition at the Harlem YMCA in 1938 and achieved national acclaim when his* Migration of the Negro *series was exhibited at New York's Downtown Gallery in 1941. New York was a frontier for him and other African American artists, providing opportunities that did not exist elsewhere in the United States in the 1930s and 1940s. Throughout his career, Lawrence focused on scenes from his Harlem background and the African American experience, creating historical series, including* Toussaint L'Ouverture *(1937–1939),* Frederick Douglass *(1938–1939), and* Harriet Tubman *(1939–1940), as well as thematic works, such as* Theater *(1951–1952) and* Wounded Man *(1968), about the civil-rights conflicts in the United States. In 1941, Lawrence married Gwendolyn Knight; they lived in Seattle, Washington, where Lawrence was a professor of art at the University of Washington from 1971 until his retirement in 1987.*

MY FAMILY WAS A PART of the migration. That is, my mother, my sister, and my brother. My father and mother were separated. I was born in Atlantic City, New Jersey. They were moving up the coast, as many families were moving during that migration. And I was part of that. We moved up to various cities until we arrived—the last two cities I can remember before moving to New York were Easton, Pennsylvania, and Philadelphia, Pennsylvania. And then we finally settled in New York City. So that was my upbringing. My young years were spent just doing that: traveling, as part of the migration, and that was it.

I was aware of people moving, older people like my mother's peers—I would hear them talk about how another family has arrived. And these were the people who would mention the fact that they had been here a few years, and they were seeing the new migrants coming in and settling or moving on. And I didn't realize what it was at the time, of course; it's only in later years that I realized what was going on.

For me, there were bright lights, the excitement, the movement, the texture, the vitality. I didn't know it in those terms then, but it's only in remembering my subconscious feeling of moving into this great metropolis or into this great Harlem community, which was a part of New York City. And that's remained with me. In fact, much of my work is based on that experience.

My mother's name was Rosalie Armstead. She was born in Fredericksburg, Virginia. My father's name was Jacob, and he was born in South Carolina. And he worked as a cook on the railroad. I was very young when they split up. We arrived in New York in 1930 when I was thirteen years of age. We were coming from Pennsylvania. I must have been six, seven, around that, when they split up. My parents were on the move, like many of the migrants were. Maybe I was like two—one or two—when they left the South.

It's only in retrospect that I can realize the significance of the migration to my own work. I couldn't analyze it like that. Not at that time. I could only see it from a child's point of view. I didn't realize the significance of it at the time. When I did the *Migration* series, of course, I realized it. But prior to that time, I did not know the significance of it. There was so much going on. The lynchings were at their peak in the South; people were talking about this. There were the Marcus Garvey people. There were black nationalists. There was just so much happening. There was so much going on that I couldn't analyze it. I wasn't a sociologist.

In New York, my mother was able to maintain us. We lived in an apartment in Harlem. I think we arrived at 137th Street, right near Harlem Hospital. We always lived up around that area. I had one brother and one sister. Geraldine was my sister, and William was my brother.

We lived in a railroad flat. When you say "small," it had two bedrooms and a kitchen and a living room, like many of the places in the Harlem community. Much was going on in that part of Harlem. You'd walk up and down Seventh Avenue or Lenox Avenue. There were so-called soapbox orators. I didn't always understand the content of what they were saying, but it was full of life, full of vitality, full of energy, and it was only later that I realized that many of them were the Garveyites, the religious people, the communists, and they were all very active. It was a very active community. And the churches played a very vital role in our community. I was baptized in the Abyssinian Baptist Church. That was Adam Clayton Powell's father's church, and then the younger Powell took over. And that was a very big church in the community. A very important church in the community.

I got placed in a foster home right after my mother and father were separated. I must have been seven, around there. That wasn't in New York. That was before we got there. My brother and sister were placed separately. I didn't know enough to be scared. You don't realize these things as a youngster; you don't realize what's going on.

But when we got to Harlem, we lived with my mother. She was a domestic. I know she didn't work in the Harlem community, because the people in the Harlem community for the most part didn't hire domestics. They were all blacks. My mother worked like most domestics; she worked, I guess, throughout the city, in the Bronx and Manhattan and wherever people could find work.

I didn't realize that I had gotten there at the end of the Harlem Renaissance. It kind of teetered off in the thirties at the beginning of the Great Depression. But the important years, I think, took place in the twenties. And after the Great Depression, what we know of the Renaissance started to phase out.

I went to Public School 68, elementary school; Public School 89, which is a junior high; and the High School of Commerce. I didn't get interested in art until I was at the Utopia Children's Center, Utopia House. My mother enrolled us there when she was working and you could go there and get lunch for a dime, the children, and there was also an after-school center that offered a program in arts and crafts. And that's when I had the opportunity. I was encouraged to work with paint. I loved color. I must have been about thirteen or fourteen years of age.

The most influential artist for me was Charles Alston. When I was thirteen, he was twenty-three, which is quite a difference when you're young. And he was taking his graduate work, I think, at Columbia University, and he was also hired by the Utopia House as a counselor, as a person who taught arts and crafts. He knew I liked color, like most kids; that's not unusual. And he encouraged me. And that's when I was encouraged to work with color, to play with color, and had a wonderful time.

My first paintings were abstract. I didn't get interested in figurative work until I started telling stories of the community, seeing people in the community, the pool halls, the churches, the people on the street, the soapbox orators, and so on. And that's what stimulated my interest to try to portray this life.

I was encouraged in my art when I was in high school, but not to the same degree as I was encouraged outside. Let's go back a moment. You know, during that period is the Great Depression. The Roosevelt administration established arts centers throughout the country, which gave people work, like teachers and counselors and people like that, to run these centers. Augusta Savage was one. Charles Alston was another. And I was encouraged to attend. After I left the Utopia House, Alston got his own place on 147th Street, and I was encouraged to come in and join the group—people of all ages. And these centers were wonderful because they gave us the opportunity—we met people of all ages. Of course, they were completely free, and if you were interested in music, dance, theater, any of the arts, performing arts like this, you attended one of these centers. And I went into one of these centers during the early thirties when I was about fifteen, sixteen years of age. I met all kinds of people, you know, not just people from the Harlem community, but people outside the community, people of all ethnic backgrounds. It was just a wonderful thing.

It was an inspiration to me. I realize it more now, I think, than I did then. Oh, I think there were many artists who got their start there and who are actually working now. Many of them are dead, of course. My wife came up during that period. There was Ronald Joseph. There was Romare Bearden, who was not a member of the center because he was a welfare worker, but he attended the center. And so there were people like that who had outside jobs. They would congregate and meet in the centers in the evening, so it was just a wonderful experience.

I didn't graduate from high school. I just left school. That must have been about the second year in high school. I sold newspapers, I worked in hand laundries, just did anything, like many young people of my age did.

But I did receive a scholarship at the American Artists' School, which is now nonexistent. It's been nonexistent for years. And I think it was a left-wing school. That was the school I attended—outside the Harlem community. When I went to the Harlem Arts Center, that was a school, too, but it was in Harlem. The American Artists' School was on Fourteenth Street in Manhattan between Fifth and Sixth Avenues, I think. I was in and out of the American Artists' School in a couple of years.

At the Harlem artists' school we had several teachers: Augusta Savage, Charles Alston, Sara West, William H. Johnson, Ronald Joseph. Many active artists. And it was free. This was under the Federal Art Project.

The first opportunity I had to show my work was in the Harlem community. It was at the James Weldon Johnson Literary Guild. And the name means just what it says. Women who were very interested in the life of James Weldon Johnson, they set up this program. And they gave me a show. It was at one of the Harlem art centers. There were about four of them. Augusta Savage had one on 136th or 137th Street. My wife went to her center. Then there was Alston's center. That was on 141st Street. And then there were two others in the Harlem community that I remember.

Harlem was very active at that time. There were so many people on the streets. People played music just like you see them play on the streets today. But then they played instruments up from the South, washboards, harmonicas, and things of that sort.

I was a young fellow then. I never thought of nightclubs or anything like that. I lived at home with my mother until I began to work on the Federal Art Project. And that would have been about when I was twenty-one years of age. That's when I established my own studio.

I was invited to sign up for the project, to get a job on the Federal Art

Project, which many people did. I was twenty-one years of age. And Augusta Savage was responsible for that. Augusta Savage was very well known, very highly respected in the black artistic community. And she was just a wonderful person. She took me down to the hiring office. She was a mentor in the community with many of the young black artists. And she had taken me down in 1936 to sign me up for the project. They told her I was too young, to come back next year. Well, I went back to Harlem; I'd completely forgotten about it. But she hadn't forgotten. And she took me down again in 1938, when I was twenty-one years of age. And I was signed up, and I made a fabulous salary of $23.86 a week, which was a lot of money then. I also served time in the CCC, Civilian Conservation Corps. I worked on a dam up in New York State. It was the first time I remember going into the countryside. It was nice. I was around people my own age. It was a good experience.

My first studio of my own was on 125th Street, between Lenox and Seventh Avenues. It was a loft apartment. I was able to get that after I received a fellowship award. At that time, my work was figurative. But first, before doing people, I just did designs, like arabesque designs and things like that. And then I moved on. I did masks—not representing any particular person or persons. And then I started doing street scenes. That was it.

I started thinking about the *Migration* series about 1939. That was completed in 1941. I was inspired by the people talking about people coming up from the South. That was a big thing on people's minds. The lynchings that went on in the South were at their peak. The *Amsterdam News* reported that almost every week a lynching was taking place. And I was doing people on the street even before that, and then I decided to do a series, and that's how the *Migration* things came out. And it shows people, North, South, North, South, North, South, with the panels alternating like that. This was happening in the South, and then we moved north, happening in the South, we moved north, happening in the South, we moved north, until the sixty panels were completed.

New York represented a frontier for these people that were coming. The opportunities, jobs, and we were going to war.

The *Migration* series brought me attention outside the community, outside the Harlem community. But I got my first attention, I'll always remember this, from the people of the Harlem community, and that's something I'll never forget. That was a very important thing, like the James Weldon Johnson Literary Guild. My support came from the black community. The life of my work was that community.

I was drafted in 1943. I went into the United States Coast Guard. And my first station was aboard ship, the USS *Sea Cloud*. That was the name of the ship. And I was stationed, I think, in Curtis Bay, Maryland. But you know, that's many years ago, so I can't remember exactly. It was segregated in the service, but this ship, the *Sea Cloud*, was an experiment, one of the first experiments to have an integrated ship, during the war. The segregation was beginning to break down throughout the army and navy, throughout the services.

I was in the service twenty-five months. I went overseas aboard a troop transport. I went to the southern port of England, Southampton. And then we went to France and to a part of India, then Egypt. On a troop transport, you really got around. It was a new experience for me. If you had to be in the war, then the navy or coast guard, any of those services, was a very good place to be. You always had clean bedding, clean clothes. And I didn't really see much warfare. When I went out on ship, the Atlantic was more or less cleaned up of submarines.

When I came back to New York, I just picked up my painting and continued to paint, got fellowships, received a Guggenheim to do my war series. And I've just been painting ever since.

The war series was done in 1946. And after that, I did a theater series and then a series on the civil-rights business in the South. It was in the sixties. And I did a piece called *Struggle*, a history of the American people. These were three of the series I did after I left the service.

I never thought I'd leave New York. But I did briefly in 1941. I got married; we went to New Orleans and then to Virginia, near Richmond. From there we came back to New York, and that's where we lived until 1971, when we moved out to the West Coast. I was invited to teach at the University of Washington, and we thought we'd be out here for three to five years, and we've been out here since then. We've been out here for about twenty-some years.

I miss New York, but being out here, it's a nice experience. There was a big migration, of course, out to Washington, too, during the war years, when so many blacks moved from places like Texas into the West and California. But this migration never attracted my interest enough to want to make paintings about it. I guess I said everything I wanted to say in the *Migration* series. There was nothing else I could add. I mean, I couldn't do it. And I was interested in painting, but not doing that again, I'll put it that way. It would have been repetitive; it would have repeated itself.

I like storytelling. I always liked that. I just like storytelling. I like history, and so I put the two together, my painting and my interest in the historical scene. And it's very exciting for me. Painting. The excitement of painting, the excitement of working with color, hoping that I'm growing, that I'm developing. And the encouragement I receive constantly. I constantly get this.

I love tools. When I was a youngster, I was around tools. I was around three brothers, the Bates brothers. There was Addison Bates, John Bates, and Leonard Bates. And they were brothers, and they were cabinetmakers. And I was around them, and I didn't realize what an impression they were making as cabinetmakers. I didn't realize at the time that this would be one of my basic subjects. And that's how that started. I just love tools; they're beautiful. I paint them.

Artists must be committed. What is the commitment to the community, to the world community? I think to show beauty, to show your insight. Always searching, always looking for something.

[Interview by Alan Govenar, September 3, 1998]

*Bruce Lee, chief of Microbiology Lab, Detroit Arsenal, ca. 1953.*

# BRUCE LEE

BIOLOGIST

*Born November 16, 1921*

*Bruce Lee grew up in the Cold Spring area of Buffalo, New York, in a "community of coloreds," whom he defines as people of mixed Native American, African, and Anglo-Saxon descent. Lee calls this region of Upstate New York the Niagara Frontier, where colored professionals came with their families to live without having to be constantly reminded of the limitations imposed by racial segregation. Lee recounts childhood meetings with W. E. B. DuBois, Eugene Kinkle Jones, Mary McLeod Bethune, and other African American leaders who were involved with the Niagara Movement and the struggle for civil rights. Lee attended a predominantly white school through the eighth grade and then went to high school in downtown Buffalo, where the colored teachers worked, although the classes had students with different ethnic backgrounds (the children of Jewish, German, and Irish immigrants). After high school, Lee enrolled in the Brockport Normal School; he received a bachelor's degree from the Tuskegee Institute and a master's and a doctorate in biology from the University of Michigan. After working for many years as a biologist, he moved in 1970 to California to accept a position with the Department of Health, Education, and Welfare. Lee retired in 1983.*

I WAS BORN INTO THE "COLORED COMMUNITY" of Buffalo. The African American community of Buffalo did not accept readily the term *Negro* that was given to us by the white world before and after the Civil War, nor did they accept the term *African American*. They preferred to be called colored—colored, meaning they knew they were the descendants of African American slaves who came here in the seventeenth and eighteenth centuries—and also they were proud of the fact that they had European ancestors and also a rich heritage from the American Indian communities. The region I came from in Upstate New York was known as the Niagara Frontier. That was the area bordered by Lake Ontario, the Niagara River, and Lake Erie.

One Sunday morning in 1952, after I had finished my doctorate at the University of Michigan, I was invited to have breakfast with Charles S. Johnson, who was the distinguished president of Fisk University and who was also a great researcher of African American history in the United States. In the early 1920s, Johnson went to Buffalo to observe the colored community. And he characterized the colored families, and the white families for whom they worked, as "peculiarly friendly." He noted that the whites sometimes attended the African American social events, which were patterned after those the whites had. These coloreds were quite familiar with the social gatherings of the aristocrats because it was their responsibility to serve at their society affairs. Colored families had a presence in political campaigns, municipal celebrations, and when receiving visitors to the city. Except for the Irish, whites seemed to tolerate these colored families. Coloreds and whites attended the same parties, where everyone spoke German.

My father was fluent in German, and many of the people of his generation were because in the schools, German was taught along with English in the early grades. The children became fluent, and they developed that peculiar relationship. I speak to it because it has influenced my life.

I came up in Buffalo, realizing that every summer, we would have a large arrival of the colored professionals from the eastern United States. There would be the physicians, the dentists, the doctors, the lawyers, and people who had other status away from manual labor and service. Many of them were graduates of the finest colleges, and they took great pride in their accomplishments. And the older colored families of Buffalo opened their homes to these people, not as roomers, but as visitors and guests.

My mother was a New York woman. She was born in Jersey City, but she was socialized in New York. My mother was a Pratt graduate from Brooklyn, New York, in haute couture, and she designed the clothes for some of the families on Fifth Avenue, Riverside Drive, and the East Side of New York City. She knew these people, and when they came to Buffalo, we were taken to meet them. All these people came to Buffalo because they were able to go to the theaters, go to the stores, use the public recreational facilities, and move without segregation. Buffalo was one of the few cities, maybe the only city in the North, which had practically open access for colored people.

As a child, I used to hear that Mother was not ashamed of the word *Negro,* but in the world of Buffalo, we seldom heard it. People referred to themselves as "colored people." And I came to look upon myself as a colored person, which I still do. It's very difficult for me to understand how people can call themselves black, which is an adjective. Chinese people aren't referred to as yellow, or Indian people as reds. This is the only group in the country that is labeled *black.* Use a term that describes them. They are colored people. *Colored* is an adjective, but *people* is a noun. They also speak to the fact that they are a group of three races. That's what the African American is, an amalgam of three races—the African, the European, and the American Indian. And it is something that I am proud of. And my family is proud. And the people I was raised amongst are proud. There is nothing to be ashamed of. It's not trying to be anything different. It's what we are.

In Buffalo, the only things that were segregated were the Christian things. The churches were segregated. We went to colored churches. The white YMCA was closed. They gave us a black YMCA that was miles from where I lived, and so I used to go over to the white YMCA with my white friends to watch them recreate. I was a spectator to sports, not a participant. They could use the pools. They could use the tennis courts. And I'd wait for them outside. They often wondered why I was never admitted. It was a question of pigmentation that kept me from participating. The Boy Scout troops you could join, as long as you remained in your own packs. You were never allowed to choose the pack you wanted to be in. They assigned you to your pack, which was segregation. The Boys Clubs were also segregated. So I took it upon myself to say, if that's what they want, they can have it. I made my own way. I looked out in the world above me, having a father who ran on the railroad. He was the chief waiter on the Empire State Express. He used to go to New York and bring back the newspapers. And he and I would assemble scrapbooks. He also opened the world to me.

I'm a descendant of one of the first of the colored families in western New York. My father was Edward David Lee Sr., and my mother was Florence Randolph Jackson of Jersey City, New Jersey. They were married in Niagara Falls in September of 1915.

There were five of us in my family—my brothers, Voyle [1918–1995] and Edward [1921–1996]. I'm the middle child, and my two sisters, Harriet Agnes Louise and Florence Lois Jane. The three of us younger ones are still surviving. Voyle and Edward died in the last two years.

My family was in western New York, and that means a lot because they were people who were there during slavery. The earliest reference in the family is 1789 on my mother's side; the gravestone is in Niagara Falls. The earliest reference in my father's family is to his great-great-grandfather Henry, who was brought over as an Ibo slave to Baltimore, Maryland. Henry escaped his captors and joined the Indian nation outside of Baltimore and married an Indian woman called Patty. And my great-grandfather Edward Cook was born in 1815, and he was baptized a Catholic at St. Charles Cathedral in Baltimore. I have his baptismal certificate with the names of his parents and grandparents on it.

Edward Cook was declared free because he was of Indian heritage; his father was Ibo and his mother was a Native American Indian. The mayor of Baltimore issued him his free papers in 1837, and this allowed him to leave Baltimore with a passport. The passport is a written statement from the mayor: "Edward Cook, behaving himself in an orderly manner, colored man, is allowed to be out until ten o'clock p.m." Signed by Mayor Smith. He used that, and he joined an overland train which went over the Allegheny Mountains, and he came to Buffalo. He established himself in 1837 as a barber at the Mansion House, one of the finest hotels in Buffalo (on the site where the Statler Building now stands). And he was there until he died in 1906.

One day in 1840 or 1843, Edward was down at the terminus of the Erie Canal, and he saw a very lovely Indian lady getting off the canal boat. He looked at her and he said, "That's the girl for me." And he started to court her. She was a Mohawk lady called Phoebe Lansing. She was born in 1821 in Fort Plain, New York, which is outside of Albany, and they were married October 29, 1845, at the Vine Street Methodist Church in Buffalo, New York. I have in my possession the silk wedding slipper she wore. It was made in Lynn, Massachusetts. I also have the wedding blanket, which is homespun and was used on their bed.

Phoebe and Edward had eight children. My grandmother Harriet Emma was born in 1850. She married my grandfather David Moses Lee in 1870. Grandpa Lee was the child of a Madagascar native who was kidnapped into slavery from Madagascar and brought to Niagara-on-the-Lake, where he was a slave until he was freed by the Canadian government about 1837, many years before the Emancipation Proclamation in the United States. Barnard Lee was his full name.

Barnard Lee was a bitter man because he could never develop the means to get himself back to his native land. In 1840, he married an English-Irish girl called Eleanor Jane McCormick. Some people call her the name McCornish. Her family came from Tipperary, Ireland. She sailed with her family to Canada from County Cork. And I have in my possession the blanket, the biddy blanket, which she wore on the voyage over. It's a Jacob's coat of many colors, made of Irish homespun. She brought with her some peasant mourning jewelry. It's made of basalt, a black material, and she wore it when people in our family died. I also have some of the cameos she had sewn onto her as buttons on her waistcoat, as well as some of her china.

Eleanor was an interesting woman. She loved Barnard Lee, but she had a hard time living with him because he was so bitter about his status. I remember that there's a story in our family that he always resented the fact that his race was enslaved in America. They were living in Niagara-on-the-Lake. And yet, I was told as a child that often people would see Eleanor out in the yard, washing his dirty drawers, and he'd say, "You see that, don't you? They've got my folks in slavery down South, but you see that, don't you?" And after a while, she decided to leave him. But before she did, they had three children. George was the oldest son. Now, George appeared to be a white man, and in the 1860s, he left Canada and sailed to England, where he settled in Liverpool. He sent three letters saying he was doing well, and that's the last we heard of him. He took the name of George Cotton.

David Moses Lee, my grandfather, was born in 1847, and in 1870, he married my grandmother Harriet Emma, who was the daughter of Edward Cook and Phoebe Lansing. Edward and Phoebe had another child, who was known as Anna. We called her Auntie. She appeared to be an Indian, although she was Malagasy-English-Irish. When she grew to her maturity, she left her family and joined the Kiowa Indian nation. We learned by word of mouth that she married a man named Douglas Harvey and settled in Oklahoma. And that's the last we heard of her.

David Lee was born in Branford, Ontario, and he came to the United States. He married my grandmother in Buffalo, New York, and they had two children. My aunt Janie, her name was Cora Jane Lee [1873–1953], and my father, Edward David Lee [1877–1954]. Aunt Janie was the second colored person to finish the Buffalo High School, which is known as Central High. She graduated in 1894. That was unique because in that year, the New York State Regents Examination in algebra was so difficult that the city had a hard time finding people who passed the examination to graduate. She was, I think, one of three people to pass, and she graduated.

My grandfather Lee was a male nurse. He worked at Dr. Pierce's hospital in Buffalo. Dr. Pierce advertised "Dr. Pierce's Golden Medical Discovery." And that "Golden Medical Discovery" was a medicine that was supposed to cure certain venereal diseases. It's particularly amazing because the leading courtesans from Europe used to come to Dr. Pierce's hospital to get cured. My grandfather used to say they got "boiled out." Apparently, what he did was to immerse them in hot water to raise their body temperatures to kill off the existing spirocete, which caused syphilis. And they felt well for a time before they went back to their professions.

In the 1890s, when David Lee was working with Dr. Pierce, a courtesan and a large retinue came from Europe, and David Lee was assigned to be their nurse to look after them. When they left, the courtesan said, "Dave, I appreciate what you've done for us. I'm going to give you something." She gave him a sunburst-of-diamonds stud and a single solitary diamond stud for his formal outfit. You see, the colored community often had formal balls in Buffalo, which were attended in exquisite clothes and jewelry.

The marriage of my grandparents foundered in the 1870s, and my grandmother separated from Dave. They did not divorce, but she lived the remainder of her life alone. My father came into his maturity in the early part of the twentieth century. And in 1915, he courted and married Florence Randolph Jackson of Jersey City and Niagara Falls. Florence Randolph Jackson was the daughter of Charles Kersey Jackson, who was born a slave around 1846 near Roanoke, Virginia. He was the grandson of John Randolph, who was a cousin of Thomas Jefferson. Randolph was the ambassador to Russia and a member of the House of Representatives from Virginia. He was supposed to never have had children, but when I heard this, I said that was incorrect. He had one child, but they often said, he didn't have any white children. He had one child by a slave. We never knew her name. But Martha Randolph was the child of this slave. Martha Randolph secured her freedom when Randolph died. He manumitted his slaves, including Martha, and she was the mother of my grandfather.

For some reason, Martha's children were never free, and they were sold into slavery. But she kept up with her children. I don't know how that happened, why she was manumitted and not the children. Martha appeared to be a white person; she was very fair-skinned. And when General Grant took Richmond, she sought out her children, gathered them, and posed as a white woman, saying, "I'm liberating these three slaves." They were in their teens. And she took them to New York City.

When Martha was growing up, her white relatives in the Randolph household did something they were not supposed to do. They taught Martha to read and to write and to do figures [math], and in New York, she became a very astute businesswoman. Within two years, she owned her own house at 220 Whiton Street in Jersey City, and the house is still standing. She set up her house with business as a modiste, making clothes for women. She taught her children that the key to success in life is to get into business and to always own your own home. And this lesson was well known. Martha had three children, James and Charles, and a girl. James and Charles grew up and owned hotels. James went to Saratoga to run a hotel, and my grandfather Charles owned the Falls House and later the Robinson House, a large hotel in Niagara Falls. They were large hotels for the white tourist trade. African American trade was impossible because of the social customs of the day. Now, my grandfather was a very astute businessman. He always resented the fact that he'd been a slave. He was barely literate; he wrote phonetically, but his speech was astute, and he was alert to any opportunity to make money. And every fall, at the end of the season, he would take a trip through the South, after closing the hotel, to visit the "Negro" colleges, looking for fair-skinned Negroes, in those days, who could pass for white persons. And he would offer them jobs the next year working for him in the

Robinson House. So the Robinson House was a hotel for white trade staffed by so-called white people, who were African Americans passing as whites and who were able to give him the standards of service that he required. They worked on the desk, as concierge. They worked all through the hotel in various occupations. Domestic work, unfortunately, was done by dark-skinned African Americans.

When we came along, my brothers, Voyle and Edward, myself, and my sisters, Harriet and Florence, some of us were fair, and some of us were brown-skinned. I remember as a child, trying to use the front steps of my grandfather's hotel and being taken by a maid off to the side down to the park to watch the falls. I think I knew more about the falls than I did any other place as a child.

And in spite of his success, my grandfather had a feeling of inferiority about himself. In his will, he said he wanted no colored man to handle any of his affairs because they knew nothing about business. And as a result, his lawyer cleaned out the estate. He died and left a huge amount of money. In those days, it must have been over $150,000 in cash and the hotel and the properties that we owned. But by 1932, during the Depression, practically nothing was left. My grandmother's last days were not what they should have been.

They had three daughters, Paulina, born in 1882, Florence [1884–1965] my mother, and Ethel [1895–1985]. Now, my grandfather, even though he was born a slave and did not have an education, he was a stickler for education. And he dressed his daughters elegantly. Their clothes were from the finest shops in New York City. He was able to give them a background that you didn't ordinarily find within the colored society of that day except in New York City. The society at the turn of the century was an elegant colored society. There was a tremendous respect for education. My mother was a member of the Scotia Scholastic Society. The Scotia Scholastic Society consisted of young colored men and women who stayed in the New York metropolitan area for education. They went to Columbia. They went to Fordham. The girls went to Barnard or they went to the normal schools there. They took advantage of the local education rather than going south. And they would give affairs during the year to try to raise money to help people who wanted to do the same things they did: stay in the North and get educated.

My mother told a story that in the early 1900s she dated an African prince. She said he had a strange name: Prince Icaca. It was about 1910, and he gave a dinner party at Columbia, where he attended. And he served strawberries in January. Well, that was in those days before there was refrigeration and freezing. You can imagine, that was considered the height of elegance.

These were the stories of my background. I try to characterize this colored world. It was a world of people who thought themselves apart. You had to be born into it and you died out of it. They were the descendants of people who were freed before the Emancipation Proclamation. Many of them were freed in the eighteenth century, and they came to Buffalo and they formed their own community. Out of a city of about five hundred thousand people, there might have been five thousand colored people. They lived downtown in the older part of the city. I grew up in an area known as Cold Springs. In my day, it was considered the outskirts of the city, but now it's the center of the city. They numbered about fifty families. We knew each other. We associated only with each other. And unfortunately, they never told us the true facts of life, of our relationship as African Americans to the world about us. We thought that everybody lived as we did, with all the advantages.

When I got into the army, I was shocked to find that there were African Americans who had never been allowed to use a library. They had never been into a store. They had never been into a theater. They never had the advantages I took for granted. Almost everything was open in Buffalo. It was one of the few cities in the country where coloreds could shop. You could go downtown to the theater, or you could eat out. In the summertime, you could take a boat ride. You could go to Canada. The Niagara Frontier was filled with the colored professionals from the South who came to the North to live without having to be reminded every minute that things were not open to them simply on the basis of their skin color.

Many of them came to Buffalo for vacation, and then they moved to the city from the South. They came to western New York. They loved to go shopping downtown. During summer vacation, people would say, "Well, where are you staying?" They never said they were rooming. Instead, they were the guest of such and such a person. To me, they were the most elegant people. I remember being taken out to meet these people. I met W. E. B. DuBois, Eugene Kinkle Jones, Mary McLeod Bethune, Mordecai Johnson, Rosamond Johnson, and his brother James Weldon

Johnson, who wrote "Lift Every Voice and Sing." Anybody who was any-body in the colored world from about 1900 to the 1950s came to Buffalo. Anybody who was civil rights or pressing for the improvement of the race, they would come to town, and my mother would march the five of us to meet these people.

Years later, in 1948, when I was a student at the University of Michi-gan, I attended a rally in Detroit to help Dr. W. E. B. DuBois fight the monstrous charges pressed against him by our government. I was a vet-eran, and I was called to help with this meeting. And he and his wife, Shirley Graham, were there. They were traveling about the country, and a group organized a mass meeting at Bethel Church in Detroit. Shirley Graham was trying to raise money for his defense. And after the meet-ing, we went back to the minister's quarters to meet them. There was W. E. B. DuBois, looking like a polished new Buddha of fine ivory. He was in his eighties then. He died in 1963; that was 1948. Oh, to see this person, who all my life I had revered, and to shake his hand. And I told him who I was, and I saw this smile come to his face.

The people of the Niagara Movement came through Buffalo. I have in my possession the loving cup given to my great-grandfather by the colored community in 1868 because of his work as a conductor on the Underground Railroad during the years of slavery. The Niagara Move-ment was the precursor to the NAACP. That's the reason DuBois was in the Niagara Frontier. My family was involved. They served as hosts for the people who came to town, and they would ferry them to Canada. They all had to meet in Niagara, Ontario, because the customs of the day made it nearly impossible for them to meet without difficulty.

They came to western New York; it was picturesque. The summer season was a time when you could spend your time being elegant. The homes of the society were thrown open to these people.

When Marcus Garvey started his improvement association in the early part of the century, many of the colored people looked at him askance because, first of all, he was dark-skinned. This colored world, I'm sorry to say, was often composed of those people who were there be-cause of their color. I also realize that I had my own prejudice about many of the people who came at that time. Was there prejudice among the colored world? Of course there was. It was based on your family background and your skin color and sometimes your hair quality and how you looked. And as children, we were amazed to hear one family member, when she was growing up, be told not to bring anybody home who was darker than she was. When my son heard this, he was appalled. And I told him, "I never practiced it."

My mother was fair-skinned, and coming from New York City, she thought that the local attitudes were atrocious. And she never allowed any of us to do anything like that. But with my father's side of the family, there was an emphasis on physical features. I recall being told this old adage, "If you're white, you're right. If you're yellow, you're mellow. If you're brown, stick around. If you're black, get back." Tragically, this kind of stereotyping happened within our community. And it even extended to where you went to church. In my youth, there was only one church to be attended to be socially accepted, and that was St. Phillip's Anglican Episcopal Church. It was the high Episcopalian Anglican. Also, it was a church, they used to say, that you were born into and you died out of. And the whole time I was there, the twenty-one years I lived in Buffalo, very few people joined the church, because they weren't welcome. The congregation didn't have to worry about paying our bills to the diocese because the white churches didn't want us as members of their church. And they'd given us our church to keep us out of their church. My mother was easily aware of what that meant. Also, there was a succession of ministers until the arrival of an outstanding man, Osmond Henry Brown, who was West Indian. He came there in the twenties, and he stayed until the fifties. He was an amazing man, and he had the most wonderful, wonderful wife, who was a New Englander. But she said to my mother, "Florence, I'm not fish nor fowl." She wasn't a West Indian and she wasn't a Buffalonian. And she was practically crucified by the viciousness of many of the people in the church. But she turned out three wonderful boys. Alan is now a physician in Georgia. And Junior, Osmond Henry Brown Jr., became a priest, and he's dead. And the last one, John, became a federal employee, and he's dead.

My mother was very much aware of what was going on and was constantly angry and doing battle with the locals. She was never really accepted into old Buffalo society, and she didn't give a damn because she came from New York society. She was very proud, and we were very proud within our family. But in the world we lived in, it was difficult. It wasn't concealed, the colored versus the new-Negro situation. The colored people lived in Cold Spring. The new Negroes, often called blacks, lived downtown. And they were called blacks not on the basis of color, but on the basis of culture. Is your culture white-oriented, or is it Negro-oriented? The church you went to, Anglican Church, was high church, English in origin. Many services were attended by white people who wanted to enjoy the high Anglican service, which they couldn't get in their own Episcopal churches. Yes, there were many mixed people.

One woman, a new member, said to my aunt, "I visited one of your old members. I come to your church, but I feel like I have a strange disease. No one will speak to me, and I've been coming for years."

So my aunt had her to tea. And she said, "Now, dear, where are you from?" And the woman said she was from Alabama. And my aunt said, "Have you told that to anyone?"

She said, "Yes." And she said, "Well, that's your trouble. You'll have to reinvent you. You were really born in New York, Rochester, Olean, Salamanca, and you were taken south as a child. Now you've come back to reclaim your heritage."

The woman said, "I think you're crazy," and left. And she joined the Roman Catholic Church. In my day, the Roman Catholic Church maintained a separate church for Negroes called St. Augustin's, which is downtown. And if you were a colored Catholic, you had to go there.

When I was in the army, down at Tuskegee, every church was closed except the Roman Catholic. On Sundays, you'd see the people going up to worship their God without fear of being arrested. And as far as the local colored population, many went to the Michigan Avenue Baptist Church. The Michigan Avenue Baptist Church was the center of the Underground Railroad in Buffalo. It was the stopping place for hiding many of the runaway slaves. And many of the older residents of the city went there, and many of the newcomers, because when they went to the Episcopal Church, they were not accepted or they were insulted. They had a minister called Elder Jesse Nash. He came there in 1892, and he stayed until 1952—a huge span of years. He was ancient. And the church is still there, but it's moved to a different location. But the building is still there. During slavery, during all the civil rights of those days, it was there.

In Buffalo, there was Bethel AME Zion, of which my great-grandparents were charter members, back in the 1840s. And my brother returned to that church when he married a Methodist girl. And he was buried at that church. In fact, the first Methodist service I went to was his funeral. I never knew my brothers well, but as I sat there during the funeral and I listened, I learned who my brother was by the testimonies these people gave. He found his heritage back in the church that his ancestors founded.

Deceased people were laid out for people to see in many of the Protestant churches. We called it the "Last Look." But we were Anglicans, and the casket was closed when you left the home or funeral home, and that was the last you saw of the person. That was sort of a social distinction; we're not like you, in other words. And the Last Look was not in the Anglican Church. When the body leaves the home or where it was laid out, the funeral parlor, the coffin is closed, and that's that for eternity.

My brother Voyle was buried Anglican, but Eddie was buried Methodist. I watched—aisle after aisle—people would go up for an hour looking at his body. And I wouldn't go, because that was not the way I felt. I remembered him as he was. I did visit homes where people used to have pictures taken of people laid out in their coffins. And I visited homes where people had the Last Look of people laid out.

In our church, I was often asked to sing at funerals. I was a boy soprano. And we'd have a high Mass. The services in our church were rigidly formal, whereas in the Protestant churches, the Baptist and the Methodist church, there's a lot of emotion. And people would express themselves and cry out. But that's typical African, and there's nothing wrong with that. That's one of the vestiges that came over from slavery which still survives. And after the Last Look, they'd close the coffin, and I think they used to sing "If I Can See My Mother Pray." They'd sing those songs that bring the tears falling. And the ministers would get up and they'd read telegrams and they'd read testimonials, and people would get up to speak about what they remembered of the deceased. But you never saw that at the Anglican church. The Anglican church would have the Credo and the Agnus Dei, and Sanctus, and then it would be over.

Buffalo was one of the few cities in the country where blacks are buried in the best cemeteries. My great-grandfather bought our lots at Forest Lawn Cemetery in 1846. There are forty of us buried there. You just bought your lot and you were buried there, and nobody said anything. But in many places, like Detroit and Cleveland, it's difficult to be buried where you want to be buried. Those cities have these black cemeteries, and I was amazed to see how poorly they're kept. Well, when you're dead, who gives a damn anyway? But the fact remains, Forest Lawn is maintained beautifully. And every time I go home, I go out and talk to my folks for a whole day. We're buried in three cemeteries in Buffalo. We're buried in Forest Lawn in two sections, and in Niagara Falls and Oakwood, where my grandmother's and grandfather's people are.

Ours was the colored world, but our interface was with the white world we lived in. We moved into an area before the whites came. The home was built out in Cold Springs in the early 1870s, and then the Germans and the Irish came and settled around us. Buffalo was the frontier in the 1870s. Buffalo was part of the Underground Railroad, the people who helped the escaped slaves row across the Niagara River. I wonder how it was done, seeing that current, it's ten miles an hour. But there must have been some skillful boatmen.

All during slavery until emancipation, my great-grandfather had to carry with him a shillelagh, and I've still got it hanging on my wall. It has a knob, and he used it to protect himself and his children. He constantly had to be on the alert. His kids had to be aware that they lived a precarious existence, to be wary of strangers, although they were free people. If they were not aware, they could be carried back to slavery.

Many colored people don't want to admit their Indian heritage. They are proud of their white heritage, but their Indian heritage is looked upon askance by many people. My Indian heritage is part Mohawk, Cherokee, and Narragansett, and I am not unique. Most of the colored people I knew had mixed Indian ancestry, and during the Trail of Tears, many of the Indians joined black families and black people. And many Indians even adopted black runaways into their tribes. Osceola, the famous chief of the Seminoles, was half-black. But some of the Indian tribes were also slaveholders, and they had families with them, too. Of course, the genes are immortal. And for that reason, you often see these high cheekbones and straight hair quality.

When I was growing up, discrimination was really twofold: one recognized and one not recognized. We just assumed white values were right. The black doctors in Buffalo had a very difficult time getting clientele because the colored people went to white doctors. You went to white hospitals. I went to completely white schools. I was one of two colored kids in my eighth-grade class. And in high school, I had all these wonderful advantages, and I didn't realize what an enchanted life I was leading.

In Buffalo, the inner city is now called Cold Spring. When I lived there, it was on the outskirts of the city. The people came there in the 1850s and they made their way. But now we're living in a world filled with problems. There are drugs, there's overpopulation and the various things which go along with economic displacement and the various things that didn't exist in my time. In my time, the school was a middle-class school, and you never thought of yourself as anything different. The only thing I did notice was when I was trying to play on sports teams, my classmates would not accept me. When the baseball season came, they'd choose up sides and say, "We don't want him. We don't want him." And the teacher would assign me to a team, and they'd say, "We don't want him." So I'd play the best I could, and when I told my mother about what happened, she said, "Well, baseball, football, and basketball are un-American sports."

"Un-American?" I asked.

"Un-American, yes," she said. "If you can't play them, they're un-American."

So I often stayed away from sports, but in my day, it was the schoolwork that mattered most. We had fantastic teachers. They were mostly older people. Then, the schools there were full of immigrants. Mostly, there were Jews. And when the Ashkenazi [Jews] first started coming to Buffalo, the older Jews were Sephardim. But when the Ashkenazi first started coming in, they settled down there around Williams Street, where my family first lived. And my aunt told me that the older Ashkenazi women would come door to door selling things, and that's when my family first became aware that there were new immigrants coming to town.

The descendants of the Christians and Jews who made their way into the city became the teachers in the schools I went to. I started off for college when I finished high school in 1939. My father had gone blind in 1933, during the Depression. It was a very difficult time for the family because we had a fourteen-room house, and my mother was forced to go to work. And she found work in the WPA, Works Progress Administration, under Roosevelt. My mother used to say to us, "We're not poor. We're broke. There's a big difference." And the people who were our social workers were our friends, and my mother would always have tea ready for them when they came. And it was sort of a social visit, trying to work out a budget for seven people to live on fifteen dollars a week. And when the grocery man took the welfare check and gave my mother the money, he said, "Trade where you wish." And my mother said, "We're going to trade right here. You're giving me dignity." This is the way we lived. Nobody knew we were on relief, because my mother had money to spend.

I went to school with kids who were very well off. My mother would give us peanut-butter sandwiches. I hated them. At lunchtime up at school, there'd be a chap named Noel, and his mother gave him a pound cake, sandwiches, and he said, "I don't want any of this stuff. You want it, Bruce?" Every day I sat with Noel, and I had his lunch, because he would buy his lunch at the commissary; he had money. And he didn't realize I ate off of him for two or three years. When we graduated, I guess the saddest day of my life was September 5, 1939, when I had to go down to the station to watch all my friends from high school go to Harvard and Yale and the various places I wanted to go. The University of Michigan accepted me, but they wanted four hundred dollars, and there was no way I could afford it.

If it wasn't for Lethia Warren, I might have never been able to go to college. Lethia was a fair-skinned person who came to Buffalo, and she ran a nightclub at the Vendome Hotel. She spotlighted people like Sammy Davis, Sr. and Jr., and Jimmie Lunceford and his band, and Bill "Bojangles" Robinson. All the people in town came to her establishment. When she left that business, she became a supervisor for the National Youth Administration [NYA] under Roosevelt. That was my salvation. I worked for a check of eighteen dollars a month. I think I worked about twenty hours a week. Well, they had what they called colored NYA projects in Buffalo, run by a minister who didn't particularly care for the older colored people and was in charge of their children. He gave me a job emptying ashes at a police station. I didn't go for that. I was breaking my back. So I went to Lethia, who was my supervisor, and I complained, and that started sixty years of friendship. She gave me a job. I had been a member of the Junior Education Department at the Buffalo Museum of Science. That's where my interest in birds and nature came from. I worked in the NYA program of the Museum of Science, and I learned how to do taxonomy, the naming of mollusks in the shell collection. At that time, I was sixteen or seventeen, and I was doing this professional work, and it was opening me to the world, into the world of science. And it was considered quite a thing because I was a colored boy working on a white project through that door Lethia Warren opened for me. And the door never closed.

So I went back to high school, PG [post-graduate] the next year, because I couldn't afford to go to college and didn't want to waste the year lacking any education. I took courses I didn't need but that interested me—in music, literature, and subjects such as that.

Later, Lethia arranged for a scholarship from the Alpha Phi Alpha fraternity (which is the colored fraternity), and I went downstate to a small normal school called Brockport Normal, which is now a state university. It's a big school now with twenty thousand students, but when I went there, they only had about a thousand. And she said, "Now Bruce, you're going there, and they don't want you down there. Remember, call me if you need me." I never had to call her. It opened doors, and there were three colored men: Dr. Edwin Harris Mitchell, who's currently chief of radiology at Meharry Medical College; Dr. Jimmy Singleterry, who's now dead, but was in the State Department at Washington; and myself. We all got our doctorates. I got mine from Michigan, Jimmy got his from Chicago, and Ed went into medicine.

When I went to Brockport, there was also a colored girl, named Norine Anderson. The school was small, in a small village that looked at us, didn't want us there. The colored students had no place to stay, so we stayed at a farm on the outskirts of town and found what you might call one of those living saints. A farmer's wife, a Mrs. Burlingame, took us in and said, "Use my cold cellar." I'd never heard of a cold cellar. It's a hole in the ground that freezes and was filled with vegetables and fatback. We learned to live very well on the produce that she put down for us. All I can say is that she was a living saint. And I stayed there a year, and I would have finished there except that it was so difficult to find anything to do in the town because the Christians didn't want us around. So I came back to Buffalo and entered teachers' college. Then World War II came.

I was sworn into the army as a "white man" (not as a colored) in those days because of the fact I'd been a museum kid. I'd been awarded medals (for achievement) from the Buffalo Museum of Science and the Junior Education Department. The head of the museum knew my grandmother. She'd worked for him and his family. His name was Chauncy Hamlin, and he gave me a card to give to the chief of the induction center. And when the person in charge at the induction center saw that name, he said, "I'm going to help you. I'm not to do anything illegal." And when my class was called up, I went down, and there were twenty-nine people from my class at teachers' college. We went through the induction. I raised my hand and was sworn into the army. And then, he said, "Now I'm leaving here, and whoever succeeds me is going to figure out what to do with you as a colored person."

Well, they called my class up in six months. I went down to the army office that day. There were crying mothers. My mother was down there. They took everybody away but me, because they didn't know what to do with this colored boy who had come into the army as a white man. I was sworn in as white. And somebody said, "Well, there's Tuskegee." And I went down to Tuskegee as a flying cadet at the army airfield. Well, the first day, the commanding officer asked me if I drove a car. I said that I never learned to drive. I was twenty years old. So I washed out the first day there in training.

When I was down at Tuskegee, P. H. Polk, who had a photographic studio on campus, made my portrait. And I still have it. I didn't realize what a fine work it was. Polk was thin and tall. And the thing I remember most about him was that he had bins that were about twenty feet long and had these long, open glass negative bins filled with the work he'd done over the years. It was just captivating for me to see his work.

Tuskegee in those days was living on a name long since past. If you've read *Invisible Man,* you know what I'm talking about. Fred Patterson was in charge, and he was trying to fit into the twentieth century with attributes of the nineteenth. And all of us boys who'd been to Northern schools were just appalled by the quality of work and the lack of understanding. We knew we were in a second-class outfit of a segregated army. We were in something called Negro Military Personnel. And when people said, "Well, I won't get into that," I had very strange feelings about this country. My first night on a Jim Crow train car was like *Schindler's List.* We rode in wooden cars behind the engine with the upper windows open. The coal dust blew in. I was in a car that was built to hold eighty people, but there must have been over one hundred fifty men jammed into it. The toilets were broken down, and there were mice and bed bugs all around. This was my first experience with Jim Crow, and these things opened my life to the fact that I lived in a world of illusion in Buffalo. My parents had carefully protected me from knowing that anything like that was out there. I had heard about Jim Crow, but I didn't know what it really was. Jim Crow was like a bad chasm that is filled with the ghosts and the refuse of what had happened to people who had aspired to dignity.

One day, coming back from furlough, I got off the train in Nashville, Tennessee, and I made the mistake of walking with the white troops into a white waiting room. Suddenly, an MP came up to me, and before I could say a word, he hit me over the head and I blacked out. When I came to, I was lying on a baggage cart, and this lovely older colored lady was leaning over me, saying, "When will you Northern boys learn?" And she had a broken cookie and a jelly jar full of water. And I tried to stand up. I had a concussion. And I had to stand on the train with a concussion from Nashville to Cincinnati until I could get some competent medical help. That was my welcome to America in October 1943.

I never had a gun in my hand. I never had any basic training. What I did when I was in the army, I collected butterflies, which are now at the University of Michigan and quite valued. You see, there were flying MATS, military air transports, planes that went from South America to Alabama. They didn't fumigate them, and we'd get these exotic tropical species breeding for one season in the Tuskegee area and then dying out when the winter came. And the ones I collected were from there, and they're now in the University of Michigan collection. So I did do something. I didn't waste my time. I was an intelligence clerk, and I served there from 1943 until 1946.

When I was discharged from the army, I found out about the GI Bill and said, "That's for me. I'm going to reactivate my application to Michigan." And I finished my bachelor's in 1947, got my master's in 1948, and my doctorate in biology, earned in 1951 and awarded in 1952, at the University of Michigan.

When I came out of the university, my professors wanted me to go south to teach. And I said to them, "Look, I've lived there. I'm not going to raise any children down there. There are no opportunities." So I took a job as a riveter and porter at Kaiser-Frazier. I told them I'd finished the fifth grade in Alabama. They hired me immediately. The plant was in Ypsilanti, Michigan. I went over there at four o'clock in the morning to get the job. I stood in line until eight o'clock. And I stayed there until I could make some money.

Well, when I was at the University of Michigan, I had befriended a young black man who'd come north for his master's degree. The black students who came from the South had never been allowed to be in libraries, because most blacks couldn't use libraries in the cities where they lived. And when they came to Michigan, they were given assignments to use the library, and many of them asked, "How do you use it?" So I said, "I'll show you." And I took groups of them to the library and showed them how to use the card catalog, the encyclopedias, and the basic reference tools that they were going to need for doing their master's degrees. And this one man I helped never forgot me. And one Christmas morning in 1951, he called, saying, "There's a job at the Detroit Arsenal in microbiology and it's yours." I said, "I've only had four hours in that." He said, "Don't tell them. Fake it." So I went there. And I spent the next thirty-five years going from job to job in government, always moving upward, moving toward one thing: dignity, learning on the job and holding responsible positions. I worked all over the world, and I have no regrets. When I walked out the door and retired, I said, "Well, you did it, Bruce." And like many people, the blacks of my generation, all of us knew when we got our doctorates, we'd never work in our field, the field in which we got our doctorate. You worked where you could, and I saw that. But I was not going to reproduce what happened to my father's generation, when I saw these people who had educations doing porter work and doing demeaning occupations. And yet they never let you know the jobs were demeaning. They were people who maintained their dignity in spite of their status. I had an aunt that used to go to work every morning carrying a violin case. They thought she was playing it at the Gypsy Tea Room. She wasn't. She worked as a maid downtown, and she carried her stuff in it. She posed as a musician with her case to keep her dignity.

I moved to California in 1970, '71. There was a job posted out here, and I had befriended a person back in Washington. When she sent me the announcement of the job—"Grants officer, Region 9, Health, Education, and Welfare (HEW)"—I said, "That's for me." I went for the interview and I was hired. I was supposed to go to Chicago, but San Francisco interviewed me first and I was offered the job. I went and my life changed. I took the position as grants officer, and I was promoted in a year to be the assistant regional director for Human Development of Health, Education, and Welfare. I had five years in that office. I was in charge of the programs for the states of California, Nevada, Arizona, and Hawaii, and the whole Pacific—Polynesia, Micronesia, and a bit of Melanesia. It was a headache in many ways, but it was also a learning experience for me because it taught me the extent of human need and the importance of being an objective yet caring and compassionate person when doing public programs and dealing with society's needs as they emerge. I had a staff of over a hundred people.

I retired in 1983. I had a wonderful boss, George Miller, a Nixon appointment, but what a wonderful man. He was one of the finest people I'll ever know. San Francisco is a very difficult region because everybody wants to come here. And they come with different agendas of why they want to be here. And it made it wonderful for me because I was able to live in a city where you can love who you wish and do the work you love.

Western New York was colored; the Bay Area is black. And you've got the people in the Bay Area from the Deep South, people who you would never know in Buffalo. They're here in large numbers, and I found friendships I never knew possible, people from Louisiana and Arkansas and Texas. Their stories, there's one from Texas, Ruth; she's ninety-two years old now. She's fantastic. She's marvelous. And she'll talk about her experience. She was raised in the cotton fields, and here she is with a beautiful home. She has her own life and still drives her own car. Then there's my friend Cora and her friend Sally, who died. All of these three women have become important in my life, people I would never have known. And there's another woman, who is partially blind, but who has an elegance about her that makes me realize that I'm blessed to have people such as these to work with, to fall in love with, and to know they are my friends.

Most of the blacks came during World War II and went to Richmond, California. Ruth said she lived in Dallas and was working in a white beauty shop. She got on a train, and when it pulled into Pasadena, she saw the flowers and said, "You know, I never went back. I called my landlady, and said, 'Send my things.' " And the landlady sent her things, and she said, "I worked at Lockheed for thirty-some years." And then she moved up and married a man in Berkeley, and he died and left her this house, paid up. All these people, they lived in paid-up houses. And Sally was this wonderful woman who came from Louisiana, and during the war and as the people came in, she'd take them into her house as roomers, and she'd say, "Look, I bought a house for you today." "What do you mean?" "I put five hundred dollars down. Now, you pay me back. But you got a house." And when she died, the church was filled with over twenty people who got up and said that she helped them become home-owners.

Every time I take these ladies out, it's a learning experience. We go to the market in Oakland and I see people. I'll say to them, "[Are you from] Louisiana?" "How do you recognize it?" There's something about the dignity of the older people that I recognize. They carry themselves with great dignity, and each one of them has a story. What I do, I go up to them and say, "I'm cooking greens today. What do I need? How do you cook that?" And before you know it, you're deep into conversation with them. And you get the story of their lives. They're amazing, amazing.

My mother, when she was a young woman in New York City at the turn of the nineteenth century, worked as a deaconess at Ellis Island. When I was at the Tenement Museum with a friend, the man said, "Any of your parents come through this house that is now a museum?" I said, "My mother probably worked here." The young colored girls who were college students from, say, 1905 to 1915, they didn't have what they call social workers; they had deaconesses. Women on the weekends would work with the Eastern Europeans as they came over. And the man said, "Well, I can't believe that. Colored people?" I said, "Yes, there were. If you come to my house, I'll show you pictures of them, the five girls. They called themselves Les Cinque—the five. And they worked down there on the East Side, when they used to move the people from the island to the Lower East Side as they started their march through American society to where they are today."

I've met the people from Texas and Arkansas who have the same history. Mr. C. Taylor was one man from Arkansas who worked for me as my yardman. Some of the stories would curl your hair, as he'd talk about running away as a twelve-year-old boy, falling off a train, and being left for dead. And an older woman picked him up, called "Auntie." He said, "Auntie took me in and brought me back to life." And he said, "You see that line of trees, dark leaves, that goes from the Bay Bridge out to Richmond? I planted every one of those trees." He's Man Mountain, a big, strapping black man, and you look at his old age. When he went through my yard, all I could see was this man mowing this yard, grabbing things up. He cleared out my backyard. When I came to the house, they hadn't kept the backyard. Within one day, all I could see was this man, grabbing and creating. And to hear his stories. I said, "What's your name?" "Mr. C. Taylor. I don't want any white person calling me by my first name." So he's Mr. C. Taylor. His name is Cal. He said, "But when I'm away from this house and away from home, I'm Mr. C. Taylor."

I work in a shop as a volunteer where we get discards from many of the fine homes in San Francisco. The things we can't use, we send to a shop out in Richmond, where the three ladies—Ruth, Cora, and Sally—and others work. It's a wonder to see how these people give love when they sell these things to the people who come to that shop. It's a type of charity, and I'm just amazed. It makes me feel good to see people who have humble beginnings living in dignity and greatness. What keeps me going is the fact that each day I'm on borrowed time now. I'm nearly eighty years old. And each day, I celebrate. I'm not a Christian, but I look upon myself as a very fortunate person, to have been born as I was, to be raised in Buffalo, where there was a charm, even though it was deceptive. And then in the army, I got my first chance to really get to know other black people and to know them as personal friends. And the academic experience and the wonderful years in the government, traveling all over the world, being sent to Paris and London, and working there and finding that there was a mecca on the West Coast, the Bay Area, San Francisco. I moved there, and I've never regretted it. I say, well, you can check out, but you can never leave that city. It's true. I consider myself to have good health. The only thing I got now, since I'm older, is my health. Money can't buy health. Nor memory. Nabokov said, "Speak memory." You mine your memory. And I think of these memories. There are tons more of them, but it's basically where I am, and I'm grateful.

[Interview by Alan Govenar, June 22, 1997]

*Jeni LeGon, Vancouver, British Columbia, 2005.*

# JENI LEGON

ACTRESS AND TAP DANCER

*Born August 14, 1916*

*Jeni LeGon is an entertainer, actress, and dancer who was one of the first African American women to develop a career as a soloist in tap. A low-heeled dancer, she combines flash, acrobatics, and rhythm dancing. Growing up, she honed her skills on the street in neighborhood bands and musical groups. When she was thirteen, she got her first job in musical theater, dancing as a soubrette in pants, and by the age of sixteen, she was dancing in a chorus line for the Count Basie Orchestra. She toured the South with the Whitman Sisters, an African American–managed company, and was part of a chorus line that, she remembers, "had all the colors our race is known for. All the pretty shading from the darkest, to the palest of the pale . . . a rainbow of beautiful girls." In Los Angeles, LeGon became known for her flips, double spins, and toe stands, and she was cast as the first African American dancer partner for the legendary Bill "Bojangles" Robinson in the 1935 MGM musical* Hooray for Love. *A year later, she performed in the London production of C. B. Cochran's* At Home Abroad. *In the 1940s, she appeared in more than a dozen movies, including* Easter Parade *with Fred Astaire. In the 1950s, she played a glamour gal on the* Amos 'n Andy *television show and established her own dance studio. In 1969, LeGon was invited to perform in Vancouver and decided to relocate there, encouraged by her friends and students. Over the years, LeGon has continued to perform and to mentor young dancers. She is the subject of Grant Greshuck's 1999 documentary* Living in a Great Big Way, *narrated by Fayard Nicholas.*

I'M NAMED FOR MY GRANDMOTHER, whose name was Jennie Bell. I was born in Chicago, Illinois. My mom's name was Harriet Bell Ligon, and my dad's name was Hector Ligon. But when I got the contract in Hollywood many years later, Luella Parsons [the gossip columnist] didn't have space to write "nnie," and she wrote "Jeni," and we had it legalized, and I started spelling my given name Ligon as LeGon because I have French blood.

My mom was just a housewife, and my dad was a chef, who also worked on the railway as a rail [Pullman] porter at one time. He died when I was quite young. He worked at one of the big hotels in Chicago. I can't remember which one it was now, but he was a chef there.

My family came from the bowels of Georgia. It was called Goose Pond, and they moved to Atlanta, and that's where my mother met my dad. My father was a Geechee. He was from South Carolina. It's an interesting culture. It's very African. And mixed.

Well, I had a wonderful childhood. We were a large family. My [maternal] grandmother was the matriarch of our family, and she used to hold court every Sunday. We had lots and lots of relatives who had migrated from the South to Chicago. And they would come and pay homage to Grandmother on Sundays. She had a wonderful porch where she lived, and in the summertime she'd have her rocking chair there, and she'd have the first cousins and seconds, thirds, and fourths, and all of them come and say hello to her and tell her what they were doing, and she'd report as to their progress and their new babies, etc. One of her brothers lived to be a hundred. And we had a wonderful, wonderful family reunion at that time, and I say, if by chance a man was shooting a movie and he wanted to have an interracial cast, he could have got it from our family because we had everything from the whitest of the white to the blackest of the black and all the rest of the hues that we are famous for.

We lived on the South Side of Chicago. I was born at Forty-fifth and Wabash. And I went to school in that section. When I was about nine or ten, my folks moved further south, and I graduated from the school across from Washington Park. The very first school I went to was called Doolittle. I went to two or three in between because we moved. During that time, there was a migration of lots of people, black people coming up from the South, and the whites were moving out and leaving us all their property, places to live. So I lived in different neighborhoods, and

I went to a school where there were more white kids than black kids. And that's how I got my good education—unfortunately, I have to say that, but that's true.

Some of my family owned their own property and some didn't. My grandmother had nineteen grandchildren during the course of her life-time. I can't remember all of them. But my mom had six sisters, and we used to have wonderful get-togethers, and we'd celebrate the birthdays in our family. If two of the kids had a birthday at the same time of the year—I had a cousin who was born in August, like me—we had a joint party. And we'd have it usually at one of the wonderful amusement parks in Chicago, either Riverside or White City, or either Lincoln Park or Washington or Jackson or someplace like that. We'd have a wonderful time. And my folks used to entertain. My brother was a singer. My sister was a singer. My oldest brother was a pianist and was a comedian and could sing, too. We used to do lots of stuff like that at our house during that time. That's how I got bitten by the acting bug.

I started dancing when I was about nine. We used to dance on the streets and do shows and stuff like that. I was a champion. We were do-ing the Charleston, the Black Bottom, and all of those wonderful things. Jazz records were out in my youth, and wonderful bands began coming up to Chicago. There was a lot of St. Louis blues and stuff like that that was popular in those days. I can't remember exactly all the music that I heard when I was growing up.

Well, I was ill at one time, and I went south. I had eczema, and our family doctor suggested that if it was possible—it was in the wintertime—I should go south and lie in the sun, and I would be cured. And this is what happened. I was about eleven years old, and a friend of my sister invited me to go south with her, to Savannah, to stay with her folks. Well, I did what the doctor said and I lay in the sun every day. And while I was there, the kids down there were very interested in show business, and at the end of school time, they had a contest between the east- and west-side kids. They found out I could dance, and so they asked me to repre-sent them on the west side, where I was living. I won. I was going to be a gym teacher. That's what I had excelled in as a kid. But when this hap-pened, I realized I was actually becoming a good dancer, and I went back to Chicago.

I didn't start remembering music until I was about eleven or twelve, when I heard Duke [Ellington] and Cab [Calloway] coming from the Cotton Club, and I began to go to the Oriental Theater in Chicago. They used to have stage shows with the movies. That was when Count Basie became popular in the late twenties and early thirties. And I used to go see all the wonderful shows and all the dancers. I got a chance to audition one time, and I was selected, and that led to my getting in the chorus line with Count Basie's band when it was presented by John Hammond at the Uptown Theater in Chicago.

Later on, I got to go to Hollywood by pure accident. I had a foster sister, and we had formed a little dance team together, where we sang and danced. Her name was Willa Mae Lane, and she was an orphan. My mother more or less let her come and stay with us. I met her at a dance audition one time, and she at that time didn't really have anyplace to stay, and I brought her home, and my mom said, "Let's keep her." And we did. And we made this little team. So what happened was, we had a chance to go to Detroit and we did. We went there. And we were working in a theater and also in a nightclub in the hotel that we stayed in.

Leonard Reed—he was the producer of both the theater and the club—and I became the MC at the club. I had some cards made, and I was spelling my name Jennie, "nnie," like my grandmother did, and it had "Jennie MC" on the cards for the hotel there. I think it was called the Watkins. I can't remember. Anyway, some friends of ours from Chicago called us to come to Hollywood from Detroit. We were working the two jobs, and we were doing pretty well. We asked ourselves, "Should we give it up or not?" And we said, "Oh, let's go," so we did. A gentleman brought us out to Hollywood, out to Los Angeles, I should say. There were eighteen of us. He was the "Some of These Days" man. Shelton Brooks. He was the star of the show that we were going to do in Hollywood. And we had a lady singer. And we had three boy dancers, my sister and me, and about three or four other people. This gentleman told us that he had a job for us, and when we got there, it wasn't true. So we had to hustle and see if we could get ourselves together. And he put us up in a hotel and paid our rent for almost a month, I believe it was. Then we heard about an audition being held by a gentleman named Earl Dancer, who had been Ethel Waters's manager. He was doing a show for Fox studio for Mr.

Will Shehan and Will Rogers on the Fox lot, and they were also going to appear at the Ebell Theater on Wilshire Boulevard. And on Sundays, at the Wilshire Ebell, at that time, most of the agents in the city could bring their people that they thought had the qualifications to be selected for movies because the casting agents from all the studios came.

So we did the show at the Fox studio, and Earl, he liked us, but he didn't like us as a duo, he liked us separately. And he hired me for my own kind of stuff, and she danced differently from me, and he hired her for her stuff. And we both were in the show, and what happened is at both Fox and the Ebell, I stopped the show. Mr. Sheehan liked me, and RKO was in the studio, and they signed me for the first movie I did, called *Hooray for Love* with Ann Sothern and Gene Raymond. I got to dance with Bill "Bojangles" Robinson.

And then, Earl was negotiating with Fox and MGM about signing, and Fox was slow in signing, so he signed me up at MGM. And then we

Jeni LeGon and Bill "Bojangles" Robinson rehearsing for the movie *Hooray for Love*, RKO Studios, Los Angeles, California, 1935.

did a concert, and Miss Eleanor Powell and I danced on the same show, and the same thing happened: I had this horrible habit of stopping the show [and outdoing Miss Powell]. So the next day, Earl was called down and told that they couldn't have two tappers on the show. But they sent me to Europe, and that's how I got started.

I was in a show that was in New York, called *At Home Abroad,* starring Ethel Waters, Bea Lillie, and Eleanor Powell. It went to Europe. It didn't actually tour Europe. We just did London. The show was renamed *Follow the Sun,* and some of the numbers that were in the original show were used.

In London, I met Paul Robeson. He lived there for years, and he was a friend of Earl Dancer's. They had met one another as youngsters. Earl was my promoter; he was my manager. I stayed in Sloan Square; it was just grand. I'd see Paul Robeson not too often, but once in a while. In America, they thought he was a communist, and they put him out of the country. They wouldn't let him come back for a long time.

I've acted since I was a kid. But the only people that I really wanted to copy were Josephine Baker and Ethel Waters. I just thought they were the grandest of the grand. They were my mentors. And I got the job with Count Basie because I did imitate Josephine.

I met Josephine [Baker] when I was in London as a kid. And on my birthday, we had a big birthday party for me, and she was living in Paris, of course, at the time, and some friends of hers and Earl's were visiting. Josephine had been in the show *Shuffle Along,* and this gentleman was one of the stars of it. Some of Josephine's friends were the big headliners on the vaudeville circuit there in London. But every year, because they were Americans, they had to go out of the country, and they always went over and stayed with Josephine. And that year, they went over, and Josephine knew about my being in the show, and on my birthday, they called me to wish me a happy birthday, and I talked to her. And then about six or seven years later, the last time Josephine was in America, she came to Hollywood, and these same people took me to see her, and I saw her in person. I had talked to her on the phone before. She was a beautiful, wonderful lady, grand, just a princess. She was very courteous and very nice to me. And I can't say any more than that. Ethel Waters was the same. She was wonderful. I met her through Earl because Earl had been her manager.

When I came back from Europe the first time [after appearing in a show with Ethel Waters], I just made different movies. I've done twenty-four movies. I have acted, and I've danced in them, and two of my movies that I danced in, the dance sections—I sing and dance—and two of the sections were disliked by the leading ladies, and so they cut out the dancing and left the singing.

The first movie was called *Fools for Scandal* [1938], and it starred Carole Lombard. And I do a number in there called "There's a Boy in Harlem." I sing and dance. And I wear a top hat and a white dress suit. And then, the other one was with Jimmy Durante and Gertrude Niessen in a movie called *Start Cheering* [1938].

These movies were mixed [with whites and blacks]. We were selected to do a part in each of the movies. Later on, the first all-black one I did was called *While Thousands Cheer* [1943]. It starred at that time the young, wonderful athlete from UCLA whose name was Kenny Washington. He was a big star athlete in football. We danced together and acted together, and then I did *Hi-De-Ho* with Cab Calloway. And I did *Easter Parade* [1948] with Fred Astaire and Judy Garland, and *I Shot Jesse James* [1948], and *Somebody Loves Me* [1952], which I liked, with Betty Hutton.

It was outstanding when I got the contract to work with Bill "Bojangles" Robinson in *Hooray for Love* [and was the only black woman to dance with Bill Robinson]. I mean, I couldn't believe it, because I was just a youngster from back East, and I hadn't really been a show host. I had just been dancing, but was never anywhere near being on a circuit or anything. So to get that particular job to dance with him—at that time he was king of tap. Bill Robinson was wonderful. Very nice.

[Being black in Hollywood] is just like the rest of America—you're separate. You're just black, that's all. You didn't socialize at all. In fact, I was laughing about that a few weeks ago because as long as I lived in Hollywood, I think the only reason Al Jolson and Ruby Keeler invited us to their home was because he and Earl were working together. Earl was hounding Ethel [Waters], and he was trying to get his foot in there, and they used to bottom and top the playbills. You know about that, don't you?

Well, what happened is that during the time of vaudeville and all that sort of stuff, if you were at the top of the bill, you were the star, and if you were at the bottom of the bill, you were the next star. And so, you wanted to be the top star, and they used to change positions [on the playbill] according to how much they were paid or how they appeared in their last gig. So Ethel [Waters] and Al [Jolson] were one of the shows. And Earl knew Al, and he invited us to their home two or three times. We had a wonderful time. I think we went two or three times. But that's the only—other than a lady that had a son in my classes when I taught, and also a gentleman I met on the show that I did called *Arabian Nights*. And those are the only white homes I'd ever been in until recently. In the last few years, I've been in a couple. But I was never invited to anybody's home in Hollywood. I never ate with anybody. In fact, when I was under contract at MGM, I was making twelve hundred fifty dollars a week, and we went into the commissary and started for the main dining room, and they told us we couldn't come in. That was Hollywood then, my dear. It was a black-and-white thing, and you did not socialize, and that was the end of it.

Same thing [on the set], same thing. You were there to do your job, and they were there to do their job, and they didn't even have to speak to you if they didn't want to. Twice, I think—like I said, this gentleman I met on the *Arabian Nights*—he and I had a conversation. One director took to me, and he talked to me during intermission and stuff, but I never spoke to the stars. That was a lot of bull corn.

[When I danced with Fred Astaire] that was at rehearsal time, and we were on the RKO lot. All of the dressing rooms in the building were where the rehearsal hall was. And Bill [Robinson] had his and I had mine, and Astaire and Rogers had theirs. And their dance studio was more or less for them, and they had two or three others, which were used like when we came in. [Bill and I] had one, you know, where we rehearsed. As I said, Bill knew Astaire from back East, and so, they were acquainted, and we would go and watch them rehearse, and they'd come watch us rehearse. And what had happened, I was touted at the time because it was quite a novelty for me—as I said, for not being known or anything—to receive such a wonderful contract and to be in the picture [*Hooray for Love*], anyway, with Bill and then to get the MGM contract. I was the first black woman to get a long-term contract. And I think I understand that at the moment now, there's a play about Lena Horne on Broadway, and she's claiming to be the first, but I was there ten years

before she was. But anyway, that was it, and Fred Astaire never acknowledged me as the person he had danced with on the lot. I couldn't believe it.

In *Easter Parade,* he [Astaire] did his own thing. I was a maid in
*Easter Parade.* I didn't have a dancing part. I was just a maid, and I only
did one scene with him alone. I'm sure if you've seen it. I did the opening scene with Ann Miller and Fred Astaire, too.

I don't know [what made tap appealing to me]. I just knew how to do
it, and that was the end of that. I didn't take any lessons or anything. I
just tapped. Well, like anything that you want to do, you have to work at
it, perfect it, stay with it, love it. If you don't like it, don't do it.

[I can't tap] like I used to. I'm too tight. What's happened is when my
film came out, the documentary called *Living in a Great Big Way* [1999], I
was rediscovered. The movie has reopened the interest in me, and since
'99, I've been invited to these tap festivals because tap fell out for a long
time. There were no tappers doing anything on Broadway or anywhere
else. But then it took hold again, and so they've been having these wonderful tap festivals all through the country and also in Europe and all
around. And I've been invited; I've collected thirty awards. It's just simply fabulous. And I've been inducted into the New York Tap Association,
and also in Chicago and also in New Orleans.

Oh, when I came to Canada, it was kind of a fluke. What happened
is, I was up here working. In the late sixties, I had a group called the Jazz
Caribe. And the reason for it was that during that time, [Harry] Bela-
fonte's stuff became so popular. And I had a mixed group playing the
steel drums, and a young man who did the limbo underneath [a bar supported by] two Coke bottles. And he could also do a fire pole two feet
from the floor. We had a jazz section, a four-piece jazz band, and I played
drums, congas, and timbales and all those shakers and stuff like that.
And we did the steel drums. I called it Jazz Caribe, and I got a job up in
Edmonton and Calgary, and the kids [the performers in my group] at
that time were from Chicago. They all went back to Chicago, and I came
back, because Los Angeles was home, and I was going home. I met a
young man in Edmonton, and he said, "Well, when you get to Vancouver,
stop and look up certain performers." And so I drove back by myself,
from Edmonton going home down to Los Angeles and getting ready to

do a new show with my Jazz Caribe, because I had been doing it for about four years, and I did the army posts and the private clubs in Oklahoma and Texas and all around down there. It was a good job, and I enjoyed it. And I played the South and all the way over to Boston and New York and all that sort of stuff. Anyway, the long and short of it was that when I came here, to Vancouver, I went to a club, and not only was my friend there, but two of my ex-students were working there, and they convinced me to stay. I was going back home to L.A. to re-form [Jazz Caribe], and they said, "Oh, stay here and teach because you have a wider variety of techniques." And they said on a Monday, "We'll get you students," and they did. And by Thursday, I had a place to teach, and when I opened the door that Thursday, I had twenty students. That was in 1969. And I haven't left. That's my story.

We're people up here [in Vancouver]. They don't have any black and white problems. I have dual citizenship. I'm both now. They won't let you in America become a complete Canadian. You have to keep your American citizenship, which is okay. I don't mind.

In Hollywood, I played a lot of different kinds of maids. I've been an Arabian maid, I've been an African maid, I've been an American maid three or four times. And then, as I said before, the hurting part was that the numbers that I sang and danced in, they took out the dancing part, which was very cruel, although I like seeing myself sing, and they're damn good numbers. My best for me was with Betty Hutton in a movie.

I met the Lindy Hopper Norma Miller many, many years ago in Hollywood when she came out to do that wonderful show *Hellzapoppin'* [1940] for Ole Olson and Chic Johnson, who were making a film of their hit musical by the same name. And since then, I have had the opportunity to dance with Norma. About four years ago, I danced with her in Seattle, and then last year, she was there when I was presented an award [in 2001] from the Flobert organization in New York. It's an organization named for Florence Mills and Bert Williams that gives awards to those of us who've made it, and I happened to be one of them. Norma was there because her dance partner, Frankie Manning, received one, too. And we were all together, and I have some pictures of us talking backstage.

In Canada, I've done lots of things. I was on a Pfizer advertisement with a wonderful gentleman—it was in *Time* magazine as well as on the screen. And the best so far this year, what's happened to me, I just came back from Ottawa, the capital here, and it was in conjunction with Black History Month. And I was invited to come, and it was called "Blacks in Canada: A Rich History," a film screening of *Living in a Great Big Way*, about me, Jeni LeGon, and *Speakers for the Dead*, by a couple named David and Jennifer Southern. And it was just simply a wonderful time. And for me to be selected, not being a native Canadian, it's an honor. I've been in a few TV movies since I've been in Canada. One was called *Nobody's Child* [1986] with Danny Thomas's daughter, Marlo, and *Cold Front* [1989] with Martin Sheen. In *Nobody's Child*, I was a resident in a home where we were all sick and stuff like that. And in *Cold Front*, I just did a couple of lines in the presence of Martin Sheen, out here in our park, Stanley Park.

I don't know [what keeps me going]. I just love it, and I keep getting called, and I say no, and then I say yes. I think I might retire. I don't know. I'll see what happens.

[Interview by Alan Govenar, March 8, 2005]

*Josephine Harreld Love, Detroit, Michigan, ca. 1980.*

# JOSEPHINE HARRELD LOVE

ARTS ADVOCATE

December 11, 1914–September 12, 2003

*Josephine Harreld Love grew up in Atlanta, Georgia. She graduated from Spelman College in 1933 and completed a postgraduate year at the Juilliard School of Music in 1934. In 1936, she received a master's degree in musicology from Radcliffe College and subsequently attended the Mozart Academy in Austria. Four years later, she met William Thomas Love (1901–1966) in Detroit, and they married in Atlanta in July 1941. William Love was a physician who earned his medical degree at the University of Michigan in 1930. Following an internship and residency at People's Hospital in St. Louis, Missouri, he moved to Detroit to open a private practice, though he also served at several facilities owned and operated by blacks, such as Kirwood General, Burton Mercy, and Edyth K. Thomas Memorial hospitals, as well as on the staffs of Hutzel Women's and Grace hospitals. Mrs. Love was a scholar-in-residence at Radcliffe College from 1966 to 1969 and completed the last year of her studies in Paris, France. Early in her career, she taught piano, and over the years, she was a tireless worker in the African American community of Detroit, sponsoring field trips to museums, plays, concerts, and other cultural events. She was a staunch supporter of the Michigan Opera Theatre and served on the original planning committee that led to the commissioning of the new opera* Margaret Garner, *with music by Richard Danielpour and libretto by Toni Morrison. Mrs. Love cofounded Your Heritage House Fine Arts Museum for Youth in 1969 and continued as its director until her death.*

I WAS ONE OF THOSE CHILDREN who did not resist the plans of a parent for his or her career. I grew up in a home surrounded by musical people and permeated by music. My father was a violinist and a teacher of music whose ambitions were for me to become a violinist. In that respect I did oppose him, but that is a story in itself. He had a quarter-size violin under my chin by the time I was three years old. However, on my own I began around age four or five to go to the piano to pick out tunes. I have always had what is known as a good ear and could play easily what I had heard.

At the time, my father had a large music studio in our home. There would be sometimes as many as five or six students playing different instruments in various rooms in the house. He was a choral conductor, head of a college music department, and often played the piano as an accompanist for soloists, Later, he headed the music departments of two colleges, was chapel organist at one of them, and music director for a graduate school.

There were a number [of musical influences in my life], but the strongest one was a remarkable woman, a pianist, whose name was Hazel Harrison. She started visiting our home when I was about six years old, [and she] was impressed by the fact that I had made a great deal of progress in learning to play the piano and encouraged my becoming a student of piano. She made an arrangement with my parents to teach whenever her tours brought her through Atlanta—the place of my birth and growing up—and extracted a promise from my father that he would pursue the matter diligently between times. She selected the music that I was to study and suggested technical approaches. The music she chose for me was delightful. When I became a full-grown professional, a pianist, and a teacher of piano, I often used these albums of music by Schumann, Tchaikovsky, Bach, Grieg, and others that I had first learned through lessons with her.

Meanwhile, my father proceeded with his determination that the violin would be my instrument. In the end, I made the choice at age ten. We were to attend a conference of the National Association of Negro Musicians in Indianapolis, and I would appear on the Children's Matinee—an established tradition of that organization's annual meeting. However, I was not staying in the home in which my parents were lodged and was therefore free to work on my own—away from my father's supervision—so I practiced only the piano, and on the day of the concert I announced to the master of ceremonies, an old family friend, the violinist and composer Clarence Cameron White, that I would play the piano, *not* the violin. I shall never forget the expression on his face when he made the announcement! He was tremendously amused, although I am not sure that he realized at the time that he was an agent of my rebellion! I have rarely in my life given a better performance!

The bargain I struck with my father after that was that I would practice the violin, but never more than a half hour per day, and that I would play in the orchestral concerts that he organized and directed at the college. Later, I played the viola in the orchestra.

At age twelve, I became a professional child, a pianist, touring frequently, giving solo recitals and playing my father's accompaniments for his violin recitals. I studied piano with my father through my college years with trips during the summer to Chicago, where I worked with Hazel Harrison. After that, I went to Juilliard School of Music. I had fine instructors there; a major influence on my musical thinking came later than that when I enrolled at Radcliffe College and took up graduate studies in musicology in the Harvard University Department of Music. There, my advisor, composition teacher, and strongest advocate was the great American composer Walter Piston. He revolutionized my thinking about music and gave gentle but firm direction to my studies.

There have been other influences, but none that equaled the ones that I have talked about. I have had many musical friends and have enjoyed a number of my teachers. Most recent were those with whom I studied at the University of Michigan during the early 1960s—Hans David, the great Bach scholar, and Eugene Bossart, a fine pianist and well-known accompanist, my ensemble coach. I cannot imagine a finer one. He spent a year helping me prepare for a series of two piano recitals with Carol Diggs, who is now, unfortunately, dead. She and I were a two-piano ensemble as teenagers, went to Juilliard at the same time, and then after two and a half decades of not playing together, came together again for a series of appearances in Southern colleges. These tours were cut short by her death.

I should add that I have been greatly moved and influenced by performers with whom I had little or no direct contact and have enjoyed a rich diversity of musical relationships.

My strongest inclination as a child of five, six, and seven was to dance! I was given no formal training. At the age when children my age were studying ballet, I was allowed to "move naturally." My parents had advanced ideas about such things. They had seen and read about Isadora Duncan, the great advocate of natural movement whose ideas about children centered around their moving naturally and as they were inclined to respond to music. It was fascinating for me only a few years ago to discover that my great musical idol, Claude Debussy, had written a ballet for children called *La boite aux joujoux*, for which he demanded that there be no ballet master—only a stage director! This was revolutionary for his time, and especially so in a country like France, where ballet reigned supreme. In college, I danced with the modern-dance group.

During my two years at Juilliard, I attended quite regularly a class in life drawing and sculpture at the Clay Club, a sculpture studio founded by the daughter of my mother's high school English teacher. They had kept in close touch. I became acquainted with an exciting group of now quite famous sculptors at the Clay Club on those Friday evenings in Greenwich Village.

Since young adulthood, there has been no equivalent in my life for the exposures and associations I had then with artists in the world of art outside of music. To name a few—Richard Harrison, who played De Lawd in *Green Pastures*. I heard him give readings when I was a child. What a thrill to be taken to New York many years later and to the theater where he was playing! He was denied access to the legitimate theater till the end of his life, but during the last three years was chosen to play the one role. He died in his dressing room while his part was being taken over by his understudy and devoted disciple.

Between Atlanta, Chicago (where we spent summers), New York, and Boston, which we visited frequently, I met most of the exciting artists of the day—Richmond Barthe, the sculptor was in Chicago as a young man. Meta Warwick Fuller, a well-known sculptor of the day, made an indelible impression when we visited her home in Framingham, Massachusetts, when I was seven. These first impressions were reinforced during return visits years later. Recently, the sculptor Elizabeth Catlett took a small plaster statue of Mrs. Fuller's which she saw in my home and had it cast in bronze in the foundry in Mexico where many of her own works are cast. A few years ago a delightful young woman visited my home and I discovered [that she is] the granddaughter of Meta Warwick Fuller. She is assembling the catalogue raisonné of her grandmother's art. Meta Fuller was a student of Rodin in Paris in her young days.

Sculptors seem to occupy a special place in this group of remembered personalities. One who must be added is Elizabeth Prophet, also a longtime resident of France, who lived and worked on the campus at Spelman College during my last years in Atlanta and was a close friend of my father. One unforgettable scene in my memory is of her struggling up the front walk of our home on my wedding day. She was carrying an exquisite pearwood statue, which she had carved many years before in her Paris studio. French pear trees grow for many decades and make exceptionally beautiful works of art when carved by artists like Miss Prophet. We had many conversations during the years that I knew her. She was a striking, impressive person in physical appearance as in spirit. Her students in the art department at Atlanta University had the rare opportunity to meet one of America's most dynamic artists. She was a native of Rhode Island—of mixed black, Indian, and Caucasian heritage.

There are many, many others—writers . . . Charles Chestnut, the black novelist, in his late years, fishing from a pier on a small lake at Idlewild, Michigan, where we went my twelfth summer to visit Hazel and Birdie [her mother] Harrison. I took a snapshot of him with my first camera! Benjamin Brawley was a close family friend. Jessie Fauset visited in our home. W. E. B. DuBois was a special friend. During his years in Atlanta, I often chatted at length with him. He would park his car at the "bottom" of the campus in order to catch an otherwise-prohibited on-campus smoke. What a giant! He was not bitter, but knew the sometimes ridiculousness of human behavior. He was master of the sardonic comment—always with the twinkle of mischief in his eye. Several years after coming to Detroit, I invited him to spend the Fourth of July in my home here. He surprised me by coming. My mother was here on a visit. His father had attended the Niagara Conference, was a leader in the movement and—like Dr. DuBois—an impeccable foe of Booker T. Washington. As a wedding present, Dr. DuBois gave me autographed copies of several of his books, among them an original printed copy of the famed Philadelphia dissertation.

During those years I knew Langston Hughes—not closely but at an admiring distance. Autographed copies of his poems are among my most prized possessions. He had tremendous influence over my thinking at the time. Ethnicity in art was the legacy of the poets of that period— Countee Cullen, Langston Hughes, Claude McKay, James Weldon Johnson, Sterling Brown, and some of the novelists such as Walter White—they were the New Front, the cutting edge of our lives for those of us who were growing up as part of the succeeding generation. As I read *God's Trombones,* I was also hearing that genre of poetry at the source—fiery backwoods preachers, or the Dry Bones sermons heard re- peatedly day in and day out on records played on gramophones in the neighborhood of my childhood, the storefront church across from our house, where an itinerant preacher held forth on Saturday nights boom- ing out fundamentalist beliefs in rhythmic and poetic cadence.

E. Franklin Frazier gave me my first intelligence tests. He insisted that I be accelerated in school. My parents followed his dicta. I was al- lowed to skip grades, some with tutoring in summer on the side porch of our house! My parents insisted that these lessons should be conducted where there was fresh air and sun. Frazier was a gently sardonic man. I can understand it all now. What the U.S.A. has done to these brilliant and accomplished black men! Denial of proper and deserved honor and elevation, set apart, not understood for what they were—global people!

My choice of literature from the age of eleven years on was guided by a close friend and colleague of my father, Nathaniel Tillman, head of the English department at Morehouse and Atlanta University. His choice for my reading, shaped to my inclination of the time, were the novels of Thomas Hardy, Arnold Bennett, Dickens, Trollope. On my own I discov- ered William Faulkner, Henri Beyle, Stendhal, Southern writers such as Lillian Smith. Shakespeare was part of daily living. The Atlanta Univer- sity Players—and before that the Morehouse drama group—did an annual production. Some of those student actors made impressive Hamlets and Macbeths.

Today, my preference is largely for biography, but I relish the novels of Nadine Gordimer, who it is rumored is up next for a Nobel Prize, and the unforgettable Toni Morrison. A few years back I discovered Nabokov, but my favorite of his books is autobiographical—*Speak, Memory.* My closest friend among writers has been [the poet] Robert Hayden, whom I met shortly after coming to Detroit. His death in 1980 was a great personal loss. He took great interest in Your Heritage House and knew in a heightened sense what it is meant to be. His generosity to our museum was on the large scale. Erma Hayden remains one of my closest friends. We have many interests and concerns in common and are part of the same profession—music. Nathan Huggins is a new discovery, a marvelous spinner of historical narrative.

Well, I love to write and am doing more and more of it. Currently, I am trying to pull together a monograph on the life of my mother. The most recent writing to be published is an article on the life and career of Hazel Harrison written for *Notable American Women,* a supplement to the original book published by Harvard University Press, for which I wrote an article on E. Azalia Hackley.

There are other subjects for which material has been gathered. I spent three years on solid research for a book on music for children written by notable French composers from the age of Louis XIV until the present. This involved research on the painters, poets, and other artists of those three centuries whose creative output occasionally centered upon children and youth.

I have a number of unpublished articles on black musicians that began as lectures and should be sent to magazines for possible publication; also articles in the sphere of the arts for children. Unfortunately, my constraints of time keep me from doing what should be done about them.

It would seem that my current occupation was once my hobby—working with children and involving them in the arts. It has become my vocation. Your Heritage House began in my childhood. I was educated by the poets—the creative, expressive people of my time. That is the goal here, to surround children with the poets, the artists, and the musicians of their epoch. My own activities with children began almost when I was a child. In my teens, I had many younger friends. I gathered them around me to teach and entertain, taking them on cultural outings of one sort or another. In college, I had a sort of adopted child, a little girl whose name was Susie May, a three-year-old whom I discovered in the course of walking to school. She lived with her family in a poor little house. I noticed her bright little face and made friends with her, took her for holidays, and finally arranged for her to enter the nursery school at Spelman College, one of the model programs of its sort in the U.S.A. at that time. When she was tested, it was discovered that she was in the highest percentile for intelligence, and the university system under which the nursery school operated agreed to guarantee her education through college and graduate school. The experiment was halted when her family was forced by the Depression to move to Huntsville, Alabama. I went there to see her when she was about ten, but that genius was clouded over by the experiences of poverty and deprivation. It broke my heart, for I had tried every possible means I could think of to keep her in Atlanta. Everywhere I went after that, I was in touch with young children. In my years as a music student in New York, I directed music programs for the Harlem Girl Scouts. During my second year in this position, I arranged and produced a pageant. Early in my career as a concert pianist and teacher of piano, there were many similar kinds of undertakings— and before and after coming to Detroit, I gave numerous recitals for young audiences in large and small urban communities in almost every part of the U.S.A.

During my first year in Detroit, I had two little friends whom I started taking to concerts and, because my car could accommodate more children, offered to take others. It ended up with my having a group of between fifty and sixty children who met me regularly on Saturdays for the youth concerts of the Detroit Symphony Orchestra, the Clare Tree Major Children's Theater performances, and for a monthly meeting held at the Detroit Urban League. The children named their club the Merry MADS—Music, Art, and Drama Society! We went not only to the concerts and plays but took in the opera, puppet shows, art exhibits—we heard Paul Robeson sing, went backstage afterwards, and had all of our programs autographed by him. (Not long ago, I gave the Paul Robeson School one of those programs for their collection of Robeson memorabilia.) Our monthly meetings were devoted to discussions of past and upcoming programs. We started what is now the Your Heritage House Library with books and recordings purchased with the children's modest "dues," which of course I had to supplement. The children took home the books and records between meetings. Following that, there were other children's clubs. It was apparent that children need more direct experience, hands-on experience, in the arts. Puppetry was the ideal mode of expression for them. It involved acting, writing, music, painting, sculpture, movement—all the arts. So we drew on the younger membership of the Merry MADS and younger brothers and sisters for formation of another club—the Merry Marionettes. These children remained together three or four years, making marionettes and producing shows. A younger group made hand puppets. They became very competent in the art under the tutelage of two accomplished artists—Mary Giovann and Emma Robinson. The first two productions were *Peer Gynt* by Ibsen and *Ali Baba and the Forty Thieves.* Our basement was their workshop, and their Friday-night productions-cum-workshops became known around Detroit. Many persons dropped in just to see their work and to view their rehearsals. One of the teenagers wrote a musical score for *Peer Gynt*—completely new and original. They also did a variety act and later went out around the city giving performances.

Some of those children from the two groups, the Merry MADS and Merry Marionettes, became professional artists. Alvin Loving Jr. was a well-known painter nationally [he passed away in 2005]; Joseph Wills is an architect in New York City. Others have a continuing interest in art and are solid patrons. The nicest tributes come from those who tell me that they are providing similar experiences for their children. My daughter, who was one of the younger ones, has served on the board of directors of the Capitol Ballet in Washington and is currently considering starting her own arts-management office to present exciting new artists in the field of music. My son, who lives in Chicago, is a supporter of the Kuumba Players, who spent over a month at the Music Hall in Detroit a few years ago. He was a member of the Mostly Music Club, formed after the children outgrew puppetry—going off to college or pursuing other interests.

This group was active during the fifties and was what the name describes—mostly about music. They were my piano students and a few others who once a year gave a music and drama production based on the life and works of a particular composer. I had two friends who were interested in the theater, Mayo and Jennie Partee. They did the staging and costuming. Their son, a member of the group and always a leading performer, is now an ace television cameraman and has won an Emmy Award. The plays the children gave were settings for formal recitals of the works of the composers—Mozart's life as a child and young composer, the family life of Bach and his compositions for family members. These plays gave lasting impressions of these musical geniuses to players and young audiences. Pathways to Music, another group of children, first assembled in my home for a class in music appreciation. The children were from the families of now well-known art patrons—the Konikows (he is president of the Detroit Chamber Music Society), the Schwartzes (a few years ago Alan and Marianne Schwartz presented funding to the Detroit Institute of Arts for the exquisite new Fine Prints Gallery), the Andersons (Victoria Anderson Davenport is a member of the Detroit Arts Commission). We did a puppet show about a little girl who dreams about the instruments of the orchestra. This class was later taken over by the Detroit Community Music School. Its final performance—just before I left Detroit in the late 1960s for a three-year stay—was a parlor version of *Hansel and Gretel* with an original opening scene in which a fat little boy played Humperdinck arriving at the home of his sister with the score of the opera stuffed into the pockets of his overcoat—a Christmas gift for the sister's children (this is based on actual fact).

In Cambridge, Massachusetts, where I lived for two years, my studio became the "children's place" for visitors to the Radcliffe College Institute of Independent Study. I taught the children of Harvard University faculty members there and had some small friends who loved to come to my studio and look at the books and pictures I kept there for them. I also had some of the recordings of music for children and toys that now reside at Your Heritage House. During all of these experiences a large collection was started, and these plus the experiences with organizing children's programs grew into what is now happening at Your Heritage House on, of course, a much larger scale. When we had the Merry MADS, the book collection was begun. Merry Marionettes was the beginning of doll and puppet collecting. Pathways to Music and piano-teaching activity were the beginning of the vast collecting of musical scores written expressly for children. The years in Cambridge and in France produced incomparable additions to the whole collection—personal collecting and numerous gifts from persons met during those years who became interested in my dream of starting a museum for children whose sole theme and raison d'être would be the arts.

Your Heritage House has brought about intensified collecting and many gifts, some quite important, single items and small collections. In France, I met people who could, in the spiritual sense, share and appreciate my dreams and goals. I was taken to the home of the composer Maurice Ravel, outside Paris. It has been preserved as it was when he was alive. The person in charge at the time of my visits was Celestine Albarez—famous as the young housekeeper who helped to care for Marcel Proust during his final years and whom he mentioned repeatedly in *Remembrance of Things Past*. Mme. Albarez opened the house for me on nonvisiting days so that I could wander freely among the memorabilia of Ravel. I wound up his mechanical toys, had them photographed, and enjoyed the ambience of his home where childhood was "preserved in amber." Ravel never forsook his own state of being a child. He understood what that meant more than others. Among his closest friends were the children of his friends. I have written about this in a catalogue prepared for an exhibit I assembled for the Detroit Symphony Orchestra Ravel Festival held a few years ago.

I met Helene de Tinan—"Dolly"—the stepdaughter of Claude Debussy and wrote a chapter of my book about her experiences as a child. Gabriel Fauré dedicated an album of his piano pieces to her when she was a baby. He was a close friend of her mother, who later became the wife of Debussy. Two young American musicians whom I met at her home confided in me that rumor had it that she was actually Fauré's child. The mother, however, was married to a prominent banker in Paris—Dolly's maiden name was Bardac. If Mme. de Tinan is still living, she is in her nineties. She cried when I read to her the chapter that I had written about her and said that no one had ever understood so thoroughly her life as a child.

I discovered in my research at that time, and at all other times, that the inspired and meaningful imperishable music and literature for children stems from the artist's close association with children. From this discovery comes my own strong belief that the artist and the child enjoy natural affinity. The barrels of materials that I have accumulated over so many years amply testify to it. Children have a capacity from childhood on to create and express in a natural way. They are always improvising—tearing apart and pulling together. It is the aesthetic process. They have their own special kind of language and movement—that's creativity! My belief is that there are natural bonds between those people who are just beginning to learn and do (children) and those people who learned how to do in special creative ways. Every kind of experience that we've had at Your Heritage House bears me out. We hire persons who employ sophisticated modes in the art of aesthetic expression who in turn are able to suggest in subtle ways the child's employment of his or her abilities and inclinations in shaping and reshaping materials, redesigning surfaces. The process is completely fascinating; the results often amazing.

The youngest children are two-year-olds who can attend a Family Arts Workshop with their parents. At four years, Creative Movement is offered, and at five years, Explorations in Art and Music, the beginning of learning about producing and putting together musical sounds. This is coupled with the introduction to visual art. Sketching, painting, sand casting and other types of ceramics, paper sculpture, collage, note reading, pitch recognition, and techniques of learning to perform on simple, easily mastered musical instruments comprise the Explorations in Music.

Around the age of eight, more formal instruction in sketching and painting are available. Puppetry and filmmaking, techniques of modern dance, piano lessons, and, as we move ahead, other forms of training in music. theory, composition, other instrumental training are already or will be introduced to the curriculum in the near future. A Young Artists' Workshop tops the course of study here. This is for those students more focused on becoming proficient artists. During the summer and during previous periods, we have offered textile art and youth drama. These will be introduced again as we find persons to conduct the workshops. There is a fine mixture of ages and races and origin within the metropolitan area in our student group.

[Other art education facilities in Detroit include] the public schools—of course, first of all when "cuts" are not in effect. The Center for Creative Studies has a youth program. Marygrove College offers work in dance. The Jewish Community Center in Southfield has a long history of effective tuition in the various arts. In the central part of Detroit, there is not a great deal available, particularly in visual arts. Some neighborhood programs, after-school centers, exist, mostly not really formalized programs offering many levels of training.

[Black children are] definitely not [sufficiently exposed to art education opportunities]. For one thing and for prime consideration is the fact that often black people feel alienated from the formal focal life of the city and its institutions. They feel unwelcome. For out-of-work persons or the many in unfavorable work situations, the arts are a luxury. However, these can be the persons most eager to enroll their children in programs like ours. Our society sets up so many barriers to open access to culture. Television's pervasive influence does little to reverse this situation. Unilateral decisions come down from on high as to what black folk really want and enjoy. In many instances, the response of the black community bears them out. However, I believe that no assumptions should be made as to who should look at or listen to or be given access to what. The church has often served as the acculturating factor in the lives of black people. It has also served to keep them apart from the total culture.

The problem is often that the art institution ignores or is ignorant of the affinity that it may have with the arts of the people of their epoch. Folk cultures of earlier times are revered, researched, displayed, performed, but those forms of culture that lie closest at hand are often not heeded.

Art is too often associated with wealth and privilege. Artists starve to death while art patrons become more affluent. They drive prices higher and higher, and consider art their exclusive private domain. There is a terrible incongruity here. We still think too little about the plight of the artist in our society. There is no law of nature or society that rules that squalor is the natural condition for those who produce great art.

I would say that the force of his or her message [makes the artist great]. I was impressed with a statement made by Elizabeth Catlett when she was here. She mentioned that she and her husband talk about an issue of ten thousand prints while it is considered that a limited edition of not more than fifty or one hundred prints is de rigueur among artists and collectors of the printmaking establishment. The argument for the accessibility and availability of art on a grand scale was most convincing.

[Art is for everyone.] True! I observed this in Mexico recently. One sees articles made of paper sold at minimal cost—beautiful objects of papier-mâché, for example, masks, puppets, bowls, figures of animals and birds—affordable by almost anyone, adults and children, rich and poor, purchasable for pennies. We don't have the equivalent of that in this country.

I think that Detroit could have a great future as a center for art. Many good things have happened. There is a groundswell of interest in the arts. Experience the evolution of Hart Plaza that made many people aware of the contribution that an artist like Noguchi could make to the interest and vitality of the city. There are few residents of the city who have not been in some way exposed to this extraordinary phenomenon. There have been other events that have had similar fallout. However, I can think of none that equal that one. The entire populace heard the name; thousands saw the sculptor [Noguchi], read about his meeting with city council, enjoyed the exhibit and the posters at the Detroit Institute of Arts. More artists could be brought here and exposed in the same way—commissions for public work, follow-up visits.

For Your Heritage House and for me, Detroit has been the ideal setting. At one time I thought of leaving, going back to Atlanta after my husband died and the children were living elsewhere. But I would not have had the resources there that this city offers—the backup of studio artists, educational institutions with strong arts resources, the developing University Cultural Center Association with which our institution is growing up, of having a voice in what is said and done. I enjoy the close proximity of Canada—the Art Gallery of Windsor is a wonderful example of a growing-up institution like ours. It has full support of the provincial government and a marvelous people-involving style of performance.

You know that one of the things we forget is that many children find their way to experiences outside of their immediate environments. For as long as I can look back in Detroit, years of living and working in the shadow of the Institute of Arts, I have seen black children going up those steps, curious to know what was happening inside and often on their own without older members of their families.

Unfortunately the reception inside has not been what it should have been for them. It was not a matter of the children being considered acceptable, but a matter of staff not always attending properly to their needs.

As a young artist, I began more and more to understand that the enjoyment of musical programs was too often limited to the more ingratiating numbers placed at the end. This sent me in search of repertory that could lead to deeper understanding of all of music.

Last year I had a most agreeable experience when I went to Washington for a dinner given by the National Black Child Development Association. There was someone present from every period of my life up to now—adults who had been children in my programs, older adults who had known me as a child, childhood playmates, and one of my own children. In the audience were three young women who were in the Merry MADS! They are educating their children in the arts as they were educated, they said.

[There] are the children whom we must go out and seek and hang on to when they show the least bit of interest. I could share with you many experiences of the latter that we have had. There have been a number of interesting recent occurrences here with young people in the immediate neighborhood identifying in a very complete way with our institution. One of our most talented students in the summer classes came to the city to spend some months with his father. He lives in California. The boy happened to pass the building, saw other young people around, came in to investigate, and returned with his grandfather the next day to register for classes. Often we have neighborhood children bring their friends to visit or, in passing by, point with pride at our building, attempting to explain what happens here—the exhibits, the classes. We have even had children return stolen items. There is definitely a message that they receive in terms of what Your Heritage House means for them.

When one considers the wide range of choices open to youth today, the shoddiness of so much of it, their wanting to be here has great implications. What is needed is an extension of this to more youth—many more.

We spend a great deal of time thinking about this. One need is for

adults to help us find youth—searching them out in their neighborhood—enlisting the help of teachers, principals, pastors, businesspeople, parents, group leaders, in recruitment. The children they meet on
the street, see in church, must be encouraged to come. I have learned
how to pass out literature on the streets. It is important that we take programs into neighborhoods. As we develop our outdoor space, we must
stage more outdoor events, children's festivals, games—days like the ones
held during the summer. We hope that our environmental program—
where children explore their environment through the arts and hopefully,
at a later date, through humanities and sciences—will enlist hundreds of
youth of the city. During the summer of 1980, a group of twenty youths
began studies in landscape art. They started a small park. We want them
to work on neighborhood history, developing a sense of the past and its
importance to the future—theirs in particular. Even more importantly,
planning and designing for the future can be a part of the curriculum.

Basically, I believe in the unlimited capacity of the individual for
self-realization, for realization of the close natural ties among individuals that need to be discovered and cultivated, and those among society
and its numerous peoples. We become so involved in petty issues among
family members, among friends and acquaintances, and among the
larger societal groups. These issues become exaggerated when countries
and groups of nations pull apart for trivial reasons. It is painful for me to
see so much division, so much evasion of the common issues that should
bind people together. That other way, the divisive way, is not the way I
want to live.

My grandson attends a school in Washington that is like a small
United Nations. It is a beautiful sight—the children outside the school
mornings and afternoons, clusters of them representing all kinds of nationalities and races. I wish that all children could have such exposures
to language, to customs, to appearances, to cultures, and to religions.
The children have so much to offer to one another at this stage of un-
selfconsciousness. It will affect their attitudes towards those other than
themselves all of their lives. On another level is my great faith in the
heroic principles of living, the need to strive for originality, the innate
capacity that each individual has for ultimate greatness of character and
achievement. There are so many dimensions of living that we lose sight

of. Pettiness and materialism are archenemies—the tendency to diminish capacity rather than to enlarge it. Our innate spirituality is so often overlooked.

In the projects that children do, they often become very personal in their expression, whether it be painting, drawing, performing, filmmaking, modeling. I try to encourage teachers not to limit this individual expression. Copying is discouraged, even in a class like the Sketching in the Galleries at the Detroit Institute of Arts, in which they are drawing from painted, drawn, or sculptured subjects. For example, one of our instructors had children sketching armor. As they worked, she had them redesign the armor, thinking of what it was enclosing—a shoulder, leg, arm, thigh—articulating the various parts covering different areas of the human body or the body of the horse on which the rider was mounted. In the course of the study, many revelations were made, such as the fact that mounted knights' armor had no metal covering the hips, or the design of a helmet to allow for seeing and breathing. This leads to observations about the nature of fighting and war—ancient, medieval, modern.

When they sketched the Diego Rivera murals, they were again expected to recompose, as one does in listening to music, but this time with the eye and pencil. It was an exciting adventure that put the young person in the place of the original artist, seeing as he or she had seen. Individual expression became greater, and none of the drawings came out looking the same. Again, the murals served as springboards for discovering the role of Detroit as the scene for manufacturer and laborer and those important issues in modern living.

Filmmaking offers even greater opportunities for expressing the spirituality of the young person. At one time several of the films done were about life in the school, about drugs, interpersonal relationships, and the environment. One beautiful film done some years ago was about litter—a child wandering down an alley filled with trash and garbage and how he learned to transcend the environment to which he had been assigned by society.

I want our film teachers to deal more than they do with reality. There is a tendency today to stress animation, trick photography, mirth and merriment. This year I am expecting more in the way of documentary and narrative of young people coping with and interpreting life.

Young people do [write things that could be perceived as being religious]. Very often, I pick up snatches of verse or prose which they have left behind or thrown into a wastebasket. Our society is not saturated with religion. It is not like fifty or seventy-five years ago when the church played a more dominant role, but young people's views are decidedly moralistic—passing judgment.

Architecture—when does one first awaken to its various manifestations? In [Atlanta], the city of my childhood, there were outstanding examples of Southern colonial. One was the home of Alonzo Herndon, mentioned elsewhere as one of the first black millionaires. Mr. Herndon owned the city's finest barbershop and was president of a large insurance company that has now become one of the nation's best-known black businesses. His shop was in the Five Points area, center of the downtown business district. Its clientele was composed of the richest white men of the city. It was elegantly appointed. When he died, the shop was willed to its employees as a guarantee that black people would own property in the downtown area.

His home was a majestic mansion—pillared, boasting a sloping green lawn, beautifully tended flower beds, and a handsomely furnished interior. My first awareness of Tiffany glass was gained there. The first and second Mrs. Herndons were ladies of consummate good taste and breeding. The first one died before I was born. She had been drama coach at the old Atlanta University. It was rumored that wealth won over education and polished manners when she chose Mr. Herndon in preference to the handsome, promising young physician just starting practice with whom she was really in love. He, incidentally, was the doctor who brought me into the world. Mr. Herndon uttered impure sentences, had a rough manner, and a heart of alloy—some gold, lots of iron. He respected learning and built his home on the block occupied by the homes of the president and a longtime professor at the university. The city never paved it during his lifetime or that of his second wife. It was a subtle, mean way of keeping Herndon in his place!

I have wonderful memories of visiting the home with my parents. My mother knew the first Mrs. Herndon. My father had known the second from his days in Chicago as a young man. Recipient of the fallout from these warm relationships, I enjoyed those luxurious surroundings.

They were the site of subliminal learning about architecture and interior design.

In the house across the street, another kind of learning took place. George Towns taught at Atlanta University for over fifty years. He was a scholar of impeccable standards. The home was filled with books and art and talk by people of great learning. It was filled with interesting young people—the Towns children, some years older than me, and their friends from the campus nearby.

The other house on the street was Bumstead Cottage, where presidents of the college had lived in succession. In my high school years, Carrie Bond Day lived there—drama coach at Atlanta University and future anthropologist. She studied with Ernest Van Hooten at Harvard and wrote one of the first books on black-white families to be published in this country—an anthropological study.

In the course of her research and writing, she received a great deal of advice and help from my mother. They were close friends. During her days as drama coach, I learned about New York theater, poring over her copies of *Theater Arts* magazine and her fine collection of books about the theater and performing arts. This became a kind of systematic training about theater arts and the work of performing artists of the day. This included those who worked in the puppet theater as puppeteers and designs—Gordon Craig, Tony Sarg, Paul McPharlin. In my junior year in high school, Tony Sarg brought a puppet production of *Alice in Wonderland* to the Spelman campus. It affected my life from that time on, as did those evenings curled up in Carrie Day's library learning about contemporary theater, becoming a reality for me when productions were brought to the Atlanta Theater—*Mourning Becomes Electra* and productions of Shakespeare by Marlowe and Southern, an eminent husband-wife acting-directing team. We traveled to New York in the summer occasionally, and I saw two memorable stage productions, *Green Pastures* with Richard Harrison and *Blackbirds* with Ethel Waters.

Outstanding among those early days were pageants given at the colleges—*The Open Door*, written by my kindergarten teacher, Gertrude Ware. These performances combined dancing and acting and were remarkably well done, at least from a child's point of view. I appeared in them as a member of the youngest dancing group. Also, my father produced musical plays in which I was cast as a butterfly or one time as Sunshine, half of a Sunshine and Shadow team, which was my first and last appearance with a male dancing partner on stage!

Mother also produced pageants that dealt with the founding of Spelman. It is from those days that I first remember Alberta King (Mrs. Martin Luther King Sr.).

This tremendous involvement of children and adults in the cultural milieu is the precasting of Your Heritage House. Our undertaking cannot have the same force within the social context of today. Ours was a segregated world that developed its initiatives out of isolation. Life today is scattered and more diffused, more complicated. People are more skeptical, more dependent on the media, more materialistic. They are, I believe, less conscious of children's real need for constant but gentle and subtle surveillance, for membership in the full family and adult circles.

My parents employed baby-sitters, but more often I went with them to lectures, concerts, exhibits, services, and public affairs and to the homes of their friends. They entertained frequently. Their home and those of many of their friends were stopping places for the persons of accomplishment of our race who were denied accommodations in the hotels of the day. What a thrill a few years ago to answer the phone in a home I was visiting in Wilmington, Delaware, and hear the voice of one of those early visitors in our home—Marian Anderson. It took me back over a half century to the times when my father arranged her tours of colleges and churches in the South and my mother took her under her wing, providing accommodations for her during and between engagements. Recently, I completed an article for publication in *Notable American Women* [Harvard University Press, 1980] about Hazel Harrison, another frequent visitor. Others came for an evening in a constant parade of vibrant, accomplished people. I was never barred from enjoyment of this adult society, as I see too often in the case with so many of today's children.

When I was ten years old, my art teacher was Mabel Brooks. Her special interest was Italian Renaissance art. I recall that the Metropolitan Museum of New York City had a traveling exhibit at this time [1925]. My mother and Mrs. Brooks, along with Alpha Kappa Alpha Sorority, were responsible for bringing this exhibit to Atlanta University. Every summer, I traveled with my parents to Chicago, and I was allowed to spend a great deal of time visiting the Chicago Art Institute, where I participated in classes for sketching. When I was an undergraduate at Spelman College, I studied African art and cubism under Hale Woodruff, who was my studio-art teacher for two years. In New York City, I was very fortunate as a young woman to study sculpture and life drawing under Hosea DeCreeft, Frank Elisue, Cornelia Denslowe, and others.

A final word is this. I'll have to live forever if I am to do what I want to do. I will say that all of these experiences constitute a wonderful opportunity. I enjoy the kind of life I lead. It has been filled with more than a reasonable share of tremendous experience. The best of this has been sharing with children, helping shape their experience, designing their lives, helping them towards self-determination and towards contributive roles. There is a positive effect. We see it here day after day. I see it in their response, their interest in continuing, their concern about what happens to their projects, the relationships that develop between individuals, their attitudes about one another, about their teachers, their observations and comments. More and more they return [to Your Heritage House] bringing their friends.

During a summer session, we saw overnight transformation—greater self-control, ameliorated hostility, lengthened span of attention, better socialization, and most of all, flowering expression. When the program was first designed, I did not anticipate such immediate apparent, visible, appreciable growth. This is an extra reward—a bonus received, not expected. From those young people who have been here and are now older and moving farther out into the world, there is remarkable testimony of what this experience has meant to them. Our charge is to make it happen again and to gain more and more!

[Interview by Marlene Chavis, June 30, 1980]

*Walter "Brownie" McGhee in the music room of his home, Oakland, California, 1990.*

# WALTER "BROWNIE" McGHEE

BLUES MUSICIAN

*November 30, 1915–February 16, 1996*

*Brown Walter "Brownie" McGhee left his home in Knoxville, Tennessee, at age eighteen to perform his self-taught blues in medicine shows and juke joints around the South. He made his first recordings in 1939. Stylistically, he was influenced by the Piedmont blues of Blind Boy Fuller, and for a brief period after Fuller's death in 1941, McGhee was billed as Blind Boy Fuller Number Two. He moved to New York in the early 1940s and teamed up with harmonica stylist Sonny Terry. Together, Terry and McGhee joined with folk blues legend Huddie "Leadbelly" Ledbetter to perform with the Woody Guthrie Singers. In 1948, McGhee started a blues-guitar school in Harlem called Brownie McGhee's Home of the Blues. In the 1950s, he was invited to perform in films, as well as in such plays as Tennessee Williams's* Cat on a Hot Tin Roof *(1954) and Langston Hughes's* Simply Heavenly *(1957). Throughout the 1960s and '70s, McGhee and Terry toured extensively as part of the blues and folkmusic revival, appearing at festivals across the United States and abroad. In 1982 McGhee and Terry received National Heritage Fellowships from the National Endowment for the Arts.*

I NEVER DREAMED OF BECOMING A MUSICIAN. But my father was a guitar player in front of me, and I liked what he was doing. I had polio when I was five. My idea of life did not know what it consisted of. I wanted to be a lawyer or doctor. A good education is what I wanted. I used to read a lot. But Mother and Father separated when I was five. So in between all of that, financial difficulties and family affairs got in the way. I got a high school education. And when I finished high school, I didn't have any money.

My daddy said, "You have to make it on your own now, son."

I thought you could go to school until you got tired of going, but I found out about tuition . . . and my family had financial difficulties. They didn't have the money. So I went out searching for a school, and religion came into it. Methodist blacks had money. Baptist blacks didn't have much. And the Methodist people had Methodist black colleges. And so if I became a Methodist, I could go to college. But I was too independent to change my way of thinking, because I felt there was something funny about religion. If there was a God and he separated us like that [into different denominations], I didn't want any part of it. So I didn't go to college, and I say that's why I picked up my guitar. My guitar was my companion.

I thought my daddy made guitars. I thought he was the originator of the guitar because he played one. There wasn't anybody else around, and he made his guitar by himself. He played bluesy, what you might call music about his daily life, what was happening at that time.

Growing up with my father was marvelous, but he wasn't a highly educated man. He was a common laborer, and he only played his guitar on the weekend. And then when he'd have problems on the job or wherever he was working, he'd come home and—I knew that in later years, but I didn't know then—but he'd come home and play his guitar, and out of that guitar would come something. He'd sing a lot. And I remember now, it didn't rhyme at times. But what he would sing, it was like he was talking. I was so impressed with what he was doing. I liked to hear him play guitar, but my daddy played more guitar during the time he was drinking. And I really enjoyed seeing him drink because he would take a lot of time with me when he drank. And he'd show me things because I'd grab the guitar. And he'd tell me what was right or what was wrong. My father never abused me when he drank.

I play like my father. I remember he said, "You cannot strum a guitar, you got to pick it." And that's what I do, though I knew I'd never end up playing exactly like him. My daddy was my biggest influence, but I was also influenced by Lonnie Johnson, whom I heard on records.

A lot of lyrics that my daddy did I put into my songs later on—the way he talked to me is what I wrote. See, my daddy told me parables. And sometimes when he talked to me, I'd say it couldn't be possible. And I learned the songs "John Henry," "Betty and Dupree" from my daddy. A lot of the lyrics I learned from my father make sense now and are lessons to live by. And the things that he talked to me about I put into a song of my own. It's called "My Father's Words," and those are the tidings that are my ethics for living.

One of these lyrics is—I didn't know what he meant when he said it— "The longer the road, the shorter the turn." Another was "The taller the tree, the deeper the roots." That was pretty strong stuff. And when I began to realize what he was saying, it followed me through the years, those words: "No matter how long you live, you'll never grow too old to learn— the blacker the berry, the sweeter the juice."

Daddy would always say, "You got to love somebody if you want them to love you, but don't ever let your right hand know what your left hand do." "My Father's Words" is on my last album, called *Blues Is Truth*.

It wasn't that tough growing up in Tennessee because I had a roof over my head, and I had plenty to eat. I never had to go from door to door. One thing about my father, if we had beans, we had a lot of beans. If we had potatoes, I had plenty of potatoes. And I always had clothes. And so it was with shoes. And I had to go to school. I never played hooky. And if I was late, I got a whipping for it. If I was disobedient at school, I got a whipping, because the teacher would come by and say, "Walter was bad," and I got a whipping that day, not the next day.

I started singing at age eight. Whatever I heard, I'd sing it. I could learn myself. And what my daddy sang, I could sing. But I wasn't to do what he did; I had to do what he told me to do. My daddy cursed every breath he drew, but I never cursed until I got older. Now, I curse when I want to. Not because I have to, because it's not a demand, but my father, I thought he had to. When he didn't do it, I thought there was something wrong.

Yeah, everything I sing about today is from my childhood [sings]: "From my childhood to where I am now, I ain't gonna worry, I'll get by somehow. My mama had them. My daddy had them, too. You know I was born with the blues."

And I used to sing spirituals. "How sweet and a-happy seems, those days of which I dream. When memories recall them now and then. And with what a righteous feat, my worried heart would beat, if I could hear my mother pray again." I sang that song as far back as I can remember. And I don't think I ever heard my mother pray. But I remember her very well. I never saw my mother anymore after about the 1920s. She died in New York State.

I was brought up during the years of discrimination. But I was taught that I was the best, I was the greatest. Daddy would say, "Nobody is as good as you, son. You are it. You're good-looking, you're intelligent, and you're everything. Love yourself, and then you can love the world and everybody that's in it. But you must love yourself first. Give away a little bit, but keep the big end. Don't ever give it all to anybody. Keep some for yourself." And today, I'm as good as any man in the world. Better than some men that don't have—I don't even realize it—I had polio.

I went through all the changes. I had an operation. Walked with a crutch and a cane until I was nineteen. I sang my way a cappella. The State of Tennessee gave me three operations, didn't cost me anything. I threw my crutch and the cane away and took to the road. My life is built on experiences of reality.

I was discovered by a talent scout—J. B. Long—in 1939, in North Carolina. I had my high school diploma in my pocket, and I was singing in a black ghetto in Burlington, North Carolina. And some black washboard player went and told the talent scout, "Man, I hear a guy down there singing something. It's different than what we're used to here in North Carolina." And I was singing a song, a poem that I had written. It was called "Me and My Dog." And I was picking up nickels and dimes [in tips] and was gonna buy me some wine.

And this black boy, Washboard George, says, "Hey, Mr. Long wants you to come down to his store, man."

I said, "Who is Mr. Long?"

He says, "A white fella, man. He might take you up to make records."

"Oh," I said. "Man, I ain't got time to bother with nobody. You see this crowd I got?" I said I was picking up the change. I was making some money. Had my cap laying down in there.

But he says, "He's gonna stay in his store tonight late. He wants you to come down."

So I said, "Well, all right, if he's there late, I will."

But anyway, after I finished playing, it was after midnight, and this guy was still hanging around. He says, "Mr. Long is right down the street here." So I followed down the street.

Mr. Long says, "What's that song you're singing up there about this dog?"

Ha, ha, ha, tickled me to death. That was the first song I ever wrote myself. "Me and My Dog."

"Oh," I said, "yeah, 'Me and My Dog.' "

He says, "Well, sing it for me."

And I sang "Me and My Dog" for him. And he said, "That's nice." And he asked me a few questions about records. I didn't know anything about records. Here I was, a black boy talking to a white man in the South in the 1930s.

"How'd you like to make records?" he asked.

"Fine," I said. But I'd never made a record and didn't know anything about it. I wished he'd said, "Do you want to go to school?" Man, that would have been the best deal.

He said, "Well, come down here tomorrow. Bring your guitar, come down, and we'll see what we gonna do," and I did.

I didn't even know what in the world was going on. I never dreamed I'd ever make a record. I didn't study music. I had four years of voice in school, singing a cappella.

Well, he thought I was great. He took me up to Chicago. And I made a record. I had never heard myself. So he said, "We're going to play this one back. Listen to it." And I listened, but I didn't know what to say.

"How'd you like that, McGhee? Yeah, that was you."

I said, "Me?" I said, "No, I can beat that."

He said, "Well, that's good. We think that's pretty good. We gonna keep that one."

I said to him, "Man, I can beat that." That was 1939. And I've been trying to beat that ever since. Competing with myself. Because I'd never heard myself before.

So everything that Mr. Long said to me came to pass. He was trying to lift me up and give me some support. I don't know what he saw in me, because when I first met him, I was thinking, What's he telling me all this bull for? I told him I finished high school. Got my diploma, had a driver's license. And he said a lot of things to me, and it went in one ear and out the other.

He said, "You're the first guy that I ever heard sing the blues that could read or write." And he had recorded many of them. He said, "I'm from Georgia, but I got my store here in North Carolina."

I was looking at him, him talking to me, wondering how much of that he thought I believed. And so he said, "Now what you can do . . ." He taught me what I know about writing my songs down. I didn't know anything about writing, how long it took and what it takes. But I learned more, and I went along with him.

Well, J. B. Long was with Okeh Records [which became Columbia]. I heard him talk to that man [from the record company] on the telephone. That man was saying, "I don't want any more of those country blues singers. They make good records, but they don't sell." And J. B. said, "I think this boy's got something. I'm going to bring him to Chicago anyway."

So I went up to Chicago with J. B. Long. Whatever I made, you understand, I was rich. Because I earned it, and I signed a deal, but the point of it was, I didn't read it. And he didn't beat me out of anything. I loved J. B. He's dead. I know his children, I knew his wife, and I knew a lot of people around him after that. But if it hadn't been for J. B., I could have been sitting on a corner in North Carolina or standing on a street in Tennessee today. But I went along with him, and I went back home. I got a hundred and some dollars for my first record session. And was I happy? I'd been singing all day and didn't make two dollars. But in Chicago I sang six or seven lyrics six or seven times, and the man said, "That's it." I didn't know how to make records, and they just cut me off. All of my first records just stopped. There weren't endings because I didn't know anything about it. I'd just sing. And J. B. gave me a hundred and some dollars, transportation to Chicago and back, a hotel, and a meal ticket. And I thought I was rich. That's the first hundred dollars I had in my life, and I earned it.

When I left J. B. Long, he said, "Now you go on, man. You know, we'll do some other things [another time], but write down your songs. Write them down; your lyrics are great. Write four verses and sing three and play one, and then sing two more and out, and you've got a complete record. Make it about three minutes."

And as time went on, I learned the skill of writing songs, and then J. B. began to call me and write me letters, telling me my song "Me and

My Dog" was out and selling as a record. "Me and My Dog" was a song about a girl I had met when I was in the hospital, having an operation on my leg, and about her leaving me and going back to her mother. And the dog was in a picture above my bed. It was the RCA Victor dog, the one in the horn of the Victrola on the RCA Victor 78 rpm record label. I had my guitar in the hospital and I sang, "Just me and my dog, we don't have no friends right now. Woman I love, she lives like a queen, but I'll get along somehow."

J. B. didn't know that I was singing about that paper dog. He thought I was a lover of a real dog. And it was years later that I told him when he asked me, "What happened to that dog?" Me and him were driving along on the highway. And I said, "Aw, man, that dog, I left that dog on the wall." It was funny. Then I told him the story, and he thought it was marvelous. So that was the first record, the first song I wrote, first record I recorded, in 1939.

Now, J. B. never did copyright any of my songs. I didn't learn to copyright my songs until I got to New York. I thought I had a contract with Okeh Records, but I was actually only under contract to J. B. Long. Well, when the war [World War II] broke out, and I got into New York, I went down to Okeh Records, and the man there says, "We don't know anything about you. Who are you?"

"I'm Brownie McGhee."

"Brownie McGhee?" Then the girl in the office called out [to one of the executives] and said, "Come down. It's one of these crazy Harlem guys down here talking about how he works for Okeh Records."

Well, the man came down and said, "Who are you?"

And I mentioned J. B. Long. He said, "Oooh. Get J. B. Long's file."

"Oh," he said, "you one of J.B.'s boys. From North Carolina. Yeah, but we don't have a contract with you. We are not even buying J. B.'s boys anymore." Says, "We had a contract, but we bought you from J. B. You're as free as a bird far as we're concerned. But I'll give you a copy of everything you ever did for J. B. Long for us."

So I got the copies. To me, it looked like J. B. made a couple dollars. But I wasn't mad at J. B. because he made some money. If he hadn't made some money, then I'd have thought it was a trick game. But he didn't give me all he made because what he spent on me is more than what he got.

Nice as he was, taking me up to Chicago and back, I know it cost more than six hundred bucks, man. I had a fine hotel. I didn't sleep in any second-grade hotels in Chicago. I wasn't dropped on the street. And I had a meal ticket. That's one thing I had. And I had cigarettes and money for a drink. J. B. had seen to that. And then I found out that J. B. Long got six or seven hundred dollars a session for me, and he gave me a hundred and something. I didn't owe him anything, and I got clothes from his store, and I got cigarettes from his store. He had a store in Burlington, North Carolina, and he didn't charge me for that. He advanced me money. So J. B. was my life.

Brownie is my name. Brown. My name is Brown Walter McGhee. "Brownie" was given to me at school. My daddy didn't like "Brownie," but the kids called me "Brownie," and my daddy couldn't do anything about it. And I accepted "Brownie." I answered to "Brownie." He always told me Brownie was a dog's name. Brown is a man's name. Brownie is a dog's name. But anyway, I liked Brownie.

Now, for J. B. Long, I was playing under the name of Poor Brown. I wanted to be called Poor Brown. But J. B. said, "Let's do this. Anybody can be Poor Brown. But there can't be but one Brownie McGhee." And that's why, he says, "I like that better anyways. Why don't we stay with Brownie McGhee?" And that was it. And I changed my birth certificate. I was grown then, but after I got up and got to New York, I wrote home and got my birth certificate changed from "Brown Walter" to "Walter Brownie McGhee." Officially signed and sealed in Nashville, Tennessee, in the archives there. I am Walter Brownie McGhee. You see, Brownie McGhee makes the money and Walter B. spends it.

There were no clubs in the South. People should realize that. A black man hardly had a place to hang his hat. The ghettos were very narrow and small. And if you played anyplace, it had to be a whorehouse, a road-house, a whiskey joint, or a gambling den, or a medicine show. And I did medicine shows. Just to get around, hustling quarters and whatever I could get. But after my first record, I went back home to sit down to write my songs down.

In late 1939, I found out about the Library of Congress through J. B. Long. [The folklorist] Alan Lomax had called [the harmonica player] Sonny Terry. Lomax wanted Sonny and [the blues guitarist] Blind Boy

Fuller to come to Washington so he could record them [for the Library of Congress]. Fuller was blind, and Sonny couldn't see either, and J. B. thought I could pick Sonny up and help him catch a train or a bus. I could buy the tickets.

J. B. said, "Well, Brownie, you catch a train. At the L&N station, Southern train station. You pick up two tickets and you get off at such and such a place and call this man."

That was a responsibility I was qualified to do. Well, Sonny was marvelous. And I met him and Fuller at the same time. And after Fuller died, I made [the song] "The Death of Blind Boy Fuller," and J. B. called me Blind Boy Fuller Number Two, which my daddy resented. I never thought about it, because [that record] was a big seller. J. B. gave me a couple or three hundred dollars, and he gave me some money to put in my pocket and travel around and promote the record in North Carolina. That's why people think I'm a North Carolinian. But I'm not. I'm a Tennessean.

Well, J. B. Long [paired me with Sonny Terry] and created [the duo] Sonny Terry and Brownie McGhee. He asked me if I would go over and see if I could be of some help to Sonny after Fuller died [in 1941]. And that's how Sonny and me got together. Sonny couldn't see well, and I was handicapped to a point, but I took care of myself. And I went over to look out for Sonny and played around Durham, North Carolina, and people began to hear us playing around there together. We made a few dollars, and I stayed there in Durham with Sonny for a while.

Sonny was an individualist. He was on his own. I had a harmonica player when I met Sonny. I had a fellow by the name of Jordan Webb, and Webb was a good harmonica player and piano player. But when I met Sonny, I stayed with him. And so me and Sonny's friendship lasted thirty-five years until he died in the 1980s.

In the 1940s, Sonny and I went to New York. Alan Lomax and Millard Lampell, a writer from California, suggested that we come to New York to meet Josh White and Leadbelly. I had met Leadbelly in Washington. But I knew he was in New York. And then I met Lee Hays, Pete Seeger, and Alan Lomax, and Alan's sister, Bess Lomax, and then I met Millard and Josh White.

Clubs weren't my bag, because I was a street player, but I developed into a club singer. I had never played a club before. I was pretty rough when I got to New York. I had a steel guitar and steel picks. I'd wham down on it, and I didn't have any sense of microphones, because I never used a microphone on the street. They'd have to move the mike so far back, the guitar distorted. I just didn't have any club technique, period. And I had to develop technique. I knew I could make it. I would listen. I learned.

I did a lot of charity work. I wasn't a politician, but what did I care if there were politicians with some money involved? I played on shows with Leadbelly, Pete Seeger, and Alan and Bess and all the people back in that day, in the 1940s. Unions were just beginning. They had these func-tions. They were just big singing functions to me. They were talking communist, but it didn't mean a thing to me. Communist—I'd never heard the word before. I thought they were talking a word that I missed in the dictionary. We didn't study it in school. And anyway, it was just singing, and I sang my same songs. I didn't change my songs.

Leadbelly was great. I never met a warmer man than Leadbelly. I started living with Leadbelly after I got to New York: 604 East Ninth Street, that was the first place, in a coldwater flat, him and his wife. Sonny and me lived down there with Leadbelly, him and his twelve-string guitar. Ah, boy, he was marvelous to live with. I wished I'd known more about him. I lived with him about almost a year. You know, on and off.

I started recording with the Savoy label on December 12, 1944, at the WOR studio in New York. I picked up an agent in New York, a West Indian fella, Sam Manning. And I was singing on the street there in New York, and I got this invitation for Savoy to make some records, and I took it. But I had to pay my agent twenty-five cents out of every dollar. I didn't care about giving him the twenty-five cents to make some records, be-cause it was easy money for me singing.

I didn't have a big hit until 1948 with Savoy, but I had some good sellers, smooth sellers, but my lyrics used to be real shoddy. I used to do a lot of risqué songs: "Bad blood, let me look under your hood," and "Big leg woman." You know, if a record went South and didn't sell, it didn't come East. It didn't come back. If it went South and became a hit, you'd find it in New York. I learned that after I got there. It had to go South first. All blues went South. My biggest song for Savoy was "My

Fault," in 1948: "I'm beggin'. It's all my fault. Just give me one more chance, and I'll correct it all. I'm beggin', babe, it's all my fault. Just one more chance, and I'll correct it all. You know it's my fault, just one more chance, and I'll correct it all." That song came out of a misunderstanding I had with a girlfriend, right down the street where I lived. Oh, that song made money, two thousand dollars in royalties, and I was getting half a cent [a record]. I didn't even know what royalties were, because I never got any royalties from Okeh for records [that were selling] at thirty cents apiece, thirty-five cents at the most. I got some money from J. B. Long. But I don't know where J. B. got it. I never saw a royalty statement from Okeh Records. In the 1940s, records sold for seventy-five cents, then they moved up to a dollar.

After I recorded with Savoy, I recorded for everybody, [using] five alias names, and then I went to England and recorded. I made records for just about every company in New York. I recorded as Blind Boy Fuller Number Two, Big Tom Collins, Spider Sam, Tennessee Gabriel, and Henry Johnson. I made records under all those names. Well, I could compete with myself. Because I was voice wise, singing, I could sing with a sixteen-piece band and strum my guitar, and you wouldn't even know it was me, unless you knew me very well. I had a way of doing it. I fixed my guitar into a different style. So if I made a record, and Spider Sam sold, Brownie McGhee would come along and do the song, but it would sound different.

I got with my wife, Ruth, in 1948. I married her after my record *My Fault* came out. Her maiden name was Ruth Dantzler. Too good for a bum like me, but we were together about thirty years. She was from South Carolina. I met her in New York. I had four kids by her. She had two small kids at the time. I raised them. And my wife died in 1974, right here [in Oakland, California]. I bought this house for her. Sweetest girl in the world, boy.

I wasn't smart enough to relax until I got married. There was something missing in my life in New York. So I got married and I thought the whole world blossomed. She was a guiding light. She wanted me to play. She loved to hear me play. And she liked to hear me write. And after I married, I stopped writing bad about women. She said, "You know, I'm a woman. I ain't gonna buy that. You have to say something good about women." And you know, she'd say, "I don't like that verse." I started changing my lyrics, and she said, "That's great," or "That's beautiful," and I'd sing a song, she'd say, "That's beautiful. Be sure to record that."

Me and my wife, we'd sit down and talk. She didn't know how much I loved her. I couldn't tell her how much I loved her. But everything she ever said to me to do, I was successful. She got me on Broadway. She caused me to come to California. She caused me to go to England.

"Do it for me," she said. "Now, when you don't want to do nothing for yourself, do it for me."

That's the way my wife was with me. She kept saying, "You can make it." And I wrote one song. She didn't get to hear it. I wrote it. I never recorded it until 1975, and she died in 1974. "The blues had a baby, and they called it rock 'n' roll." See, that was before rock 'n' roll. And when rock 'n' roll started, I wrote this song, and we were up in the Berkshire Mountains, had the kids with us. And I said, I got an idea and I wrote it.

She said, "Oh, honey, why don't you record that? That's great." She always said, "That's the best idea you've had in a long time."

I said, "But, honey, if I record it now and then rock 'n' roll don't last, it's a dead idea."

She said, "Well, anyway, preserve it." She kept telling me, and I said, "Ah."

And I told her, I said, "If it lasts fifteen years, I'm gonna record it. I'm gonna give rock 'n' roll a chance. I'm gonna give the baby long enough to get fifteen years old." And so I copyrighted it. And in 1975 I recorded it.

I'll be seventy-five this year [1990]. Everything is still like it was with my wife. My house is just like it was. I got my family; all my children are grown. I've got twenty-two grandchildren and six great-grands, and I'm a proud old man. I'm a happy old man, too. I'm not greedy and I'm not worldly. I've had a good life. Not a bored life. I haven't looked back. Nobody did me so bad that I hate anybody. I love everybody; see I love myself, that's why. That's what makes me love people, because I love myself. Money has never been an obstacle. I've never let money get between me and happiness. I can't take it with me. I can't buy a passport to heaven and can't ship it ahead and have no fun where I'm going. So I stay here and enjoy life as long as I can and forget the rest of it.

What do I want to retire for? I'm the boss. I can play when I get ready. You know, I play piano, and I play my guitar. I play all the time. I don't want to prove a point. I ain't got any points to prove. I paid my dues. And I said something. And I've still got a lot to say. Can't leave me out. I'm the captain. I'm what it is. I'm the blues. I don't care who plays it, or how they do it. It ain't me. I know who I am. I am the blues. Blues is America. And the blues is me. I'm an American. I'm not an import. I'm real. Don't tell me that I'm old. I'm not.

Blues is truth. Blues is not a fairy tale, it's not an imagination. Blues is real. Blues is people. It's a living thing. You know, you can't get rid of it. If you get rid of the blues, America's dead. And America will never die because of the blues. The blues has made America, and America has made me. You can't tell a lie about it. And you can't get away from it; you can't go around it. It's too wide. You can't get over it. It's too high. You can't go under it. It's too deep. See, I don't care what other people do and say about it. It doesn't insult me at all. Blues will never die.

I'm not a musician; I'm an entertainer. What I get out of life is the way I feel. I'm not afraid to make an error because there are no errors in the truth. I know who I am. I can look at myself with my eyes closed. I know I'm happy because I am. It's not money. Nothing worldly makes me happy. I got plenty to eat. I got a couple of bucks. All of this is my philosophy. I live with this. I'm not ashamed to look back because I left footprints in the sands of time. I can turn around, and I can go back the same way I came. I haven't done anything in life that I regret. Happiness. That's what keeps me going. I have made it this far. It's the sunshine that makes me feel good every day. I can go to two or three banks and get me some money, but that doesn't make me happy. I'm so glad that I'm alive. I may not even get to the bank, but they'll say, "You know, McGhee was smiling." That's my life. That's where I am. Right here in this chair. This is heaven on earth to me.

[Interview by Alan Govenar, March 17, 1990]

*John McLendon, Chicago, Illinois, early 1980s.*

# JOHN McLENDON

BASKETBALL COACH

*April 5, 1915–October 8, 1999*

*John McLendon moved to Kansas City after the death of his mother when he was three years old. He attended elementary and second- ary schools in Kansas City and enrolled as a physical education major at Kansas University. McLendon attended Kansas University from 1933 to 1936 and studied with Dr. James Naismith, the inven- tor of basketball. In 1937, he began graduate school at the University of Iowa. After receiving a master's degree in physical education, he was hired as an assistant basketball coach at the North Carolina College for Negroes (now called North Carolina Central). McLendon is credited with desegregating basketball by challenging white-only teams to compete against his champion African American players. For McLendon, competitive sports presented a frontier where racism could be confronted and overcome.*

I NEVER SAW AN INDOOR BASKETBALL COURT until I got to seventh grade. And that was when I fell in love with it. My father and I were tour- ing the new junior high school to which all of the black kids in the city were going to go the next year. They had already gotten their staff to- gether in that other school, and when we were touring the building, in the middle of the floor was a man shooting a basketball. From where he was shooting, it would be four- or five-point shots (if there were such a thing). And he was making them. It fascinated me to the point where I decided I'd like to do whatever he was doing. He was a physical trainer. He wasn't even called a basketball coach.

His name was P. L. Jacobs. He'd come there from Washington, D.C., and brought this sport. He was going to have basketball in the junior high school. Well, the senior high school had it earlier, but now the ju- nior high school was to be incorporated into the senior school league.

P. L. Jacobs was my first coach, but when I went out for the team, he told me I'd do better in gymnastics. So I went out for gymnastics and made a letter in that. But I was student manager in basketball, and then when I went to Summer High School, A. T. Edwards was there. He was one of the most successful coaches in Kansas in the segregated league— the Kansas-Missouri Athletic Conference. But after I couldn't make the team, I had an agreement with him that I'd be his student manager. And I got to sit next to him during games, and I got to learn some of the best coaching that was going on at that time. I tried to learn everything about the game.

I wanted to go to Springfield College in Massachusetts because that was where Dr. James Naismith invented the game of basketball. But my father didn't have enough money, and I didn't either, even after working and putting aside money for college. But in the meantime, my father researched where Dr. Naismith was. He said, "Why go where basketball was invented when we can go right up here at Kansas University?" He found Dr. Naismith, and luckily for us, he was only forty miles away.

Well, when my father took me to the university, he told me to look for Dr. Naismith. He said, "Tell him that he's to be your advisor."

And I did just that, but Dr. Naismith asked me, "Who told you this?"

So I told him, "My father," and he replied, "Fathers are always right."

I went to Kansas University from 1933 to 1936. Kansas University was mixed, black and white. But there were only sixty blacks out of a total of four thousand students. I couldn't play basketball at Kansas University because they wouldn't let blacks play in any competitive sports. I just went there because Dr. Naismith was there. I wanted to be a basketball coach.

Now, when I went to Kansas University, Dr. Naismith had just started the physical education program through which you could get a degree, that is, if you combined it with health and some other minor subjects. My major was physical education and my minor was education and sociology. He got the university to approve the degree, but I had to take courses like anatomy and kinesiology, which were his main subjects.

Dr. Naismith said that he invented the game of basketball at Springfield College [in Massachusetts] in 1891. He had been a football player; he and Alonzo Stagg invented the football helmet. He was a football player when he was in college. So when he got to Springfield College, they told him his job was to find something for football players to do inside, and he came up with the game of basketball. The football players were unruly in the dormitory at night. They needed an indoor game after the football season ended to kind of wear the players out so that when they went to their rooms to study a little bit, they'd go to sleep instead of staying up all night being boisterous and rowdy. He tried indoor soccer at first. But it was too rough, and then he tried basketball, and that worked. Soon after that, Dr. Naismith brought basketball to the YMCA system, and the YMCA spread the game across the country.

Kansas was one of the first schools to have a competitive basketball program, starting in 1898. You see, after Dr. Naismith left Springfield College, he worked in Denver, Colorado, at the YMCA, but then he left the Denver YMCA and came to Kansas University as an instructor and also worked as a basketball coach and a physical education professor. He coached basketball at Kansas for a few years. He was followed by Forrest "Phog" Allen, who today is considered the father of basketball coaching, because he refined the game and developed strategies for making the game more competitive.

The main thing I got from Dr. Naismith was how to coach, the psychology of coaching, and knowledge of human anatomy and kinesiology. Well, the best philosophy for coaching is to get an understanding with your players. Understand what your goals are and merge their goals with yours. But also, teach the game. In a way, Dr. Naismith didn't really believe in coaching. For years, you couldn't have a time-out in a basketball game where the players could come to the sideline, because the players were supposed to have been instructed beforehand what they were going to do. And when they called time-out, the coach couldn't go out on the court, nor could the players come to the sideline. As a coach, you had messages that you sent—signals—and sometimes you wrote on little boards.

Dr. Naismith discouraged the coach from being such a big part of the game. He believed players should have a game plan that you gave to them. And they went out on the court and carried it out. Well, Dr. Allen came along and said, "No." It took a long time for them to follow Dr. Allen's advice, that you could have a time-out and the players could come over to the sideline and the coach could reconstruct the game or decide on a different strategy and so forth. Well, Dr. Allen was the first coach to start that level of involvement. And Dr. Allen and Dr. Naismith were in the same building, right down the hall from each other. I took classes from Dr. Allen—physical therapy and athletic administration—and I took principles of physical education from another teacher there in the building. So I got the whole picture. I was very fortunate, really.

When I graduated from the University of Kansas, Dr. Naismith asked me what was I going to do. He told me I should go to graduate school, but I said I'd have to go back home and go to work. I had been working at the packinghouse, Cudahy's packinghouse, in the summertime. And he told me it wasn't a good idea. He said, "You shouldn't discontinue your studies. It's hard to go to work and then come back to your academics." So I asked him, what could I do about it. I didn't have any way to go to school. He said, "Step in my office here a minute."

He called up a man named Ed Schroeder up in Iowa. They have a

John McLendon beside a photograph of James Naismith, Cleveland, Ohio, 1990s.

building on the University of Iowa campus named after him. But anyway, Dr. Naismith called him and said, "John McLendon will make a good student for you." Well, they knew each other, apparently, because Mr. Schroeder said for him to send me on. And I went to Iowa University because of a telephone call. But mainly, Dr. Naismith wanted me to go to Iowa because there was a man named C. H. McCloy teaching there. He was the leading researcher in physical education at that time. That was during the 1930s. Dr. Naismith had talked about him in class. And when I went there, I met Dr. McCloy, and we became very good friends because he had very special people in the graduate class. It was an opportunity to be friends and at the same time have a top-notch instructor. The only thing I had to pay to go to the University of Iowa was room rent. That was in 1937.

I went to graduate school through some difficult times. Those were the years of the Depression. And there was a lady there named Miss Lemmie, and she took in black students because they didn't have any residence accommodations for black students on the campus in Iowa. Years later, they named a school after her. Of course, she carried such a load for years. Practically all the black students came to her house. She had a big old house with about ten or twelve rooms in it. That's where I stayed. And she charged $10 a month per person. For my roommate and me, that made it $20 a month.

While I was a student in Iowa, I met a fellow named—well, he became Dr. William F. Burghardt. We were classmates, and we got to be great friends, so much so that that's how I later ended up in North Carolina. He was a distant relative of W. E. Burghardt DuBois, and he could trace his ancestry back to 1700-something. Of course, that name was the key to being able to do that.

He got a job at North Carolina College for Negroes. Today, it's North Carolina Central. And he sent for me after I finished my degree at Iowa, and I came out there as his assistant from 1937 to 1941. Then, he left to pursue a doctor's degree, which he finally got, and I became head of physical education and head basketball coach in 1940, '41. And I stayed another twelve years.

Well, North Carolina was heavily segregated when I got there in 1937. We were all members of what in those days was called the Colored

Intercollegiate Athletic Association. The name changed in 1945 to Central Intercollegiate Athletic Association (CIAA). We had about sixteen colleges in the CIAA. And it stretched all the way to West Virginia—West Virginia State and Bluefield State. In the north, there was Lincoln University of Pennsylvania and the University of Maryland Eastern Shore—they came in later—but Howard University was one of the schools. And there were five others in North Carolina, the largest of which was North Carolina A&P State University.

At that time, playing games between races was forbidden. It was against the law. But I had been trying to get my team to understand that basketball was a game that really needn't be segregated. The other side (the white league) was always in the newspaper, and the players were big heroes, and we didn't have any publicity. You would think each of us was playing a different game. I won the CIAA championship and never even made the newspaper once.

In North Carolina, I was able to put all that I had learned into action. I had been working on developing the fast break. I knew the fast break was a winner because it could use the few special abilities of an individual. It seemed more practical from a coaching standpoint than a system that depends on the all-around ability in all players.

My first coach, A. T. Edwards of Sumner High School, introduced me to an emphasis on superior conditioning. Then my junior college coach in Sumner Branch, Beltron Orne, a part-time psychology teacher, found a place for me, a small player on that team, by assigning me to out-race the defense and score on the close shot. Naturally, I became an early devotee to a system which utilized my meager talents, speed, and stamina and helped to achieve team success.

So often, especially in the early practice season, players may fail to attract attention because their one or two special abilities may be overshadowed by other players who can execute several skills, if not exceptionally, at least reasonably well. Wherever there is a lack of players with multiple skills, individuals who can execute one skill very well may be molded together for the fast-break offense.

There are some few who speak derisively of the fast break, but there are none who refuse to use its techniques if and when circumstances are presented for the quick, easy layup shot on the end of a long pass or two. Contrary to its reputation, the fast break is not an aimless, helter-skelter, run-and-shoot game except in the appearance of its rapid, often demoralizing action. It is a planned attack.

So in 1942, I challenged all the teams that I could think of to come to Washington, D.C. Washington, D.C., was supposedly a neutral ground, and I challenged any team to play my team because I had just won the CIAA championship my first year of coaching. We had a 14–0 record in the CIAA conference and won the conference championship.

The only response I got was from Brooklyn College, who had defeated all the schools in New York, all the schools that had a record of any kind, and they had beaten them. But they said they would play us in Washington, D.C., since it was neutral ground and so forth, and it wasn't against the law there. I invited Eleanor Roosevelt, but she couldn't come, and she sent Harry Hopkins, her State Department representative. He came to the game. And we played the first integrated college basketball game in the District of Columbia, but it didn't have as much impact as I had hoped.

It was known to students who came to play for the North Carolina Central Eagles that I was interested in integrating the schedule someday. One of my goals was to stay as ready as I could, so anytime it ever happened, we'd come off pretty good. In the meantime, this player of mine went to a YMCA meeting, which was actually more dangerous than you might think. Sometimes the black students had to lie on the floor of the car going to those meetings so that the police didn't see them. Durham, [North Carolina], was very segregated. Well, at this meeting, one of my players, George Parks (he's still living, in Orange County, California), heard one of the players from the Duke Navy Medical School say that they were the best team in the state because they had beaten all the teams in the state. And Parks took exception.

He said, "Well, you haven't played us."

So he came back and told me that we, our team, had challenged them. But they didn't have anywhere to play. They needed to play in our gym at a time when nobody would notice. And that turned out to be at eleven o'clock on Sunday morning. Just about everybody in Durham was in church on Sunday morning. So the Duke Navy Medical School team came over, and we played a regular game. This was unheard of. It was on March 12, 1944.

We didn't want spectators, but the word got out to a few, though the police and the newspapers never picked up on it. The players never paid any attention to them. Actually, I don't think the players had seen the spectators when they came in because they hid until they got inside, then they got on boxes, barrels, crates, and ladders and everything to look in the windows. The windows were about six feet off the ground, and it was hard to see in. We thought that if we played the game without spectators, they might not be so hard on us if we were discovered playing. But anyway, nobody ever discovered it.

Fact of the matter is, the writer Scott Ellsworth was the first reporter who ever asked me about it. At the fiftieth anniversary of the CIAA tournament in 1996, he came up and said, "What does this mean?" I had 523 victories listed in my bio, and in parentheses, just facetiously, I had added, "plus one, if the secret game was counted."

Well, the game started out slowly. My players were shaky because they had never played basketball against white people before. They didn't know what might happen if there was a hard foul or if a fight broke out. But we had two players from the North, Henry "Big Dog" Thomas and James "Boogie-Woogie" Hardy, and the players from the South looked to them to see what to do. We had some real standouts—Floyd "Cootie" Brown, George Parks, and Aubrey Stanley. Stanley was only sixteen and was the Eagles' youngest player, and it took him a while to realize we could beat these guys. By the second half, we were scoring on nearly every possession. We played the kind of fast-break basketball we were accustomed to. We did our cutaways and reverse pivots, moving the ball up the court as quickly as we could. And at the end, the scoreboard read: Eagles 88, Visitors 44. The Duke team was stunned.

At that time, the Klan was pretty strong in North Carolina. In fact, our student manager recalled that the Klan had had a meeting on the outskirts of Durham just the week before. Furthermore, it hadn't been very long since a bus driver had murdered a black soldier for not moving on the bus. The jury only debated twenty minutes and freed the guy. It was a pretty tough time. One thing though, in our favor, was that there was a black colonel who was stationed there at Camp Buckner, about twelve miles north of Durham. That was something for us to be very proud of. He came in there about the time this soldier was shot. And so he sent his entire company into Durham to ride the buses. They rode the buses all over for a day or two. And nothing happened. But they were ready. They were going to counter with promised drastic action if anybody was not treated fairly. Anyway, it was at this time that these white guys said, "OK, we'll play you." And they came over, and since that time, I've counted them very special people. I think they were. They were very special to even take the chance, because they would have been penalized worse than we were. They would have been socially ostracized and everything else. At that time, that was the main punishment—ostracism and name-calling. The only thing that might have happened to us was—and I never even thought about it at the time—our appropriation might have been slashed, from the state department of education.

I was in North Carolina from 1937 to 1952. Head coach from 1940 to 1952. I played the first public integrated basketball game in the state of North Carolina against the Camp Lejeune Marines in 1949. That was not long after Executive Order 8802 was put forward by Harry Truman to integrate the armed services. And various military bases around the country put out the word that they would entertain "integrated" sports on any level—any sport, including college teams. So we contacted the Camp Lejeune Marines and asked them for a game, and they gave it to us.

Around that time, I started a committee, called the National Basketball Committee, which later became the National Athletic Steering Committee. Its main purpose was to integrate sports on a national level. And in 1952, I left North Carolina and went to Hampton University in Hampton, Virginia. Now, Hampton was where the first black-college basketball program existed. They started in 1909. There was a man name of U. V. Henderson, and he got the colleges organized enough to play and engage in competition.

I stayed at Hampton for two years. I went there by choice, because after I left North Carolina, I wanted to coach in a school that didn't give scholarships, to see how it would be. At Hampton, at that time, you couldn't get in without a B average, and you couldn't get in without the proved fact that you had enough money to go there. In other words, you had to pay to go to school, and I think their initial fee was $342. There were no scholarships or grant aids or anything given until you paid that money.

I went to Hampton because one of my best friends was athletic director there, and another friend was head coach. So I went to Hampton. Of course, it was one of the best schools you could go to, and still is. But while I was at Hampton, Tennessee State's athletic director and president contacted me and said, "If integrating basketball is going to be the mission of your life, you better come on out here. We have the athletes; we have the government behind us. Here, you can manage this on a national level, and this is the place for you to be." Tennessee State was practically number one in all sports. So I left Hampton and went to Tennessee State.

Well, the Boston Celtics were the first National Basketball Association [NBA] team to integrate when they signed Charles "Tarzan" Cooper, April 15, 1950. Cooper had played on the Duquesne University team. A year later, the Washington Capitols signed Earl Lloyd of West Virginia State and Harold Hunter of North Carolina College. And on October 31, 1950, Lloyd became the first African American to play in an NBA game.

So when I was at Tennessee State, we had the best black-college team in the country. And that's when we were finally able to integrate college basketball on a national level. The National Association of Intercollegiate Athletics [NAIA] finally granted us an opportunity to play in the tournament in Kansas City during the 1952–53 season.

It's a long story, but we put the proposition to them that we should be in integrated sports on a national level. We had tried the other organization, the National Collegiate Athletic Association [NCAA]. However, when the NAIA invited us in, two years later, the NCAA started the college division tournament in Evansville, which was then open to everybody. The NCAA started it in 1956, where the NAIA had its first black team play in the tournament in 1953.

Clarence Cash was the coach at Tennessee State then. And when the NAIA opened its doors, the conditions were that the eighty-six black schools had to decide on one team to go to Kansas City and take one place in the thirty-two-team bracket. That wasn't really integration, but it was the beginning.

When you reflect back on it, if you think like we do today, you might say, "Never mind, we're not coming," but that was our first foot in the door, and it created within us a great spirit of competition, which improved our team, because you had to win the Negro National Championship to get to that NAIA tournament in Kansas City.

I think a number of organizations around the country, a number of communities, were influenced by the executive order [that integrated the armed forces], as a result of the war and the experiences in the war, where black soldiers were fighting without full rights of citizenship. And this was actually the beginning of the social revolution that extended on to the sixties, in my opinion. That was the catalyst.

So athletics played its part when the NAIA integrated its tournament on a national level. And when the NCAA found out what the NAIA was doing, they then created the tournament in Evansville. Besides that, there were several hundred schools that didn't belong to any organization. And they built their membership up from that beginning, when they opened up the doors for their own schools.

I went to Tennessee State in 1954, and the year I went there, the NAIA had a Christmas tournament, which is like the National Intercollegiate Tournament [NIT]. They chose the teams that they felt had performed well in the previous spring tournament. And Tennessee State was one of those teams. Clarence Cash's team had performed what they considered very well in Kansas City, although they didn't win the tournament. I received the invitation that was for Clarence. Clarence had left Tennessee State, and I had taken his place. But when they called and told me that I was invited to the NAIA tournament, I refused to come if they didn't integrate the Kansas City hotels and restaurants. And they said I just had to come or I wouldn't be able to compete, but I said I wasn't coming unless they let us stay in the same hotels and eat at the same restaurants as the white teams. See, we had to be the best of all the Negro schools to get one place in a thirty-two-team bracket. Tennessee State had won the Negro National Championship in 1953 and 1954.

And my assistant coaches said, "Well, we're with you, Coach. If you don't want to go until we can do better with our accommodations, well, we'll be with you."

I never did take this up with the administration, because I knew one thing: If they said no, that would have been an impasse. If they said yes, then they would have gotten in trouble with the state authorities. So it was better for me to do it and get fired or get chastised or reprimanded or something than for the president to get involved because he could always say, "Well, I didn't know anything about it. I didn't have any idea he'd do something like that." And when he heard about it, that's what he said he would have said.

The late Al Duer, who was executive secretary of the NAIA at the time, was the one that called me and told me that my team was supposed to take part in this tournament. And I told him, yes, I knew it, but I wasn't planning on coming.

He said, "What's the problem?"

I told him.

So he said, "How long will you be by the phone?"

And I told him, "All day, if necessary."

He said, "I'll call you back in twenty minutes."

In twenty minutes, he canvassed the chamber of commerce, junior chamber of commerce, and his committee, who had apparently been studying this anyway, and called me back and said we could stay at the Hotel Kansas Citian, and we could eat at any of the restaurants that the other teams do. And that's how Kansas City was integrated. That was 1954. Up until that time, even Lena Horne couldn't stay in downtown Kansas City.

Well, I stayed at Tennessee State for five years. I went from there to a new opportunity, which gave black guys a chance to coach beyond the college level. I joined the Cleveland Pipers in the National Industrial League. This was the league that stretched from coast to coast and was sponsored by big corporations and industry, like Goodyear. Semipro, they called it. It was a step forward for all of us, and it was quite challenging, so I went. And one of the conditions I had then was I had to bring some of my own players with me. I took four players from Tennessee State into that experience. The Industrial League was integrated. That is, they were integrated to the extent that they could be if they wanted to. I think one team had two black players, and another six didn't have any.

I stayed with the Pipers about two years. I won the championship in the second year. And that league broke up because the pros didn't like it. There were better players in that league than there were in the pros at the time. So they [the professional teams] took all of them; they made big offers to the players and that broke the league up. My team won the last NIBL [National Industrial Basketball League] championship. Then I also won the AAU championship the same year. The team was bought by George Steinbrenner. And we didn't get along very well. At the end of the first half of the season, my team won the Eastern Division championship.

After I left the Pipers, it wasn't long before I had another opportunity. I was called by the State Department and asked to teach basketball to the coaches of Southeast Asia. I went to Malaysia for six months. And it was a great experience. Then I came back to Tennessee State, where my two assistants had played for me before. For years, I wouldn't have any assistants unless they had already played for me. That saved a lot of arguments and problems. Anyway, they were being successful with the team in my absence, and even though they asked me to take it back, I told them no. So the president made me head of everything—the graduate school and undergraduate school—for that year. And then the president of the athletic council, and also one of the leading professors in the school, was called to Kentucky State to be its president. And I went on up there with him.

I was at Kentucky State for three years: 1963–1966. Well, I had great success there. Fact is, I took the team to Kansas City. Won one game and gave me the record, which hasn't been broken, seventeen straight victories in the national tournament. That's not likely to be broken anytime soon. But anyway, then I left Kentucky, and I went back to Cleveland, because Cleveland State, where I am now, had a new president. And when he came in and found out that no predominantly white school in the United States had ever hired a black basketball coach, he said, "This has got to end." He called me up on the telephone and said, "You've got to get up here to Cleveland. It's very important. I want to talk to you." So I went up there, and that's what he said. "You've got to be the new coach."

And since then, I've been at Cleveland State off and on. I left Cleveland and went with the Denver Rockets in the ABA [American Basketball Association] in 1969–70. Then I went with Converse [athletic-shoe company] for one year and stayed with them for twenty years. I was their national basketball rep, and international rep as well. They sent me everywhere, all around the world, teaching basketball and coaching all-star teams. I became a member of the Olympic Basketball Committee for ten years, did all the scouting for the Olympic team during that time.

I came back to Cleveland State in a year; I got here around 1990. This is my seventh year back. And for the last six years, I've been either athletic adviser or teaching in the athletic department. But the last five years, I've been teaching in the history department. I'm teaching a course that nobody knows anything about, believe it or not, the history of sports in the United States and the role of minorities in their development.

I've had some great players. They've told me. One of them calls me up every now and then, says, "Don't forget who put you in the Hall of Fame." Aubrey Stanley. He's a member of that team that played that secret game. His nickname was Stinky. But he was a great one. On my 1959 team, four players went in the NBA: John Barnhill, Ben Walley, Dick Barnett, and Porter Merriwether. I coached Sam Jones [star of the Boston Celtics] in 1950. In fact, I recruited at North Carolina Central and coached him in 1950, 1952. He went in the service in about 1956 and played his rookie season in 1957 for the Celtics. Sam Jones was one of my miracle players. But it took him about eight games to make the starting lineup on my team. Then, of course, I've had a lot players nobody ever heard of. But they could play ball.

Teaching and working with young people keeps me going. It helps.

[Interview by Alan Govenar, April 6, 1998]

*Geraldine Miller at Smith College, 2003.*

# GERALDINE MILLER

HOUSEHOLD TECHNICIAN AND SOCIAL ACTIVIST

*January 7, 1920–March 28, 2005*

*Geraldine Miller was an activist and advocate for women's rights for decades. She grew up in a small town in Kansas and eventually settled in New York, where she was a domestic worker in hotels, kitchens, and private homes. In 1971, Miller founded the Household Technicians organization to help attain equal rights for women who were nannies, maids, and cooks, often without benefits. Household Technicians pressed employers to comply with minimum-wage standards and Social Security laws, and in 1974, Miller worked closely with U.S. congresswoman Shirley Chisholm to ensure that household workers would be included in the Federal Minimum Wage Act.*

*Miller founded the Bronx chapter of the National Organization for Women (NOW) and was the first to chair NOW's Women of Color Task Force. She served several times as chair of NOW's committee on Eliminating Racism and presented numerous workshops for NOW members and leaders on ending racism, developing a project called Race, Class, and Cultural Conflict. Miller was inducted into Smith College's Women of Color Hall of Fame in honor of her efforts for household workers.*

LIFE IN KANSAS WAS GOOD for me as a child because I didn't know that I was supposed to be a Negro at that time. The children that I played with were all blue-eyed and blond-haired. I was born in Sabetha, Kansas, in 1920, the same year women got the vote. Sabetha is close to Atchison, Kansas, close to St. Joseph, Missouri; that's the only way I can describe it. My mother's name was Gertrude Davis, and I was born out of wedlock.

My mother did anything just to make enough money to get by. Anything. And I did, too. As a child, I had to work alongside her and cooked and did housework and all of that. We moved around a lot. We were in Atchison, where my mother worked at a hotel, for a year or two, and I got my first start in school there.

I used to love to dance, and my cousin and I became a dance team. We were called the Sunflower Girls. We did the Charleston and the dances of that time for a big event at the school, and we were asked to travel around Kansas for a year and perform. I was in kindergarten, and we ended up getting some money to perform. I'll never forget how proud I was, because my mother used that money to pay for my first-grade clothes. I'll never forget it. When I went into the first grade, my mother kept telling me, "This is your money that you're wearing. This money that you made has bought your clothes."

I was constantly trying to learn how to do different things. I was taught to take care of myself. And that's what I did. A boy taught me to box; [he was] a Golden Gloves champion. I was pretty good. He used to tell me, "It's time to stop now," and I said, "I didn't tell you to bother me." I remember that, and laughing. Well, boxing was to keep people off of me, to keep them from getting me in any scrapes.

My auntie had taught me how to read poetry. And I was a pretty good singer, up until the day my mother died, and I cracked my larynx because I screamed so loud. I was brokenhearted. I was seventeen when she died. It was very sad.

My grandmother was named Eva. But I never really knew where she was from. My mother never got around to really telling me everything. I was too busy trying to find out who my father was. My mother was only thirteen years old when I was born. My father was my step-grandfather. I didn't find out that [it was incest] until I was grown. They were scared to tell me.

When my mother died, I was living with relatives in Omaha, Nebraska, but my mother was in St. Joseph, Missouri, where she had a restaurant. She wanted me to live in Omaha because she thought I could get a good education there. I went to Central High School in Omaha. I learned to tap-dance in Omaha, and I worked for the National Youth Association. We made eighteen dollars and seventy-five cents a month. Omaha really had a lot of wonderful people in it. There were different couples that would take me in and talk to me. There was even a Jewish couple that had a little dress store on Twenty-fourth Street in Omaha, and from them I learned to eat gefilte fish and chicken soup and all the good things for the Jewish holidays. I think of that with really fond memories. I could go in [to their store] and pay a little bit on a dress, and it might take me a couple of months [to pay for it].

I didn't graduate high school. I dropped out of school at seventeen [not long after my mother died]. My mother was poisoned by another woman for her man. I don't know [what she was poisoned with]. I know I was in the room when she died. I had just reached St. Joseph, Missouri. I had just left Omaha. Good thing it was a Catholic hospital, because they were wonderful. I think if it hadn't been for them, I might have just gone to pieces for real. My mother was poisoned in St. Joseph.

In addition to being a cook, my mother was an entertainer. One little song I remember is "Dragging My Poor Heart Around." I actually heard her sing this on the radio. She let me know that she was doing this, and I remember it well. And another special song I remember is, I think it was called "My Mother's Eyes." She taught this to me at a very early age. And I've never forgotten it. "Just like a wandering sparrow lost in the woods, I'd walk the straight and narrow, just to reach my goal. God's gift came from above, a real unselfish love, I found in my mother's eyes." I think of it and sing it to myself at times.

So after my mother passed, I did a lot of jobs. I danced at night. I worked in clubs. I'd learned the Lindy Hop, and there was a bunch of soldiers that were coming in around that time and I'd dance with them. At age eighteen, nineteen, I was a real buzz saw. I didn't know whether I was coming or going. I was drinking. I thought I could drown my sorrow. Then, one day, I looked at myself in the mirror and said to myself, "Your mother wouldn't want you to do this. She wouldn't want you to do what you're doing." And I just stopped. I stopped drinking and tried to find a little work here and there.

I did housework, see, because at that time, blacks weren't able to get much work. But I was one of the first people that broke the barrier with elevator [operators] at a hotel. And the reason why I got the job is, I walked in and told the man that he wasn't born to the seat he was sitting in. And he said that he used to sell papers outside this hotel, and he figured if I could tell him that, then I needed the job.

I got married when I was twenty-one. My husband's name was Leslie

Ervin Oliver Miller. I don't remember what day I got married, but it was in St. Joseph, Missouri. I just went into the justice of the peace and got married. And after I got married, I had an opportunity to travel south with the Hennie Brothers carnival.

I was with what they called the jig show. Well, it was the colored people's little show—we had chorus girls and all of that. We had a band, a small one, with about six men. I was pretty good at learning [dance] steps. If I could hear the steps, I could, you know, walk you through them. So it wasn't long before I was teaching others how, when they joined the show, one by one. And we traveled that summer and that fall.

One day, we had "colored people's day," and I said to one of the [white] men working there, "Wonder where all the people are?" He said, "Well, girl, let me tell you. It's going to be like a black cloud under the gate." And I said, "Black cloud?" He said, "Yes." And I said, "All them people going to come out because it's colored folks' day?" And I just stood there and looked at him. I said, "This man has no idea who he's talking to. I'm one of them. I am one of them." But I just stood there and looked at him. I was just dumbfounded.

Another time, some man walked over to me and said, "You mine." I said, "No, I'm not." He said, "You're mine for the evening." I said, "No, I'm not." So I found out that one of my fellow workers had told him he had sold me to him. But I wasn't going to let him get away with it. I put a stop to that right away.

Maybe there was something [sexual about the dancing], because we didn't have on that many clothes. We had a couple of long gowns. We had some short things. You know, you could not bump forward, move your body to the front. You could go side to side and back, but you couldn't bump forward. That was against the law. We traveled all over the South. We were in Alabama, Louisiana, and Mississippi.

I remember Mississippi because I didn't like it. Our bus turned over between Greenville and Greenwood, Mississippi. We fell down this embankment. The bus driver wanted to take a little nap. It was raining; it was nasty. And that was my first time hearing people saying things about us. They wanted to know if those "niggers" down there, any of us, were dead. And that angered me. I said, "Instead of helping me up this incline, they were talking about me and the other people there." So I was angry, and it just happened that one of the men saw me. They said, "Oh,

God, here comes trouble!" I was coming up, climbing up that embankment with a determined look on my face. I think I would have slapped the man if I could have got up there. But they just picked me up and carried me off the other way because I didn't weigh that much.

I had told everybody else what to do. I found out that the seats were bolted to the floor, and when we started to turn over, I woke up, and I yelled at everybody. I said, "Grab the handles, and press your feet against the floor." So when the bus turned over, I didn't turn over. And a lot of others didn't turn over. There were only the few in the front who got hurt because they were thrown up against the window of the bus. And some people got hit by flying luggage.

Later on, we were in some other place in Mississippi, and I walked by [a store] and looked at these dresses and suits and things they had in the window. A woman came out and got me by the hand, she said, "Y'all come on in here and look at these things." She said, "Now, when you get through picking them beans, you can come in here and buy it on time." And I'm looking at her, and everybody was trying to say to me, "Don't you dare open your mouth." So, finally, I couldn't take it any longer. I said, "Lady, I didn't intend to buy, I was just admiring the way your window was dressed." And she just dropped my hand like it was a hot potato. She said, "Oh, my God, where y'all from?" And I said, "We're with Hennie Brothers. You need to come down and see us."

She brought her family, the whole store, and I broke that barrier because I'm not that dark, but I'm brown-skinned. So I broke the barrier of our line, the chorus girls' line. All the dark girls would be in the back, and all the light-complected people would be in the front. And the people carried on so bad and stomped and screamed and hollered, said, "Bring that one out front," because I was in the back, whooping it up, you know, like yelling and having fun. See, I started breaking barriers when I was young because I didn't really pay attention all the time. I wasn't really hung up on color. Color didn't ever bother me. As long as you treated me right, you were all right with me, and it didn't matter what color you were.

I think "breaking barriers" is kind of a motto for me. I don't know where it came from, but if something was an obstacle for me, I'd try to find a way to get around it and do what I wanted to do. I think that makes a lot of sense. For some, it's hard to break out of being passive. And that's the reason why we [African Americans] have a lot of problems. Because

I do a lot of talking to young black women, trying to get them to speak up for themselves and to stand up for themselves, not in a dirty way, but in a nice way. I want people to get the idea that they don't have to be talked down to or treated differently.

I quit the [Hennie Brothers] in Hot Springs, Arkansas, and then came back home to my husband. I was living in Council Bluffs, Iowa, which is right across the river from Omaha, Nebraska. At that time, my husband was working at the wheel foundry. And he soon lost that job because he was a womanizer and what have you. I'd say I was married for two years. But I didn't stay with the man two years. I started figuring out how I was going to get away. So I went back to Omaha, and a friend and I rented this house and then paid for it by doing housework. But see, I was also dancing at night or whenever I could to make up for the money that we really and truly needed, but didn't have.

I moved to Ocean City, New Jersey, in '54, '53. And I stayed there a couple of years, doing housework and hotel work. Then I worked in Atlantic City and a couple of the other little suburbs around. I'd work for people, and then I happened to get a letter from the people I had worked with on the show. I found out that New York was close to Jersey, so I decided to go visit them. And I came up here, and I kind of liked the atmosphere, the beat of the town. You know, a lot of cities have what they call a beat that you either like or don't like. And I kind of liked that beat, even though I was around some people who didn't like me. I would have problems with jobs and all that. I worked in several big places. I worked in a lot of restaurants. And I refused to dance in New York because they work you to death. So I did mainly housework. I could get enough work to kind of sustain me. There are times when I lived off, like, seven dollars a week, food-wise. I was in Harlem. Then I left Harlem and came to Brooklyn. From Brooklyn, I went back to the Bronx, because I'd been in the Bronx before. And then I moved back and forth between the three places, and I ended up in the Bronx. I'm in Brooklyn now. See, I had a cancer operation, cervical cancer. I had to get to where people were, where I could have some help if I needed it.

I've always enjoyed talking to different people, especially the younger people, and telling them there's nothing they can't do if they put their mind to it. I like to tell them how I became a social activist when I founded the Household Technicians organization in New York State. I was on my way to work at a job I had up in New Rochelle, and a woman asked me, wouldn't I like to have fringe benefits? And the more I thought about fringe benefits, the more I wanted them. So what I did is, I went to that first meeting. And the other woman who was with me started working for one of the other groups there in the Bronx, which left me all by myself to do what I could. And we went to this first meeting that was held in Arlington, Virginia, for household workers. And I found out that five hundred women, black women, were there at that conference, and that was just the thrill of my life, to see that many women and listen to their stories and how hard it was for some of them. They raised their children on starvation wages. And some of their children became doctors and lawyers and teachers. Well, the more I heard their stories, the more I thought that we should have fringe benefits. Health insurance. Paid vacations. Not to take my vacation when you wanted it, but when I wanted it.

I started working with Shirley Chisholm, and she finally got us covered under the Federal Minimum Wage Act. That's what Shirley was able to do. I think of her often with that dark skin. Given the history of skin color, she had an extra ladder to climb and did so with relish. She saw herself and the needs of what she was doing not only as African American but also as woman. And so there were two obstacles there. It's really something to think about. I just think the opportunity presented itself to her to become involved in politics, and she acted upon it. It's the same with me. The opportunity presented itself to become an organizer, and I did it. I founded the Household Technicians because the opportunity was there. And once I found out I could get fringe benefits, I went haywire—I was determined because I wanted those benefits.

We took the name of Technicians because we figured we were capable of working with little or no supervision. We knew what we were doing. The first meeting was in Virginia. It was called the National Committee on Household Employment, and it was based in Washington, D.C. And the Ford Foundation funded it. That was in 1971. And I came home July 25 and founded the Household Technicians in New York State. It was not a union. We were just a big organization.

We incorporated Household Technicians as a nonprofit in July 1971. We had quite a few members from the Bronx, Manhattan, and Brooklyn. But some of the people didn't like me for some reason—well, probably because I was a day worker. And I didn't work for anyone rich at that time. I just worked for anybody that would pay me what I thought I should have. So I worked for a lot of couples. I would work for a man, just like I would for a woman. I didn't care. I would work for a black, whereas a lot of the others wouldn't. I served parties, I cooked, and I did a lot of things, just to make a living. And I love children, so if people had children and I was around working, I would be in seventh heaven, because that would be as close as I could get to a baby and be able to care for it a little bit. That was something that I enjoyed. See, I don't have any children of my own, but I have children, because I claim them even after they get grown.

I was the founder and president of the New York State Household Technicians. But I had so much opposition, it was hard to stay involved. In less than a year, they had me out as president and tried to run it themselves, and they found out that they couldn't. So they used to say, "Well, Miss Miller sure knows how to get the media." And in 1972, Shirley Chisholm and I were two of ten black women recognized by Channel 13 [PBS]. Shirley was running for president, and I had started the Household Technicians in New York State.

Shirley Chisholm was just a little tough cookie. She was just nice as she could be, but she didn't take anything from anybody. She came out of Brooklyn. For her to succeed, she had to be a little strange and certainly extraordinary. She was one of those people who was just out there fighting for what she believed in. She said that people should have more than what they had—they shouldn't always be poor. And once Shirley got into Congress and all, she worked on that. She was elected to the House of Representatives from Brooklyn, New York, in 1968, becoming the first black woman elected to serve in Congress. She was eighty when she died January the first of this year [2005]. She was an outspoken advocate for the disadvantaged and the underdog. She was not big. She wasn't tall, but she was dynamite. She was dynamite.

See, I didn't know anything about politics. I had learned all there was to learn about show business. I could put a show together, but I wouldn't know how to go about doing politicking. Shirley Chisholm was a tireless worker. But she came out as a woman who was not only working for women who were black, but she was also working for women, for them to have more and not be beat up every time they turned around.

**Award**
**OF MERIT**

*This is to certify that* Geraldine Miller

**HAS BEEN PRESENTED THIS AWARD**

*for organizing household technicians and lobbying for their rights*

*Awarded by* Bronx N.O.W.

Date Oct. 5, 1975        Signed Katherine Todd

Geraldine Miller's award of merit for organizing household technicians and lobbying for their rights, Bronx NOW (National Organization for Women), October 5, 1975.

I just think I wanted to find out more about what women could do to-gether. And I find out that's a very hard thing to do, that women are not taught to work together. They're taught to be destructive and not willing to work together like they should. There seems to be jealousy. They're like little kids at times. These are grown women, acting like something's wrong with them. And see, men—I used to run with a bunch of boys. Never have I ever had the same type of treatment that I got from the boys. They would kind of look out after me, and I'd look out after them, but in a different manner. Women have a habit of talking about one another, of tearing each other's characters down, and I just think it's terrible. Looks like men are taught to kind of like look out after each other. Men know if you're best friends, you're going to be there for your best friend. My best friend, if it's a woman, might decide to turn on me and leave me hanging.

As I say, I enjoy being around certain people. I like the idea. I claim many a woman as my child, and I say God gave them to me. And I don't care what nationality they are. I have a daughter who's not a daughter, but she's from India. She's a beautiful young lady, smart as a whip. And she just called me on my birthday, from India. Now you know that was a joy. And she was born on Christmas Day, which makes her a Capricorn, like me. So, I'd ask her to tell her mother, "Thanks for the Christmas gift."

I'm still involved in women's advocacy and social issues, more or less. I get kind of tired at times, though. Some of the nonsense has carried on. I have a lot of the women that are really good about pooling their thoughts or what have you and working together for the betterment of all. And they're all nationalities. So if we could get more than just those people, we would have really something great.

I am not really a churchgoer. I say it like this, I believe in God, and I think my body is a temple, and I think God is with me. I don't think I have to look, search, or hunt for him. He's right here.

When you think of freedom, you don't think of people not being free. I've gotten a chance to learn some of this. It really and truly makes me feel as though I'm doing something great or good when I get other people to find out, to accept the fact that we must work together. We either hang together or we hang separately.

We have been striving to achieve, but it looks like almost every time we get up so far, there's somebody up there. Shirley Chisholm said at one time or another that people were like crabs in a barrel.

I remember when I traveled around, speaking to groups of people, I said, "That's what we're doing. We don't let anybody get up so high before we pull them back down." We're not willing to use that as a vehicle to be able to come out of this misery because sometimes it is miserable to be stuck in this. You're, like, stuck in time. It's like a time capsule. There you are; you're stuck. You want to get out of that. I want to move forward. I don't want to be sitting around, looking sorry and feeling sorry for myself. That's not going to help me any. Even as old as I am, I still don't want to be sorry for myself. I want to do what I can and help somebody else to get where they need to be. And I've done that. And I feel good about it, see?

I've worked hard for people who do household work; that's a very tough way to live. You know, most of these women are having problems like I'm having now. I need to have my teeth taken out. I've got a cold. I'm not eating. I've lost weight. Now I'm scaring myself. See, I brought this on myself. It's because I have not done what I should do. But I hate for somebody to nag at me. I don't like that. I'm used to being alone. I'm not used to being with people. I'm used to being alone and thinking for myself and doing what I think is necessary.

Doing household work, you're alone a lot. But I don't think you really have time to think. My auntie once told me, my aunt Retta, who was a beautiful little old woman, said, "Think of this house [where you're working] as yours until you're through. Then step out the door and then step back in and see what you've done. Now, if it meets your approval, then you know you did a good job." We can be a good judge of what's right and what's not right. You or me. I had an uncle that was just neat as a pin. That's right. My uncle Luther was just—oh!—he was so clean. He could cook. He was self-sufficient. He could take care of himself. And he didn't have a wife. But he took care of himself and his home. He was very quiet, worked hard, had very little to say sometimes. But he was just my ideal of what a man should be.

Oh, boy, was Retta ever a doll. She pounded the English language and everything else into my head. She saw to it that I learned. She was not going to have a dummy in her house. And there were other aunts. There was Aunt Agnes, who I stayed with, and there was my grandmother I lived with for a short time when I was very little. I remember, I think I was in kindergarten when I stayed with her. And they had taught me, because I was an only child, they started teaching me to share. And to this day, I'm still sharing.

A lot of the women who have to do household work to support themselves are single women like me. There weren't a lot of opportunities. When I got here to New York, I went in looking for a job at one of the stores. And the woman said, "I would love to be able to hire you, but . . ." I could type because I learned it in high school. But I didn't get that little piece of paper because I was just too torn up [about my mother dying] to try to finish my years in high school. And I didn't know where I was going to live or what kind of money I would have. But people used to tell me, these people I talked about, how they would have helped me had I said I wanted to go back to school. There was that Jewish couple I knew in Omaha, they said, "Gerry, you need to go back." And I told them I didn't want to.

A lot of Jews were involved in the civil-rights movement. And, see, I have a friend whose name is Sarah Curry Cobb; she's an administrative aide to one of the women that's an elected official from the Bronx. She was with Martin Luther King. I didn't meet him, but I met Sarah, and some of the things that she has told me are just frightening, scary. You know, those marches and what have you. I participated in marches. Oh, did I ever! Bella Abzug, I met her early on. Flo Kennedy scared me to death, but she was my friend. I could ask her to do something for NOW [National Organization for Women], and NOW couldn't get her to do it. I marched for the ERA, March for Women's Lives. I was at the last march.

Bella and I both went to the United Nations. I was there to help Bella when she'd run, if I stuffed envelopes or talked on the phone. Didn't matter because Bella treated me very good. She yelled and screamed at a lot of people. I was one of the people she didn't yell and scream at. I never will forget. We had a Bronx People's Fair up here in the Bronx. And guess what? We hadn't been open too long, and in comes Bella. "Hey, Gerri Miller! It's me! It's Bella!" And everybody turned around.

Flo Kennedy was another one I worked with. She was scary in certain ways. Once, I couldn't figure out why I couldn't get anybody on the phone when we were trying to get to Albany. And come to find out that Flo had a picket around this building, which housed Avon. Avon told these people, "Give that woman what she wants and take that picket away from our door." Just that quick, Flo had a picket going.

Thank goodness that Shirley Chisholm and Florence Kennedy and Bella Abzug and other women who were with the veteran feminists were able to help me so that I could do what I needed to do to be able to help others. Well, I wanted to inform people about what needed to be done and maybe sometimes how it needed to be done. There's a lot of things that got done. One would tell somebody, and then somebody would tell me, and then I would tell a number of people. And it worked.

I think that there weren't enough people to really champion the cause, you know—like I had one black woman say, "What do you say you did?" And I told her. She said, "Well, who does that anymore?" I said, "Well, then, who cleans your house?" You're a homemaker, you definitely have somebody cleaning your house. The idea is, the house doesn't clean itself. It's not self-cleaning, like an oven. It has to have a human being to see to it that things are where they should be. Right? Well, she just looked at me, like she thought I was crazy. See, what she wanted to do was to not have to deal with that. She didn't want to be bothered with the thought of a household worker being thought of as a person. In other words, she didn't do that type of work. That was not her job. But it was our job to do it. That was our job. And we did it, many of us.

There's a group now . . . I would have called them, but I didn't want to get myself back in the fight in Unity for Dignity, Domestic Workers

United. And they had a march not too long ago, October the 23 [2004]. I might have been there, but I could really and truly have messed up my life, because I think they would have hung on and worn me down. See, I also helped the home health-care workers get together. I told them that they needed to know how to take care of those people who were disabled. I remember being sent to a home from the New York State unemployment office to take care of this disabled woman who would sit and play in the bathtub, take her heels and let them slide back and forth, and then expect me to lift her out. And it would put too much weight on me. And so, I told them, I said I couldn't do that; I wasn't trained to do that. I didn't want to drop the woman. She was frail. But she got the biggest kick out of scaring me. And don't think it didn't scare me because I didn't know if I could hold her or not while she played in the water. This was a grown woman. She just was up in age and not able to take care of herself. See, those are the things that bothered me. I didn't want to make things any worse for somebody. I would like to see if I could help make things better. I don't even think we should be here if we can't be doing something for someone else. That's a big thing in my life. I often think, maybe there's something I can do to make things better for you or someone else. It doesn't have to be just for me.

We can't worry about what people think about who we are. We have to make the most of our time on this earth, because once we're gone, we're gone. And while we're here, we do not need to make it difficult for someone else. That's not going to help me, and it won't help you.

I used to talk about the household workers who were standing on the streets there in the Bronx years ago, before I came to New York. Well, the women who were going to hire them would come by and inspect them. It was on Walton Avenue. I can't give you the exact year that it happened, but a man once told me that he remembered the corner as a youngster in the thirties and forties. Anyway, the women would stand on this corner and wait to see if they were going to get a job. And the women who were going to hire them would stop their cars and get out and look at their knees to see if they were properly scarred, because at that time, women cleaned floors on their hands and knees. Well, when I got to New York, I started introducing household workers to mops. See, I never was one to stand back and not say anything. So I was able to get that done. Mops took longer, because the floors usually had a buildup of wax and dirt and grease, and you'd have a hard time getting that stuff up. See, the wax messed up the floor. I don't care what kind of flooring you had. So you had to try to scrape off that wax buildup. And years ago, it was done on hands and knees. And that's the reason why a lot of us have arthritis early.

Sometimes the only work we got was by going to the unemployment office. There's always a place there for you to get work. And then there would be word of mouth. Somebody was always in need, and you would come and you'd tell me, or you'd tell somebody else. In other words, word of mouth. It was just like, if you need something, and somebody's there to help, if this person hears about it, they can help you.

I didn't work for too many bad people. I had a pretty good group of people I worked with. Household Technicians was a national organization. Josephine Hewlett, who lived in Ohio, I think is still around. She was very active nationally. She was just one of them special women that could just pull people together. And when Household Technicians began to fall apart around 1977 and Ford [Foundation] didn't want to fund us anymore, they had to have somebody to take over. She had it down pat about what to do with the group, but no one wanted to give her the support she needed, and Household Technicians went under. But as long as I live, I'm the founder of the Household Technicians in New York State.

I really and truly felt as though I did something important. It's like giving birth to something, saying to yourself, "Well, this is what we must do at this time," or, "This is something we must have at this time." And I just think I was there, and I understood. It's like my mother was a household worker, my grandmother was a household worker, or a hotel worker or whatever, and then they also cooked and served. And that was just part of my background because when I was real little, I had a little cookstove that I used to put mud pies in. If I made my mud pies and if you didn't eat them, I'd get mad at you.

We can either try to make things better, or we can sit home and cry. And I don't think tears are going to bring me anything. Tears are not going to bring me nothing but sadness. And I don't want to be sad. I want to get what I can out of life. And to the best of my ability. That might sound far-fetched, but it's real. It's the way I feel.

I'd like to get my health in some better shape right now. They've been renovating here, and all the dust—I'm in my eighties, for God's sake. You know, I feel like a dust ball. They've renovated the whole first floor. And all that dust has been traveling around for some time now. I'm going to find a machine that I can use to pull this dust out of my room and try to clean up some.

I like to think for myself. I don't mind thinking at all. I like thinking and doing, not only for myself, but also for others. And I want to have a free rein to do that. I don't want anybody in my way. Don't be putting up any obstacles. I don't need that.

I used to wonder why the colleges would have me at these colleges speaking about what I had done. I've been to God knows how many colleges. And I'm not college material. But what I've done is real. Right?

I guess I give the students something—I mean, I shut a woman up who was a professor. She was rolling on and on and on about her theories, and boy, did she ever get on my nerves. And then she put me to sleep. And I must have slept for about two or three minutes. And I said, "Oh, my God, I've been asleep." I waited till she took a deep breath and then just cut her off.

I told her, I said, "What have you done with your theory?" You know, having a theory and doing something with it are two different things. I think that sums it up, what we're both talking about. It's the thinking about it, the theory, putting it down on paper, and doing nothing about it means nothing. But having a theory and then trying to see how it will work is different.

I think it's time that we get things together in a better fashion than what we have done before, because I feel as though we've got to figure out ways of working together. We have got to do that. We cannot allow fighting against each other because we are all in the same boat. None of us has so much money that we're going to be sailing along by ourselves. We're not rich. We're not going to get rich overnight. So we've got to find a way of working together for the betterment of all of us, not just for, say, one or two people, but for all. Each time I've run for the board of the National Organization for Women, I have said, "All women." A-L-L, I even put it in big letters.

[Interview by Alan Govenar, January 14, 2005]

*Rupert Richardson, Baton Rouge, Louisiana, ca. 2002.*

# RUPERT RICHARDSON

*Born January 14, 1930*

*Rupert Richardson has lived most of her life in Lake Charles, Louisiana. Her mother, Mary Ernestine Samuels, was an educator, and her father, Albert Sidney Richardson, was a dry cleaner and tailor. Both of her parents were active in the NAACP, and Rupert became involved at an early age in the civil-rights struggle in Louisiana. She worked with the NAACP Youth Council and eventually became state president of the organization. She was national president of the NAACP from 1992 to 1996 and currently serves on its national board. Richardson discusses the changing role of African American churches, civil-rights leaders, needs in the educational system, and the strategies she has used in the pursuit of social, economic, and political justice.*

I DIDN'T KNOW ANY of my great-grandparents. None of my grandparents were slaves, and I don't know exactly why, given their ages. In fact, my paternal grandfather, whom I don't know, was a free person of color. He came into New Orleans, and all I know is, when I was growing up, they would say he came from the islands. And I didn't realize the importance of finding out exactly what islands he was from until it was too late. But with a name like Essex Richardson, I felt like it had to be one of the English-speaking islands, because my great-grandfather was Essex Richardson as well. But on the maternal side, I do know that my great-grandmother was a slave child, reared in Master's home, but those are just stories I've heard.

I was born in Navasota, Texas, but I only stayed a few months. Mother only went out there to be with her mother while I was being born, and my granddaddy was a section foreman on the railroad, and they were repairing the railroad in that area. And near the end of her pregnancy, she went there to be with her mother. And then when I was a few months old, she brought me back home to Lake Charles, Louisiana.

My mother was Mary Ernestine Samuels Richardson and my father was Albert Sidney Richardson Sr. My maternal grandparents were Ernest Thompson Samuels and Florence Parker Laws. And it's so interesting that she held onto that maiden name. Nobody was doing that then. But she used that whole name. And on the paternal side, my grandmother was Sara Richardson and my grandfather that I never knew—he died before I was born—was Essex Richardson.

My paternal grandfather was from a little place called Washington, Louisiana. That's out from Opelousas. And my grandmother was a native of Lake Charles. My maternal grandparents were from Louisiana, likewise, from the northern part of the state, a little town called Keatchie. But they lived all of their married life in DeRidder.

My mother was a teacher and a principal, an educator, in other words. My father worked at a dry cleaners, and he owned a dry-cleaning business before the Depression, a little neighborhood dry cleaners, but he wasn't able to maintain that during the Depression. So he went to work as a dry cleaner and dyer and tailor at a laundry in downtown Lake Charles, and that's where he worked until he died. And Mother retired from teaching, I guess, thirty years ago. But she lived to be almost ninety-six and died this July [2004].

Growing up in Lake Charles, Louisiana, it was very racist. And the unfortunate thing was, you kind of saw it as a way of life and seldom questioned it. I was in my teens before I really knew this was not right. Now, having said that, my father, we would go and meet him on payday to walk home from the laundry and cleaners, and we would see different places we wanted to stop. That was treat day, and we would have a hamburger. And he would always tell us, he'd never go into these places where we had to go in the back door, and we would walk home. And now that I look at it, that was quite a little walk.

When I was very small, we didn't even have city buses. But at any rate, my father would always say to us, "No, let's walk on over to Reverend Miller's and Reverend Moore's." They were two black preachers that had a restaurant. He'd say, "We can go in the front door and sit down and be waited on and enjoy it." But periodically, we would get to this place they called the Broken Drum, and the hamburgers would be coming out there, and we would ask if we could stop, and he would reiterate his message that we would spend the same amount of money at Reverend Miller's and Reverend Moore's, but be treated with dignity.

I remember Mother used to tell us we shouldn't drink colored water. There was a fountain, and she would say, "Oh, we can make it a little longer till we get home." And she would make a little joke, say, "I don't know what colored water is like. It might make us sick." But those kinds of things reminded us that it wasn't quite right, even though we just went with the flow. I think school was the worst thing because we used to get hand-me-down textbooks. Some had pages missing. Others had ugly little racial epithets. I think that was the hardest, because every time you picked up a textbook you were reminded that you were second, that you were not deserving of the very first round. It was ugly. But schools were segregated all of my life and through some portion of my children's lives.

My father was an activist in the labor movement. He led the first labor strike in Lake Charles, at the laundry where he worked. He was never in civil rights. He had a membership, though, in NAACP. But he organized that [strike], and I'll tell you, the boss, Mr. Cline, I can remember him being one of the "good" white folks, and he came to the house during the strike to say that he didn't mean to get my father in trouble, but that he had been very good to my daddy, and he didn't understand why my daddy could do that to him. And Daddy explained that it wasn't about him, that he had a respect for him and whatnot; it was about the working conditions of many of the people.

You had little tiers. And like my father and the folks in dry cleaning and dyeing and blocking hats and all of that, that was kind of a top tier. And they supervised other black folks. But they couldn't supervise whites; whites who should have been under them doing the same thing that all the blacks were doing had to report to a white, who wasn't even on duty all the time. He was the son of the owner. But yes, Daddy was very involved in that, and Mr. Cline was very, very hurt and pretended, at least, not to understand the difference. Because I was a big girl [nine or ten] when that strike happened, and I remember eavesdropping on every bit of it.

My mother was active with NAACP all of my life, and at one point, she was the state secretary. In fact, she was one of the founders of the Lake Charles, Louisiana, NAACP. And I don't know what year that was. I just remember learning about it from reading articles because I must have been too small to know about the founding. But I do remember when *Crisis* had to come in a plain brown envelope. I mean, really, the *Crisis,* the *Pittsburgh Courier,* and there was the *Chicago Defender.* They were newspapers that were really kind of national for black people. And I can remember how much information we would get, but all of that was mailed to us. And the *Crisis* was really supposed to be a subversive magazine, but we got it. And it gave us such insight; I guess that's when my eyes started to open that this is not just wrong, this is a big, big deal. As I got big enough to read those articles—I can remember a big series during World War II about giving our boys a chance to fight because black soldiers weren't going into combat. I guess that's around the time, and in '41, I would have been eleven. I think that's around the time that I knew how evil segregation was. It was more than just second-hand books; it was something systemic.

Well, when my mother retired, she was vice principal at a school, Cherry Street Elementary School, in inner-city Lake Charles. She had gone back to school late after my father died. When my father was alive, he didn't let her work. He always said, "People will think I can't take care of the family if you go to work," so she really didn't work. And that was a dual thing, because Mother was pretty strong, and I think she would have put her foot down that we needed the money, but the dual thing that was going on was that married teachers were asked not to apply because they had husbands. It's amazing the new world that it is. Because they had husbands to take care of them, but the single ladies who came out of college had no source of income, so they would ask the married women to defer in even applying, in favor of the single teachers. So there was that dual thing that kept Mother out of the classroom. Mother had a two-year degree then, from what she called "normal school," and God knows, I don't know exactly what that is and where that would have been. But she continued, even while Daddy lived, to go to school and get her degree so that when he died, she was prepared to go to school. And then she was a single woman and put at the top of the hiring.

I was sixteen when my father died. Isn't that the worst time in the world for a girl to lose her daddy? I have one sister who still lives in Lake Charles. Her name is Kermit Richardson Stevens.

I first went to a small black Baptist college called Leland College. But it is no longer in existence. A black college. That was in Baker, Louisiana. And I went there a little over a year. And then it lost its accreditation. That's something I wish you could kind of look into sometime, because the white Baptist missionaries had given that school so that black people could get an education, and then they kept it like a lot of years, from the early 1800s until 1946, '48, maybe. But there was a phaseout on their contribution to the life of that school. They did it a hundred percent at first. And then later on, there was a phaseout and the Baptists of Louisiana, the black Baptists, were supposed to match it. And I don't know what went wrong monetarily. I'm sure I can make a lot of enemies by saying something went wrong, and the match was not there, and that's how the accreditation was lost, and eventually, that university was lost. But that's where I went at first. Then I was transferred to Southern University here in Baton Rouge. And that's where I got my baccalaureate in science education, really, chemistry education.

I did work as a teacher, but as an aside, I tried to work as a chemist. I graduated in '52. Segregation was still rampant. And my father-in-law was a business agent for laborers at plants. And all the laborers were black. So that gave him a professional position, but with the limitation of being over blacks. But he would go by the different offices and look up opportunities and whatnot for folks who wanted to move beyond labor, and in the early 1950s, he was told by someone at one of the plants that the Atomic Energy Commission had sent forth an edict—and I can't say it was a real directive, almost a strong suggestion—that if they could find blacks with a background in the sciences, that they should "consider" hiring them.

I taught in Lake Charles, but not right away. I have eight children. So I would do a little substitute teaching to bring a little money in, but I really didn't go into education, per se, till all my children were in school. And I taught in the Lake Charles area at two different schools, though not for very long, because in '65, the doors opened up, soon after the '64 Civil Rights Act. I had gotten my baccalaureate, and then I had gone back and gotten my master's in counseling and guidance at McNeece State University there in Lake Charles. And so after I got the kids off to school, I would go to school, and later when the door opened, I was ready to walk through. So I was able to get a professional position and employment security as a counselor. And I never went back to teaching after that.

I've had a membership in the NAACP all my life, and at one time, we had a youth council. But I was quite small then and belonged to the youth council and did whatever little drives and whatnot the youth council did. My antenna really went up during the desegregation of the schools of Lake Charles. And I had children who were in attendance at Lake Charles High School. The first year of desegregation, '64, a few—two or three of them—went. The next year, my children along with, I guess, a dozen children went to Lake Charles High School. And the petty things that were happening were so bothersome that I decided to be involved. I went with a complaint to the branch about the way black children were being treated. And of course there was not one black teacher to whom they could go. So I showed up at the NAACP, and they took on my complaint and helped me to investigate it and to resolve it, but then, they said, "Could you be the education chairman?" And that was in the early sixties, maybe '66, '65, and I've never looked back. I mean, I took that position, and I held it, and I held it until I moved from Lake Charles, even though I was also first vice president and liaison to our regional office and different things. But I kept that education chairman seat until I relocated from Lake Charles. In fact, that's where my life membership is to this day, Lake Charles, Louisiana.

There was this shift around that time from overt segregation to segregation no less. And it was so much harder to fight. When I first started, it was very clear. When you went to the school board, it was because your child and three others were the only black children on the cheering squad, and on a bus trip, those four were given the backseat. But then it got to be little subterfuges and really denial of scholarships and later on, with my youngest child, all at once creating a co-valedictorian kind of thing because they were not exactly tied. My child had a few points more because of the level of the grades she took. It got to be so subtle, and the biggest challenge was to confront yet have enough dignity and even enough composure that you could stay in the room and deal. And that was a hard lesson to learn because you start off almost as a street fighter. "Hey, this happened. This bus driver of the city bus slapped this lady." With an incident like that, you've got the law on your side. You've got some public sentiment on your side, but at least the black and the white of it, no pun intended, are clear. But the black and the white became less clear as people hid behind laws and exceptions. So overall, and very generally, that is still the biggest challenge.

The reason I was a little behind today was that I was at the Louisiana Supreme Court yesterday for a hearing on a judge that had gone to a private Halloween party in another city in Louisiana dressed in blackface with an Afro wig and orange jumpsuit—I'm talking about a sitting state-level judge—an orange prison jumpsuit and in handcuffs. This caused such consternation that the way the NAACP found out about it was other whites who attended the party told us and gave us pictures. So, to me, that's so fifties; things are going backward. So the legal judiciary committee is recommending one year and a day suspension for this judge. And while he is admitting that it showed "poor taste," he is saying that a letter of reprimand will suffice. So the Supreme Court heard the case yesterday. And there's no time limit when they can give a ruling. But from the questions on the court, it sounds like the maximum penalty is going to be imposed. At least four judges really raked his lawyers over the coals. But that's the kind of thing, when you think you've come so far and then you have something like that happen, most embarrassing and hurtful. But when it's so bad that your colleagues, other lawyers, come back to the NAACP and say, "Look, this is a funny little club in a funny town, and I'm not filing a complaint with you. I'm giving you this information for you to look into because this happened." And I don't know what I started off to answer, but that was why I was late, because the court didn't adjourn till around, I guess, five. Not bad, but I'm the kind of person, if I'm there, and I can kill another bird or two with some stones, that's what I did. While I was in New Orleans, I had two other meetings and was very late getting back here. But that's what I mean by the overt—win, lose, or draw, that was easy to fight. But most cases are not like that. They're promotion denials, they're even, oh, sexual harassment. They're all those kinds of things that are not clear-cut, and the battle is really challenging.

Well, those are the kinds of difficulties we're still having. Now, when I served as state president of NAACP, some people, some connected to a university and some alums, filed a complaint with me against Southern University, a historically black university that is still, I guess, 99 percent black, saying that women were not permitted to participate in the marching band. Now, that's segregation at a school that ought to be sensitive to it. The band director was in college with me, and he was a little older than I, but he was a dear friend. And I thought, oh, this is just the easiest thing to rectify. I picked up the phone and called my friend and he said, "Oh, but women can't keep up. Men step at so many miles a minute, and women just can't do that and blow." And he just didn't understand why it was a question in anyone's mind. When I couldn't prevail upon him on behalf of the female applicants and the NAACP, I then went to the university [administration]. But there was a male president who didn't care, and he didn't last long. While this investigation was still going on, a female president came in. And she said, "I'm going to deal with this in bits and pieces. But this piece about women not marching in the band just goes to the top." Because we had prepared a Title IX education discrimination complaint. She asked me if I would just give her X amount of days before I filed the Title IX with the state department of education, she would "fix" it. And she fixed it. Now, bread cast upon the water—one of whom is my granddaughter. So finally that door is open. But it was difficult for me to prepare to file against my alma mater, an organization made up largely of black people, filing a Title IX complaint against a school that was made up of, I guess, at that time, all black people. Very, very painful fight. But that's the kinds of things we had—mostly during my tenure as state president, which has been up about ten years now. There were mostly job-discrimination things, class action. We did file against the state department of education when the tests for high school graduation were first instituted. Now, we did not say . . . I don't believe in all this racial bias and all of that in tests—and yes, there's some there. There has been some work to overcome some more. But by and large, the job in education is very, very clear: Teach good, basic education, and then, parents, expose your children to things in the world. Don't bog down on tests. They're here to stay, and we've just got to pass them. But what our lawsuit said—and I still contend to this day it is unfair—

those tests apply only to people in public schools. Private and parochial schools are exempt, and I think that is so wrong, but the courts didn't agree with me. Of course, the Catholic diocese in Louisiana is very strong and influential, but we did file against that. If there's anything I can say was a victory, it was that we filed—we being Louisiana State NAACP—we filed a suit against electing judges at large in the state. We got single-member districts. As a result, we went from two black judges on the bench to where we are now, around thirty-nine or thirty-eight. Victories don't come often in civil rights, but that's a major victory.

Now, in my position on the national board of the NAACP, we are starting to do futuristic or strategic planning. It's hard because the problems that are on your plate today are so pressing and just so visible. But we do try to think progressively and proactively, number one, by trying to train our young people to look at the frontier. That expression's new to me in this context. But a lot of our emphasis is with our youth and helping them to understand the kind of world that they will step out into and what the challenges are and the need for that preparation, the need for futuristic thinking. I chair the National Health Committee, and when I tell you that it's hard to look futuristically with what is happening to people, to health care in the present in this country and in the very near future, it's pretty hard. But our health committee is taking on—it has just passed a resolution to look at, and it's the present, but it will only open the door for the frontier—to look at the diversity of the teaching hospitals because that's going to be our future. And the diversity, or the lack of it, with the data that we have, points up that there's a great lack in the ten leading teaching hospitals. But we feel like if we can make a dent there so that the schools start to be more aware and to recruit more and to go back to the high school level and help us to prepare students more, at least in the health field, I think the future is going to brighten.

That's the way I think about it, but I guess we're on the frontier now in another sense. We've not only got to fix now but look toward tomorrow, or we're going to be constantly working last year's problems, last month's problems. So that's where the futuristic piece comes in with me.

My world has been Louisiana and the Deep South except for a brief stint where I spent a summer in Oregon, at the University of Oregon. I don't have any other frame of reference. And even that was a university, a closed and a different experience, because I don't think I'd ever lived in an all-white world, which is what that turned out to be. But no, my true base of knowledge is Louisiana, from experience.

You have to have an eye toward the past to live in the present and work in the future to be effective in civil rights. You've got to work in the present, but you've got to look both backward and forward. There are precedents back there that will help you to solve today's problems, and they say you're not supposed to look back. I have to be reminded just enough to keep a little sub-anger, just the least little bit, because I don't want to get too, too comfortable. I think I take a forward look but a backward glance and try to work right here in the present.

I've made a lifelong commitment to justice and fairness and peace. I have eight children—seven still living—who are achieving, working, functioning adults. Staying in contact with them every day is such a source of pride that it keeps me going so that hopefully their worlds will go very well. And, of course, they have their moments when segregation will rear its ugly head in its new, subtle clothes. But then I have my grandchildren, fourteen in all, that hopefully will have a better world. And the memory of my parents, who had the nerve back in the day, as the vernacular says, to push for better working conditions on the job, to work in political campaigns even though it was against the rules of the school board, to make a better world. I have their memory to salute and my personal integrity and commitment and then the future for my grandchildren and children yet unborn. It's a burden, but it's a challenging and sometimes rewarding burden.

I'm very much a churchgoer, but I think I'm much more a person with a moral compass, because if you don't have that, you don't have anything. With a true belief in a higher power—and I have nothing against organized religion—I go to church, I contribute to my church. I don't attend or work in activities as much as I should because church things are largely on Sunday, and I travel most weekends for something related to some of my children because all of them don't live in Louisiana, or I attend to NAACP responsibilities. But yes, a higher power is where I find my strength.

The role of the church has been strong in the civil-rights movement. But I almost have to say "has been." Frankly, I don't see as much

now as I saw when the battle was hard. We knew if we got an NAACP notice to the churches for Sunday morning, that X, Y, or Z was happening.
It wouldn't just be an announcement that was read. It would be a part of
the sermon. It would be pushed. We would hear back from pastors individually.

I was married for twenty-five years to a man from Lake Charles
named James Clemons Jr. And the pastor would say, "Mrs. Clemons,
what else do you need?" or, "I've got twenty names for you." That's not
there [today]. I'm not sure why it's not there. I do know I have been to
church when my pastor definitely communicated something of a civil-
rights issue. Churches are a little hampered now because their 501(c)(3)
status is easily threatened. There was a time pastors would just get up
and say, "Now, you go vote for John Doe. You've just got to. His materials
are in the back; he's been here. This is the best person to serve us." Because we didn't have many blacks running for office. They can't do that
now; they'll be shot down. There are listeners for the IRS for just these
kinds of things. So, the government has—and, I think, rightfully, at least
legally so—put a damper on it. But over and beyond that, I'm not sure the
motivation is there. Seems like our churches are into these great cathe-
drals that they build. And I just heard last night in a conversation with a
minister that some churches have ATMs in the lobby so that the excuse
that you forgot your checkbook is no excuse. You can get some money out
and put it in the plate. It's become pretty mercenary. And I can certainly
say, for whatever reasons, black church ministers are not as effective in
the movement as they were at one point in time.

The women's tea had a very important role in civil rights, and later,
toward the end of our struggle was when we started trying to get the ERA
[Equal Rights Amendment] passed. And the white women's tea was important in the women's movement. It wasn't fashionable for these lovely
white ladies with the hat, bag, and gloves to come out and say things
publicly to support the civil-rights movement, but around their little tea
parties they not only said things, they found ways to help. They found
ways through sending money [to the NAACP] anonymously through
their housekeepers. Some were bold enough to come to some meetings
and have input. But there was a lot of national moral conscience at those
ladies' teas. Now, there were also the ladies' teas with the Daughters of

the Confederacy. I don't know exactly what that organization does. But with the folks who still thought about white supremacy, there were those tea parties too, where things were discussed and, I'm sure, applauded. The funny thing about servants is that whites treated them as if they were nonexistent. I've experienced that. I've never worked as a servant. My daddy used to say, "If you want to clean a house, come in here and help your mama with this one." But I experienced it in politics. You're at dinner with the governor, and there are a lot of you, and you're discussing things of the utmost privacy. And I mean, outright discussing them and calling people's names, and here are these servants, these black prisoners, putting things on the tables and, oh, just being ever so removed and so polite. I've seen that, and I've wondered, do you think these people are dumb? Do you think these folks aren't listening? I have had the opposite experience where others were there, and the prisoners who worked at the mansion would call and tell me, "They are plotting this, that, and the other." So that servant factor was the way we heard about a lot of things, not only during the movement, but politically right now. Unless this administration—and we have a female governor, she might well be smarter—but that kind of plotting was still going on at least during the last administration. Just discussing political, very private matters, lawsuits, everything, in the presence of those "trusted" prisoners as if they were just not there.

They [the maids and servants] came to [the NAACP] as individuals. They wouldn't come to a meeting and say it. No, they have a rapport with me, so they tell me, or if they have a rapport with Mrs. Jones, they tell Mrs. Jones. But they would get the word back to the civil-rights movement, and even now these prisoners get the word back to the community at large of what the private discussions are.

I've been told, "They're drawing up a lawsuit against the NAACP for whatever, and so-and-so is going to be their lawyer, and they expect to file it about such and such a date." So then we had a head start on getting our response ready. The silent servant, I guess, is a name for that syndrome. But yes, it exists. The power brokers, because it's not just whites any longer, underestimate not only the intelligence of those who serve them but the loyalty to certain causes.

Sometimes I think Lake Charles (which was racist when I was growing up) could become progressive, and other times, I just don't know.

But here's what would happen. Every time the NAACP was planning something [a sit-in or march], the power brokers of Lake Charles came and met us and gave us a compromise. We never had a chance to organize around an issue during my whole number of years in Lake Charles, and that was all of my life until thirty years ago. There was only one march. And I really don't remember exactly what it was about now, but it's the one march that didn't get cut off by the white folks sending us the answer before we could demonstrate. And it was very smart of the power structure. That way, Lake Charles never got the momentum around any civil-rights organization. And the reason I question it is, was that better than the dogs and the hose, and then the world saw, and they were forced to do something about it? I think we had, if not tolerant leadership, a very at least reasonable leadership in the white community that was going to avert confrontation at all costs. I don't know if they didn't want to lose; I don't know if they didn't want to be exposed; I don't know if somewhere in their heart of hearts, somebody had a conscience.

I never did [go to sit-ins or marches]. And I would liked to have. But I had a marriage that was straining at the seams already because of travel and activity and a different philosophy about some things. I was determined that I was going to do what I needed to do in Lake Charles and to a lesser extent in Louisiana, but I never went to other demonstrations in Louisiana. I served on other blue-ribbon committees and task forces and whatnot after there had been unrest, but I was not free between the size of my family and the philosophical differences on some of these issues with my husband. I wasn't free to go and do things. I remember so well some of the things that happened. Once, it was threatened that some of the white citizen-council groups or somebody was planning something in Plaquemine, Louisiana, because Dr. Martin Luther King was supposed to come. Well, there's Plaquemine, Louisiana, a town, then there's a parish that had real bad racial relations, and it is Plaquemines, the same spelling with an *s*. And the person who came to meet Dr. King's lieutenants went to the wrong Plaquemine. And I was just dying to go to that. And I would have been at the right one because I knew from the SCLC [Southern Christian Leadership Conference]. But I wasn't—I almost have to say I wasn't free to do those things and then be free to maintain a household and a marriage and effectiveness in my own community.

Through my NAACP actions at one time, we had correspondence with Thurgood Marshall, but I didn't meet him. And no, at that time, in my view, Malcolm X was something radical and wrong, and it took a lot of education and time for me to see the effectiveness of his role, albeit different from ours. There were these kinds of people at NAACP national meetings. But then, I was a little delegate from a little branch in the little state of Louisiana. You know, I saw a lot of people speak, but I did not have much interaction with them. By the time I moved up to the top, the leadership had shifted.

I was national president of the NAACP from 1992 to 1996. It was a challenge because the presidency at that time was supposed to be something almost ceremonial. The CEO then was the person in charge. And I had to develop that into something meaningful. I had to find a role for the president. It was fun because I led us into the economic arena in a more advanced way. And the thing I did during that time that I was most proud of was that I was the liaison to the African National Congress in South Africa, leading up to the free election, the end of apartheid. It was during that tenure. But I do know that that gave me a whole new insight into women's rights. We may be behind—we're still behind—but it was nothing compared to that, where you couldn't even talk to a woman unless she got her husband's permission. And even when you persuaded the husband to let them register to vote, they weren't sure on any given day that the husband would say, "Okay, you can go to the polls." I think that was the most fascinating experience that I had during the time. But I certainly carved out new ground for the president of the association not to sit up there and put on a pretty hat and preside at general meetings. I really found a way for the president to have an impact on the policy, and that worked out just very well. Now, we changed our constitution after that when we went on the search for a new president that led us to Kweisi Mfume because some persons on the search committee felt that we should have a structure more like the Urban League and SCLC and other sister agencies, where the CEO was also president. And I very willingly withdrew as president and supported a constitutional change to get that because there's no way they could have gotten a two-thirds vote to change the constitution if I didn't lead that fight. But I felt like if indeed our structure was in some way hampering, however falsely, these applicants—if indeed the good applicants that were the cream were rising to the top—I felt strongly that if they wanted the title president/CEO, I had no problem giving it up. But it was a challenging job while it lasted.

Julian Bond and I have a relationship from back in the maybe late seventies, early eighties, and maintain it to this day, an excellent working relationship. Philosophically we're together. I've known Julian through the years. I made it to the national board in 1981. Dr. Hooks was the new executive director, Ben Hooks. And so, therefore, anybody kind of before that time, I didn't have the privilege of knowing or interacting with very much.

The main role of the NAACP is the same as when we started, to ensure political, economical, educational justice for disenfranchised people with an emphasis on people of color. That has not changed. What has changed is that now we look at economic implications, whereas at one time, we really didn't. We looked at jobs as economics. But now we see economic development in terms of not only the education of our people but also ensuring opportunity, also getting companies to be more aware of diversity and actually putting out report cards—not so much on hiring; that's the tier where we let the locals work. But what we try to do is to find opportunities for investors or investments. We try to look at the bigger money, the decision-making money. That is certainly an explosion and an expansion of where we were with economic development a few years ago. But also now we have to look at the treatment of other classes, other classes besides people of color. We indeed have an obligation to say something about women's rights, regardless of color.

And a not-too-popular decision that was made, brought to the board through my health committee very recently, was that we take a position on choice. We're having backlash from that. But the board voted that we would participate in the women's march. Do you remember when that was held in the spring? We took a position to participate, and in our policy, we said that because a woman has a right to choose. Now there are some of our folks who are more than a little displeased with that, but the board sets policy. And that has been the policy. But I felt as chair of the health committee, that if not now, when? We've dodged the question of choice for years, but always ended up tabling it. Well, I was brave enough with Julian Bond—boy, the e-mails flew for days—to get that to where I could get it through the board, maybe with a big fight, but get it through. But there was no big fight. So we've got to look at stuff like that, and we've got to look at stem-cell research that affects the masses. We can't just stay in our little bitty black world. And of course, we have not really taken a position on sexual orientation. When gay people decided they were going to push for—what was the military response? Ask but don't tell. Anyway, the NAACP spoke up for the rights of people of any sexual orientation to have every right that everybody else had. We didn't discuss marriage and cohabitation and any of that. Marriage has become a question that Julian only has addressed, that it's a civil-rights matter and people ought to be permitted to marry. We never took a position on the general question of sexual orientation, but we took a position a long time ago that people who were of gay or lesbian persuasion should have every right, every privilege, that everybody else should have. We're broadening, and I think that's the true mission, to be more inclusive but to continue to fight for full freedom.

[Interview by Alan Govenar, July 14, 2005]

*Richard E. Stewart at home, Nashville, Tennessee, 2005.*

# RICHARD E. STEWART

ARMY CHAPLAIN

*Born September 23, 1932*

*Richard E. Stewart is a retired army chaplain. Both his father and uncle were ministers, and he knew from an early age that he wanted to become a pastor as well. He attended Wiley College in Marshall, Texas, from 1950 to 1954, and after graduation, he enlisted in the United States Air Force. He was stationed at Lackland Air Force Base in San Antonio for three years, and when he was discharged, he enrolled in the Perkins School of Theology at Southern Methodist University. While he was a student, he became involved in the civil-rights movement. After receiving his divinity degree from SMU in 1960, he worked at Wiley College as dean of the chapel, and then went into the army to become a chaplain. He served in the armed forces for twenty years in Korea, Vietnam, and several posts in the United States.*

I GREW UP IN TEXAS, forty miles south of Houston on the Gulf Coast in a little place called Angleton. My father was a United Methodist pastor. He and my mother had eight children, and I was the seventh of the eight. My parents were Timothy Marshall Stewart and Malinda Stewart. Angleton is forty miles south of Houston toward Freeport and Velasco. My father had a church there, Wards Chapel United Methodist Church. I don't know how it got started, but I imagine by the time they moved there from a place called Live Oak, Texas, near Bay City, that church had already been there. So he eventually became pastor there. In the United Methodist Church, the bishop appoints our clergy, so that's how he got there.

My father grew up near Bay City, and my mother was from a little place out from Angleton named McBeth. McBeth was a black town. As a

matter of fact, it was named for my mother's great-uncle, Preston Mc-
Beth. It still exists today. When it was founded, it had two churches
and a little school, a little post office, a little train station, and so forth.
The two churches and a cemetery still exist. They're right outside of Angleton.

I'd imagine the black population in Angleton was about 40 percent.
Schools were not integrated at the time I was growing up, of course. That
didn't occur until long after I had been graduated from there.

My father got his training as a minister in Gulfside. It was an opportunity for African American clergy of the United Methodists who did not
go to seminary to go and receive what they called a "course of study
training" in Gulfside, Mississippi. It was a Methodist training ground. It
was before I was old enough to know, so I imagine about the 1930s,
sometime in that time frame.

In Angleton, you really were aware of racism and segregation because the lines were pretty clearly drawn, and you simply did not step
over them. You were aware that you went to a school that was inferior.
Your white friends went to a school that was different from yours and
was obviously much better than yours. But you got along very well with
everybody, and you played with each other and had fun, but you always
knew that there were two places that you were not going to be with them.
One was at school, and the other was at church.

I went to a school called Marshall. It was all on the same campus,
from elementary through high school. They were in different buildings,
but they were on the same general grounds. The teachers were trained at
Prairie View A&M College or at Huston-Tillotson or at Texas Southern.
And they got their graduate degrees from elsewhere, usually up North.
Columbia is the only one I can recall offhand. But I remember one of my
coaches went to the University of Minnesota.

I started Wiley College in Marshall, Texas, in 1950. I graduated high
school in 1949. But I had been injured, so I was out for a year. I got hurt
playing football and I had to have a knee operation. And at that time, you
couldn't go to Wiley at midterm; you had to go at the beginning of a year.

Wiley College was the greatest experience of my life. Again, I was
aware that it was not the best school in the world. I realized that the
buildings were old, etc., etc., but it was a very, very rich experience, and

I was fortunate. I was able to sing in the choir at Wiley and do some other things. I did join a fraternity. But they had other kinds of clubs there, as well, so I was involved in several of those. Student life was very rich at Wiley. The socioeconomic divisions were not as great, so although you were very poor, it seemed not to matter very much. So if you had the desire, you could just do a whole lot of things that made life very, very rich for you.

I'm just going to have to guess what it cost. Maybe a thousand dollars a year. But a thousand dollars a year in the early fifties was very, very difficult to come by and to spare. I majored in religious education and philosophy. The teachers were outstanding. We had some very good professors. A man named Carlos Smith who taught German, he was outstanding. A woman named Thelma John Newton taught sociology. J. Otis Erwin was the campus minister. A man named Calvin Reese taught sociology. We had plenty of white teachers. That was a godsend for Wiley because accreditation depended on Ph.D.'s. We were fortunate that we had whites, who made that "sacrifice" and came to Wiley and taught, which allowed us to keep our accreditation.

What was especially good about the faculty was that they wanted you to succeed so much, and they just put their all into that. Probably the only way you could fail at Wiley was to just really screw up, be lazy, something of that sort. But they took great interest in you and worked real hard to have you work for yourself, to make certain that you made it. It was like a village.

But the surrounding community of Marshall was rigidly segregated. Although Angleton, as I said, was segregated, it wasn't as pronounced. You just never had problems of the sort that we had in Marshall. I'll tell you a quick story. We had several students from Nigeria, and they didn't know the customs of the South, so they went to a movie theater and went in the wrong door. They were set upon and beat quite severely. The British Embassy entered that fracas, and [it was] interesting how changes began to occur slowly when people had to distinguish, of course, which students were British subjects and those of us who were not. Several of us began adopting a speech pattern that could confuse people as to whether they should accost us or whether they might be confronting British subjects. But it was very "funny" for us that if you were an American black, that's tough. If you were an African black, they treated you much more carefully.

Most of the students from Nigeria were in other fields, in the sciences, and were extremely bright, *extremely* bright students. I imagine that the only way they could be chosen to be sent here, though, was to be the cream of the crop. They were all very bright.

There were [civil-rights] protests after I left Wiley in the latter 1950s. The protests were pretty silent, but we think pretty effective. For instance, there was a segregated bus which came through our community, came right by our campus, and picked us up. And we'd get on the bus, and the man would tell us we had to sit at the back of the bus. So we'd tell him, give us our dime back. Sometimes he would just ignore the fact that we were not sitting at the back of the bus. But sometimes he would take us up on that and make us get off and give us our dime back. I think he was aware that that was a pretty silly thing, a bus rambling through a large part of the city empty. But again, that was before protests reached the kind of stage that led to the changes that came later.

Our [activism] consisted mostly of registering voters—again, the silent protest I just mentioned—and representing the college in national kinds of student-movement meetings. I was very fortunate to be able to do that quite often out of that little school. I went to Methodist Student Movement meetings, or Interscholastic Student Movement meetings, YMCA meetings; they were always integrated meetings. White students from white schools in Texas met with us, or we'd meet with them.

I did meet James Farmer; he was [originally from Marshall, Texas,] and was the founder of CORE [Congress on Racial Equality]. I graduated from Wiley in 1954. That was a very important year. I remember the Supreme Court decision *[Brown v. Board of Education]* when it came out. I was happy for my nephew, who was about four at that time, and I was thinking about the fact that he was going to have the opportunity to go to the kind of schools that I could not go to. A very interesting thing happened. Many years later, when he became a senior in high school, he did go to an integrated school in Angleton. The year was 1968, so fourteen years went by without his being able to receive benefits of the 1954 decision. But I remember on May 17, 1954, how excited we all were about the fact that our brothers and sisters and kindred would have an opportunity for much better schooling than that which we had. At that time, I was a student at Wiley when the *Brown v. Board of Education* decision was handed down by the Supreme Court, and I graduated in the summer of 1954.

Our assumption was that the Supreme Court decision was going to be resisted in Marshall, Texas, like it was in Mississippi. And of course it was. But we didn't pay a whole lot of attention to how the townspeople reacted to that because we were very certain that the *Brown* decision was going to be resisted at all costs.

[After graduation] I went into the United States Air Force and served for three years. And when I was discharged, I went to the Perkins School of Theology at Southern Methodist University [SMU]. I was stationed at Lackland in San Antonio for the whole time. With people of my own age, it [military service] was great. With some others, there was racism, but the federal government was very, very clear on its policies, that there was not going to be segregation. So persons who had problems with that, of course, that was for them to deal with. I did not encounter it blatantly, but I was aware of it.

I'd always wanted to go to SMU. When I was growing up, Doak Walker and Kyle Rote were fantastic football players, and I'd listen to the games. There was an announcer named Kern Tipps, and he made the games just come alive on the radio. So being a United Methodist, I certainly wanted to go to SMU. But the only schools open to blacks at that time were the school of theology and the school of law.

I started at SMU in 1958. The students, for the most part, and the faculty, for the most part, seemed aware that the campus was an island of tolerance, which, when you stepped off, it vanished. So, for the most part, you didn't encounter racial conflicts at all. In the city itself, of course, it was different. But those were great years. I enjoyed it. One of the most wonderful things that ever happened to me was I was on the student government. I represented the Perkins School on the student government. And they had a welcoming committee. And when big wheels came into the city, students would get in this big Cadillac, and we'd go out to the airport—it was Dallas Love Field. And we'd greet this big wheel and bring them onto the campus. That was a wonderful experience. The wheels seemed to have accepted my being a part of that as being a very, very natural thing.

SMU had some pretty important people come to its campus. I remember Dr. Ralph Bunche came. Just amazing to me. Jackie Robinson came to SMU in 1958. The United Methodist Church had a conference. But at any rate, it had to do with integration, and they wanted to meet at SMU. At that time, as I said earlier, the only schools that were open to blacks were the school of theology and the school of law. And the question was raised at that conference with an insistence that the university fulfill its responsibility to be a university and open up all of its doors. That was a good experience. One of the things which had occurred was, I found, quite interesting. SMU in those days had the most outstanding swimming team in the Southwest Conference. And they had a place called Perkins Natatorium that had a little swimming pool. And when that conference was held there, I went swimming in the pool. The next week, no more conference, and I go to go into the pool, and the coach says I cannot swim in the pool. I said, "Coach, I swam in the pool last week." He says, "I know." "But you're telling me I cannot swim in the pool now." He said no. Well, those kinds of frustrating experiences occurred every now and then at school.

There was a store in downtown [Dallas] called H. L. Green's. We didn't picket. What had happened was we had tried several restaurants closer to the university that were not making much progress [with integration]. So two of my white buddies and I, both students at the school of theology, went downtown to Green's. I had been told that the Citizens Council of Dallas (not to be confused with the White Citizens' Council, which was a segregationist group)—the Citizens Council of Dallas was a group of businessmen who were determined that the unrest that was occurring in Birmingham, etc., etc., etc., was not going to occur in Dallas— they had impressed upon the businesses of Dallas that if black persons came to those particular institutions for service, that we should be served. And when we first went in, a young lady greeted us and told us that they were not going to be able to serve us. That's when we informed them that there was a new policy in effect. She went and checked with her manager, and when he came back, he assured her that was correct and that she should serve us. So there wasn't any kind of problem.

Well, it took a lot of courage because we were seniors and about to be graduated, and there was always the possibility they might not let you graduate if you got sent to jail or got in trouble. But from the other point of view, as students, you were pretty much in a different world from what the townspeople of Dallas were facing. That was in 1960. I graduated from Perkins [School of Theology] in '60.

My father's a minister, my uncle is a minister. Of course, that will not make you a minister simply because of that. You have to have a desire in you to want to live that kind of lifestyle because you do not get rich. And you have to pay quite a cost, you and your family, in order to do that. But I felt that that was a good way to serve and do something that I loved very, very much. Interestingly, I was a stutterer. As a matter of fact, I still am. So going through that and trying to be a preacher was not an easy thing.

About the only people who can tell I stutter are speech pathologists. I was stationed in Korea, and I never will forget, I had this young man in my choir. And we had gone to eat lunch. And this young captain comes up and says, "Chaplain, you are a stutterer." I said, "Yeah, man, but how in the world do you . . . ?" He says, "Because you speak too precisely." He says, "You form your words with great difficulty." And I say, "Well, you're right. But I had no idea that it was that difficult to do." He says, "Yes." He says, "I work with people who have speech-pattern problems." Well, I was touched by the way he phrased that. I thought I had masked it very well.

When I first got out of SMU, I went to Wiley College in Marshall, Texas, and I worked as the dean of the chapel for two years. And then I went into the army. I became an army chaplain. I was in the military for twenty years. I was in Korea, and then I was in Vietnam and in several posts in the States.

I was stationed in Fort Bliss, Texas, and this beautiful young lady and her beautiful twin sister came in the chapel with their mother. And lo and behold, she ended up being my wife. We were married in 1966. Her name is Jeanette Anderson.

[After we got married], we were at Fort Polk, Louisiana; Fort Dix, New Jersey; Fort Alexander Hamilton, New York; Walter Reed, D.C.; Fort Sill, Oklahoma. She wasn't with me in Korea and Vietnam. Those were very tough assignments. Very scary.

[All of the civil-rights activity going on in the United States did affect things at military bases.] I'll give you a quick story. I had some

Reverend Richard E. Stewart, South Korea, 1965.

friends stationed at Fort Polk, Louisiana, and they brought a complaint, and the Department of Defense moved them away from there. Not the Department of the Army, the Department of Defense. When we were stationed at Fort Polk, Louisiana, and I was getting ready to go to Vietnam, we attempted to get a house for my wife and our baby daughter in Temple, Texas. When we'd call, there'd be a house available, but when we showed up, it had just rented, just been let, just been sold, etc., etc. So we were not able to get a house for them. Fortunately, my father-in-law had a house that he let my wife and daughter stay in while I served in Vietnam. Now, I didn't have sense enough to raise the kind of hell which I should have raised about that. I'm certain that the army would have taken steps. As you may know, they can put a town off limits, a whole city off limits. There's a great big post near Temple, Texas, Fort Hood. So that commanding general could have put the whole thing off limits. I regret very much I did not push that.

I won't say I was co-opted by the army, but things in the army were not nearly as bad as they were on the outside. I went into the army because I felt that there was a great need. I had always been aware that we send our young people off to fight wars, and they don't have a choice, but if you're an officer, you can choose whether you want to go into the military. You can't choose the place that you want to go to, but you can always choose to resign your commission, etc., etc. So there's a whole lot more freedom available to officers as far as choices are concerned, which are not available to eighteen- and nineteen- and twenty-year-old enlisted people.

After I left the army, I worked at Southern Methodist University for two years and then at Parkland Hospital for two years. I then worked at the Methodist Medical Center. Then we came to Nashville from Dallas in 1986. In Nashville, I had the opportunity to serve with the same board that endorses chaplains and functions with chaplains all over the world, the United Methodist Board of Higher Education and Ministry. I worked with the chaplains' division, and that's the division in which we have chaplains all over the world, in the armed forces, VA [Veterans Administration], in medical facilities, etc.

I retired in 1999, and then worked at Fisk University for three years as the dean of the chapel. And now, I'm retired [from Fisk] and writing and reading and painting. I've been very fortunate. I thank [God] for that. I tell people all the time, God has been better to me than I could have dreamed, better than I could have asked for, and certainly much, much better to me than I could have deserved or earned. I have been very blessed. I have been so blessed. God continues to use me in ways that I find fascinating. My wife and I sing with a contemporary gospel

Religious service led by an unidentified army chaplain, North Africa, ca. 1943–1944.

ensemble. It's called Agape. And it's essentially twelve soloists who are able to blend their voices in ways that are just utterly amazing. So we've enjoyed that very much. Our daughter has given us two little grandchildren; one is five and one is three. And our son has given us a little girl who is five months old.

My oldest [child] is Janet. She went to Southern Methodist University. Our son is named Richard Jr. And our youngest is a daughter named Laiandrea. She's a third-year medical resident in radiology. So they've all been just a real blessing to us.

My wife teaches first grade; that is her ministry. Every now and then, she'll run into kids who she taught ten years ago, fifteen years ago, and they're now big people. And they still love her. You know, I tell her all the time, that's a blessing. She got a bachelor's at Cameron University in Oklahoma. She got the master of science in professional education at UTD [University of Texas at Dallas]. And she got a doctorate at Tennessee State University in Nashville. She's much younger than me.

In the armed forces, [the biggest challenge] was knowing that you were part of a system that is designed to inflict death and destruction upon others and to realize that that same death and destruction is aimed toward you. As chaplains, you cannot engage in killing, you cannot engage in fighting, you cannot engage in damaging persons or property, but you must stand with those who have that responsibility, that as long as young men and young women are sent out to fight wars brought on by old men and old women, then it's your responsibility to be there with them. Doesn't mean that you're not scared, because believe me, those were the scariest days of my life, and so I pray that the war [in Iraq] will soon end and that we don't do this anymore. When our son was born, I was so happy, I was just grinning and giggling. And my wife was crying, and she told me that she prays that she has not brought into this world a son that's going to go off and fight in wars and kill and be killed. In those days, only young men were being sent to war. But I thought her reaction was so interesting, which I hadn't thought about at all, although she suffered every day I was in Vietnam. She was scared. And then she thought about the fact that her son might face that same future.

My daughters tell me I'm the youngest seventy-two-year-old man they've ever seen in their lives. I have faith in God and the goodness of people, and the hope that things will be better for my children and my grandchildren keeps me going. I am hoping for a better world for them and for all people.

[Interview by Alan Govenar, February 1, 2005]

*William H. Waddell IV in military dress, ca. 1930s.*

# WILLIAM H. WADDELL IV

VETERINARIAN

*Born August 9, 1908*

*William H. Waddell IV grew up in South Richmond, Virginia, in a family of mixed black-white racial ancestry. At age fourteen, he enrolled in the Manassas Industrial School in Manassas, Virginia, where he became interested in veterinary medicine. After graduation, he went to Lincoln University near Oxford, Pennsylvania. At Lincoln University, he met Langston Hughes and Thurgood Marshall. In 1931, he was the first black student to attend the University of Pennsylvania School of Veterinary Medicine since 1913. He received his DVM degree in 1935 and was hired to teach at Tuskegee Institute in Alabama, working with George Washington Carver and Booker T. Washington. He later became the first African American to practice veterinary medicine in West Virginia. During World War II, he served in the army as a Buffalo Soldier in the same company as Joe Louis and Jackie Robinson. After World War II, Waddell worked in Alabama, West Virginia, and North Dakota before settling in Hawaii in the 1960s. He retired in 1973. In 2004, Waddell received an honorary doctor of science degree from his alma mater, Lincoln University.*

I WAS RAISED IN A HOME that believed in values and discipline. My father was William H. Waddell III, and my mother's name was Sara. There were eight in my family, and I am the only living one. My father worked at one place all of his life. At eighteen, he went to work at Wingo, Ellett, and Crump Boots and Shoes in Richmond, Virginia, and he worked there until he died. My mother was a cook for the bosses of that company—one meal a day, at noon. And she did that for years. She was an excellent cook for these people my daddy worked for, as well as for her children as they grew up. She taught all the girls how to sew, wash, and iron. All the rich girls, she taught them how to do that. The relationship at that time in Richmond, Virginia, among blacks and whites was very good in that everybody respected each other. When you got sick, be you white or black, they would come and ask you, "Can I do anything for you?" And they would come and sit and bring you food or whatnot. And if people, black or white, would die, they would go to each other's funerals, although the blacks would have to sit in the "backup" in the attic, but they would be there. They were invited. It wasn't as bad as other parts of the South. But you knew you were in the South. The relationship, I think, was on a much higher level than further south.

Now, William H. Waddell I was born and reared in Wales. He never got married, but he lived with two women that were ex-slaves. However, he was very fertile in that he impregnated at least eighteen or twenty white women. All in a little town in North Carolina. These women had to leave town because in those days, when you got pregnant and you weren't married, you left town. And I had the privilege of meeting them later on in life.

My grandfather was born and reared in Amelia County, Virginia. He was a tobacco farmer, sawmill man, and truck farmer. Amelia County is located between Richmond and Danville. My grandmother was a slave, but my grandfather was not. He was born a year or so after slavery ended. His mother was a slave, who was impregnated by William H. Waddell I.

All that part of my grandparents' family looked white. And when my grandfather died, he left all of his land, over eight hundred acres, to his colored offspring, and they still own that land today in Amelia County, Virginia. A lot of them have died off.

Of the children on my father's side, my father was the oldest. All of the siblings worked and cooperated with each other. My father was the leader of the family, and if anything happened, they would not do anything until my father was consulted. My father had four brothers. My father's name was William, and his brothers were George, Edward, Joe, and Allen. And he had five sisters: Frances, Rosa, Louise, Helen, and Ellen.

At the age of thirteen and a half years, I was helped by a lady by the name of Grace Walker, who was trained in Boston, Massachusetts, at the school of public speaking, better known as Emerson. Her father was the first black lawyer to pass the state board exam in Virginia. Well, this lady thought it would be nice for them to get me away from Richmond, Virginia, because I was much advanced over the students that went to the same school. Grace Walker did a lot to motivate me to go to the Manassas school.

I went to the Manassas Industrial School in Manassas, Virginia, when I was nearly fourteen. It was also known as the Old Battlefield School because it was built on the fields where the Battle of Bull Run was fought. The daughter of an ex-slave established that school in 1893. Most of the teachers at that school were teachers from Howard University. The president of the trustees of that school was an outstanding white man from the North by the name of Oswald Garrison Dillard. He was the grandson of William Lloyd Garrison, the abolitionist during the Civil War. He and John Brown were two of the greatest abolitionists of the North.

I had the opportunity of being exposed to some of the greatest black teachers in the world at that time. Such people as Alain Locke of Howard University; Carter G. Woodson at Howard University; E. E. Just, a biologist from Howard University; James Henderson from Howard University; Monroe Gregory, the captain of the Amherst baseball team, from Minor Normal College; Sterling Brown from Howard University; Dr. Charles Drew, the founder of the blood test; and W. E. B. DuBois. As a matter of fact, Manassas ended up getting all of the people who came to Howard University as part of their program. Manassas was only thirty miles from Howard University.

At Manassas Industrial School, upon my arrival, they had training, military training, which is very good in the life of a child of fourteen. They believed in good, old-fashioned training, which I will never forget. Now, not all these people that were at Howard University, the outstanding people, were on the faculty. They did what we called in those days bootlegging. They would come down to Manassas once a month or twice a month because they had full-time jobs, and some were professors at Howard. Strange as it might seem, in those days, they came down for five dollars a day to lecture, two dollars for gas, and as much food as they could eat for free. It was only then that I found out that city people didn't eat as much as country people, because I've never seen people eat as much as some of those men at a meal.

I was very fortunate at Manassas that I met a lot of people who had gone out in the world and were not trained to do anything, but came back in later life to pick up trades. Those people served as big brothers to me, and as a matter of fact, one of them recommended me to a job at the age of fourteen. I got a job as a porch boy at the Homestead Hotel, one of the most outstanding hotels in the world. And during those years, I worked hard and I met such interesting people from such companies as Sears Roebuck, Marshall Field's, and Anheuser-Busch.

At the Homestead Hotel, I was the porch boy and the bellboy at the same time because I could make more money. This hotel was a huge place that employed three thousand people. They raised their own food. They had the national tennis tournaments, golf tournaments, and bridge tournaments there. And bar associations from all over the world would come there. And I got to meet the rich people. I waited on Franklin Delano Roosevelt when he was the governor of New York. I waited on Warren G. Harding when he was the president of the United States. I waited on people like that. And I learned a lot. It prepared me to be a better man because I saw these rich people every morning and watched them read the papers about stocks and bonds and whatnot. I found out that in order to be successful in life, you had to get into the mainstream of American life. You just couldn't make a few dollars and say, "Well, I'm going to live by myself, among my family, among my people." To be successful you got to get out there in the gravy, where the stuff is. And I learned that. And I learned how to get along with people and work with people, to communicate, to cooperate, to coordinate. And compromise. I learned such things at Manassas and at home.

At the Manassas school, I watched the big boys. It was at Manassas that I became interested in veterinary medicine. A cow by the name of Minnehaha tried to calve, to give birth, and she had difficulty. So the big boys came to my room and took me to the dairy barn and told me what to do. In other words, the neck of the calf was blocking the vulva so she couldn't get her head through. And her feet would knuckle under her. They couldn't get their arms in the cow to get them out, and I had a small arm. So they told me what to do. They gave me some small manila rope, they called it, and as the cow would stop laboring, I would push her back by the muscles on the chest. And I put a rope around each foot and brought the foot that would knuckle under her out toward the opening of the vulva. And after I got the legs straight to come out, then I put a rope around the calf, which was toward the right. I straightened it up to be parallel with the spinal cord above. And then they pulled her out, and we had a live, big, beautiful calf. And I decided on that day that I wanted to be a veterinarian.

During my stay at Manassas, the school didn't have a very good football team. Until I got to be a sophomore, we had hardly any team. Everybody beat us. But as time went on, and particularly during my junior and senior years, I was captain of the football team, and we were never defeated in northern Virginia. I was also captain of the baseball team. And in track, I ran pin relays and we won at all the races. That's when we put Manassas on the map, those of my generation. And when I graduated, the day of graduation, Oswald Villard, the president of the trustee board, told me he had been reading about me and had written about me in his book *Atlantic Life*. And he said to me, "Keep up the good work."

My coach wrote a letter of support for me to enter Lincoln University of Pennsylvania. I had to write a paper about why I selected Lincoln, and I did and I was accepted to be a student.

When I got to Lincoln University, I had no trouble. But when I got ready to take veterinary medicine, I had trouble getting in because the last black man who went there was from a rich family and looked like he was white. Well, he made it bad for everybody who followed him. But I worked at it. And I was the first black student to attend the University of Pennsylvania School of Veterinary Medicine since 1913, up until 1931, when I went there. Eighteen years, nearly, had passed.

At Penn, however, before my time, John Baxter Taylor, the world's best, fastest quarter miler, became one the first blacks to win the Olympics. And we had a man named Augustus Lushington, who was the first black to graduate, 1897, at Penn. Then John Baxter Taylor was a year later. Then, after Baxter, we had another man, and then this man who caused all the trouble. But he came from a very rich family, of Wilmington, Delaware, and his uncle married Marian Anderson, the singer. But Fisher was his name. He just caused a lot of trouble. And nobody in his class liked him. Of course, he was a smart man, too, because he'd studied veterinary medicine at Penn. But he wasn't too successful in life, I think, because he was a playboy, and he had too much money. He married white, which was all right. I have nothing against that. But they didn't find out he wasn't white until he died. They went to look for his body and couldn't find it till one man remembered that there was a bunch of Fishers that would look half-white and owned the town of Wilmington, Delaware, nearly, so he recommended his wife go to that place, and that's where they found his body, at a black undertaker's place.

When I was at Penn, I had to uncover, break down, and build up everything that went wrong. Now, those men before Fisher, all of them turned out to be very good men. All of them had wonderful jobs and did wonders for our race. But the little things that Fisher did stayed there all those years, and I had to break it down. However, I'm happy to say that during my tenure at Lincoln University, Pennsylvania, where I graduated, my record was terrific. All white professors except one. It was located near Oxford, Pennsylvania.

While I was there, I had the privilege of rooming for a while with Langston Hughes. And I had the privilege of knowing Thurgood Marshall.

Well, a lot of people—I've had over two thousand people nearly, white people—write me and ask me if Langston was a "sissy." Was he a homosexual? No, he was not a homosexual, as far as I knew. If he was a homosexual, he had the ability to make women yell at him, or holler, "Ow." So I figured he was no sissy. Or he could have been bisexual, but I didn't know anything about that. I would say the man was like anybody else. Just a scholar who had been exposed to a different type of life and had a mama who had been harassed quite a bit in her life, and he was just different.

Langston wrote a book while he was there, *Not Without Laughter*, a novel. And then he was writing all these other poems and whatnot. I don't remember them all. I remember some, but not all. But he was busy then trying to build a public relationship between the white and black worlds. He was going around speaking at white schools and going to football games and all, trying to get recognition for Lincoln.

Thurgood Marshall was also at Lincoln at that time. I got along with Thurgood very well. I get along with people. Thurgood was supposed to have finished Lincoln before I got through. But he came down with tuberculosis. And he stayed out two years. He was supposed to have finished the class of '29. But instead, he finished with the class of '31, my class.

From Lincoln, I went to veterinary school at University of Pennsylvania. I was there for four years. University of Pennsylvania was a Quaker school. It's over 290 years old now. They gave me a medal ten years ago.

They were nice to me when I was in school there. I respected myself. You got to respect yourself first. That's the first law of nature: Respect yourself. My rich white benefactors got me to the University of Pennsylvania.

I graduated from Lincoln in '31. I graduated from the University of Pennsylvania June 19, 1935. And I became second lieutenant of the Officers' Reserve Corps of the University of Pennsylvania. They called it ORC then. Well, while I was at Penn, I met a man who was a captain in the United States Army, and he told me about the Ninth and Tenth Cavalries. He'd visit and lecture on campus. So, on the day of my graduation from the University of Pennsylvania, I went down and volunteered for duties with the Ninth and Tenth Cavalries.

The night of my graduation, I went to see Mrs. Bond—she was my chief benefactor, a rich Quaker lady. She said, "Well, what are you going to do now?"

I said, "Well, I've made arrangements to go into the army. The Ninth and Tenth."

She said, "Well, I think it would be wise for you to break that because we made arrangements for you to go to Tuskegee Institute. We knew Mr. Washington, Booker T. Washington. And we knew him when he used to come to our churches and beg for money, and we gave him money and whatnot. And we feel like that with your training and what we have done for you, you should go to Tuskegee Institute."

So I got in touch with the people in the army and told them that I'd be in touch, but I had to go to Tuskegee, which I did. I worked there; I went straight to Tuskegee. And there I taught veterinary sciences. I was also working with Dr. Carver and his peanut oil that was used to remove blemishes as well as to correct wrinkles in your face. I worked with him for two and a half years, until he died. And then I drew up plans for the school of veterinary medicine.

At Tuskegee, they made me the director of the veterinary division. And the veterinary division had about four hundred or five hundred cows. They had sheep of all breeds, hogs of all breeds, cattle of all breeds. So I was in charge of all that. Not only did I do that, but I also had a hospital there, which was not to my liking. That's when I first had my trouble at Tuskegee with the people. Not with the people, but the president. Because in those days all these black schools wanted me. Tennessee wanted me. Albany wanted me. And even in Oklahoma, Langston University wanted me. But you know why they wanted me? The president of the school would build a hospital or a place up for you to work with at the school's expense or the state's expense, and then you gave them one-half the money you took in. That's the reason I didn't work at Tennessee State. They wanted me there. They gave me more money. They offered at least three hundred more dollars than I was getting at Tuskegee. And any outside practice I did I had to share with the president. That was Dr. Daniel Hale, when he was there.

I stayed at Tuskegee until the beginning of World War II. I had joined the Fifth Brigade, though my time in the army was delayed by work at Tuskegee. The Fifth Brigade was located at that time at Brackettville, Texas. But as reserve officer, I had been also to Fort Riley at Junction City, Kansas. Then I went to Leavenworth. When I took short courses, the army sent me to different places. They were preparing me to be the first black brigadier general.

Being a Buffalo Soldier was terrific. Well, a man has not been a soldier or any part of the United States Army in any division or any department unless he's been a Buffalo Soldier. To be a Buffalo Soldier it meant, number one, that you had to discipline the men. It meant getting out and riding horses every day. It meant having sham battles every day. It meant twenty-four hours a day of work, which they don't do now, because you had your horses to take care of as well as yourself. And we didn't have a lot of crap like you're having now because we didn't have women. We had nurses, but they weren't at station hospitals. You soldiered and you worked. And you had discipline. And you had values. My life at Brackettville was a hell of a life because we were up at five-thirty every morning, and we soldiered up until six in the evening.

In those days, the morale of the cavalry depended upon money, food, and [the availability of] women. They encouraged that. And every company had its own cooking outfit, and every outfit had damn good cooks. You ate well. You soldiered well. And you never had any time off. Even on Sundays when you were supposed to be off, you had to take your troops to Ciudad Acuña, Mexico. That's right across from Del Rio, Texas. We'd take our men down there every Sunday for sex [with prostitutes]. They'd go to Mexico, and they'd spend the whole day on Sunday. We'd get the money changed up for them, two-dollar bills, and they'd go over and have sex all day. You'd take them at eleven o'clock in the morning, and they'd leave at eleven o'clock at night. And then, you had to have them ready to get up at 5:30 A.M. for those damn big-eyed horses the next day. That's what Brackettville was like. Armadillos. Rattlesnakes. Yellow snakes. Coyotes. Mosquitoes.

There were some black Seminoles around Brackettville. Some would serve as scouts. As a matter of fact, I saw one here two years ago, lectured at the universities. He lives down there now at Del Rio, I think. His family served as scouts there. And I knew where the family lived, and I knew where the graveyards were. But now it's a dude camp down there.

The black Seminoles were very close together. Much closer together than most black people. Because black people as a rule, they're close for a while, but once some of them become educated, they forget all about where they came from. But the life at Brackettville, basically, was a rough, tough life: riding, bivouacking, going out, coming back, being eaten up with ticks all over your damn body. The first time I went out, I came back that night, I had about forty ticks on me. I was out for three days. And then I learned how to deal with them. You take chloroform and ether and put it on them. And get them drunk and then pull them out. If you don't pull them out right away, you could get infected, highly infected, with so many of them on you. But then I learned how to take care of them. I learned how to fix my clothes and fix myself up so that they wouldn't bother me or the men. Well, I was new the first time that happened. And I wasn't properly prepared for the bivouac I went on.

Life at Fort Clark in Brackettville, Texas, was a rough life. We'd eat well; we played hard. And Joe Louis was in our outfit. Yeah. So was Jackie Robinson. Jackie Robinson was a gentleman then and a gentleman all the way through life. He'd worked and gone to school. Whites knew how to get along with him. And he'd beat the hell of them at table tennis. You talk about a man playing with a table-tennis racket. I saw him win as much as five hundred dollars from those young white boys.

Joe Louis was a gentleman too. Very nice, very refined. I even knew Joe before he went in the army. I met him at a fight in New York. And I went round to his house, and I found out what he liked. He liked quiet. I went to a party they gave for him, and the house was just packed up with celebrities, both white and black. And you know where he was? Back on the couch in the den, eating an apple and looking at the funny papers.

The first woman Joe married wasn't for him. I met her, too, at the port of embarkation, or at San Antonio, one night coming back. I saw her there with another guy, and I knew. I had met her at her house. Ruth Brown was Joe Louis's second wife. She was a nice woman. She was a lawyer, educated. And she kept him straight.

I was a Buffalo Soldier from the time that I started after graduation from Penn, though I did work for a while at Tuskegee. But as part of my training as a Buffalo Soldier, I had to take different short courses here and there. Everything had to do with horses and warfare. I had to go to the Carlisle Barracks to learn how to put my ass on a horse—and how to deal with the use of gas in warfare and what to do about burns. And then at Fort Leavenworth, I learned about the business of being an officer.

Well, Kansas was just a prejudiced damn place. We couldn't even go to the officers' club in town. And those who went down there nearly got into fights and didn't go back anymore. And of course, the people in Junction City, Kansas, they were a little better because they depended upon the military men for money. However, they still had segregation. And it was that way at Fort Benning, Georgia. I was there, too.

I played baseball over there at Fort Benning with the faculty baseball team at Tuskegee. And I played baseball against Satchell Paige and all those guys, Jackie Robinson and Roy Campanella. I was manager of the faculty baseball team at Tuskegee.

When I was a Buffalo Soldier, we had to patrol the U.S. border with Mexico to keep the Mexicans out. We kept them out. We chased them with horses, on horseback, and they had better damn horses. And they ran. And they wouldn't come back anymore when you chased them forty yards on a damn horseback. We were not trying to hurt them.

One time, when we patrolled the borders of Mexico, we went out looking for Pancho Villa's son or cousin, or relative, who was causing a lot of trouble on the border. He had been an officer in the Mexican army, but he deserted and decided to go out for himself and get rich. All I knew, he belonged to the Pancho Villa family. And Pancho Villa was the one that General Black Jack Pershing chased before my time.

I had met Black Jack Pershing when I was a porch boy at the Homestead Hotel. He was a fine man. The thing I didn't understand about him was that he came over and looked at me and started smiling and asking me questions. I answered him and he rubbed his hand through my hair. Now my hair wasn't that good. Wasn't nappy, either, but it wasn't good hair, wasn't straight, you know. And he just said, "You're a nice boy." And I gave him his newspaper and thanked him. He gave me a dollar, which was a lot of money back then.

Well, after World War II broke out, the Buffalo Soldiers headed overseas. En route, however, we stopped at Fort Patrick Henry, Virginia. We were supposed to be there for two weeks. And we got in a riot there. The boys in my outfit, Company B, went up to the PX, just getting off the train, and wanted to get something cold to drink and whatnot. And the paratroopers that were white, that we went on maneuvers with, and beat their butts down in Louisiana that same year, they decided to take the boots off our boys. They took the boots off a sergeant of ours. And he walked back to our company and got our boys, who went back up there and broke their damn place up. And then we refused to go into the dining room to eat because they wanted to separate our boys from their officers. We always ate with our officers, but they didn't want us to. So we wouldn't go in to eat. Well, they finally made up their mind, after they had that riot there, and we nearly beat up the paratroopers, they let us in to eat together.

From Fort Patrick Henry, we went to Casablanca in Morocco. And we were there for two days, and then they moved us out the third day, because we had trouble again. We went down to the Casablanca Club, where they had made the movie *Casablanca*. The officers in our outfit went down there, and some white officers tried to stop them. So we broke up that place. And they got us out of there the next day. But before we did, we got to see the prince of Morocco, who had a house where he had all of his wives. One of the prince's Arabian horses had gotten sick at the University of Morocco, and they came out to see whether or not we had a veterinarian.

Well, the general recommended me. They had a horse, a very beautiful horse, that they were having trouble with, and they wanted me to come over, and they were a quarter of a mile from where the railroad train was, and I went over in an American jeep that they had. And there were all these pretty women. I had never seen so many pretty women at one time as I did at that university. So I finally got to the horse, and the man told me he was wild and whatnot. So I reached in my pocket and got out some sugar lumps that I generally carried around with me for the horses in our outfit. And that Arabian horse ate a little of that sugar, and I started away. I knew what was going to happen: he started following me. And when I stopped, he stopped and was reaching at me for more sugar, and I gave him a little bit more. And then I told the owner, or the manager, to hold the horse and let me look at him. I picked up a pan with some grain, gave it to him, and the horse ate that grain because it was ground, and I gave him some corn to take to the horse, hard corn. And the horse ate some of that, and I saw he was having difficulty chewing. So then, I told them to bring me a bucket of water and some grease. And they did. And I soaped my hand and arm down. And I went over to the horse. First, I gave him sugar, and he ate that. Then I put my hand in his mouth, and the people started screaming. And I put my hand down because it was exciting the horse. And I looked, and they said, "Oh," in relief: They thought the horse was going to bite my arm off. But they didn't know that I put my hand on the side of the horse's mouth and the teeth were on the inside of my hand and the outside of my skin was on the mucous membrane of the horse; the horse couldn't bite me. And I found out what was wrong with the horse; its tooth was about a half an inch or more too long. And he couldn't chew. So then we opened up the bag I had there, and I cut that tooth off, and then I called that veterinarian over, who was from the university, and had him grind the teeth down, trim them, and make them even. And that horse was beginning to eat when I left, and he came over and licked me. I gave him more sugar, and we left, because the train was pulling out. That took four or five hours. And it was the talk of the town. Nobody had ever seen a man put his hand in a horse's mouth. The only way he could hurt me was to rear up. And he didn't do that because I'd been giving him sugar, and he wanted the sugar. That horse had more sense than some people. So we left from there and went on to Oran, and we started fighting in North Africa.

Well, anywhere they're fighting and are being killed is a bitch, man. It's terrible. I saw hard men who fought and were dying. We lost a lot of men in North Africa. In Oran, we were running out the Germans and Italians that were there and got stranded and couldn't get out. And after we cleaned up the fighting in Oran, North Africa, they put us on a ship and we went to Livorno, Italy.

In Livorno, we had to fight and drive the people from out of the hills there and make it possible for the citizens to come back to their homes. And when we finished helping the people living in Livorno, we went on over to Rome, and then to Salerno and Pisa. In Italy, I had two or three jobs. I did reconnaissance on horseback to look and see how close the enemy was to us. And then I was with the mule-pack outfit. And I was with the battalion that unloads ships coming in and inspecting ships. When you're qualified, they take advantage of you.

It was rough in Italy, because those Germans were smart as hell, excellent fighters. And they were much smarter than the Italians. The only thing you had to get accustomed to was the German 88. That was a type of cannon that they shot at you. But we fought them, and we lost a lot of men.

I went home when the war was over in Italy; that was in 1945. Brigadier General Raymond Kelso, a graduate of the University of Pennsylvania, wanted me to come to Washington to be his successor. He was planning on retiring, and he had recommended me. However, Tuskegee had put in a request for me to come and work. They were in distress because the board of education in the South had given money to open up the veterinary school, and they wanted to start it. So I went in October of 1945. I reported to Tuskegee and started work right away.

I had my problems with Tuskegee, but I went back. I had originally gone to Tuskegee on a contract. But after the president of the school was in trouble financially with a lot of stuff, he brought in his brother-in-law to help him. His brother-in-law was a very dear friend of mine. His name was Bob Moten, and he told the president how much money I was making and that I had money in all the banks around there, because I was the veterinarian in four counties—all white. In that area, Negroes didn't do anything, veterinary-wise, so if their animals had a problem, they let them die. I did work for rich white people. And some of them I'm still very friendly with throughout the South. They were good, the better type of white person. Let's put it that way.

Well, at Tuskegee, the president called me one day. I had a house I built from scratch, not myself, but I had the white people and black people do it. An eight-room house on eighty acres of land with big pecans all the way around it. And the president had a place about a quarter of a mile from my house where he had tried selling souvenirs from the school, but he failed. He tried the restaurant business and failed; he tried a nightclub and he failed. So then his brother-in-law wanted me to go into a veterinary business with him and give him half of the money. Well, I objected to that very strongly. I didn't like the idea of working, doing all that damn work, and giving half of the money to somebody else not doing anything. But what happened was I showed him that I didn't like the deal and that I wanted to talk it over with my wife. My wife taught French at Tuskegee. So he told me he'd made up his mind. I was making eighteen hundred dollars a month, and he agreed to take that up to twenty-five hundred. I told him I would do it, but I didn't like doing it. And he just smiled and said, "Well, do you have a choice?" I said, "Not right now." Well, in the meantime, being a reserve officer, when they called me, I talked to some of my white friends that were in charge, and they wanted me. They said, "You don't have to go, Doc. We're going to save you. You're going to stay here. We don't have a veterinarian." So I talked with them and told them I had to go. But I was also running the school's veterinary hospital, mind you, a clinic for all of their animals. They called it Tuskegee Animal Hospital, the first in the South.

When I finally left Tuskegee, the government wanted to send me to India to be in charge of a program. But I didn't go. Ed Evans did. Evans recommended me. I was under him then at Tuskegee. Edward Evans had been at Prairie View A&M in Texas, and while I was overseas, he took over the veterinarian program at Tuskegee. Evans was an educated man, a damn good veterinarian. But Evans was a man that had sixty-four teeth instead of thirty-two. In other words, he talked from both sides of his mouth. And we didn't get along too well.

Well, I was giving Evans so much hell that he recommended to the government that I was the logical man to go to India or to Liberia. But I refused to go because the government called me to go back because of the Korean War. And I went to work as a meat-inspection specialist. I went to Morgantown, West Virginia, and was in charge of the shipments of meat. I examined the meat that was being shipped to Korea. I grabbed that opportunity because I didn't want any more of that fighting and fire.

Then I decided that I would open up a veterinary practice. I opened a small veterinary hospital in Philippi, West Virginia, to have a little practice on the side, and the government gave me the permission to do so. And then the practice got so big there, I decided I had to get away from that place or work myself to death. I went to Morgantown and built a hospital. It was one of the most beautiful places. I took care of a hundred animals. I stayed in West Virginia for ten or eleven years.

I've had a successful life. I became one of the first black Kiwanis in the world. I was president of the Junior Chamber of Commerce. I've been involved in many different service organizations. I've got 150 citations or awards on the wall here. I have five pictures from Clinton himself.

I came to Hawaii in 1963. My daughter was here, and I'd come out here for vacation every year. Before Hawaii, I was in Fargo, North Dakota. The United States government had sent me to do epidemiology work in the north central states. It was quite a big job. I started there in 1963. And in 1973, I retired in Hawaii, but before I retired, I wrote a book called *The Black Man in Veterinary Medicine.*

A man from Mississippi once asked me what keeps me going. He fellowshipped with me every day, and he wanted to know. I told him,

"Hell, man, you're looking at an old man. You got to go back and start eating raw, with vinegar, salt and pepper, pine nuts. Raw pecans. Stuff like that." I was just kidding him. I just eat well. I drink what I want and eat what I want to. And I eat well. I do everything well.

[Interview by Alan Govenar, March 27, 1998]

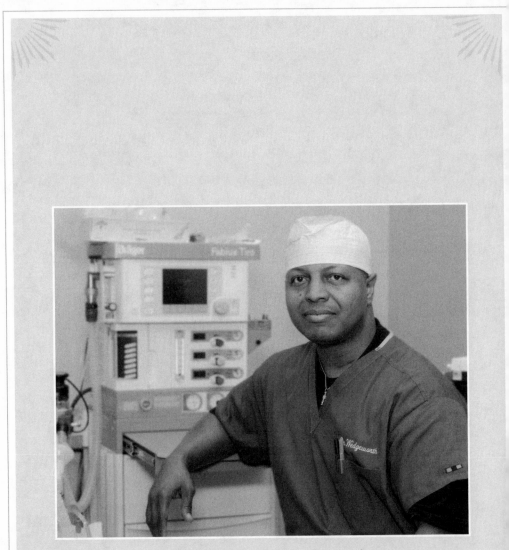

*Richard J. Wedgeworth II, Denton, Texas, 2006.*

# RICHARD J. WEDGEWORTH II

PHYSICIAN

*Born April 12, 1953*

*Richard J. Wedgeworth II is an anesthesiologist. He received a bachelor's degree from Dartmouth University in 1975 and an M.D. from University of Texas Southwestern Medical School in Dallas in 1979. After working as an emergency-room physician at a hospital in Denton, Texas, he accepted an anesthesiology residency at Parkland Hospital in Dallas, which he completed in 1984. He opened a solo practice in Denton, and eventually, he hired associates and formed his own group of anesthesiologists. In the mid-1990s, Wedgeworth decided to diversify his practice and joined a larger group of physicians who together were able to build a doctor-supported, -funded, and -owned short-stay hospital, North Texas Hospital, in Denton.*

MY FATHER DIED IN KOREA when I was three months old. I was born at Baylor Hospital in Dallas to Barbara and Willie Hugh Wedgeworth. My mother was nineteen. But I'm not exactly sure how old my father was. Maybe twenty. And my mother later remarried.

I grew up in South Dallas and Oak Cliff. As a matter of fact, I really never had any contact with Caucasians in the classroom or in any significant way until I was in the seventh grade. I was going to R. L. Thornton Elementary School, and there were white students in my class. That was my first real significant contact.

At that time, I was really unaware of racism. I lived, for the most part, in the black community. All my teachers were black. Everyone I knew of any significance was African American, so I wasn't really aware of segregation, per se, though I did, in the early sixties become familiar with the racial strife because of the civil-rights movement, by seeing strikes and protests on television. But I was never touched by it.

My mother was an elementary school teacher. By that time, she had remarried, and my stepfather's name is Floyd Patrick. He was a postal clerk and businessman. He was a real estate broker and entrepreneur.

Busing was initiated about the time I was in the seventh grade. And there was a move to integrate my school. Fair housing was, I believe, an issue, and so that area of South Oak Cliff began opening up to African Americans. And when we moved there, there was a significant Caucasian population. However, within three years, it was essentially all African American. White flight had taken place.

I felt that whites didn't like blacks and didn't want to live in a neighborhood with blacks. And for me, coming from a black community, it was pretty much okay with me. So, basically, I was in a community that was predominantly or totally African American, and within two years, I was in another community that was predominantly African American. The community had changed, and it went from integration back to segregation with white flight.

I went to South Oak Cliff High School in the same area I had gone to middle school. It was a good experience. I was very comfortable. There were several middle schools that fed South Oak Cliff, and there continued to be a few Caucasians in our classes. And we had some Caucasian teachers who were still at South Oak Cliff. In the late 1960s, it was interesting because a lot of the upperclassmen I looked up to were officers in the ROTC program. And they were graduating from high school and were getting into good colleges; they were going to Ivy League schools. I really looked up to these guys. They were African American, and I got a sense of what was possible from seeing them do well. They studied hard, they got good grades, and they were being accepted at very good colleges. So I had every reason to think that that's what I would do. I basically modeled myself after the guys that I looked up to, and they happened to be in ROTC and were officers. So I joined ROTC. I hung out with these guys, and these were my buds, and I patterned my expectations after them. And one thing following those guys did was, it got me into clubs outside of high school. I was in Junior Achievement and was very active in Junior Achievement all those years. I was in Junior Toastmasters. I think Junior Toastmasters was sponsored by the Kiwanis. I did those types of things, and I worked extensively with Junior Achievement all through high school.

In Junior Achievement, we were put into groups and then formed our own companies. We decided on a product. We kept records. We wrote checks. We did everything—we modeled entrepreneurial activity. We made personalized decks of cards. That was one product that we had, and we sold them. We sold the cards to family, friends, and door to door. We would bring the money back to Junior Achievement and bank it. We had sales contests and had a lot of fun. And there were different businessmen and entrepreneurs, corporations, who volunteered their time and sponsored each of our companies. And so they guided us through our activities. I participated in the national Junior Achievement conferences, and we traveled to different other regional conferences. It was great fun.

In 1968, the assassination of Martin Luther King Jr. upset me. And the riots that followed. I was particularly upset by that. Things were changing. And some of the white students clearly had racist ideas and perspectives that they probably innocently attained from listening to their parents. I was very angry, very bitter. I thought, What a violent country that people are killed for their ideas. Martin Luther King taught that nonviolence was the only technique to bring about the liberation of our people, but it brought only violence from our enemies. I really didn't know that much about the nonviolent contribution to the civil-rights movement. I was learning. I was just mature enough to begin to understand. And the fact that someone who was a model for nonviolence suffered an assassination seemed terribly tragic.

Well, during my junior year of high school, I was on the debate team, and I remember taking a course called Problems of Democracy. And in Problems in Democracy, we discussed the Daniel Webster case. The name of the case was *Dartmouth v. Woodward.* And it was one of those early constitutional challenges. And later that year, Dartmouth actually sent me a letter and asked me to apply. I think it was through my counselor. They were looking for good students.

Many of the upperclassmen that I looked up to had gone to very good schools. A couple had gone to Princeton, and others had been accepted to Brown or Harvard in past years. So I was aware of the Ivy League because of them. And so when Dartmouth sent me a letter, I thought, "Okay, yeah, I'll try that." I also applied to Rice and the University of Texas. I applied to Princeton, but I did not get in. My best friend from high school was accepted at Princeton. He and I were very competitive students, and so we were always best friends, but we always competed to see who was getting the best grades, and so we were very close. We actually both graduated with 4.0 averages. But he got to be the valedictorian, and I got to be the salutatorian, since they couldn't have a tie.

Moving to New Hampshire and going to Dartmouth was quite an experience. I'd never been to New England. As a matter of fact, I didn't even visit the college before I went there to start my freshman year. I got a need-based scholarship, and because my father was killed in Korea, my mother had saved all of his benefits and Social Security and stuff like that. So I was able to pay for my college with [the scholarship] combined with my father's death benefits and Social Security.

I loved Dartmouth and New England. It was very different—the architecture and the difference in speech for people in that region. I just took to it. I really enjoyed it and I didn't get homesick or anything. I was having a good time. Even the snows—and you know New Hampshire. It gets cold, but that didn't bother me. I took it all in stride and enjoyed it.

Probably my senior year of high school, I decided I wanted to be a physician. But when I was a junior I thought that I wanted to be an electrical engineer. That was in '69, '70, and I started hearing about Ph.D.'s that were employed in the military-industrial connection losing their jobs. Ph.D.'s were looking for work—I'm not sure exactly what was happening with the economy, aside from the Vietnam War, but I decided that I didn't want to pursue a career that would place me in a difficult employment situation. I wanted to be my own boss. I didn't want anyone else signing my paycheck. I enjoyed the sciences, and I enjoyed taking care of people, so I thought that medicine would give me the opportunity to solve problems for people, take care of patients, and be independent. It would allow me to make a contribution to society and not be at the whim of an employer.

I graduated from high school in June '71. I graduated from college in '75. And then I went to University of Texas Southwestern Medical School in Dallas. Southwestern Medical School was probably one of the highest-rated medical schools in the country at that time and probably still is the premier in Texas, though I don't know how it rates nationally. But at that time, the tuition for [Southwestern's] medical school was very attractive as well. So all of that combined to make Southwestern a top choice.

I graduated from medical school in '79. In my senior year of medical school, I thought I wanted to be an ER physician. I did my internship at Methodist Hospital in anesthesia. But I wasn't really sure that I wanted to be an anesthesiologist. At that time, there was a job opportunity to be a full-time emergency-room doc in Denton, Texas. I'd been doing some moonlighting during my internship in the ER at a hospital in Denton. It was called Westgate Hospital then. So when there was an opportunity that came up, I thought, "Ah, I think I'll do it." So I actually dropped out of my anesthesia program after finishing my internship and went to work full-time here in Denton.

After about a year, I decided that I really didn't want to be an ER doc; I wanted to be an anesthesiologist. So there was a spot open in what must have been in September or October of '82. And so I returned to Parkland Hospital for two more years to finish my anesthesia residency. And I finally finished in November of '84 and then started a solo practice in Denton.

Over time, I've hired associates, and then a small group joined with some others, and we formed a larger group of anesthesiologists and then merged again with another large group, and so now we're about two hundred M.D.'s. Our group is called Pinnacle. We had been based at one hospital called Westgate, or Denton Regional Medical. It probably had changed to Denton Regional Medical Center at that time. And we were working in about a 120-bed hospital. It had changed corporate hands a few times. So we had moved to a new hospital, where we had an exclusive contract for providing anesthesia services. But we had a rather capricious CEO who was not very friendly to us as anesthesia providers. And because of a few conflicts over the years, we started to realize that it was very important for us to diversify our practice. An exclusive contract was starting to be a liability and was actually, instead of providing security, becoming rather risky. So we started looking at going to other hospitals and doing anesthesia. We were developing a little bit closer relationship—because most of the doctors in Pinnacle are located in the North Dallas and Plano area—with places like Baylor Grapevine, Garland, Las Colinas, Presbyterian on Walnut Hill, Presbyterian Plano, and Trinity Medical Center, places like that. We were probably one of the outlying divisions, and we didn't have as much contact with the other divisions in Pinnacle, except at board meetings. We didn't really go to their hospitals. We started developing some other relationships, and because of numerous other conflicts, we decided that we should diversify our practice. We were having some problems with our office in the Medical Office Building, and we decided that we wanted to move our office, and there were several other surgeons who were also thinking about building offices. So we thought, well, why don't we get together, a few of the surgeons and us, and we'll build an office building. Then, as part of our effort to diversify, we considered building an ambulatory surgery center, basically a place with a couple of operating rooms for some plastic surgeons and podiatrists and others who might want to otherwise do office-space surgery and anesthesia. We realized we could provide these services with a safer alternative that was also convenient and might allow them to invest. That grew. Several of the surgeons who we were talking to asked, "Why don't we just build a short-stay hospital?" And we looked around the room and looked at each other and said, "Yeah, why not?" So our organization grew from an office building to an office building with a couple of operating rooms and a surgery center into a short-stay hospital.

It took us about two and a half years, until 2003, to implement our plan. It's called North Texas Hospital. [Soon after we got underway], the federal government, in response to the hospital lobby, put a moratorium on short-stay specialty hospitals. And they basically halted any investment by surgeons or any investment by physicians. Every hospital needs to have a Medicare license. And in order to have access to managed-care contracts, they need to have a Medicare number. [By determining who gets those licenses and numbers], the government can control what hospitals actually are allowed to flourish. So the federal government actually has a moratorium on that.

The moratorium started in September 2003, but we already had all of our work done by July—all of our investment, our land purchased, the whole nine yards. So we basically got in under the wire. But that was because we put up the money ourselves because we didn't have all the investors in place, but we had enough of the dollars so that we could actually get the thing started, get it rolling, while investors continued to come in. All of our investors were surgeons. Ours is a doctor-supported, -funded, and -owned hospital. We have a limited partnership, but we have a general partner, which is Cirrus Health.

North Texas Hospital, Denton, Texas, 2006.

We wanted to do a short-stay hospital. It's basically an upgrade of a surgery center. If you go to an ambulatory surgery center, they do cases where patients can go home the same day. But occasionally, patients need a night or two of care before they can go home, and that's what we provide.

There are other specialty hospitals in this area—Trophy Club has one. There's one in Frisco, Texas. There's another short-stay just recently opened at Presbyterian Hospital. So they're popping up all over.

As a short-stay hospital, we can actually offer our services at lower cost because we don't have an ICU; we don't have an obstetrics ward; we don't have a lot of the types of patients that drive up the cost in a medical center. A lot of major medical centers will charge the patients that have premium insurance high prices so that they can cover the patients who have only Medicare or no insurance. We don't have that problem, so we can afford to offer care at a lower price, which is why managed-care companies like our organization. That's why managed-care companies like ambulatory surgery centers, because their patients can go and get their hernia fixed for maybe half the price of going to a major facility. And so if you need a hysterectomy and you need a couple of nights' stay, we can do the same thing. We've got general surgeons, we have podiatrists, we have gynecologists, we have GI [gastrointestinal] doctors. We have some back surgeons. We've got a good mix.

I've taken a serious look at the European health-care system, and the Europeans are just wild about their system. But the costs of providing universal health care—I mean, they've got to pay. Someone has to pay the cost. I really don't have an answer for that. I really don't have a solution. But I think that what we as a nation have to do is provide an economy where gainful employment is available to a majority of the populace, enough employment so that the individual can afford to take responsibility for their health-care choices. And they should be able to shop with their own dollars for their health care and allow a little bit of competition.

I don't think that this particular hospital addresses any problems that African Americans face, health-care issues, other than the fact that it might be lower-cost health care. If you're working and you're uninsured and you need a procedure, you need something that's not too major, this is a good place; this will save you money. But that cuts across racial lines.

I don't get the sense that the American Medical Association [AMA] has limited the numbers of doctors [admitted to medical schools around the country]. But I think that the distribution of health care is a problem for the U.S. It's popular to want to be in an urban area, but there are places that need health-care providers that don't have them, and there are individuals, because of insurance, who may live in the inner city who won't see a physician until perhaps it's too late to adequately treat a lot of their problems. So the distribution of health care is an issue. I don't know that the AMA has really addressed the problem of making health care available to more people who need it.

What keeps me going is my family. I've got two boys and a beautiful wife. My mom's still alive. My stepfather passed away about seventeen years ago. And I have a twenty-five-year-old and a seventeen-year-old. I have a child by a prior marriage. My first son went to Dartmouth and works in banking in New York City, lives in Queens, works in Manhattan. My other son is considering a career in medicine and, at least at this point, has ranked Dartmouth as one of his top choices for undergraduate school.

I have some strong ideas, strong opinions, about what African Americans need to do to continue to make progress. I would say that if you look at the different camps among African Americans, you've got an integrationist camp [and] you've got a more nationalist camp. Of course, "the integrationists" is probably the wrong label to apply now. But then, you've got a younger generation that doesn't really belong to any camp. I guess they're sort of the hip-hop generation, and I think that a lot of African Americans need to eliminate any values or behaviors that are either self-destructive or counterproductive. Are you aware of Kwanzaa, the principles of Kwanzaa? Though I don't think that it's complete as a holiday, I think that the principles expressed in the celebration of Kwanzaa are very important. I'm in favor of what Bill Cosby is doing. I think that he's sparked some criticism, but I think such controversy is good. A lot of African Americans are unhappy with him for airing our dirty laundry nationally, but actually, the dirty laundry needs to be washed.

Did you ever read *Pedagogy of the Oppressed* by Paulo Freire? In the book, Freire points out that it's hard to have an oppressor when the oppressed don't participate in that dynamic. So I think that as African Americans, we have to identify the values and behaviors and attitudes that contribute to our own oppression. We have to evaluate; we have to identify and evaluate and eliminate anything that contributes to our own oppression, that lands more African American men in jail than in college, that raises the teen pregnancy rate, and that damages our communities. This does not take the responsibility away from those who have oppressed us in the past but have failed to repair the damage done; this doesn't take any of that responsibility away. But we have a certain responsibility to ourselves, to fix what we can fix. And I think that that's what we really need to focus on as a community.

I would be in favor of reparations for the descendants of slaves, but not a cash payout, but a real repairing of the mental and psychological damage. There is a need to address the absence of African Americans in a meaningful way in this nation's history. Aside from Black History Month in February, the real contributions of African Americans need to be highlighted throughout the year. The education that African Americans receive in this country is horribly Eurocentric. And I think that in order to correct some of the attitudes that we find ourselves carrying that are counterproductive or self-destructive, I think we have to know ourselves better. We have to know our greatness. We have to know what made us great even before slavery in order to have a change of attitude. And we're not getting that with the Eurocentric education. The Eurocentric education is good for Europeans, but in some instances is not the type of education that is good for African Americans. But we don't have a culture; our culture was destroyed. We don't have a culture to pass on in the family. We don't have a language as other ethnic groups do. So we're particularly damaged in that respect. So we have to synthesize; we have to create something new out of nothingness. A Eurocentric education really disables us in that regard. Am I saying that separate but equal is the way we should go? I don't really know, but I think that if we looked honestly at ourselves we would consider the reparations movements as a way to really repair the damaged psyche and the damaged culture that we've suffered that makes us vulnerable to continued oppression.

This is not to take away from the fact that there are some strong, wonderful African American families. The community is a hardworking African American community to have survived all this. We had to be strong. We had to have endurance. We had to have a sense of hope and spirit that allowed us to emerge from the decimation of our family, of our culture, and create a new culture similar to the birth of jazz and the blues, creating something out of nothing. And that's a strong people that can come through that. There are some things that we still need to fix, and that's what I'm about. But I would never want to take anything away from the sacrifices, from the heroes and heroines that have allowed us to get where we are. We're not fixed yet. And there's another phase to go, and so I always want to make sure that I give credit to the ancestors who sacrificed and who bled and died, as my father did. I mean, I probably would not have been able to do the things that I have done had my father not bled and died on the battlefield. And one of the reasons that my aunts told me he wanted to go to the Korean War was a sense of proving manhood for the African American male. It was an opportunity. Blacks integrated the armed services in 1948, and the Korean War was the first war in which there was an integrated armed services. And my father chose to go to war; he volunteered. But he paid for it, and because he paid that price, I am where I am today. And obviously, my mother made sure that his price, that the price he paid, would not be squandered. My grandmother and grandfather worked in the factories during World War II, and my grandmother owned her own beauty salon so that my mother was able to go to college even after I was born. My mother came back and started a career in teaching. So there are a lot of unsung heroes and heroines who made it possible for people like myself to be where I am today. I always want to make sure that I give credit to our ancestors.

[Interview by Alan Govenar, June 1, 2005]

*Lawrence Douglas Wilder, ca. 2004.*

# LAWRENCE DOUGLAS WILDER

MAYOR

*Born January 17, 1931*

*Lawrence Douglas Wilder has devoted himself to public service for more than four decades. The grandson of slaves, he was named after the poet Paul Laurence Dunbar and the abolitionist and orator Frederick Douglass. He grew up in Richmond, Virginia, and attended George Mason Elementary School and Armstrong High School. He then enrolled in Virginia Union University, where he earned a B.S. in chemistry in 1951. Wilder served in the Korean conflict and was awarded a Bronze Star. Soon after his discharge from military service, on May 17, 1954, the United States Supreme Court announced its decision in the case of* Brown v. Board of Education *that "separate educational facilities are inherently unequal." This ruling, which denied the legal basis for segregation in Kansas and twenty other states with segregated classrooms, inspired Wilder to pursue a law degree himself and to become more actively involved in the "advancement of African Americans through the legal system." Wilder attended Howard University School of Law under the GI Bill, graduating in 1959 and cofounding the law firm Wilder, Gregory, and Associates.*

*In 1969, Wilder won a seat in the Senate of Virginia in a special election and was the first African American state senator from Virginia since Reconstruction. He served in the state senate until 1985, when he was elected lieutenant governor of Virginia. In 1990, Wilder defeated the Republican Marshall Coleman to become the governor of Virginia, a position he held until 1994. Wilder is the first African American to be elected governor of a U.S. state.*

*Throughout his career, Wilder has worked to overcome partisan politics. He was elected governor as a Democrat, but in the mid-1990s, he challenged fellow Democrat Chuck Robb and supported*

*Republican Mark Earley. In 1992, he ran for president of the United States, but withdrew from the race. He considered running for the U.S. Senate in 1994, but instead decided to accept a teaching position at Virginia Commonwealth University. Since serving as governor, Wilder has declared himself an independent.*

*In 2004, Wilder was urged to run for mayor of the city of Richmond, Virginia, which had approved a mayor-at-large referendum a year earlier. Wilder received 79 percent of the vote and was the first directly elected mayor in Richmond in sixty years. As mayor, he is committed to fighting corruption in city government, improving the quality of education, and empowering neighborhood communities.*

GROWING UP, I THOUGHT IN TERMS of a new frontier. I knew there were wider horizons, mostly by indirect means, from readings and descriptions. Fortunately, when I was in high school, I was able to take an elective course in Negro history, and I read some of the writing of Carter G. Woodson [*The Negro in Our History* (1921), *Negro Orators and Orations* (1926), and *Negro Makers of History* (1928)]. I shudder sometimes to think of what little we know and how little we would still know if it had not been for Dr. Woodson and his vision for recognizing that the history of African Americans was essential in the building of this country.

What has happened over the years in terms of the evolution of thinking about African Americans is that what was thought to have been the key prior to slavery, during slavery, and after slavery was education. That is still the key. That has never ceased to be the key. And yet there is not the same thirst for knowledge that there was years ago when the idea of the New Frontier was envisioned. Some people feel if you don't have an education, you don't have to have it, as long as you make some money. The great educator Benjamin Mays described education once as being intrinsic. If nothing else, education is something that no one can take from you.

My parents, particularly my mother, who had gone through the educational system in New Jersey, instilled in me the importance of education. She grew up in New Jersey. Her mother had gone to New Jersey and married someone there, and my mother went to school in the white system. I think she was the only African American in her class, and the education was different. There's no question about it. She was naturally bright, so, consequently, coming back here to live and to raise a family, she recognized early on that if you were not educated, you would be left further behind.

In my neighborhood, when I was a kid, the barbers behind my house allowed their barbershop to be a forum for me to expound on what I knew and to challenge them. And if someone tried to cut me off, they'd say, "Hey, listen, let the kid speak. Let the boy talk."

So even though in the barbershop there were persons who had more education than me, they wouldn't speak as much as I would because—you know how kids are; they don't have anything to hold them back. A lot of times, people who were educated didn't want to speak because they didn't want to give the indication that they were talking down or looking down, and they weren't.

When you read the stories of the slaves who were thirsting and hungering to have the so-called Northern liberators to teach them, you realize the power of education. It was a crime to educate slaves or to teach slaves—punishable by a fine or prison time. The Northerners were surprised by the hunger of the slaves to learn. They never understood that it was those same slaves that would steal away to read in the forest, the woods at night, by campfire and candlelight so as to be able to carry the message [from one generation to the next] and to carry the word [if they were able to escape].

My paternal grandparents were slaves, and so my father would tell those stories. And he told me about his brother who was able to go to medical school and to eventually become a doctor, but died at a very early age. My father wanted to go to law school, but because of his big family, he couldn't [because he could not afford to do so]. Education was never a question in my household.

I have a problem today with people who debate whether or not to get an education. We have people here in my state [Virginia] giving high fives, particularly in my city [Richmond], because of the number of students who pass standardized tests. Are they crazy? This limited ability to read and write and understand only certain things is not enough.

Whether it's apocryphal or not, you can see the value of an education. Abe Lincoln, for example, never had the formalities of an education, other than that which was engendered at home. When I was growing up, I remember reading the Declaration of Independence and trying to understand the word *inalienable*. I asked my mother, "What does that mean?" and she said, "It means that no one can take it from you."

I said, "Well, is that a right that I have by virtue of being born?"

"Yes, that's what it means." When you instill that in a kid at an early age, it stays with him for life, and it stayed with me.

My father was Robert Judson Wilder. My mother was Beulah Olive Richards Wilder. My grandfather's name was James, and my grandmother's name was Agnes. Those were my paternal grandparents. My father was the youngest in his family of thirteen. And they were dead when I was born, but that's the reason slavery is so close [to me]. The younger siblings [of my father] may have been born after slavery, though the older brothers and sisters were born in slavery.

My grandfather was from Louisa, Virginia, which is about thirty-five miles away, but ultimately, his family came to Richmond. My mother was born in Richmond. My grandmother was from Richmond. And so my grandparents lived together in Richmond for most of the time. But then they were separated sometime after they were married. My grandmother was sold to Bragg's farm in Ashland, Virginia, in Hanover County. And my grandfather stayed in Richmond, and he would take off and go the twenty miles or so to see her on the weekends. And he'd come back late, but the overseer knew he wasn't going to run away. But the overseer had to, on occasions, according to my father, act as if he was whipping my grandfather even if he was not, and my grandfather was supposed to cry out as if he were being whipped when the saddle actually was being whipped. And sometimes, he had to actually administer the punishment. But then after the Civil War, my grandfather went up, reclaimed his family, brought them back to Richmond to live, and built a house. That's where he started the rest of his family.

My mother grew up in Newark, New Jersey, and after her mother died, she moved to Richmond. She came to live with her aunts in Church Hill, east of Richmond. My father was already here in east Richmond, and my mother would say he would show off by getting his surrey, his horse and buggy. He'd get the horse all shined up all pretty, too—the horse was black—and would parade his nephews in the back, showing off, and the people would say, "What a fine young man, taking his nephews out." My mother liked to say he was promenading so he could attract attention from young ladies like herself, which he did, and they ultimately married.

My father was in insurance. He worked with the Southern Aid Life Insurance Company. He was an insurance salesman. Ultimately, he was promoted to supervisor. I think he never made over fifty dollars a week in his life. But it was regular work, and there were opportunities for him to go into forming new companies. The Virginia Mutual Life Insurance Company started, but he didn't have the money, didn't feel he could chance it, and so, he didn't do anything. There were kids. The two died, one at three years old, the other at a couple of days after childbirth. And then there were eight of us siblings—one brother, ten years older, and six sisters. I was next to the youngest.

When asked how I became in involved in politics, I often say I had a dream and went crazy. I never really wanted to be in politics. I had an undergraduate degree in chemistry. And as a matter of fact, after coming home from the Korean War, I worked in the state medical examiner's office in toxicology for two years. I'd always been interested in the social sciences. I didn't love chemistry and all the sciences. But we didn't have counselors in school, and everybody said, "What are you going to do?" "Well, I'm going to be a doctor," or, "I'm going to be a dentist." "Well, what are you going to do?" And I said, "I'm going to be a doctor." Why? Because everyone else was saying that, so I went that route. But throughout high school and college, I was more interested in the social sciences, philosophy, history, and political science.

The *Brown v. Board of Education* decision [1954] came down just after I got back from Korea, and I said, "My God, you mean you had black lawyers do this? I can't believe it." I had given up on the system; I had given up on everything. I'd been sent to Korea fighting for freedoms and rights for a country when I couldn't experience the rights myself in my own country. I was very bitter. But then when that decision came down, it just was like a lightning bolt hit me, and I thought, "There's a need for more people to be involved in the advancement of African Americans through the legal system, because this system can work."

So, I applied to law school and was accepted at Howard University, and after I graduated in 1959, I practiced law for about ten years with no intention ever of being in politics. I never wanted to smile and shake hands and grin and beg for votes and beg for money. I wanted to be involved in my family. I wanted to be able to afford the kinds of things that weren't usually afforded in my family. And after about ten years, I was doing fine with the law practice. But I was still grumbling and griping and complaining about things. So people would say, "Look, why don't you run?" They didn't mean for me to run for office, they meant run away and quit bugging them. I'd write letters to the editor, and many times they'd get published. But I found out that you couldn't stay on the sidelines and complain if you weren't willing to be a part of correcting the problem. So the *Brown* decision didn't occasion my becoming involved in politics, but it did motivate me to become involved in law. And as a lawyer, I wanted to be involved in the totality of representing people in court and making certain that they had access to the judicial system. Sure, I involved myself with a number of civil-rights cases. I was the registered agent for the state of Virginia for the NAACP fund after Spottswood Robinson left, because he had asked me to work with him and help him, and I was privileged to work with such a great man to understand civil-rights cases. I had occasion to meet all the civil-rights lawyers from around the country, out of Chicago, out of Louisiana, out of Delaware, out of New Jersey. Then, when I met Thurgood Marshall, this giant of a man, he said to Spott, "You've got this young fellow working with you," so Spott recommended that I be the guy that would take Spott's place when he left. He said, "Fine, good. Done." So my involvement with politics was more like quicksand: You take a step, and the more you stepped in, the deeper you got, and to get out requires as much effort as to go further. So I said, "I'll go a little further."

I've been very fortunate, and I've had the support of a whole bunch of people, usually whom I've never even mentioned, whom I've never even involved—the faceless, nameless, standing out in the cold, registering people to vote. We ride on their shoulders. We take all of the accolades. We take the so-called credits that come our way.

There were those of us who felt that there needed to be further advancement by African Americans—ultimately, to the benefit of the nation itself, to transform America from being a place that was envisioned by some, for some, when it should be for all. And I think we're still in the throes of bringing that change about, and that's the challenge that we all face today, particularly young African Americans who may feel that the battle is won. It's not won; it's far from being won. And America has never been the place of one race, one language, one culture, never has been, and never will be. America is the greatest place on the face of the globe. But great only to the extent that we remember from whence we've come and for whom we're to make this country great.

[When I ran for governor of Virginia], I'd been in the state senate for sixteen years, and I was chairman of just about every committee that I'd served on. I had earned so much seniority that I was even chairman of the committee that assigned other members of the senate to committees. There wasn't too much further for me to go, other than to get a gold watch for being the longest-serving member of the senate. So that wasn't in my mind, and I decided, as far as minority aspirations are concerned, I needed to run for governor, but first, I had to show proficiency at a lower level. So I had to run for lieutenant governor to show that I could represent all of Virginia. And Virginia having the lowest number of African Americans in any of the Southern states, I knew that my appeal had to be wider and more pervasive and less concentrated in the urban areas. I had to get out and meet the people and let the people see me. And I did that in '85 and was, fortunately, successful.

I had previously described the position of lieutenant governor as vacuous, having very little authority in Virginia, very little power in Virginia. And quite frankly, if you run for lieutenant governor, the only thing you could be interested in is being governor. But still it was a surprise to some when I said, "Now, I'm going to run for governor." It wouldn't be a surprise in ordinary circumstances [among white politicians] because people expect that if you're attorney general or you're lieutenant governor, you're not there for life; you're there to move up. So I felt it was a natural progression. And that's what I did. I tried to have a record that would show that I was outreaching and not constrained or confined. I knew the entry-level problem [I faced as an African American] because that's been the case in America, whether it's with Irish Americans, whether it's with Asian Americans or Italian Americans. You had to show that you could be something else first and could perform at some degree of proficiency [before you could move up]. And then after that, you could be judged for your merit and accomplishment.

Then in 1992 [I decided to run for the presidency]. Virginia's the only state now that limits the governor to one four-year term. And we were going through some considerable financial throes, which I was addressing. I thought that I could run. I thought that people would say, "Hey, this is great. Other governors are doing it." Bill Clinton was running, and other people were running. I knew that the time was ripe for a non-Washingtonian to run because they were a part of the problem. I knew Bush Sr. could be beaten. But the people in Virginia hated the idea [of my running for president]. My friends didn't even want me to do it. But I announced that I was going to do it, and I started traveling around a bit. I qualified in New Hampshire for the primary and set up everything to do the same in Iowa. I was leading in the polls in Maryland. I was leading in the polls that were taken in South Carolina. Super Tuesday hadn't come about. And yet there was little emotional support for me to run in my own state of Virginia. I announced I was going to run in September. But the loudest applause I ever got was at the joint session of the Virginia legislature when I made my statement at the opening of the State of the State address that I was no longer seeking the presidency of the United States. They went crazy. "Yay!" They loved it. "Stay here!"

I enjoyed running for president a great deal. I learned a great deal and would take nothing for the experience. But it was ill timed, and it was something maybe I should not have done, but I don't regret it.

The most amazing thing is that now, at my age, I run into people who say, "Would you run for president?" I say, "Are you crazy?" They'll say, "Well, no, but we just think that . . ." And I don't think it's a question of age that they're talking about. I think it's a matter of saying—how would I describe it—I have a view toward being a representative of the people to the extent that I am not solely defined by race. A lot of people support that. And I suggest the first African American president will be that type of person, someone who's not defined by race but who is clearly identified by race. They're two different things. One cannot hide from the fact that he or she is of African descent, but that fact doesn't have to dictate what you do. You wake up in the morning; you don't wake up as anything other than a human being. And in my judgment, the way that I react to issues affects all of society.

I never really wanted to be a part of running for a city position, particularly a city council; that's a two-year term. Once I got involved in state government at the legislature, I did everything I could to represent the interests of the city. But I didn't want to get involved in the squabbles and all the day-to-day city operations. I tried to bring about a better understanding, but that was not always possible, and sometimes my ideas were rejected.

About ten years ago, I worked to find people, particularly younger African Americans, and to bring them together. [On the state level], we had changed the government in the city [of Richmond] to make certain that there would be African American leadership. There were several court cases about the city being divided into wards and ensuring that all districts had fair representation. But the overall performance levels were highly questionable—a councilman going to jail, other persons being indicted, and all sorts of things relative to corruption. So I had come to describe the city as being a cesspool of corruption and inefficiency, and I sought to change the way by which the city was represented from a council selecting the mayor from among its nine members to a strong mayor, which the city had not had since 1948. But the change to a strong mayor had to clear the Justice Department, since we're under the Voting Rights Act. And it was strongly resisted by African American leadership, almost overwhelmingly—the NAACP, the teachers' union, the clergy, the elected officials themselves. But the people, the citizens themselves, wanted it; 80 percent of the people in the referendum voted yes. And in the election, we carried every district. We lost only seven out of ninety-two precincts. And in those seven, some we lost by only a handful of votes—that meant that the public was crying out for this type of change.

So after that victory in the polls, the job was: Who is going to do it? Who is going to run for mayor? At the time, I was not even living in Richmond. I was down in Charles City on the river near Williamsburg. I had gone into some degree of retirement. I was teaching at Virginia Commonwealth University—I loved doing that because it was keeping me relevant. The kids [my students] didn't let me get away with anything, nor did I let them get away with anything, so we challenged each other.

I tried and tried to find the kind of person who could really commit to running as a strong mayor. We [those of us who had worked to initiate the strong-mayor referendum] looked and looked. And ultimately, I was prevailed upon to do it, and I said, "Well, you know, I've got to move back into the city, get a condo or an apartment, and I'll try." So I decided to run for mayor of Richmond. The thing that was driving me most, though, was the need to prove that African Americans can govern, that we can govern at all levels, and that we don't have to be elected from specific districts to ensure that. It was important to show that we could bring stability, we could bring effectiveness, we could bring efficiency, and we could bring integrity to government, run with an administration headed by an African American or with a majority of the council being African American. So I guess it was a combination of all of those things that operated to convince me that I ought to run for mayor. Ultimately, this is the city that's given me the opportunity for everything—a good legal career, a great political support mechanism. All of the things that I've ever achieved came as a result of the people in the city of Richmond. I owed it to them not to go back on that sideline and sit and carp and criticize as I did in the ten-year period prior to my entering politics while I was practicing law. I said, "Wait a minute. I'm returning to be the same kind of guy I was before. I can't afford that."

My first goal as mayor [for the city of Richmond] is to be able to show that we will make a difference, that we can have a school system that doesn't give high fives, as I said, over standardized testing, but one that can produce competitive students; that we can have a safe, clean city; that we reduce the murder rate; that we make certain that we're not going to tolerate our neighborhoods and our streets being taken over by those who, for whatever reasons in crime, choose so to do; that we will encourage people to invest in our city; that the economic engine is still fueled by education. I was very pleased by Philip Morris announcing to investors its research-development center in downtown Richmond, a $330 million project that they've already started the construction on. It's this type of revitalization, this type of reemergence, that can make Richmond a beaconlike city, that can make it a desirable place to live, and that can foster the beginning of a different frontier of urban life. We can overcome the blight, the social neglect, the political neglect, and the flight to the suburbs. I want to see people come to believe that we can have effective cities and that Richmond can serve as a model for addressing similar problems in cities all over the country.

I have worked to reach out to the people. I started off by asking people to assist me in study committees. I asked a finance-review team to help me look at what we were doing in terms of how we operate the city. They comment free of charge. They're charging you absolutely nothing, experts from the various corporate heads and boards and things. I've asked people from the health community, "Come in and show me what we need to do to improve health." Social services. Education. I'm saying, "Look, you don't have to live in the city of Richmond to tell me what we need to do in the city of Richmond." I'm asking retired principals, I'm asking corporate executives, I'm asking people who are retired teachers, people who may have been on boards when they were appointed and when they were elected, "Let's evaluate our system of education. Let's see what it is we *don't* need. Let's see what it is we *do* need."

I went to the legislature and said, "I want monies. I want to make Richmond a pilot city for truancy." We were number one in the state in truancy and dropouts and low graduation rates. "Give me some money. Don't give it to the school system. Give it to the city, and I will comport with the state board of education to form a team to combat the truancy." I did the same thing with the federal government. I said, "I need money so we can fight gangs." I want our police department to work with the area police to combat crime, not driving it from one sector to another, but shrinking it so that we let people know that a life of crime isn't going to be rewarding. Reduce the problems we have in the housing projects and the developments by making other types of mixed-use housing available for our young kids, making certain that the inroads of crime don't exist, by reducing the avenues and the streets in those areas so that people can patrol and get in there, making the school system [stronger]—our school system wasn't even taking truancy reports or roll call until 11:30 in the morning. And they had all kinds of excuses for it.

So reaching out, involving yourself with the community, letting people know that you want their help, is critical. And I can tell you the response has been tremendous. There's not a single person that has been asked to help that has refused to do so. The only reservations have been on occasions when there have been conflicts in the past, when people just felt they could not resolve the problem at hand without being criticized.

[It seems that, sadly, teachers are almost an underclass in American society. They're poorly paid, they're not appreciated, and they're not treated like professionals.] That's absolutely right. Look at your product. Look at what you produce. Look what the end result is. Look at your dropout rate. Look at your graduation rate. Look at how many of these kids are going to be acceptable to college. Accentuate more vocational education. I'm starting a charter-school piece now that the secretary of education, Margaret Spellings, has already authorized. The state has given us a little grant money to start organizing a public charter school for people in the inner city, who feel that they are trapped in some system where discipline is such a problem. Give us a chance to show them what we can do, and we can be a part of the governance of that school.

I've asked for our budget and our council, I'm saying, "Look, we're not giving monies to any groups until we have someone vouchsafing for their efficiencies and the various capacities and the various neighborhoods, and it's not a matter that we won't fund them. But we're not just going to be spending money for salaries. We're not going to be spending money for office space. We're not going to be spending money for grandiose ideas that you could get off the Internet."

But sometimes you've got to step on a whole lot of toes. You know what that's like. I describe Richmond as socially a viscous place as you're going to find in terms of change. And they will tell you, "We've always done this this way." Well, it doesn't mean that it's been right.

[Interview by Alan Govenar, August 11, 2005]

*Marvin Williams wearing the hat given to him when he
tried out for the Boston Red Sox, 1945.*

# MARVIN WILLIAMS

BASEBALL PLAYER

*February 12, 1920–December 23, 2000*

*Marvin Williams was raised in Conroe, Texas, the son of a domestic and a sawmill laborer. At an early age, he was interested in baseball, and by the time he was a teenager, he was playing for a local team called the Pine Knots. When he was twenty-two, a friend from Houston recommended him to the Philadelphia Stars in the Negro League. He was asked to try out, and in 1943, he joined the team in Philadelphia. In a relatively short time, Williams established himself as a talented player, and in 1945, he went with Jackie Robinson and Sam Jethro to try out for the Boston Red Sox. Despite their abilities, Joe Cronin, the manager of the Red Sox, was unwilling to take the risk of hiring black players and trying to integrate Major League Baseball. Disappointed, but not deterred, Williams returned to the Negro League, where he continued to play until 1947. The Negro League was phased out soon after Robinson was signed to play for the Brooklyn Dodgers. Williams played for semiprofessional teams in the Arizona and Mexico League, the Pacific Coast League, and the Texas League. After his retirement from baseball in 1962, he went to work as a deliveryman for Sears, Roebuck, and Company and retired in 1981.*

MY FATHER WAS NAMED FRANK WILLIAMS, and my mother was Eva Williams. I didn't know my grandfather, but I knew my grandmother. And she passed away when I was nine years old. Her name was Edna Nichols. She had remarried. I don't believe she was born during slavery. She never talked about it, and I don't think so. But I don't really know what her birth date was.

My grandmother was a wonderful, wonderful woman, I'd say, because she let me have my way. And we didn't live too far apart from her. And when my mother and daddy gave me a bad time, I'd go to Grandmama's house, so I could have my way. And I didn't get any whippings there.

My daddy worked at the sawmill. It was pretty bad. Mother and Daddy were real poor. My grandmother walked about a mile and a half to work. And she worked for three dollars and something a week. She cleaned up houses and cooked meals for people. And the people she worked for didn't have any car to come pick her up, and that's why she had to walk to get to the job. There was plenty of discrimination. Blacks and whites were mostly separated from one another, so they didn't have too much do with each other. Racism was there, but you didn't run into it if you were able to stay away from it. Only thing different was that when you went to the courthouse, we had separate water fountains. One was painted white; other one was painted black.

When we were in Conroe, Texas, during the oil boom [of the 1930s], they supposedly burned a black guy alive in the courthouse, right downtown. Some white lady said he was looking at her. He didn't touch her, didn't say anything to her. Just staring at her. And they made a big deal out of it. And that's what happened, now, and that's what I was told, but I didn't see it.

Well, when I was coming up in Conroe, the superintendent of the sawmill liked to watch baseball. And we had enough guys there to play ball. And he liked to watch us play. In Conroe, they had a white team, and we had a team. And so the superintendent said, "I'm going to build you guys a park. Give you enough lumber." And our team was named the Pine Knots.

I started playing, and they thought I was good. And I kept playing, and then when I got a little older, twenty-two years old, I had played against a guy in Houston, and he recommended me to the owner of the Philadelphia Stars. And so they came down and asked me did I think I could play major-league baseball.

I said, "Well, those guys up there are playing. I think I can do what they're doing."

They said, "Well, OK, we'll give you a try. You want to go try out?"

I said, "Yeah."

Unidentified baseball player, ca. 1910–1920.

So I went, and they said, "Well, you're not up here to play around. If you don't make it, we're going to send you back to Texas."

I said, "I understand. But I want the chance. You give me the chance, and then if I don't make it, I won't feel bad."

So I was lucky and good enough my first year, and that's how I started playing—with the Philadelphia Stars.

I had gone to black schools in Conroe. Booker T. Washington was the name of the high school there. But I never did finish, and I didn't go to college. I went through the tenth grade. Times were so hard. And my father was working twelve hours a day, I think for a dollar. I tried to give as much help with the house as I could. And I know now that was a mistake, but at that time, I was thinking about helping my mother and father. And I just thought that helping them meant more than finishing school at that time. I know better now. But then I didn't.

During World War II, they called me to enlist, and I think one reason I didn't go, before I went up, I had an operation in '42 for a peptic ul-cerated stomach. And they called me to go in the service. When I went to do the examination, they wanted to know what that scar was from. So I told them I had an ulcer, and they put me in 4F.

They said, "We can't give no special treatment. You got to have milk and this and that, we put you in 4F. If the war gets that bad, that's the only way you'll go."

So anyway, when the baseball scout came to me and asked me to go to Philadelphia, he said, "I'm going to talk to your parents."

And he went and talked to my mother and father. And they didn't want me to go. And they said, "We're going to pay him $375 a month."

So my mother said, "I still don't want him away from home."

I said, "Well, I got to go one day. Let me go try." And I said, "I will send you some money on the fifteenth, first and fifteenth."

And she said, "No, I don't want you to go, honey, but we'll make it."

So some of our neighbors and friends found out, and they wanted me to go, and they insisted to her to let me go. And she told me, "If you get up there, don't get hungry. Let Mama know. We'll find a way to get you back home." And so I was lucky and I made it, stayed, and sent her a lit-tle money on the first and helped them out on the fifteenth.

When I started, I played shortstop. And I spent my first winter in Philadelphia in '43. And during the winter of '43, a few guys from the Negro League went over to the Panama Canal to play baseball. And when they came back, they started telling Eddie Godley, the owner of the Philadelphia Stars, about a young man named Frank Austin. So Eddie Godley sent Frank Austin a ticket. And he came to Philadelphia. And during the spring training, he was the shortstop. And he could hit the ball real good. So Eddie called me in the office and asked me, said, "We want Frank Austin. He can't play no other position. Will you go to second base and let him play short?"

I said, "Yeah, help the team. Don't make me any difference."

He said, "You hit good and he hits good. We have a good team."

I said, "OK." So that's how I wound up playing second base.

I hit about three-something my first year; it wasn't that high of an average, but I was hitting pretty good and had a pretty good batting av-erage. And after my first year, they said, "I think you done made it. We are going to give you a contract for next year. We're going to give you a raise. We'll give you four hundred dollars."

I said, "Great."

In the winter of 1944, after the season was over in the States, they called me to come to Puerto Rico—San Juan, Puerto Rico—to play winter ball. So I would go to Puerto Rico to play winter ball, then come back to Philadelphia and play summer ball. That's what we call it: winter and summer. And then that's the way it went the whole time. I was that good, and that's the way they wanted me. That's how I got to go to all the different countries—Venezuela, Cuba, Puerto Rico, and Mexico.

Well, I played in the Negro League through 1947, and then I went and played winter ball in winter of '47. And then I got a tryout with the Sacramento and Pacific Coast League. And then I went back and had contract trouble with my boss man in Philadelphia. There were two owners there, a black guy owned it, and Eddie Godley, he ran the team. And they didn't want to pay my salary, what I wanted.

And so I said, "Well, Eddie, you can't pay me. I can get paid in Mexico." I said, "Will you release me?"

In the confusion, he said, "Well, let me talk with them." So Eddie talked with the Pascal brothers, I remember, in Mexico. And he found out what they'd pay me, what they wanted to pay me, and so he said, "Well, I can't pay you for that. We're losing money, and I don't think the league's going to last too much longer."

He said, "You go ahead and play this year and see how we're going to come out. And if we get started building back up, then you come back." But every year, they were losing money, and eventually, in '50, they just folded.

I was getting six hundred dollars in Mexico with all expenses paid. And even if you make six hundred dollars in the States, you had to pay your own expenses. That's the reason I played in all them different countries.

I never hit too many home runs in one year. The most home runs I hit was in the Arizona and Mexico League, after the Negro League broke up. They had games in Phoenix and Tucson, El Paso, and a little town in Mexico called Chihuahua. I hit forty-five home runs that year. The Arizona and Mexico League was made up of American and Cuban ballplayers.

I met Jackie Robinson—I believe Jackie started in either '43 or '44 with Kansas City. But I didn't meet him until we played against each other—Kansas City and Philadelphia. But I got to know him personally a little better in the winter of '45. The Negro League took an all-star team to Caracas, Venezuela, and Jackie Robinson was on it, Sam Jethro was on it, and I was on it. Jackie played shortstop and Sam was in the outfield.

Not long after that, Jackie Robinson, Sam Jethro, and I got a chance to try out for the Boston Red Sox in '45. You see, they had this paper in Pittsburgh called the *Pittsburgh Courier,* and they were trying to get the major league to let the black ballplayers play in the major league. Wendell Smith was the editor at that black paper, and he talked to Joe Cronin in Boston. At that time, Joe Cronin was the general manager of the Red Sox, and he said he would like to have three players try out for the team.

So I was invited to come try out with Jackie Robinson and Sam Jethro. That was in 1945. We had batting practice and took infield, ground balls, and that was all. And then we were going to have three days' tryout. But the first day we were there, President Roosevelt died. And that killed everything. That shut down everything. So we just had that one day. But they were real nice.

And Joe Cronin told us, he said, "There's no doubt in my mind that you guys can play major-league baseball. It's just that, what owner's going to take the chance of putting all of you on the team?" He said, "That's the problem. See, there are sixteen teams in the league. Well, who's going to have the nerve to put you on the team?"

Well, it wasn't until a year later that Mr. Branch Rickey had the nerve. I'd say every black athlete, I don't care what the sport is, has to give credit to Mr. Branch Rickey of the Brooklyn Dodgers. He signed Jackie Robinson. He took the chance and put Jackie in Montreal, in the minor league, in 1946 and then brought him up to the major league in 1947. And Jackie turned out okay.

Jackie Robinson was a great guy. But he wasn't the kind that wanted to go out and have a lot of fun. He would socialize with you. Don't get me wrong. But some of us, when we checked in a hotel, some of us would go one way and the others go another. Jackie always had those pocket books. He'd always read on the bus or read in the hotel. He bought all the Mickey Spillane books. And he just liked to read all the time.

The first year Jackie played for Brooklyn, I stayed in touch with him. And when they played the Phillies. You know, Philadelphia had two teams. And when they traveled there, I always made it my business to contact him. Jackie had some pretty rough times. But his wife, Rachel, was wonderful. She stayed right with him.

She said, "You're going to make it."

But I tell you, after what he went through, you could only take so much. He took a lot. They went into Philadelphia, and they were trying to hurt Jackie in the game. Then it got kind of nasty. So the report came out in the *Philadelphia Inquirer.* Pee Wee Reese said, "Jackie, you took enough. We are with you all the way now." And I think this is why some people might say he got bitter. He had to take a lot to make it.

But Jackie had his wife right there. You can give her credit. Because she said, "You can handle it. Show them you can handle it. And you can do it. I'm going to be with you. You can do it."

And he said, "Well, if you say I'll make it, I'll make it."

And she said, "I'm going to be with you. Every step."

When Jackie was signed in '46, and when he went to the Dodgers in '47, Eddie Godley told me that he believed the New York Yankee scouts were watching me. But no one ever did contact me. The Yankees wanted "Suitcase" Simpson when he was playing for the Black New York Yankees. But the owner of the Black Yankees wanted too much money to let Simpson out of his contract.

Suitcase went up for a tryout to see if he was worth that much. But he never did make it. That's why they called him Suitcase Simpson, because he didn't make it with the Yankees. And he went back to the Black Yankees, but he traveled quite a bit, different teams.

Josh Gibson was the greatest hitter I've ever seen. He was a big guy, about six four, and 240 pounds. Josh and I were in Puerto Rico the same year, the first year I went down there. Josh was a catcher.

And the best pitcher I ever saw was Satchel Paige. I played against him. Knew him, too. He was real nice. He helped a lot of ballplayers. Satchel was making lots more money. He and Josh were making more money than any other players. And those other players lived in Kansas City, where he lived, and he would help them out a whole lot, financial-wise.

In the Negro League we would play mostly four games a week. We'd start Thursday and then play Friday, Saturday, and Sunday. Most of the time, we'd be traveling on Monday and Tuesday, trying to get to the next place. We went by bus, and we'd stay in either a black hotel or in someone's rooming house. Sometimes we couldn't all be together because the hotel or the house was too small for everyone. But we wouldn't be too far apart.

The living conditions were pretty bad. And actually, we didn't check in too many places. We slept on the bus. And let me explain why I mean on the bus. Say we play ball here in Dallas this afternoon. And after the game we would go somewhere and eat. Not anyplace, just some barbecue place or go in the grocery store and get some baloney or stuff. Now, if we had to play in Houston tomorrow, after we eat, we'd get on the bus. The pitcher who would start the game the next day, he would get on the back-seat—that's the long seat—and sleep. We'd have eighteen players. All the regulars would have a seat to themselves. They were kind of like recliner seats. So we would just drive from here to Houston. By the time we'd get there, it would be just about time to play. So that's the reason I say the conditions were kind of bad. We didn't have the money to stay in too many hotels because we weren't making that much [and there weren't many black-owned hotels].

They gave you, I think, a couple of dollars a day to eat. That's when you're on the road. You'd feed yourself when you're at home. And when I was in Philadelphia, I couldn't afford an apartment. When they knew I was coming to Philadelphia, I had a friend of mine, Red Parnell. He lived with a lady who had an apartment, a three-bedroom apartment. And when I got there, Parnell was going to retire and he was moving on. And he recommended that the lady let me live with her, renting a room. And so I stayed there. She was a settled lady, and she didn't have nobody but her daughter and granddaughter living in the house with her. And she was ill. And she welcomed someone being in the house. So I roomed with her.

Well, if we played Kansas City, we'd either play in the Polo Grounds or the Yankee Stadium or at Connie Mack Park. That's the only way we could make money. People were going to come out to see Satchel Paige pitch. So we had to be in a major-league ballpark in order to get the people to come. But now, when we weren't playing Satchel, we'd go across the river there to Camden, New Jersey, and play a semipro team. And you wouldn't have too many people there. But they would guarantee us a certain amount of money.

I played semipro, too. We had a team in Brooklyn that was semipro. All of the players had a job there at the factory; they didn't play anywhere else. And we had a good crowd; we'd draw a good crowd there.

Teams in the East and the West, we couldn't play each other too much, because there was too much distance, you know. From one team, you come up and play one game. And you didn't have the money to be staying two or three days in the hotel. And you could barely get a hotel. So what we would do, we would book Kansas City or Birmingham in their home city with the Philadelphia Stars, and we'd have a doubleheader. We'd play in Birmingham the first game; then Kansas City would play somebody the second game. That's how we'd get the people in the ballpark. We played different teams in a doubleheader. And the people go to see two games for the same price.

At some of our games, they had Jesse Owens to perform [after he had been in the Olympics]. He'd run against somebody before the game. That was another way to get the people to the game. They'd advertise Jesse Owens was going to be there. But after he raced, he would go home, leave the ballpark.

There were different leagues around the country where you could play winter ball. In the West, they had what was called the Pacific Coast League. And we played in cities out on the coast of Mexico. Nogales and Hermosillo and Obregon. They called that the coast. I liked playing baseball in Mexico, but the first year was kind of hard because I couldn't get used to the food. And I couldn't speak the language too good.

After the Negro League folded in 1950, I went with the Texas League for summer ball. The Texas League had Tulsa, Dallas, and Fort Worth. San Antonio, Austin, Victoria, Houston. There were the Tulsa Oilers . . . the Austin Senators. Oh, it started in March, and by September, I think, it was over. Labor Day. Then I'd go to Mexico, Puerto Rico, somewhere to play in the winter.

I played three years in Tulsa, '56, '57, and '58. And I went to Victoria, Texas. They bought my contract from Tulsa. The Victoria Rosebuds.

I played, I think, two years with them, and then when the Texas League broke up, I went back to Mexico and played until I retired in 1962.

The best thing about the Negro League, I believe, was playing against certain teams and wanting to win. Like the Homestead Grays. Just to win, you know. It was fun to win. Yeah. They would brag about them going to beat us, and we'd try to disappoint them.

Baseball's a lot different today. I never seen so many guys, the money they make, come up with Charlie horses, pulled muscles, and pulled groins. I don't understand it. I don't think they're in shape. See, you get in shape in spring training, that's what you go for. And if you get the kind of injury that keeps you out that long, there's something wrong. It wasn't that way when I was playing. I might have a little sprained ankle. But we didn't have a trainer. You had to miss a few games, but if you had a sprained ankle, we had a little foot tub. Fill it up full of ice. Put your foot in it. Put a foot in that tub, kill the nerve, and kill the swelling and the soreness, and tape it up real good. You could play some the next day.

I just loved the game. Just wanted to play. And it was the only thing I knew to do. So I just kept it up.

[Interview by Alan Govenar, December 6, 1997]

# BIBLIOGRAPHY

Abbot, Lynn, and Doug Seroff. *Out of Sight: The Rise of African American Popular Music, 1889–1895.* Jackson: University Press of Mississippi, 2002.

Anderson, Jervis. *A. Philip Randolph: A Biographical Portrait.* New York: Harcourt, Brace, and Jovanovich, 1972.

Andrews, William L. *The Concise Oxford Companion to African American Literature.* New York: Oxford University Press, 2001.

Athearn, Robert. *In Search of Canaan: Black Migration to Kansas, 1879–80.* Lawrence: Regents Press of Kansas, 1978.

Barr, Alwyn. *Black Texans: A History of Negroes in Texas, 1528–1995.* Austin: Jenkins Publishing Company, 1995.

Berlin, Ira, ed. *The Black Military Experience.* New York: Cambridge University Press, 1982.

Berwanger, Eugene. *The Frontier against Slavery: Western Anti-Negro Prejudice and the Slavery Extension Controversy.* Urbana: University of Illinois Press, 1967.

———. *The West and Reconstruction.* Urbana: University of Illinois Press, 1981.

Bogle, Donald. *Toms, Coons, Mulattoes, Mammies, and Bucks: An Interpretive History of Blacks in American Film.* New York: Viking Press, 1973.

Bontemps, Arna. *Black Thunder: Gabriel's Revolt—Virginia, 1800.* Boston: Beacon Press, 1968.

———. *God Sends Sunday.* New York: Harcourt, Brace, and Company, 1931.

Bontemps, Arna, ed. *The Harlem Renaissance Remembered: Essays with a Memoir.* New York: Dodd, Mead, 1972.

Boyd, Herb, ed. *Autobiography of a People: Three Centuries of African American History Told by Those Who Lived It.* New York: Anchor Books, 2001.

Brown, Elaine. *A Taste of Power: A Black Woman's Story.* New York: Pantheon Books, 1992.

Brown, Elsa Barkley, and Thomas C. Holt, eds. *From Freedom to "Freedom Now," 1865–1990s.* Vol. 2, *Major Problems in African-American History.* Boston: Houghton Mifflin Company, 2000.

Broussard, Albert. *Black San Francisco: The Struggle for Racial Equality in the West, 1900–1954.* Lawrence: University Press of Kansas, 1993.

Bryant, Clora. *Central Avenue Sounds: Jazz in Los Angeles.* Berkeley: University of California Press, 1998.

Bunch, Lonnie, III. *Black Angelenos: The Afro-American in Los Angeles, 1850–1950.* Los Angeles: California Afro-American Museum, 1988.

Bunch, Lonnie, III, Lawrence P. Crouchett, and Martha Kendall Winnacker. *Visions Toward Tomorrow: The History of the East Bay Afro-American Community, 1852–1977.* Oakland: Northern California Center for Afro-American History and Life, 1989.

Callahan, John F., ed. *The Collected Essays of Ralph Ellison.* Preface by Saul Bellow. New York: Modern Library, 1995.

Cohen, William. *At Freedom's Edge: Black Mobility and the Southern White Quest for Racial Control, 1861–1915.* Baton Rouge: Louisiana State University Press, 1991.

Colburn, David R., and Jane L. Landers, eds. *The African American Heritage of Florida.* Gainsville: University Press of Florida, 1995.

Collins, Phillip, and Alan Govenar. *Facing the Rising Sun: Freedman's Cemetery.* Dallas: African American Museum and Black Dallas Remembered, 2000.

Coughtry, Jamie, and R. T. King, eds. *Lubertha Johnson: Civil Rights Efforts in Las Vegas 1940s–1960.* Reno: University of Nevada Oral History Program, 1988.

Cowen, Tom, and Jack Maguire, eds. *Timelines of African-American History: 500 Years of Black Achievement.* New York: Roundtable Press, 1994.

Cox, Thomas C. *Blacks in Topeka: A Social History.* Baton Rouge: Louisiana State University Press, 1982.

Crew, Spencer R. *Field to Factory: Afro-American Migration 1915–1940.* Washington, D.C.: Smithsonian Institute, 1987.

Cribbs, Thomas. *Slow Fade to Black: The Negro in American Film, 1900–1942.* New York: Oxford University Press, 1977.

Crouchet, Lorraine J. *Delilah Leontium Beasley: Oakland's Crusading Journalist.* El Cerrito, Calif.: Downey Place Publishing House, 1989.

Daniels, Douglass Henry. *Pioneer Urbanites: A Social and Cultural History of Black San Francisco.* Philadelphia: Temple University Press, 1980.

Davis, Charles, and Henry Louis Gates Jr., eds. *The Slave's Narrative.* Oxford, England: Oxford University Press, 1985.

De Graaf, Lawrence B., Kevin Mulroy, and Quintard Taylor. *Seeking El Dorado: African Americans in California.* Los Angeles: Autry Museum of Western Heritage, 2001.

DuBois, W. E. B. *The Souls of Black Folk.* New York: Random House, Inc., 1996.

Dunbar, Paul Laurence. *The Collected Poetry of Paul Laurence Dunbar.* Charlottesville: University of Virginia Press, 1993.

———. *The Heart of Happy Hollow.* New York: Random House, 2005.

Duster, Alfreda M., ed. *Crusade for Justice: The Autobiography of Ida B. Wells.* Chicago: University of Chicago Press, 1970.

Ellison, Ralph. *Invisible Man.* New York: Random House, 1952.

Emanuel, James A. *Jazz from the Haiku King.* Detroit: Broadside Press, 1999.

———. *Whole Grain: Collected Poems, 1958–1989.* Detroit: Lotus Press, 1991.

Fabre, Michel. *The World of Richard Wright.* Jackson: University Press of Mississippi, 1985.

Fayer, Steve, and Henry Hampton. *Voices of Freedom: An Oral History of the Civil Rights Movement from the 1950s through the 1980s.* New York: Bantam, 1990.

Franklin, Jimmie Louis. *Journey Toward Hope: A History of Blacks in Oklahoma.* Norman: University of Oklahoma Press, 1982.

Franklin, John Hope. *Mirror to America: The Autobiography of John Hope Franklin.* New York: Farrar, Straus, and Giroux, 2005.

Freire, Paulo. *Pedagogy of the Oppressed.* Translated by Myra Bergman Ramos. Rev. ed. New York: Continuum, 1973.

Genovese, Eugene. *Roll, Jordan, Roll: The World the Slaves Made.* New York: Vintage Books, 1976.

Govenar, Alan. *African American Frontiers: Slave Narratives and Oral Histories.* Santa Barbara, Calif., and Oxford, England: ABC-Clio, Inc., 2000.

——. "African American Ranching in Texas," in *Ranching in South Texas: A Symposium.* Edited by Joe S. Graham. Kingsville: Texas A&M University Press, 1994.

——. *The Early Years of Rhythm and Blues.* Atglen, Pa.: Schiffer Publishing, 2004.

——. *Meeting the Blues: The Rise of the Texas Sound.* New York: Da Capo Press, 1995.

——. "Musical Traditions of Twentieth Century African American Cowboys," in *Juneteenth Texas: Essays in African-American Folklore.* Edited by Francis Abernethy, Patrick B. Mullen, and Alan Govenar. Denton: University of North Texas Press, 1996.

——. *Osceola: Memories of a Sharecropper's Daughter.* New York: Jump at the Sun, 2000.

——. *Portraits of Community: African American Photography in Texas.* Austin: Texas State Historical Association, 1996.

——. *Stompin' at the Savoy: The Story of Norma Miller.* Cambridge, Mass.: Candlewick Press, 2006.

Govenar, Alan, and Jay F. Brakefield. *Deep Ellum and Central Track: Where the Black and White Worlds of Dallas Converged.* Denton: University of North Texas Press, 1998.

Greenbaum, Susan D. *The Afro-American Community in Kansas City, Kansas: A History.* City of Kansas City, Kansas, 1982.

Hahn, Steven. *A Nation under Our Feet: Black Political Struggles in the Rural South from Slavery to the Great Migration.* Cambridge, Mass.: Harvard University Press, 2003.

Hall, Gwendolyn Midlo. *Africans in Colonial Louisiana: The Development of Afro-Creole Culture in the Eighteenth Century.* Baton Rouge: Louisiana State University Press, 1995.

Hanes, Bailey C. *Bill Pickett, Bulldogger.* Norman: University of Oklahoma Press, 1977.

Harris, Richard E. *The American Odyssey of a Black Journalist, 1933–2003.* Apache Junction, Ariz.: Relmo Publishers, 2003.

——. *The First Hundred Years: A History of Arizona Blacks.* Apache Junction, Ariz.: Relmo Publishers, 1983.

——. *Politics and Prejudice: A History of Chester (Pa.) Negroes.* Apache Junction, Ariz.: Relmo Publishers, 1991.

Harris, Theodore, ed. *Negro Frontiersman: The Western Memoirs of Henry O. Flipper, First Negro Graduate of West Point.* El Paso: Texas Western College Press, 1963.

Height, Dorothy. *Open Wide the Freedom Gates.* New York: Public Affairs, 2003.

Higgins, Chester, Jr. *Echo of the Spirit: A Photographer's Journey.* New York: Doubleday, 2004.

Hine, Darlene Clark, Elsa Barkley Brown, and Rosalyn Terborg-Penn, eds. *Black Women in America: An Historical Encyclopedia.* 2 vols. Bloomington: Indiana University Press, 1994.

Hooks, Bell. *Black Looks: Race and Representation.* Boston: South End Press, 1992.

Huggins, Nathan I. *Harlem Renaissance.* New York: Oxford University Press, 1973.

Hurston, Lucy Anne, ed. *Speak, So You Can Speak Again: The Life of Nora Zeale Hurston.* New York: Doubleday, 2004.

Johnson, Charles, and Patricia Smith. *Africans in America: America's Journey through Slavery.* New York: Harcourt, Brace & Company, 1998.

Johnson, James Weldon, ed. *The Book of American Negro Poetry.* Rev. ed. New York: Harcourt, Brace & World, Inc., 1969.

Johnson, James Weldon, and J. Rosamond Johnson. *The Books of the American Negro Spirituals.* New York: Da Capo Press, 1969.

Jones, LeRoi. *Blues People: Negro Music in White America.* New York: William Morrow and Company, 1963.

Katznelson, Ira. *When Affirmative Action Was White: An Untold History of Racial Inequality in Twentieth-Century America.* New York: W. W. Norton & Company, 2004.

Kilian, Crawford. *Go Do Some Great Thing: The Black Pioneers of British Columbia.* Vancouver: Douglas and McIntyre, 1978.

Kotz, Nick. *Judgment Days: Lyndon Baines Johnson, Martin Luther King Jr., and the Laws That Changed America.* Boston: Houghton Mifflin Company, 2005.

Larsen, Lawrence H. *The Urban West at the End of the Frontier.* Lawrence: University Press of Kansas, 1978.

Lerner, Gerda, ed. *Black Women in White America: A Documentary History.* New York: Vintage Books, 1972.

Levine, Lawrence W. *Black Culture and Black Consciousness: Afro-American Folk Thought from Slavery to Freedom.* New York: Oxford University Press, 1977.

Limerick, Patricia Nelson. *Something in the Soil: Legacies and Reckonings in the New West.* New York: W. W. Norton & Company, 2000.

Litwack, Leon. *Been in the Storm So Long: The Aftermath of Slavery.* New York: Vintage Books, 1979.

Locke, Alain, ed. *The New Negro: Voices of the Harlem Renaissance.* Reprint ed. New York: Touchstone, 1999.

Marlowe, Gertrude Woodruff. *A Right Worthy Grand Mission: Maggie Lena Walker and the Quest for Black Economic Empowerment.* Washington, D.C.: Howard University Press, 2003.

McLendon, John B., Jr. *Fast Break Basketball: Fundamentals and Fine Points.* New York: Parker Publishing Company, Inc., 1965.

McMillan, James B. *Fighting Back: A Life in the Struggle for Civil Rights.* Reno: University of Nevada Oral Reading Program, 1997.

Miller, Loren. *The Petitioners: The Story of the Supreme Court of the United States and the Negro.* New York: Pantheon Books, 1966.

Milner, Clyde A., Carol A. O'Connor, and Martha A. Sandweiss. *The Oxford History of the American West.* New York: Oxford University Press, 1994.

Moore, Shirley Ann Wilson, and Quintard Taylor. *African American Women Confront the West: 1600–2000*. Norman: University of Oklahoma Press, 2003.

Nankivell, John H. *Buffalo Soldier Regiment: History of the Twenty-fifth United States Infantry, 1869–1926*. Lincoln: University of Nebraska Press, 2001.

Natanson, Nicholas. *The Black Image in the New Deal: The Politics of FSA Photography*. Knoxville: University of Tennessee Press, 1992.

Obama, Barack. *Dreams from My Father: A Story of Race and Inheritance*. New York: Three Rivers Press, 1995.

Overstreet, Everett Louis. *Black on a Background of White: A Chronicle of Afro-Americans' Involvement in America's Last Frontier, Alaska*. Anchorage: Alaska Black Caucus, 1994.

Painter, Nell Irvin. *Creating Black Americans: African American History and Its Meanings, 1619 to the Present*. New York: Oxford University Press, 2005.

———. *Exodusters: Black Migration to Kansas after Reconstruction*. Topeka: University Press of Kansas, 1986.

Robinson, Armstead L., and Patricia Sullivan, eds. *New Directions in Civil Rights Studies*. Charlottesville: University Press of Virginia, 1991.

Royster, Jacqueline Jones, ed. *Southern Horrors and Other Writings: The Anti-Lynching Campaign of Ida B. Wells, 1892–1900*. Boston: Bedford, 1997.

Salzman, Jack, Adina Back, and Gretchen Sullivan Sorin. *Bridges and Boundaries: African Americans and American Jews*. New York: George Braziller, 1992.

Salzman, Jack, David Lionel Smith, and Cornel West, eds. *Encyclopedia of African American Culture and History*. 5 vols. New York: Simon and Schuster, 1996.

Smith, Jessie Carney. *Black Academic Libraries and Research Collections: A Historical Survey*. Westport, Conn.: Greenwood Press, 1977.

Smith, John David. *Black Voices from Reconstruction 1865–1877*. Gainesville: University Press of Florida, 1997.

Starling, Marion Wilson. *The Slave Narrative: Its Place in American History*. Boston: G. K. Hall and Company, 1981.

Sterling, Dorothy. *Speak Out in Thunder Tones: Letters and Other Writings by Black Northerners, 1787–1865*. New York: Da Capo Press, 1998.

Still, William. *The Underground Railroad: A Record of Facts, Authentic Narratives, Letters, Etc.* Chicago: Johnson Publishing Company, 1970.

Stuckey, Sterling. *Slave Culture: Nationalist Theory and the Foundations of Black America*. New York: Oxford University Press, 1987.

Taylor, Quintard. *The Forging of a Black Community: Seattle's Central District from 1870 through the Civil Rights Era*. Seattle: University of Washington Press, 1994.

———. "The Great Migration: The Afro-American Communities of Seattle and Portland during the 1940s." *Arizona and the West* 23 (1981), 109–126.

———. *In Search of the Racial Frontier: African Americans in the West, 1528–1990*. New York: W. W. Norton Company, 1998.

Tye, Larry. *Rising from the Rails: Pullman Porters and the Making of the Black Middle Class*. New York: Henry Holt and Company, 2004.

Williams, Nudie E. "The African Lion: George Napier Perkins, Lawyer, Politician, and Editor." *The Chronicles of Oklahoma* 70, no. 4 (Winter 1992–93), 450–465.

——. "Black Men Who Wore White Hats: Grant Johnson, United States." *Red River Valley Historical Review* 5 (Summer 1980).

——. "Black News Journals and the Great Migration of 1879." *Kanhistique: Kansas History and Antiques* 13, no. 9 (January 1988), 4–5.

Willis, Deborah. *Reflections in Black: A History of Black Photographers, 1840 to the Present.* New York: W. W. Norton, 2000.

Willis, Deborah, ed. *J. P. Ball: Daguerrean and Studio Photographer.* New York: Garland Publishing, 1993.

Willis, Deborah, and Roger C. Birt. *VanDerZee: Photographer, 1886–1983.* New York: Harry N. Abrams, 1993.

Wilson, Joseph T. *The Black Phalanx: African American Soldiers in the War of Independence, the War of 1812, and the Civil War.* New York: Da Capo Press, 1994.

Wright, Richard. *Native Son.* New York: Harper & Brothers, 1940.

Wondrich, David. *Stomp and Swerve: American Music Gets Hot, 1843–1924.* Chicago: Chicago Review Press, 2003.

# PHOTO CREDITS

p. 174.   Courtesy Marian Kramer.

p. 190.   Courtesy Marian Kramer.

p. 194.   Courtesy Texas African American Photography Archive.

p. 204.   Courtesy Bruce Lee.

p. 228.   Photograph by Marc Royce. Copyright Marc Royce. All rights reserved.

p. 233.   Courtesy Jeni LeGon.

p. 240.   Photograph by Hugh Grannum. Courtesy Marlene Chavis.

p. 262.   Photograph by Alan Govenar.

p. 276.   Courtesy Joanna McLendon.

p. 280.   Courtesy Joanna McLendon.

p. 292.   Courtesy Texas African American Photography Archive.

p. 301.   Courtesy Texas African American Photography Archive.

p. 308.   Courtesy Rupert Richardson.

p. 326.   Courtesy Richard E. Stewart.

p. 334.   Courtesy Richard E. Stewart.

p. 335.   Courtesy Texas African American Photography Archive.

p. 338.   Courtesy William H. Waddell IV.

p. 356.   Photograph by Alan Govenar.

p. 363.   Photograph by Alan Govenar.

p. 368.   Courtesy Lawrence Douglas Wilder.

p. 382.   Courtesy Layton Revel.

p. 385.   Courtesy Texas African American Photography Archive.

ABOUT THE AUTHOR

ALAN GOVENAR is the author of numerous books, including *The Early Years of Rhythm and Blues, Stoney Knows How: Life as a Sideshow Tattoo Artist, Meeting the Blues: The Rise of the Texas Sound, Portraits of Community: African American Photography in Texas, Stompin' at the Savoy: The Norma Miller Story,* and *Extraordinary Ordinary People: Five American Masters of Traditional Arts.* He is the president and founder of Documentary Arts, a nonprofit organization that seeks to present new perspectives on historical issues and diverse cultures. He lives in Dallas, Texas.